NATIONAL GEOGRAPHIC
# TRAVELER
# Arizona

# NATIONAL GEOGRAPHIC
# TRAVELER
# Arizona

Bill Weir

# Contents

How to use this guide 6–7    About the author 8
Arizona's regions 47–234   Travelwise 235–64
Index 265–69   Credits 270–71

Page 1: Saguaro cactus
Pages 2–3: Grand Canyon from Mohave Point on the South Rim
Left: Spring in Phoenix's Papago Park

# How to use this guide

See back flap for keys to text and map symbols.

The *National Geographic Traveler* brings you the best of Arizona in text, pictures, and maps. Divided into three main sections, the guide begins with an overview of history and culture. Following are seven regional chapters with featured sites selected by the author for their particular interest. Each chapter opens with its own contents list.

The regions and sites within the regions are arranged geographically. Some regions are further divided into smaller areas. A map introduces each region, highlighting the featured sites. Walks and drives, plotted on their own maps, suggest routes for discovering an area. Features and sidebars give intriguing detail on history, culture, or contemporary life.

The final section, Travelwise, lists essential information for the traveler—pre-trip planning, special events, getting around, and emergencies—plus a selection of hotels, restaurants, shops, activities, and entertainment.

To the best of our knowledge, all information is accurate as of the press date. However, it's always advisable to call ahead when possible.

## Color coding

**206**

Each region is color coded for easy reference. Find the region you want on the map on the front flap, and look for the color flash at the top of the pages of the relevant chapter. Information in **Travelwise** is also color coded to each region.

**Powell Museum**

www.powellmuseum.org

✉ 6 N. Lake Powell Blvd., Page

☎ 928/645-9496 or 888/597-6873

🕐 Closed Sat.–Sun. & mid-Dec.– mid-Feb.

💲 $

## Visitor information

Practical information for most sites is given in the side column (see key to symbols on back flap). The map reference gives the page number of the map and grid reference. Other details are address, telephone number, days closed, and entrance charge in a range from $ (under $4) to $$$$$ (over $25). Other sites have information in italics and parentheses in the text.

## TRAVELWISE

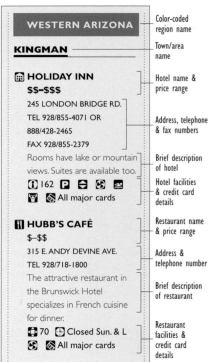

Color-coded region name

Town/area name

Hotel name & price range

Address, telephone & fax numbers

Brief description of hotel

Hotel facilities & credit card details

Restaurant name & price range

Address & telephone number

Brief description of restaurant

Restaurant facilities & credit card details

## Hotel & restaurant prices

An explanation of the price bands used in entries is given in the Hotels & restaurants section (beginning on p. 241).

## REGIONAL MAPS

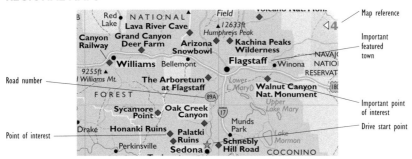

Map reference

Important featured town

Road number

Point of interest

Important point of interest

Drive start point

- A locator map accompanies each regional map and shows the location of that region in the country.
- Adjacent regions are shown, each with a page reference.

## WALKING TOURS

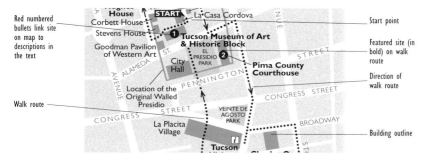

Red numbered bullets link site on map to descriptions in the text

Start point

Featured site (in bold) on walk route

Direction of walk route

Walk route

Building outline

- An information box gives the starting and ending points, time and length of walk, and places not to be missed along the route.

## DRIVING TOURS

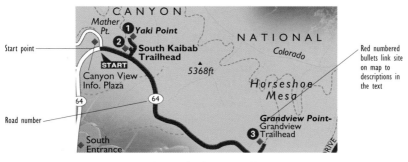

Start point

Red numbered bullets link site on map to descriptions in the text

Road number

- An information box provides details including starting and finishing points, time and length of drive, and places not to be missed along the route, or tips on terrain.
- Where two drives are marked on the map, the second route is shown in blue.

NATIONAL GEOGRAPHIC

# TRAVELER

# Arizona

## About the author

Bill Weir discovered travel while still in school and has never tried very hard to settle down. A bicycle ride across the United States with Bikecentennial in 1976 inspired the idea of the ultimate ride—a cycle tour around the world. He got started writing guide-books on that trip in 1979 by sending suggestions to the author of the *South Pacific Handbook* while island-hopping there. That led to paid assignments with the publisher to update parts of the *Indonesia Handbook* for five cents a word. When Bill returned to Arizona after four and a half years of travel, he started thinking of places about which to write a guidebook. Realizing that the best one lay under his feet, he wrote the *Arizona Handbook*. Utah beckoned next, and Bill completed the *Utah Handbook* a couple of years later. His bicycle Bessie collected dust for a while, but they returned to Asia in 1995 to finish the round-the-world ride via the Middle East and Europe. Back in Arizona, "The Grand Canyon State," Bill's next project focused on that spectacular region, and he came out with the *Grand Canyon Handbook*. Bill is based in Flagstaff, Arizona, but you are more likely to find him on the road or trail.

# History
# & culture

**Hopi basket detail**

# Arizona today

A HEADY MIX OF RICH CULTURAL TRADITIONS AND STUNNING LANDSCAPES forms the basis of Arizona's great appeal to visitors. The names of natural wonders such as the Grand Canyon, the Painted Desert, and Monument Valley can only hint at the grandeur here. Pictures of them are familiar throughout the world, but they really do have to be seen to be believed. Large areas of Arizona are the domain of Native American tribes, still following many of their old ways and practicing traditional crafts—a delight for visitors. Along with Spaniards, Mexicans, and Anglos, the tribes have left an enduring legacy that has shaped Arizona's character and is cherished and presented in museums and historic monuments all over the state.

Accounts of early explorers, amply embellished by Hollywood, provide much of the popular perception of present-day Arizona. Images come to mind of cowboys herding cattle amid scenic splendor, travelers fighting off Indians, gunfighters settling scores on the dusty streets of Tombstone, or miners seeking gold in forbidding mountains. These mental pictures have some truth, but they reflect southern Arizona—the area known to most early explorers and settlers. Lonely outposts of the Spanish Empire had reached this far, and later groups of Mexicans and Anglos preferred the region. Hostile tribes and lack of precious minerals in the northern half of what is now Arizona discouraged outsiders until well into the 1800s.

Yet it's in the north where you'll find the sparkling mountain streams, alpine meadows, snowcapped volcanoes, and the world's greatest expanse of ponderosa pine forest. Vigorous rivers in this northern high country have cut immense canyons that hold beautiful worlds of their own. Although you won't find an ocean in Arizona, the Colorado River emerges from its gorges to become the state's "west coast"—hundreds of miles of watery playgrounds and tranquil wildlife sanctuaries. Arizona's immensely varied topography creates many different natural environments and climates; you can come any time of year and find one to your liking.

**This mosaic of the Arizona State Seal lies under the rotunda of the 1900 capitol.**

Each region has something to offer. The remote Arizona Strip in the far north holds canyons, plateaus, and volcanoes in wilderness areas that many travelers have yet to discover. Just south of the Strip, the Grand Canyon's sheer size and beauty make it one of the great natural wonders of the world. You'll appreciate it best if you make time for contemplation, hiking, mule riding, or river running. Navajo lands begin on the east edge of the Grand Canyon and stretch across most of northeastern Arizona, a stunning region of rock and sky with such beautiful spots as Monument Valley and Canyon de Chelly. Within this land you'll also find the Hopi tribe, whose villages rise from the mesa tops as they have for centuries.

Moving south from the Grand Canyon and Native American lands, you'll reach Flagstaff, a mountain town with a lively university and a strong sense of the outdoors. Winter skiing, hiking, camping, boating, and fishing are all within easy reach of the town. Volcanoes in

**Landscaping and fountains of the Arizona Center provide a restful retreat in downtown Phoenix.**

**Watch out for those horns! Cowboys show their skills in amateur and professional rodeos across the state.**

the region and farther east make up the rooftop of Arizona, with heights to 12,633 feet. Craters abound—not only volcanic cones such as Sunset Crater but also the world's best preserved impact structure, Meteor Crater. The high country finally drops off in the spectacular cliffs of the Mogollon Rim, a long sweep of forests and canyons, including the red-rock country around Sedona and the less well-known Sycamore and West Clear Creek wilderness areas.

Over in the west, the Colorado River's gentle flow brings life to the hottest and driest part of the state. People come here to splash in the water during summer and soak up the sunshine in winter. Yet the harsh desert takes over just a stone's throw from the river, and here you can find ghost towns and old mines that mark prospectors' dreams of gold and silver. In the desert heart of Arizona, the skyscrapers of Phoenix mark the dynamic hub of the state's largest metropolitan area and a

multitude of fine museums, scenic parklands, and stylish nightspots. Scottsdale's luxurious resorts and Tempe's large university add to the sophistication. Miners dug gold out of the surrounding ranges, where you can visit the old sites or perhaps search for the mysterious Lost Dutchman Mine.

Wildly twisting roads—the Apache Trail and other highways—lead to eastern Arizona's Apache tribes, who have opened much of their scenic mountain and desert lands for outdoor recreation. Farther east, the Coronado Trail, now a paved highway through rugged hills and pretty forests, follows the route taken by Spanish explorers in 1540. In the Sonoran Desert of southern Arizona, national parklands have been set aside for stately saguaro and organ pipe cactuses. "Sky islands" punctuate the desert with alpine forests on their lofty summits and diverse wildlife within their canyons. Exceptionally clear skies in the area have attracted astronomers to study the heavens at several major observatories you can visit. The Spanish have left their cultural imprint on the architecture, religion, and language. Tucson, or the Old Pueblo, as it is sometimes called,

**A Native American dances in traditional dress at a powwow.**

still has historic neighborhoods reminiscent of Spanish colonial days. As Arizona's second largest city and home of a major university, Tucson offers much to see and do in the worlds of art, nature, and history.

## ARIZONANS

Who are they? The answers are many, because groups have migrated in and out of this area for millennia. Hopi can trace their clans back at least 2,000 years to inhabitants of ancient village sites widely scattered across northern Arizona. To the south, O'odham (AH-tomb) are thought to have descended from an early civilization that had mastered skills of irrigating crops in the desert.

Most of the tribes in western Arizona appear to have arrived many centuries ago too, though their nomadic lifestyle has left few traces. Navajo and Apache probably drifted into eastern Arizona from the east between A.D. 1300 and 1600—about the time the first Spanish explorers arrived.

The Spaniards kept mostly to the southeast corner of Arizona, especially after their missions were destroyed during revolts in Hopi country to the north and Quechan lands to the west. Spanish religion and culture did take root among some of the O'odham, who still worship at the 18th-century Mission San Xavier del Bac near Tucson. The legacy of the many Spanish soldiers, missionaries, and settlers who came to the region continued to have an influence despite the change to a Mexican flag in 1821 and finally, in 1847–48 and 1854, to the American Stars and Stripes.

Pioneers, including many recent European immigrants, joined Mexican communities in the mid-19th century and adopted their architectural styles, foods, and customs—all well suited to this desert climate. American influence increased with the opportunities the new railroads offered to townspeople, miners, and ranchers. Finally, air-conditioning after World War II made year-round living in the desert a more attractive proposition.

A small number of blacks arrived here too. Estévan, a Moorish slave in an advance party of Fray Marcos de Niza's 1539 expedition, was

probably the first non-Indian to enter Arizona. Black people of the area are remembered for their heroic service as Buffalo Soldiers with the U.S. Army from 1866—when Congress passed legislation establishing six (later consolidated to two) regiments to be made up of African-Americans—until statehood.

## ARIZONA'S ETHNIC INFLUENCES

Hispanic people make up about one-fifth of Arizona's population. Family life is a central feature of their society, and they are more likely than their Anglo neighbors to stay near home. Mexican cuisine attracts fiercely loyal adherents—you're rarely far from a good enchilada. Fiestas and major events in towns with Hispanic populations bring out mariachi bands and *folklórico* dancers to entertain appreciative audiences. Mariachi, played with guitars of different sizes, violins, trumpets, and sometimes a harp, has roots that go back to 18th-century Spanish orchestras. Good

places to experience Hispanic culture include the Museo Chicano in Phoenix (see p. 147), the historic districts of Tucson (see pp. 198–201), and the mission of San Xavier del Bac (see p. 222).

Native American homelands cover about 27 percent of Arizona on 23 reservations. A visit to a tribal cultural center or museum is a good introduction to traditional ways of life. Also recommended are the Museum of Northern Arizona in Flagstaff (see pp. 94–95),

**Navajo lands extend to the very rim of the Grand Canyon.**

the Heard Museum in Phoenix (see p. 150), and the Amerind Foundation, southeast of Tucson (see p. 234). Native artists and craftspeople create many beautiful pieces, which are sold directly or at galleries or trading posts.

Majestic scenery also draws visitors to Native American lands—the Navajo Nation, Havasupai, and Hualapai reservations all adjoin

the Grand Canyon, and the Navajo lands include Monument Valley and some impressive cliff dwellings. Forests, lakes, and mountain streams on the lands held by the Apache in eastern Arizona provide many recreation possibilities. A visit to a traditional Hopi village, hundreds of years old, is an experience no visitor will forget.

Hopi have the longest record of Arizona's tribes—both in their oral history and in archaeological findings. They successfully farm at high elevations with only meager sources of water. Navajo and Apache, who entered present-day Arizona about 500 years ago, have been forced to undergo a transformation from a nomadic existence to a settled one. The Pai (including the Paiute, Havasupai, Hualapai, and Yavapai) traditionally lived in

**Fry bread contest at the Navajo Nation Fair in Window Rock**

small family groups, practiced a little agriculture, and made seasonal migrations to hunt and gather wild foods. Today they are settled and follow a modern lifestyle. Paiute live on the Arizona Strip near the Utah border. Havasupai reside in beautiful Havasu Canyon, off the Grand Canyon, Hualapai are near the South Rim of the western Grand Canyon, and the Yavapai have several reservations in central Arizona. Yuman-speaking tribes—the Mohave, Quechan, and Cocopah—have lived and farmed along the Lower Colorado River for hundreds of years. Chemehuevi relinquished their nomadic life in the early 1800s and settled on the Lower Colorado; they are related to

status in 1978, and they now live near Tucson and in the town of Guadalupe, between Phoenix and Tempe; they are noted for their Easter ceremonial dances.

Most tribespeople have found a balance between tradition and modern life, working at regular jobs yet honoring the religion and customs of their ancestors. They welcome visitors who respect the privacy of people living on the reservation and follow tribal laws. You'll need to get permits or permission and pay a small fee to hike, camp, fish, hunt, or leave the paved roads. Always ask before taking a photo of someone, and be prepared to pay. The Hopi, overwhelmed by photographers in the past, now prohibit the taking of pictures, sound recordings, and even notes.

## SOUTHWESTERN CUISINE

Dining reflects Arizona's heritage. Mexican food, especially that of nearby Sonora, has a large following. Cafés serve old standbys, while chefs at more sophisticated restaurants strive to create new and more flavorful dishes featuring Southwestern ingredients, such as chilies, beans, corn, cilantro, tomatillos, pine nuts, and even prickly pear cactus. Cowboy fare makes a big hit with both locals and visitors—steak, ribs, chicken, or trout grilled and served with beans, biscuits, potatoes, and gravy; some places entertain with songs and skits from the range. Native Americans have their favorites too, such as fry bread, which can be a snack or—when topped with meat, beans, cheese, lettuce, and tomato—a filling meal. The Chinese have been running restaurants here since territorial days, and their cuisine can be found in almost every sizable town. International flavors, such as those from India and Japan, are becoming more common, most often in cities with universities.

## GOVERNMENT & POLITICS

A relative youngster in the Union, Arizona became the 48th state on St. Valentine's Day, 1912. Early politics tended toward populism, and the state was solidly Democratic, but during the 1950s, as many retirees and other newcomers swelled the cities, the state became increasingly Republican. Through the years, Arizonans have reflected their conservative side in Senator Barry Goldwater, their liberal

the southern Paiute. Maricopa once lived along the Lower Colorado, but they gradually migrated up the Gila River Valley to escape their aggressive Mohave and Quechan neighbors and now live with the Pima. The O'odham of southern Arizona, who farm the Gila and Salt River Valleys, call themselves Pima or Akimel O'odham (River People), while those who live in the deserts prefer Tohono O'odham (Desert People) rather than the old name of Papago. Outsiders have often wondered how the Tohono O'odham could exist in the harsh Sonoran Desert, but one member stated, "We don't think of ourselves as surviving in the desert. It is our home, we *live* here." Yaqui, fleeing Mexican persecution, began arriving after 1878 and into the 1920s. The federal government gave them tribal

aspect in Governor Bruce Babbitt, and their independent streak in Senator John McCain—all former presidential candidates. Generally, Arizonans believe they can manage fine without being pushed around by big government, a sentiment of self-reliance perhaps influenced by long years of frontier existence.

## THE OUTDOORS

Experiencing Arizona's natural wonders provides some of the greatest inspiration—and perspiration—the state offers. The rewards of close encounters with the Arizona outdoors make any extra efforts worthwhile. Viewing the Grand Canyon from a roadside overlook is fine, but you'll experience it more fully on a walk into its depths. Instead of seeing it as just a giant, colorful cavity, you'll know firsthand that it's an intricate system of canyons within canyons, each with its own mix of plants, wildlife, and presence or absence of water. Other canyon, mountain, and desert regions

**The way to go: drifting peacefully past the sandstone cliffs of Monument Valley**

offer their own beauties and mysteries. Your options range from easy strolls on paved trails to adventurous treks into wilderness areas. Mountain bikers can pedal down quiet lanes in a national forest or challenge daunting trails. Kayakers and rafters can take on the rapids of the Grand Canyon's Colorado River or float on placid streams and lakes.

Humans need to adapt to the different environments here just as other living things have learned to do. Hiking guides offer advice, and rangers and other backcountry travelers will suggest ideas on how to avoid the dangers of heat exhaustion, hypothermia, lightning, flash floods, and venomous reptiles and arthropods. If you're new to these outdoors, consider starting with short trips, then attempt the more challenging routes as your experience grows. ∎

# History of the land

IT MAY NOT BE TOO REMARKABLE THAT THE LAND OF ARIZONA HAS A LONG history, but what is noteworthy is that much of it can actually be seen today. Uplift by subterranean forces and downcutting by rivers have revealed the geologic layers like an open book. The arid climate has made this possible—the rock tends to break off in vertical faces and is usually free of vegetation.

The visible geologic story begins about two billion years ago with the base layer of mountain ranges, now exposed as granite, schist, and gneiss at the bottom of the Grand Canyon. Erosion wore down the mountains, and the sea moved in and out over the following millennia. Limestone and other sedimentary rocks document the history of the oceans during the Paleozoic (570–240 million years ago). The graceful lines of sand dunes once blown by desert winds lie preserved in crossbedded sandstones. Rock layers of the Mesozoic (240–66 million years ago) record the dinosaurs and other strange creatures of their time. Periods of volcanism occurred throughout geologic history, sometimes forming underground intrusions, erupting at other times in furious clouds of incandescent cinders or as gentle flows of lava. The restless crust squeezed up blocks into mountains or plateaus, often creating geologic puzzles for scientists to figure out.

During the Cenozoic (66 million years ago to the present), a massive uplift in northern Arizona created the Colorado Plateau, where the Colorado River and its tributaries began carving the Grand Canyon. Arizona's youngest volcanoes lie atop the Colorado Plateau; the newest of these, Sunset Crater, last erupted only about 700 years ago. The plateau, which extends into neighboring Utah, Colorado, and New Mexico, ends at the dramatic cliffs of the Mogollon Rim on the south and the Grand Wash Cliffs on the west. Beyond these cliffs, faulting of the Earth's crust across the rest of Arizona has formed countless mountain ranges interspersed with desert valleys. The highest of these exceed 9,000 feet in elevation and are known as sky islands because they support forests and wildlife now isolated by the surrounding desert. Most rivers in the state flow to the west or south and meet in the southwest at an elevation of only 70 feet.

## CLIMATE

Arizona's skies above the broad horizon often blaze with stars at night, radiate a deep blue by day, and present gorgeous sunrises and sunsets. Don't put too much faith in what you read about the state's average temperatures: In the deserts, low humidity combined with a lack of insulating forests can cause swings of 40°F between day and night. A warm jacket will be useful even in summer for drives or hikes into the mountains. Winter storms can bring snow to the high country as late as April, though they rarely last more than a few days. The sun prevails everywhere in the state, bringing warmth and brightness even in January, when the highs between storms run in the 40s and 50s in the high country and 60s and 70s in the low deserts.

The plateaus and mountains enjoy springlike weather in summer, with highs in the 70s and 80s. Meanwhile, the desert areas bake in highs regularly topping 100°F. The desert can still be enjoyable in summer—just set your alarm clock early to be out at first light, then retire to the air-conditioning by late morning, when the sun hammers down. Many outdoor attractions in the desert, such as zoos and gardens, have early opening hours in summer. Residents and visitors cope by making bad jokes about "it's just a dry heat."

Elevation greatly affects precipitation, which ranges from about three inches annually in the southwestern deserts to more than 30 inches in the White Mountains in eastern Arizona. Precipitation can vary considerably from one year to the next. Most arrives as gentle rain or snow during winter or as late summer thunderstorms. April, May, and June are the driest months.

**Swirling lines of ancient sand dunes, now Navajo Sandstone, lie in Coyote Buttes of the Paria Plateau in far northern Arizona.**

Black bears *(Ursus americanus)* live in remote mountain forests and usually avoid people.

The comical roadrunner *(Geococcyx californianus)* prefers to speed across the desert on its legs rather than fly.

Too close for comfort: Eleven species of rattlesnake *(Crotalus sp.)*, including this western diamondback, live in Arizona.

## VEGETATION & WILDLIFE

The spectrum of life zones extends from the lower Sonoran Desert of southern Arizona to alpine conditions atop the San Francisco Peaks in the northern part of the state. At low elevations, which seldom experience extended freezing conditions, saguaro cactuses and other plants of the Sonoran Desert thrive (see pp. 216–17). If winter rains come in the right amounts and at the right times, beautiful floral displays cover the desert from about February through May. The ephemerals (annuals that can complete their growth cycle very quickly) bloom first; they need to grow,

Unprotected by a cloak of vegetation, rock layers erode into spectacular features. The more weather-resistant strata break off in vertical slabs, creating sheer cliffs. Weaker rocks may transform into fanciful pinnacles and other shapes known as badlands.

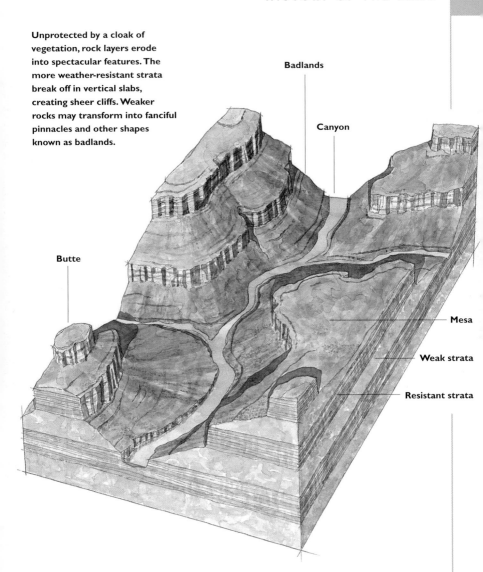

Badlands

Canyon

Butte

Mesa

Weak strata

Resistant strata

flower, and produce seed before the hot sun dries them out. Cactuses and other perennials follow. The giant saguaros bloom last, around May, when spring gives way to summer. Higher desert areas support grasslands (a favored habitat of the speedy, antelope-like pronghorn), chaparral (a tangle of manzanita, oak, and shrubs), or woodlands (pinyon pine, juniper, and oak). Here, too, agave plants shoot up their tall flowering stalks. Sweet-smelling ponderosa pine covers much of the plateaus and mountains between 6,500 and 8,000 feet. Dense forests of aspen, spruce, pine, and Douglas and other firs cling to the cool, wet slopes of the higher mountains. In summer, meadows display colorful shows of wildflowers, such as pentstemons, lupines, daisies,and sunflowers, followed in autumn by shimmering groves of aspen turning to gold. Above about 11,500 feet, on the San Francisco Peaks, trees give way to tundra.

**Spring in the Sonoran Desert at Organ Pipe Cactus National Monument in southern Arizona: Winter rains have brought out the bright yellow flowers of the brittlebush.**

Opportunistic animals such as the coyote and the common raven seek food nearly everywhere, while others have adapted to certain environments. Some subspecies in forest areas have been isolated atop sky islands or plateaus surrounded by desert. On the South Rim of the Grand Canyon, for example, you'll see large Abert squirrels with a mostly gray body, except for white on the belly and underside of the tail. The similarly sized Kaibab squirrels on the North Rim have a dark gray belly and an entirely white tail. Their ancestors may have crossed from the South Rim during cool periods of the Pleistocene epoch (1.6 million–10,000 years ago), when the canyon would have had extensive forests.

Reptiles proliferate in the warmer regions of Arizona. They include 11 species of rattlesnake, all of which are born live and can live up to 20 years in the wild. Within the Grand Canyon you might spot the shy Grand Canyon or pink rattlesnake, a subspecies of the western rattlesnake that lives only here. The Sonoran coral snake has venom, too, but is less of a threat; it has a black head and rings of alternating red and black separated by narrower rings of yellow. Don't toy with a Gila monster either—it has razor-sharp teeth, strong jaws, and venom. The lizard reaches 9 to 14 inches in length and has a black and pink (or orange) beaded skin. Desert tortoises, which dine on grasses, herbs, some shrubs, wildflowers, and cactus fruit, can live 80 years and reach 14 inches in length; they are now threatened in southern California, Nevada, Utah, and northern Arizona but seem to be doing well in the Sonoran Desert, south and east of the Colorado River.

The roadrunner, a comical member of the cuckoo family, sometimes flies but, like its Warner Brothers counterpart, prefers a speedy gait across the desert. In the mountains and the deserts you're also likely to encounter mule deer with their outsize ears. Elk—shy but large and imposing animals—roam the high forests and meadows. Black bears, also brown or cinnamon-colored, live in mountainous areas but are rarely seen, though you should heed warnings on signs at campgrounds and trailheads. Mountain lions live in the remotest areas; they are likelier to spot you than you are to notice them. Southeastern Arizona is famed for its birds, which congregate in the canyons and mountains during the warmer months. Of the large number of species, several are found only rarely elsewhere in the United States.

## ARIZONA STATE PARKS

You can enjoy some of Arizona's most intriguing historic sites and natural areas, along with fine facilities, at its state parks. Historical parks relate the history of Pueblo Indians, Spanish colonizers, the territorial years, or mining. Nature parks include scenic desert, mountain, and canyon areas and a beautiful living cave. Recreation parks feature lakeside and riverside locations ideal for water sports. About half the parks offer campgrounds. The main office of Arizona State Parks in Phoenix has an information desk and gift shop *(1300 W. Washington St., Phoenix, AZ 85007, tel 602/542-4174 or 800/285-3703 in Arizona beyond the Phoenix area, closed Sat.–Sun., www.pr.state.az.us).*

## NATIONAL PARKS, MONUMENTS, & FORESTS

Besides the well-known Grand Canyon National Park, the National Park Service *(www.nps.gov)* looks after spectacular ancient pueblos, a Spanish mission ruin, colorful petrified wood, a volcano, Sonoran Desert regions, and other scenic and recreational areas. If you plan to visit many of these, ask about the National Parks Pass, which gives 12 months of entry for a flat fee. Seniors (U.S. citizens 62 and older) can get a lifetime Golden Age Pass, and people with disabilities are eligible for the Golden Access Pass.

National forests cover large areas of the high country in Arizona, offering opportunities for scenic drives, hiking, mountain biking, fishing, and camping. You can visit any of the U.S. Forest Service offices or visitor centers for maps and recreation information, or check the Internet *(www.fs.fed.us/r3)*. Expect to pay a fee in the more heavily used areas.

The Arizona Public Lands Information Center is an excellent source of information, maps, and books for all the federal and state

**Hiking at Devil's Bridge in the red-rock country surrounding Sedona**

areas *(222 N. Central Ave., Suite 101, Phoenix, AZ 85004-2203, tel 602/417-9300, closed Sat.–Sun., www.publiclands.org).*

## ARIZONA TRAIL
Nearing completion, this challenging 790-mile trail offers hikers, mountain bikers, and equestrians an opportunity to see Arizona up close. Unlike other major trails that follow a single feature, the Arizona Trail winds through a variety of terrain. Its south end touches the Mexican border in Coronado National Memorial, and its north end is on the Arizona Strip near the Utah border. In between lie many mountain ranges, some desert sections, plateaus, and the Grand Canyon. Contact the Arizona Trail Association *(P.O. Box 36736, Phoenix, AZ 85067-6736, tel 602/252-4794, www.aztrail.org).* ■

# History of Arizona

THE HUMAN STORY IN ARIZONA SPANS AT LEAST 12,000 YEARS OF TRIUMPHS
and retreats as people sought new or better opportunities. Farming, and precious water, became
the means for complex societies to develop in early times and to progress to the present.

## THE FIRST TRIBES

Nomadic hunters once roamed a green landscape in search of big game such as mammoth, bison, pronghorn, and camel. The
bands lived along streams and lakes, leaving
few traces other than projectile points and
animal bones at their camps. By 8000 B.C.
most large animals were extinct. This, and a
drier climate, caused the tribes to rely more on
gathering wild plants and hunting small game.
A detailed knowledge of the land guided the
people on seasonal migrations to harvest
ripening seeds, nuts, and berries. Most likely
they traveled in small bands with minimal
possessions and lived in caves or brush shelters. Some tribes in Arizona pursued this existence into the late 1800s.

## GROWTH OF THE GREAT PUEBLOS

Farming may have started as early as 3000 B.C.,
but it did not provide a substantial part of the
tribes' diet until about 200 B.C. The people
planted their fields in spring, continued their
seasonal migrations in summer, and returned
in autumn to harvest their crops. Cultivation
of corn, beans, and squash became increasingly important over the centuries and made
sophisticated cultures possible. Agricultural
skills and pottery making probably originated
in Mexico. By A.D. 200, the tribes began building small villages of pit houses—partly underground dwellings roofed with sticks and
mud—near their fields.

Three distinct farming cultures emerged,
classified by archaeologists as the Anasazi (ancient Pueblo people) of the Colorado Plateau
in the north, the Mogollon (MUG-GY-own) of
the eastern uplands, and the Hohokam of the
southern deserts. Trade among the cultures
and with Mexico brought new ideas and goods
to the villages. Already skilled in basketmak-
ing, the tribespeople also learned to grow and
weave cotton. Their decorated pottery was of
such high artistic quality that it is greatly
admired today. Masonry and adobe houses

replaced pit houses as villages grew in size
and became more widespread between A.D.
500 and 1100. Complex religious ceremonies
evolved, and kivas—underground rooms reminiscent of pit houses—served as ceremonial
chambers in the uplands. The Hohokam built
platform mounds and oval ball courts that
probably had religious purposes. These desert
dwellers also developed extensive networks
of irrigation canals to channel water from the
Salt and Gila Rivers to their fields. Their simple adobe structures disappeared long ago,
but a huge Great House has survived at Casa
Grande Ruins National Monument (see p.
173).

The cultures reached their peak of craft,
masonry, and agricultural skills about 1100,
but then a series of migrations left nearly all
the villages abandoned. The Mogollon had
apparently vanished by 1200 and may have
been absorbed into Anasazi and Hohokam villages. By 1400 the Hohokam culture had also
collapsed. Spanish explorers in the following
century found the O'odham (AH-tomb), also
known as Pima and Papago, living a simple
existence along the rivers and in the desert.
O'odham legends relate a revolt against op-
pressive villages. The Anasazi consolidated on
the Hopi mesas and in the pueblos to the east,
where they live today. Hopi oral tradition tells
of their ancestors migrating as part of a great
plan. Archaeologists suspect that drought, soil
erosion, overpopulation, disease, and dwind-
ling food sources may have contributed to this
large-scale abandonment. Schisms, which have
occurred in modern times, likely had a role
too. Navajo and Apache had begun moving
into eastern Arizona at about the time the villages were vacated, but there is no evidence
that they affected the upheavals of the pueblo
cultures.

**Prehistoric tribes have left records, such as
these petroglyphs at Wupatki National
Monument, in every part of the state.**

## SPANISH CONQUISTADORES, MISSIONS, & PRESIDIOS

In 1539 the viceroy of Mexico, on hearing tales of the treasure-filled Seven Cities of Cíbola to the north, sent Brother Marcos de Niza to investigate. After losing some of his party to hostile Zuni Indians in present-day New Mexico, Niza returned with reports of a great city of stone. The following year Francisco Vásquez de Coronado set out from Mexico with 336 soldiers and nearly a thousand

**Dreams of gold and fame led Francisco Vásquez de Coronado and his huge company into unknown lands. Frederic Remington painted this scene in 1905.**

Native American allies to conquer the cities. But instead of magnificent wealth, Coronado found only poor villages. His fruitless search lasted two years, and he reached the area of modern Kansas before returning to Mexico.

Despite the disappointments, Coronado's

expedition greatly increased knowledge of these new lands among the Spanish. A detachment under Garcia López de Cárdenas had visited Hopi villages and continued west to the Grand Canyon. Meanwhile, Hernando de Alarcón—who had sailed along the west coast and traveled a short way up the Colorado River—added this new area to the maps, even though he didn't reach Coronado's men.

In 1629, Franciscans opened the first of several missions among the Hopi. They were reasonably successful in gaining converts until some Hopi joined the large, well-organized Pueblo Revolt of 1680 and killed or threw out the friars and many of their followers. Missionaries tried again with the Hopi in 1700, but villagers promptly destroyed the mission. In the south, Father Eusebio Francisco Kino achieved good relations with the O'odham by introducing cattle and new crops from 1691 until his death in 1711. The work that he started led to the later construc-

**Mission San Xavier del Bac's richly painted statues and walls have told the story of Christianity to Native Americans for more than 200 years.**

tion of Mission San Xavier del Bac, in which the O'odham worship today. Relations between the Spanish and the O'odham took a turn for the worse in 1751, when the tribe staged a major revolt, but the Spanish stayed on, making some reforms and establishing presidios (fortified military camps) at Tubac, Tucson, and other sites. A revolt by Quechan against the Spanish in 1781 on the Lower Colorado River brought mission work there to an end. The Spanish then kept to the Santa Cruz River area for the rest of their time in Arizona.

## A MEXICAN INTERLUDE

When Mexico won independence from Spain in 1821, mission work declined as funds were cut and foreign-born missionaries were expelled. Political instability in Mexico City resulted in a failure to uphold peace treaties with the Apache, who then besieged the unfortunate settlers. American traders and trappers, discouraged earlier by the Spanish, began to sneak in and got to know the land. Many of these mountain men, including Kit Carson, Jedediah Smith, Joseph Walker, Bill Williams,

and the unusually named Pauline Weaver, paved the way for later American military expeditions. Arizona came into the Union almost by accident—the Mexican War of 1847–48 had ceded not only the desired Texas and California but also everything in between.

The U.S. government paid little attention to Arizona, which was part of New Mexico Territory after 1850. What is now southern Arizona came into American hands with the Gadsden Purchase in 1854, but for most early travelers the territory was just an obstacle to be crossed on the way to Californian goldfields. In the 1850s, gold strikes along the Lower Colorado River, steamboat service, and the establishment of Army posts attracted the attention of prospectors and farmers. The taking of land by the newcomers soon upset the Native Americans, who began sporadic warfare that would last three decades. The Civil War made life much worse for the settlers after Army troops headed east to fight. Residents tended to favor the Confederacy, and Rebel captain Sherod Hunter received a fine welcome at Tucson in 1862. He had hoped to ally California with the Confederacy, but that plan fell through, and he could only delay the 2,000-man Union force headed his way from California. The Battle of Picacho Pass on April 15, 1862, took place between detachments of

Kit Carson (1809–1868) came west as a mountain man to trap and hunt, then earned fame as a guide for explorer John C. Frémont.

Mountain men groups keep the old skills and dress alive.

both sides (see p. 174). The Californians lost three men, but the Confederates, knowing that Union reinforcements would soon arrive, beat a retreat back to Tucson and on to Texas.

## TERRITORIAL YEARS

Arizona emerged for the first time as a separate entity during the dark years of the Civil War. President Abraham Lincoln signed the bill establishing Arizona Territory on February 24, 1863, bringing hope for both law and order and federal representation. The promising mining area of Prescott became the territorial capital a year later; Tucson lost out because it had leaned too much toward the Confederacy. Although the Indian wars continued to slow development, the arrival of railroads across southern and northern Arizona in the late 1870s and early 1880s opened up the land to large-scale ranching, mining, and logging. People could now import material for stylish Victorian houses instead of living in adobe or log structures. The mining of gold and silver, then copper, propelled the economy.

Members of the Church of Jesus Christ of Latter-day Saints (more commonly known as Mormons) from Utah, seeking new opportunities and freedoms, arrived in 1864 at Littlefield, in Arizona's northwest corner, only to see their farms washed away in a flood three years later. Other Mormon groups pushed south, setting up Lees Ferry across the Colorado River, above the Grand Canyon, and progressing as far as St. David in southeastern Arizona. Hard work and a strong sense of community enabled most Mormon settlements to prosper, but their practice of polygamy greatly offended their neighbors until the Mormon Church, under federal government pressure, outlawed it. Some members refused to go along and broke away from the main church; you'll see their unusually large houses on a drive past Colorado City in Arizona's far north. Many settlements in the territory became thriving cities, including Springerville (founded 1871), Mesa (1878), Snowflake (1878), and Show Low (1890).

Conflict between the Army and Native American tribes persisted. The Army ended Navajo resistance in 1863–64 with a brutal campaign that removed the tribe to a camp in eastern New Mexico, but renegade Apache

In this meeting between Geronimo (seated, left) and Gen. George Crook (in pith helmet on right) on March 25, 1886, the Apache leader agreed to surrender.

continued to attack outsiders until their leader, Geronimo, surrendered to the Army in 1886. Arizonans had lobbied for statehood since 1872, but primitive roads, outlaw and Apache troubles, and feuds kept delaying the goal. Even though citizens largely resolved these problems by the end of the century, Eastern politicians turned a deaf ear. Admitting Arizona would have adversely affected the Easterners' preference for the gold standard (Arizona was pushing for silver) and Republican values (Arizona was Democratic).

Meanwhile, the territory's citizens had no vote in Congress nor any say in who would be appointed governor. When the country needed volunteers for the Spanish-American War, Arizonans quickly signed up to show their loyalty. Prescott's William "Buckey" O'Neil, a popular former sheriff, newspaperman, and politician, led troops into battle in Cuba, earning admiration from the press, who called his group the Rough Riders. A Spanish sniper cut him down on San Juan Hill, but he died a hero.

Surely, Arizonans felt, they would be awarded statehood now, but Washington bigwigs continued their delaying tactics. It took Congress until 1910 to pass the Enabling Act; with a constitutional convention and a little more wrangling, the statehood bill was ready to be signed on February 12, 1912. The 12th turned out to be Lincoln's birthday—a holiday—and the following day an "unlucky" 13th, so President William Howard Taft waited until the 14th to give Arizona its Valentine's Day gift.

Wild celebrations broke out across the new state as soon as the news arrived at telegraph offices. One young Phoenix couple, Joe Melczer and Hazel Goldberg, had planned to have the state's first wedding. They had patiently waited, along with their three-year-old ring bearer, for the message. When it came, little Barry Goldwater presented the rings, and the couple exchanged marriage vows.

## STATEHOOD
On statehood day, Governor George W. P. Hunt led a triumphant procession to the Capitol in Phoenix. Though one of the richest men in Arizona, Hunt had arrived in the territory 31 years earlier as a penniless miner. He had worked his way up to become a successful merchant, banker, territorial representative, and president of Arizona's Constitutional

The first state legislature gave women the right to vote in 1912 (eight years before national suffrage), and in 1914 voters elected a woman to the Arizona House and another to the Arizona Senate—the first and second in the nation to hold such offices. World War I inspired another round of patriotism with heroes such as aviator Frank Luke of Phoenix, who shot down 14 German observation balloons and four planes in just 17 days. Forced down behind enemy lines, he pulled out his revolver and died fighting the German infantry.

Relying heavily on its mining industry, Arizona, the Copper State, benefited or suffered according to the metal's price. Cotton, especially long-staple Pima, led agricultural production. New dams on the Salt, Gila, and Verde Rivers supplied the water necessary for continued growth. The Great Depression hit Arizona hard, causing crop prices to plummet and forcing many mines to close. Tourism helped in the 1920s and 1930s, when fashionable resorts opened, catering to wealthy Northerners who spent winters under the palms. Dude ranches offered the romance of the Old West to those who came to ride the

**George W. P. Hunt, who later became the state's first governor, presides over the Arizona Constitutional Convention at the Territorial Capitol in 1910.**

range. The clean, dry desert air also drew "lungers"—people suffering from tuberculosis—to recuperate. Governor Benjamin Moore, a country doctor from Tempe, helped the state along during the Depression years by slashing property taxes, adding luxury taxes to keep needed programs afloat, and holding free medical clinics for the poor in the Capitol's rotunda.

### WORLD WAR II & POSTWAR BOOM

Arizona once again jumped at the opportunity to serve the nation. The Army Air Corps trained an estimated 60,000 in the state's sunny skies. Gen. George Patton prepared his men for the invasion of North Africa by rehearsing in the demanding deserts of southwestern Arizona. The desert also seemed a logical place to house German and Italian prisoners of war. Its aridity was the undoing of an escape plan by German submariners from Papago Park in Phoenix: U-boat commander Capt. Jürgen Wattenberg and 24 fellow prisoners managed to tunnel 180 feet to freedom, only to find their plan

**Giant B-52 bombers overflow Tucson's Davis-Monthan Air Force base in 1995. Most have since been scrapped.**

to raft down the Salt River to Mexico thwarted by a bone-dry riverbed. All were recaptured.

The desert also became an unhappy home for thousands of innocent Japanese Americans. Their Poston camp in western Arizona once ranked as the state's third largest city.

Of the many Arizona heroes fighting overseas, perhaps the most unusual were the Navajo Code Talkers. The Japanese had been intercepting American radio transmissions in the Pacific and using the information to attack and confuse troops, so Navajo in the Marine Corps developed a code in their native language. The Japanese never broke it, probably saving the lives of thousands of soldiers, sailors, and marines. Ira Hayes, a Pima (O'odham), helped raise the flag on Mount Suribachi during the battle for Iwo

Jima in 1945; he's the last in line with upraised hands in the famous photo.

By war's end, many servicemen and women stationed in Arizona had grown to like the state, so they settled in. Manufacturing had more than quadrupled over the war years as aeronautical and other defense industries built new factories. Most of these new industries stayed too, adding high-tech to the state's previous mix of copper, cotton, cattle, and citrus. Year-round living in Arizona became an attractive proposition for the first time, thanks to air-conditioning. Retired people, many weary of shoveling snow in northern climes, began moving to the desert, and entire cities blossomed to hold them. The state has continued to develop at a rapid pace, generating loud debate about growth and urban sprawl. Planners wonder when the supply of water will run out. Yet the career opportunities, sunny climate, outdoor recreation, and luxurious resorts continue to attract new faces. ■

# The arts

ARIZONA'S NATURAL SETTING INFLUENCES THE PERCEPTIONS OF NEARLY all who come here. The light and the way nature's hand has sculpted the landscape into wonderful forms inspire people to portray them. Art also reflects the mystique of Native Americans and cowboys, symbolizing the close relationship between humans and nature. Additional inspiration comes from the state's many historical periods.

## VISUAL ARTS

Early tribes, who had perhaps the closest connection with the land and its life, carved or painted thousands of enigmatic geometric, animal, human, and anthropomorphic designs in cliffs and boulders. The Hopi recognize some of these as clan symbols, but many others challenge us with their mysteries.

Landscapes continue to delight artists and make up a large category of regional art today. Western or cowboy art stirs up both derision and admiration. Some see it as just an assemblage of stock images—the cowboy or Indian with a horse in the desert or mountains and perhaps a sunset. Others admire the painter's skill and the qualities depicted. They feel nostalgia for a time past, when a simpler world knew self-reliance, untrammeled nature, and purity of purpose. Native American artists have extended their traditional crafts to fine jewelry, sculpture, and paintings. Tribal people have also been subjects themselves—portrayed both romantically in paintings and, perhaps more honestly, by skilled photographers.

To experience the work of regional, national, and international artists, visit the Phoenix Art Museum (see p. 149) and the Tucson Museum of Art and Historic Block (see pp. 200–201). The Scottsdale Museum of Contemporary Art (see p. 163) displays cutting-edge work in the fields of art, design, and architecture. Northern Arizona University in Flagstaff (see p. 97) offers changing and permanent collections in Old Main and a changing gallery in the Fine and Performing Arts building. Arizona State University (see pp. 161–62) in Tempe, east of Phoenix, offers several exhibit venues, including the architecturally striking Nelson Fine Arts Center. The University of Arizona (see pp. 198–200) in Tucson features diverse collections in its Art Museum and outstanding photos in its Center for Creative Photography. The Old West lives on at the Phippen Museum near Prescott (see p. 119) and at the Desert Caballeros Western Museum in Wickenburg (see p. 152). Three museums present outstanding traditional and contemporary Native American art: Flagstaff's Museum of Northern Arizona (see pp. 94–96), Phoenix's Heard Museum (see p. 150), and southeastern Arizona's Amerind Foundation (see p. 234). Art galleries abound in Sedona, Scottsdale, Tucson, and Tubac, on the Hopi and Navajo lands, and in the former mining towns of Jerome and Bisbee.

**Artists made the rest of the country aware of the majestic landscapes of the West. Thomas Moran painted the Grand Canyon in "Under the Red Wall" in 1917.**

## ARTISTS & PHOTOGRAPHERS

Much of early Arizona's art documents 19th-century expeditions and reveals the sense of wonder the artists felt. Explorer John Wesley Powell understood the importance of showing the West to people elsewhere when he invited artist Thomas Moran (1837–1926) to join him on a river expedition in 1873. Moran painted a magnificent canvas of the Grand Canyon of the Colorado the following year. The work, measuring 7 feet by 12 feet, portrayed the canyon bathed in warm light with a thunderstorm above and roiling mists in the abysses. It was hung in the lobby of the U.S. Senate in Washington, D.C., where it caught the attention not only of the public and lawmakers but also of Santa Fe Railroad officials, who later promoted the Southwest as a tourist destination.

Also in the late 1800s, artist Frederic Remington (1861–1909) earned fame for his realistic portrayals of Native Americans, cowboys, soldiers, horses, and other aspects of the West in sculptures, paintings, and illustrations. In 1900 photographer Edward S. Curtis (1868–1952) set out to record all 80 tribes active in the United States, an ambitious project that would last 30 years and produce 20 volumes. Much of his early work was done in Arizona, where Curtis lived and traveled with the tribespeople to earn their trust.

**A Navajo weaves in her canyon home in this photo by Edward Curtis.**

Contemporary artists continue this tradition of Western art and landscape painting. Howard Post (1948–) learned to rope and ride as a cowboy in southern Arizona, then began to portray range life on canvas. His mastery of light shows people living with nature as they take care of their livestock. Robert Daughters (1929–) uses bold strokes and vibrant, contrasting colors to depict the many facets of the craggy landscapes he paints in impressionistic style. Photographers strive to capture the people and land of Arizona too; many of their best shots appear on the pages of *Arizona Highways* magazine, where you'll see the work of such artists as Jerry Jacka, Gary Ladd, Jack Dykinga, Josef Muench, and Muench's son David and grandson Marc.

## NATIVE AMERICAN ARTS

Of all Arizona's tribes, the Hopi and Navajo create the most artwork, and many families rely on sales as a major source of income. You may see pieces by other tribes too, such as beadwork by the Apache, pottery and basketry by the Maricopa and Pima, and basketry by the Tohono O'odham. Some Native American artists now realize their visions in paintings,

sculptures, furniture, and stained glass that fuse modern elements with traditional motifs.

Hopi pottery reflects both a 2,000-year-old tradition and contemporary visions in its geometric patterns and figures from Hopi mythology. In the late 1800s, the Hopi craft of pottery making began to decline as modern cookware replaced the old pots. Soon only the women of First Mesa were still making and selling pots to other villages for cooking stew and cornmeal mush. During an excavation of nearby Sikyatki Ruin in 1895, however, one of the village men took some decorated pottery sherds back to his wife, Nampeyo, a skilled Tewa potter. She adapted the designs to her own work and, with the encouragement of trader Thomas Keams, perfected her re-creations of the old shapes and patterns. Brisk sales of her work encouraged other potters to take up the "new" Sikyatki style.

The Hopi also create fine basketry—one of the oldest Native American crafts—in both coiled and wicker forms that display bold patterns and colors. Cotton weaving—traditionally done by men in their kivas during the winter—is an old skill too, . During the 1890s the first Hopi silversmiths learned their skill from the Zuni, who in turn had picked it up from the Navajo, and all three groups initially produced similar styles. Staff at the Museum

**Older Navajo women often dress in the style of 19th-century army officer wives. This woman is carding wool, which she will make into yarn with the spindle whorl beside her, then weave into a rug.**

of Northern Arizona in Flagstaff saw the need for the Hopi to develop a unique style; they suggested that the Hopi adapt pottery and basketry designs for their silverwork by cutting the patterns in sheets of silver, then soldering them onto the main body of the piece as an overlay. The idea took off after World War II, when Hopi veterans returned and joined a G.I. training program. In 1949 the new Hopi Silvercrafts Cooperative Guild further helped the artists by providing a place to purchase supplies, work, display, and sell their work. Artists also experimented with gold and new techniques such as colorful inlays of gemstones. Kachina dolls, carved from cottonwood roots, originally served to educate children about the spirits in the Hopi religion. They were usually flat or cylindrical, with just enough decoration for identification. When visitors started purchasing them, artists began carving increasingly realistic representations. Some figures now boast exquisite detail. The Heard Museum in Phoenix devotes an entire room to kachina dolls.

Navajo weavers, traditionally women, at first produced fine blankets using wool from sheep obtained from the Spanish and weaving skills learned from the Pueblo tribes. In the late 1800s, factory-made blankets greatly reduced demand, so traders suggested making rugs instead. These became a great success with collectors, and more than a dozen

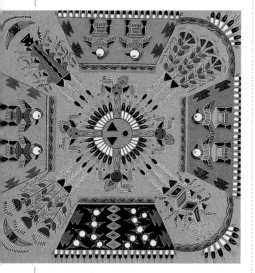

**Navajo use sand paintings in healing and other ceremonies. The colors and symbols portray the four directions, corn, spirits, and other elements.**

regional styles have emerged across the vast Navajo Nation. Silversmiths developed distinctive wares such as the squash-blossom necklace with its horseshoe-shaped pendant. Turquoise is the gemstone of choice for Navajo jewelry. Sand paintings of Navajo deities and symbols play a role in healing ceremonies; they are also mounted and sold.

## ARCHITECTURE

Prehistoric cliff dwellings with their multi-story towers still impress people today at Montezuma Castle National Monument (see pp. 112–13) and other sites across the Southwest. A later wave of people—the Spanish—constructed Mission San Xavier del Bac (see p. 222) in the late 1700s, a great domed monument to their faith. The sheer

visual impact of the ornate interior, with its many statues, murals, and decorations, was intended to make the Catholic religion appeal to the O'odham people of the time. The church's beauty and size are even more impressive in light of the fact that workers built it under the shadow of Apache raids at the edge of the Spanish empire.

Before the railroads, Americans made do with simple adobe houses in the desert and log structures in the forested uplands. Victorian houses became the fashion in the late 1800s, adding a comforting touch of civilization to the frontier. By 1900, Arizonans sought a regional identity and went through phases of Mission Revival from 1900 to 1915 and the more romantic Spanish Colonial Revival between 1915 and 1930. City planners then decided they needed more "serious" buildings and adopted less colorful modern styles—undistinguished "boxes" with little or no ornamentation. Up at the Grand Canyon, architect Mary Colter (1869–1958) had been designing distinctive public buildings using Southwestern themes or elaborate stories. She worked hard to get the details just right, even choosing the interior furnishings and colors. When called upon to design a Native American art gallery at the South Rim, she patterned the 1905 Hopi House (see p. 51) after structures in the Hopi village of Old Oraibi. Hermit's Rest (1914), another tourist facility on the South Rim, was made to look and feel as if a recluse had just decamped the premises. La Posada (1930), a luxurious railroad hotel in Winslow, may have been Colter's grandest commission—a vast hacienda designed to make guests feel as though they were the personal guests of a Spanish don.

Architect Frank Lloyd Wright (1867–1959) had already achieved worldwide fame when he opened Taliesin West (see p. 164) near Scottsdale in 1937 as a winter home for both his family and his school of architecture. Tours offer an introduction to Wright's philosophies and designs, in which he allowed his organic architecture to "grow" from the inside out.

**This statue of Gen. Francisco "Pancho" Villa caused quite a stir when it went up in downtown Tucson in 1981: The general once led raids on U.S. soil.**

**Touring in style, 1929: Architect Frank Lloyd Wright, with his wife, Olgivanna, and daughters, Svetlana and Iovanna, visit Ocotilla Desert Camp near Chandler.**

You'll see how his buildings fit gracefully upon the land and look different from every angle. Wright had a hand in the Biltmore Resort in Phoenix and designed the Gammage Auditorium (see p. 162), one of his last major buildings, on Arizona State University's Tempe campus. Also worth seeing at ASU, the Nelson Fine Arts Center (see p. 161), built in 1989 by architect Antoine Predock, offers a contemporary vision of the Southwest.

### WRITERS

Author Zane Grey (1872–1939) turned out so many romantic novels about the American West that he is often credited with inventing the genre. While working as a dentist in New York City, he tried his hand at writing *Betty Zane* (1903), a novel about pioneer life based on an ancestor's journal, then plunged into writing full-time and came out West. With his wife taking care of editing, marketing, and family, Grey was able to write more than 80 books, creating a backlog for his publisher that lasted for 20 years after his death. Grey's passion for fishing, hunting, and collecting

stories took him on wide-ranging travels that included Arizona. He built a lodge beneath the Mogollon Rim; here he researched some of his most popular novels. Historic events that had taken place nearby inspired *To the Last Man* (1922), his graphic depiction of the tragic Pleasant Valley War between sheepmen and cattlemen. Grey portrayed Arizona's social problems in books such as *Under the Tonto Rim* (1926), also set below the Mogollon Rim, and *The Call of the Canyon* (1924), which takes place in the Oak Creek Canyon area. Even if his publisher balked, he was not afraid of tackling controversial issues encountered by Native Americans: *The Vanishing American* (1925) and *Captives of the Desert* (1952) both present the difficulties faced by the Navajo people on their reservation.

Historian, folksinger, and educator Marshall Trimble (1939–) has probably done more than anyone to make Arizona's history enjoyable. He wrote in an informal story-telling style that brings to life people who walked and rode through the past. His books include *Arizona: A Cavalcade of History* (1990) and *A Roadside History of Arizona* (1986). His stories also appeared in *Arizona Highways* magazine and in the books *Law of the Gun* (1997) and the entertaining *Never Give a Heifer a Bum Steer* (1999).

Novelist Zane Grey loved the outdoor life. Some of the earliest Western movies were based on his stories.

Edward Abbey enjoyed the solitude of working as a lookout in fire towers, such as this one above Globe, Arizona.

Edward Abbey (1927–1989) captured the imagination of many who reveled in nature's wildness, as expressed in his iconic *Desert Solitaire* (1968). Later works, such as *The Monkey Wrench Gang* (1975) and its posthumous sequel, *Hayduke Lives!* (1989), added impetus to the environmental movement. Abbey's sharp wit and lively prose balance out his cynicism.

Arizona's landscapes, people, rivers, wildlife, and plants have inspired a great many writers to describe the natural world in books such as Ann Zwinger's *Downcanyon: A Naturalist Explores the Colorado River through the Grand Canyon* (1995), Craig Childs' *Grand Canyon: Time Below the Rim* (1999), John Alcock's *In a Desert Garden: Love and Death Among the Insects* (1997), and Janice Emily Bower's *Fear Falls Away; and Other Essays from Hard and Rocky Places* (1997).

## DREAMERS

Italian-born architect Paolo Soleri (1919–) has lived most of his life in Arizona pursuing a dream. Not content to do the usual house and building designs, he offers ideas for futuristic cities that will provide integrated total environments to maximize beneficial social interaction while minimizing land use and damage to the environment. The ideas provide alternatives to the urban sprawl and reliance on automobiles that plague cities today, and they point toward a future in which humans can seek their full potential. His dream is now taking shape in the desert of central Arizona through an urban laboratory called Arcosanti (see pp. 122–23). Dedicated workers at the site test the ideas of "arcology," a concept of architecture and ecology working together as a single process. Success here could revolutionize the way people build their cities.

Arizona's people, living mostly in urban settings, often dream of finding a place in the natural environment, yet earlier cultures sometimes knew best how to fit in. The alcoves that sheltered their cliff dwellings gave shade in summer but let in the low winter sun—a concept reborn in the apses of Arcosanti. Adobe villages of the Pueblo tribes featured closely spaced houses that shaded each other, protecting their inhabitants from temperature extremes and maximizing the land available for agriculture. Spanish settlers introduced to the Southwest the shady walled courtyards of the Mediterranean, an architectural style worthy of a comeback. Native plants, with their beautiful shapes and colorful flowers, seem a much better alternative to lawns and gardens imported from the humid Midwest or East. As Charles Bowden wrote in *Blue Desert:* "Here the land always makes promises of aching beauty and the people always fail the land." Thirst for water has dammed all but a handful of rivers and destroyed most of the native riparian forests. Desert grasslands are still recovering from the overgrazing of a century ago. Arizonans have responded to these challenges by setting aside natural areas as preserves and thinking hard about how to meet water and land needs.

### PERFORMING ARTS

Classical music fills the halls during performances by the symphony orchestras of Flagstaff, Phoenix, Scottsdale, and Tucson.

**John Wayne—posing on the street named for him in Prescott, Arizona—rode across the sands of Monument Valley and into movie legend.**

Arizona Opera and Ballet Arizona stage productions in both Phoenix and Tucson. These cities also host classical and contemporary plays staged by the Arizona Theater Company. All three universities—Flagstaff's Northern Arizona University, Tempe's Arizona State University, and Tucson's University of Arizona—host a varied program of concerts and plays by students and visiting artists. Local tourist offices can advise on upcoming music and fine arts festivals.

### LIGHTS, CAMERA, ACTION!

Arizona's cinema history began in 1923 with *Robber's Roost,* based on a Zane Grey outlaw story and filmed in Oak Creek Canyon. *The Vanishing American,* another silent picture portrayal of a Zane Grey story, was filmed two years later at Monument Valley, a scenic region that later became synonymous with Westerns.

Director John Ford (1895–1973) delighted in working at Monument Valley, declaring it the "most complete, beautiful, and peaceful place on earth." Westerns were no longer in fashion when Ford arrived at Monument Valley in 1938, but he had a promising script about a disparate group of travelers taking a stagecoach through hostile Apache country. Local traders Harry and Leone "Mike" Goulding had made a successful sales pitch to Ford about their beloved valley and convinced him to come out and see it.

The Great Depression had brought difficult times for the Navajo. Many faced starvation; they needed the jobs that a movie production would bring. *Stagecoach* was nominated for seven Academy Awards when it opened in 1939 and transformed the career of 31-year-old actor John Wayne. The movie also ignited a love affair between John Ford and Monument Valley that lasted the rest of his life. The appreciative Navajo made him a member of their tribe with the name Natani Nez, "Tall Soldier." He made his last Western, *Cheyenne Autumn,* a sympathetic story about a Native American tribe, here in 1964, then returned one last time in 1971 to appear in a Peter Bogdanovich documentary called *Directed by John Ford.*

In southern Arizona, 21-year-old William Holden and 31-year-old Jean Arthur starred in *Arizona,* the 1939 epic about bringing civilization to the Arizona frontier. Rather than tear down the set after filming, the movie company decided to keep it as a permanent studio. Old Tucson Studios has hosted more than 300 films and television shows since and is now a major tourist attraction (see p. 207). ∎

The raging Colorado River has carved a "geologic book" out of the colorful rock layers of the Earth's crust to create the Grand Canyon. This awesome natural wonder has entranced its many visitors for generations.

# Grand Canyon Country

**Memorial plaque, Lake Powell**

# Grand Canyon Country

GRAND INDEED ARE THE GRAND CANYON'S STATISTICS. THE GREAT CHASM extends 277 miles across northern Arizona, with an average width of 10 miles. At the bottom, about a mile below the rim, the Colorado River roars through 70 major rapids in the course of its 2,200-foot descent through the canyon. Stunning figures—yet they scarcely hint at the magnificence of the spectacle itself.

That the Grand Canyon provides such an incredible geologic record is due to its arid climate and sparse vegetation, which have left the layers of rock clearly visible. Lying one below another are deposits of ancient seas, rivers, sand dunes, volcanoes, and—at the very bottom—the roots of a mountain range more than one billion years old.

Native Americans lived here thousands of years ago, leaving behind split-twig animal figurines and stone tools. Ancient Pueblo people (Anasazi) arrived by A.D. 500 and stayed until about 1150. You can still see their masonry villages and granaries. About 1300, the Havasupai moved in from the west; they have lived in Havasu Canyon—a major tribu-

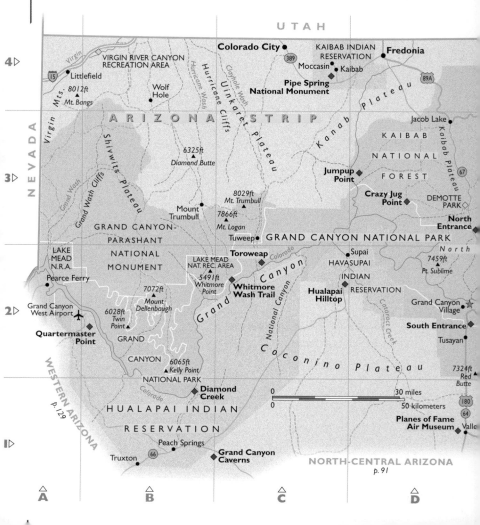

tary of the Grand Canyon—ever since. You can hike in, visit their village, and view the spectacular waterfalls and travertine pools (see pp. 56–57). Other tribes live near the canyon: the Kaibab Paiute to the north, the Navajo to the east, and the Hualapai to the south.

Spanish explorers first saw the canyon in 1540, when a detachment of Francisco Vásquez de Coronado's expedition arrived but could not find a way down. From the 1880s on, American prospectors following old Indian trails struck silver, copper, lead, and asbestos. Getting the ore up and out of the canyon was tough work, however; many of the miners found guiding tourists more profitable. Early visitors faced an all-day stage ride from Flag-

staff to the South Rim, but that changed in 1901, when the first train puffed in. Conservationists such as Theodore Roosevelt urged government protection of the canyon. It became a forest reserve in 1893, a national monument in 1908, and a national park in 1919.

Today Grand Canyon National Park receives about five million visitors each year. It's wise to plan ahead, especially in summer, when parking spots, accommodations, and campgrounds all fill up. You can often find solitude on Kaibab National Forest lands adjacent to the park on both rims. Relatively few visitors know about the viewpoints, trails, camping, and beautiful forests there.

The great barrier of the Grand Canyon separates the lonely country of the Arizona Strip from the rest of Arizona. People on widely scattered ranches and in a handful of small towns scratch out livings on the strip's 14,000 acres of rugged plateaus, mountains, and canyons. Historically, the region has far closer ties with Utah, whose Mormon explorers and settlers ventured here in the second half of the 19th century. ■

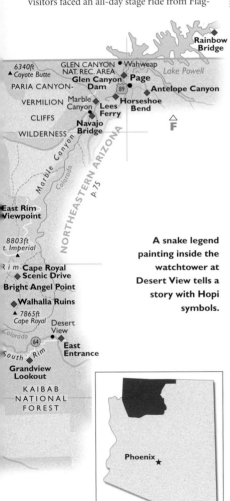

A snake legend painting inside the watchtower at Desert View tells a story with Hopi symbols.

Area of map detail

Hikers enjoy the spectacle of a Grand Canyon sunset from Yaki Point on the South Rim.

# South Rim

"DO NOTHING TO MAR ITS GRANDEUR FOR THE AGES HAVE been at work upon it and man cannot improve it. Keep it for your children, your children's children, and all who come after you."
—President Theodore Roosevelt (1858–1919)

The Grand Canyon's easily accessible South Rim has many scenic overlooks and extensive visitor services. It lies at an elevation averaging 7,000 feet, covered with ponderosa pine forests and pinyon-juniper woodlands. You'll find the **South Entrance** 58 miles north of I-40 Exit 165. Tusayan, 1 mile south of the South Entrance, offers many places to stay, a campground, restaurants, stores, an IMAX theater, and scenic flights. The **East Entrance** provides an alternative connection with Flagstaff and is closer to the North Rim and to Navajo and Hopi lands. Desert View Drive connects the South and East Entrances. At either entrance, pick up a map and *The Guide*, a handy newspaper that lists ranger programs, places to visit, suggested hikes, and park news.

The Park Service offers free **shuttle service** on parts of the South Rim to alleviate traffic congestion. In the future, parking for the Grand Canyon Village area will be shifted to just outside the park in Tusayan, and buses or a light rail line will bring visitors to Canyon View Information Plaza, just south of Mather Point, whence they can head off on a shuttle to their desired destinations.

**Grand Canyon Village** is the heart of South Rim sightseeing. From here and nearby viewpoints, you'll see the great expanse of canyon, points, buttes, and what are known as temples—majestic remnants of canyon rims isolated by erosion. Panels outside the new **Canyon View Information Plaza** indicate sightseeing and hiking possibilities, and details of

**Tusayan Ranger Station, Kaibab National Forest**
www.fs.fed.us/r3/kai
✉ Just S of the South Entrance (P.O. Box 3088, Tusayan, AZ 86023)
☎ 928/638-2443

ranger programs; step inside for the information desk and additional exhibits.

For walkers, the **Rim Trail** is the best way to see the Grand Canyon and points of interest in Grand Canyon Village; it's paved and nearly level on the 4 miles between Mather Point to the east and Maricopa Point to the west. Cyclists may not use the Rim Trail, but they can ride roads and paved trails farther back from the rim.

Several points of interest line the rim near **Bright Angel Lodge.** Step into the rustic lodge to see early tourism exhibits and a geologic fireplace (made from Grand Canyon rocks layered in the same sequence as in the canyon) in the Bright Angel History Room. The 1914 stone **Lookout Studio,** just to the west, blends in well with the rim and has a viewing platform and gift shop.

Next is the **Kolb Studio,** first opened in 1904 as a photographic studio of the Kolb brothers and now a hall, showing temporary exhibits, and bookstore. The **Bright Angel Trail** (see p. 54) drops off the rim nearby and switchbacks down to Indian Garden and on to the Colorado River and Phantom Ranch. East along the rim from Bright Angel Lodge, you'll come to the unique example of rustic elegance that is **El Tovar Hotel,** the top lodging in the park. Visit its lobby for the cathedral ceiling and log walls even if you're staying elsewhere.

**Hopi House,** just beyond, opened in 1905 as a place where members of the Hopi tribe could live, demonstrate their work, and operate a sales gallery. It's modeled after structures in the ancient Hopi village of Old Oraibi. You'll find beautiful Native American art and crafts for sale on two floors. More Native American work can be seen next door in **Verkamp's,** run by the same family since 1905. ∎

**Grand Canyon National Park**

🅰 48 C3, D3

**Visitor information**

www.nps.gov/grca

✉ P.O. Box 129, Grand Canyon, AZ 86023

☎ 928/638-7888

💲 $$$$ per vehicle or National Parks Pass, Golden Age, or Golden Access

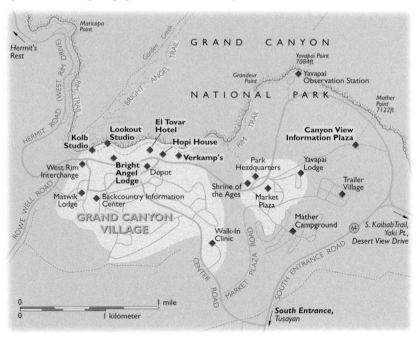

# Two South Rim drives

Two drives follow the South Rim of the Grand Canyon past many overlooks, each offering a different perspective of the canyon's spectacular scenery and geology. You can start from Grand Canyon Village, where the drives join, or at Desert View on the east end, 33 miles from Cameron.

## DRIVE ONE:
### Hermit Road (West Rim Drive)

Most visitors have to use the shuttle bus to travel this 8-mile road along the rim west from Grand Canyon Village. The bus solves parking problems, and you can hop on and off as you please. Private cars can use the road only in winter, when the shuttle isn't running, though disabled visitors may obtain a special permit from the visitor center. Bicyclists may ride the road but must pull off to let large vehicles

pass. For walkers, the unpaved **Rim Trail** (see p. 51) parallels the Hermit Road.

Besides breathtaking views of the canyon at stops along the way, you'll see the **John Wesley Powell Memorial** ❶ and **The Abyss** ❷, where the ground falls away from the rim in a 3,000-foot sheer drop. The drive ends at **Hermit's Rest** ❸, a 1914 stone building named for prospector Louis Boucher, who lived in the Grand Canyon for 21 years. Nearby is the start of the **Hermit Trail,** taking walkers all the way to the Colorado River, and connecting with other trails on the way. ■

**DRIVE ONE:**
- 🅰 Also see area map p. 48 D2
- ➤ Grand Canyon Village
- ↔ 16 miles round-trip
- 🕐 1.5 hours
- ➤ Hermit's Rest

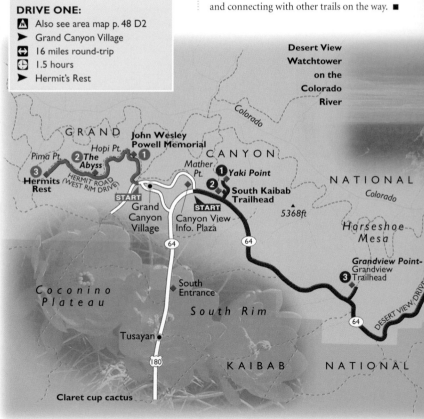

Claret cup cactus

## DRIVE TWO:
### Desert View Drive (East Rim Drive)

This 25-mile drive begins east of Grand Canyon Village and continues to Desert View, the highest viewpoint on the South Rim and one of the most spectacular. The many overlooks on or just off Desert View Drive each provide a different perspective of the canyon. Shuttle buses run to Yaki Point and South Kaibab Trailhead only.

The first overlook east of Grand Canyon Village is **Yaki Point ❶**. (Disabled visitors may obtain a permit.) A branch of the Yaki Point Road goes to the **South Kaibab Trailhead ❷**, where the South Kaibab Trail follows a ridge into the canyon. Cedar Ridge is a good day-hike, three hours round-trip.

About 8 miles farther along the drive you'll find the well-named **Grandview Point ❸**. From 1892 to 1907, miners worked copper deposits on Horseshoe Mesa and brought the

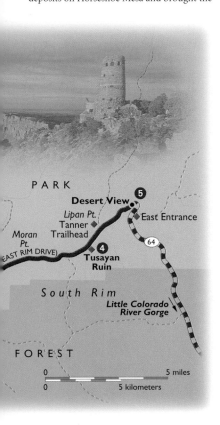

**DRIVE TWO:**
- ⚑ Also see area map p. 48 D2
- ➤ Grand Canyon Village
- ⟷ 25 miles
- 🕐 1 hour plus stops
- ➤ Desert View

**NOT TO BE MISSED**
- Grandview Point
- Tusayan Ruin
- Desert View

ore up on the Grandview Trail, a former Indian route. **Tusayan Ruin ❹** marks the site of a village built by ancient Pueblo people about 1185, according to tree ring dating of the roof beams used. For almost 40 years they coaxed a meager living from their fields and surrounding countryside, then migrated elsewhere. Exhibits in a small museum introduce the ancient and modern peoples of this region. A short self-guided tour takes you around the plaza and foundations of living quarters, storage rooms, and kivas (ceremonial rooms). *The Guide* lists times of ranger walks and storytelling held in peak season.

At **Desert View ❺**, a 70-foot stone watchtower, built in 1932, stands on the canyon's edge like a prehistoric guardian. On the walls and ceilings inside, you can try to decipher hundreds of painted designs created by Hopi. The log ceiling in the adjacent gift shop is patterned after traditional Navajo hogans. The tremendous 360-degree panorama from the watchtower's viewing platform takes in the Grand Canyon to the north and west, volcanoes of the San Francisco Volcanic Field to the south, and the Painted Desert to the east. Facilities at Desert View include an information desk, a snack bar, store, campground *(closed in winter)*, and service station.

Beyond Desert View, just north of the highway on Navajo land on the way to Cameron, are two overlooks of the **Little Colorado River Gorge**. The most popular is between Mileposts 285 and 286, with a short walk to the viewpoints; the other is between Mileposts 280 and 281, where you need to walk about a quarter-mile to see the gorge. ■

# Inner Canyon hiking

**Backcountry Information Center, Grand Canyon National Park**
www.nps.gov/grca

✉ Located at Maswik Transportation Center on South Rim & at North Rim Ranger Station; P.O. Box 129, Grand Canyon, AZ 86023 (for permits)

☎ 928/638-7875 Call Mon.–Fri. 1–5 p.m.

**The vistas from Cedar Ridge on the South Kaibab Trail make it a fine day-hike destination.**

TRAVELING ON FOOT IS ONE OF THE BEST WAYS TO appreciate the small details of the Grand Canyon—its wonderfully sculptured side canyons, its wildlife, its colorful flowers, its sounds, and its silences. Walking also reveals its grandeur and immense scale. Each of the canyons within the canyon has its own personality; you would need a lifetime to experience them all.

To enjoy a hike within the Grand Canyon's depths, plan ahead and bring the right clothing and gear for the season in this desert land. If required, obtain a backcountry permit. Water should be the heaviest item in your pack because reliable sources in the canyon may be many miles apart. Energy foods, a hat, sunscreen, and comfortable, sturdy shoes or boots will enable you to enjoy hiking to the full. Weather can surprise you in all seasons, but good rain gear will fend off any passing storms.

Spring sees wildflowers and generally pleasant hiking temperatures throughout the canyon, though some roads on the North Rim may still be closed; good hiking conditions return in autumn. In summer the lower part of the Grand Canyon becomes an oven; hikers cope by traveling early or late in the day and by drinking extra water. Winter often brings a beautiful soft light and crisp days. Snow and ice may make trails slushy or hazardously slippery, and most roads on the North Rim will be closed.

The National Park Service publishes the free newspaper *Grand Canyon National Park's Backcountry Trip Planner* with lots of good advice, trail information, maps, and permit details; it's available in the park, by mail, and on the Internet. You won't need a permit for day hikes or if you have a reservation at **Phantom Ranch** (see p. 243) in the bottom of the canyon, but all

other overnight trips require one. Demand for permits far exceeds the supply, so obtain them well in advance.

All trails entering from the rims offer good day hikes—remember to save two-thirds of your water, energy, and time for the hike back! Many hikers are tempted to go from the South Rim to the river and back in a day, but the distance and elevation change are too great to do this safely; such a trip would be very dangerous in summer.

Park rangers highly recommend that first-time hikers use trails in the Corridor Zone—the **Bright Angel** (7.8 miles) and **South Kaibab** (6.3 miles) **Trails** from the South Rim and the **North Kaibab Trail** (14.2 miles) from the North Rim. Well maintained and easy to follow, these trails offer spectacular scenery but are sufficiently well trodden for help to be around in case of trouble. All three meet at two footbridges across the Colorado River near **Bright Angel Campground** and Phantom Ranch. Many guidebooks describe trails and routes in the Grand Canyon, but it's worth talking with a ranger about current water sources and trail conditions.

If you are fit, you can make a great day-hike loop by descending the **South Kaibab Trail** 4.4 miles to the **Tonto Trail,** turning left and going 4.1 miles on the Tonto to **Indian Garden,** then ascending the **Bright Angel Trail**

4.6 miles back to the South Rim. **Plateau Point,** a 3-mile round-trip from Indian Garden, is a popular side-trip for hikers on Bright Angel Trail; it features a stunning 360-degree panorama of the Grand Canyon. A rim-to-rim hike is a grand adventure that takes three days one way; to explore side canyons and attractions such as **Ribbon Falls** en route requires additional time. ■

**A short hike leads to a spot for quiet contemplation.**

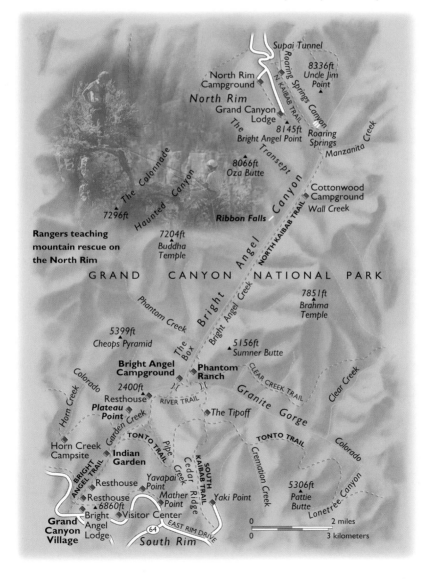

Supai Tunnel

8336ft
Uncle Jim
Point

North Rim
Campground

Roaring Springs Canyon

N KAIBAB TRAIL

North Rim
Grand Canyon
Lodge

8145ft
Bright Angel Point

Roaring
Springs

The Transept

Manzanita Creek

8066ft
Oza Butte

The Colonnade

Haunted Canyon

Bright Angel Canyon

Cottonwood
Campground
Wall Creek

7296ft

Ribbon Falls

NORTH KAIBAB TRAIL

**Rangers teaching
mountain rescue on
the North Rim**

7204ft
Buddha
Temple

G R A N D     C A N Y O N     N A T I O N A L     P A R K

Phantom Creek

Bright Angel Creek

7851ft
Brahma
Temple

5399ft
Cheops Pyramid

The Box

5156ft
Sumner Butte

Colorado

**Bright Angel
Campground**

**Phantom
Ranch**

CLEAR CREEK TRAIL

Clear Creek

2400ft
Resthouse

RIVER TRAIL

Granite Gorge

Colorado

**Plateau
Point**

Garden Creek

The Tipoff

Horn Creek
Campsite

TONTO TRAIL

TONTO TRAIL

Horn Creek

**Indian
Garden**

BRIGHT ANGEL TRAIL

Pipe Creek

Cedar Ridge

SOUTH KAIBAB TRAIL

Cremation Creek

5306ft
Pattie
Butte

Lonetree Canyon

Resthouse

Yavapai
Point

Resthouse
▲6860ft

**Grand
Canyon
Village**

Bright
Angel
Lodge

**Visitor Center**

Mather
Point

Yaki Point

64

EAST RIM DRIVE

**South Rim**

0        2 miles
0    3 kilometers

# Havasupai Indian Reservation

A HIKE INTO HAVASU CANYON, ON FOOT OR ON HORSE-
back, can be a transformative experience. Towering rock walls enclose
Supai village and an oasis of lush vegetation, glistening waterfalls,
and blue-green pools rimmed by travertine. The beauty and remoteness invoke the dawn of time.

**Havasupai Indian
Reservation**
📷 48 C2
**Visitor information**
www.havasupaitribe.com
✉ Havasupai Tourist
Enterprise, P.O. Box
160, Supai, AZ
86435
☎ 928/448-2141

An 8-mile trail (one way), steep at
first, leads from the trailhead at
5,200-foot **Hualapai Hilltop**
down through spectacular canyon
scenery to the village. To reach the
starting point, take Route 66 (Arizona 66) northwest 28 miles from
Seligman or northeast 55 miles
from Kingman, then turn northeast
and go 60 miles on Indian 18. No
gas, food, or water is available along
this road or at the trailhead.

Horses or mules will be waiting
for you if you've made a reservation
for them with the Havasupai Tourist Enterprise (if camping) or the
lodge (if staying there). The trail
descends 2,000 feet between the
start and **Supai** village. Always
carry water; in summer, avoid the

heat of the day for the climb back
up, as there is little shade.

As you enter **Havasu Canyon**
you see and hear sparkling Havasu
Creek on the approach to Supai
village, reached only by trail or
helicopter. About 500 Havasupai
(from *havasu*, meaning blue-green
water, and *pai* for people) live in
Supai and still farm in the canyon.
They welcome visitors year-round.

Reserve in advance at the
**Havasupai Lodge** *(Tel 928/448-
2111)* in the village as well as for the
campground, 2 miles farther down
Havasu Canyon between Havasu
Falls and Mooney Falls.

**Navajo Falls** is 1.5 miles
downstream from Supai. The name
of the braided 75-foot falls com-

memorates a 19th-century Havasu-pai abducted as a child and raised by Navajo. When he grew up and learned his true origin, he went back to the Havasupai, who made him a chief. Half a mile farther on, **Havasu Falls** gracefully cascades a hundred feet to a large turquoise pool rimmed by travertine—an in-viting spot for a swim or a picnic. Continue another mile through the campground for **Mooney Falls,** the highest, with an awe-inspiring 196-foot plunge to travertine pools. In 1880 prospector Daniel Mooney

tried to descend the falls on a rope, but it jammed in the rock and later broke, plunging him to his death on the rocks below.

Havasupai know the falls as "Mother of the Waters." A steep, rough trail with a chain handrail winds to the bottom. If you feel like more hiking, an even rougher trail continues downstream 2 miles to small **Beaver Falls** and a good swimming spot just below. Four more miles of walking takes you to the Colorado River at the bottom of the Grand Canyon. ■

**Havasu Falls plunges into a travertine-rimmed pool in a scene reminiscent of Shangri-la.**

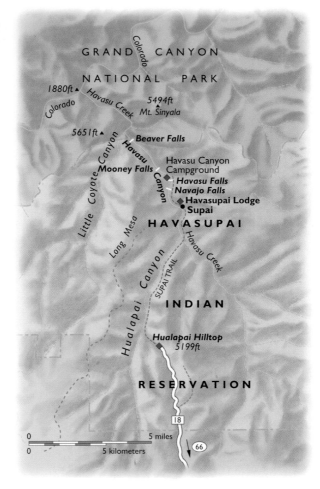

# Hualapai Indian Reservation

RELATIVELY FEW PEOPLE HAVE SEEN THE MAJESTIC panoramas from the South Rim of the lower Grand Canyon. Nor have many visitors driven Diamond Creek Road to the Colorado River at the canyon's bottom. These attractions lie on the lands of the Hualapai (Pine Tree People), who once roamed over much of northwestern Arizona.

Most of the 1,500 members of the Hualapai live in **Peach Springs,** a town lacking in charm but possessing a good motel and restaurant where you can obtain information and permits. Peach Springs sits at 4,797 feet right on Route 66 (Arizona 66), 49 miles northeast of Kingman and 34 miles northwest of Seligman.

### GRAND CANYON WEST

The Hualapai tribe offers a tour from a remote airport terminal at Grand Canyon West to overlooks nearly 4,000 feet above the Colorado River. You can fly into the terminal from Las Vegas or drive one of four routes to get there—all of which have some dirt road. Each route takes about two hours one way. Because of the distances, call the reservation first to check road conditions and tour times.

On the tour from the terminal, a bus takes you the 4.5 miles to Guano Point for a barbecue lunch and views of the lower Grand Canyon. In the late 1950s, a company called U.S. Guano built a series of towers for a tramline that carried bat guano (used for fertilizer) from a cave on the north side of the Grand Canyon. The system is no longer in use, but you can visit the tower at Guano Point

**Hualapai Indian Reservation (Grand Canyon West & Hualapai Lodge)**
www.hualapaitours.com

🏔 48 B1, C1

✉ P.O. Box 538, Peach Springs, AZ 86434

☎ 928/769-2230 or 888/255-9550

**Burning cryshed at the Hualapai Memorial Pow-Wow, near Peach Springs**

and see the machinery inside. The tour also includes a stop to view Eagle Point, a long neck of land curving far out into the canyon.

On your own with a permit, you can drive 3.4 miles from the Grand Canyon West terminal to **Quartermaster Point** for an outstanding panorama of the Grand Canyon farther upstream. A quarter-mile trail leads down to the best viewpoints.

From Peach Springs, the best approach to Grand Canyon West turns north off Route 66 between Mileposts 74 and 75 to unpaved Antares Road, which you follow 33 miles to paved Pearce Ferry Road; turn right (northeast) and go 7 miles, then keep right on Diamond Bar Road/Indian 1 for 21 miles to its end. The unpaved first 14 miles of this road cross a scenic area of Joshua trees, their spare, angular branches uplifted as if in supplication, and follow a canyon through the Grand Wash Cliffs. Buck and Doe Road, shorter but rougher, can be impassable when wet; it turns north between Mileposts 100 and 101 on Route 66.

From Kingman, you could take the partly paved Stockton Hill Road north to Pearce Ferry Road and Diamond Bar Road/Indian 1. Or from US 93 between Kingman and Las Vegas, take the paved Pearce Ferry Road 26 miles to Diamond Bar Road/Indian 1.

## DIAMOND CREEK ROAD

Diamond Creek Road turns north from Peach Springs and gradually descends into the Grand Canyon. The earliest tourists came this way in 1883, and from 1884 to 1889 the Grand Canyon's first hotel operated near the confluence of Diamond Creek and the Colorado River. The 21-mile road is unpaved and may require a high-clearance vehicle or four-wheel-drive after rain. Staff at the Hualapai Lodge can inform you of road conditions; they also sell permits for driving, camping, and fishing.

To see the lower Grand Canyon at river level, sign up for a day-long raft tour with **Hualapai River Runners** during the March to October season. Overnight trips to Lake Mead can be chartered. ■

**The Hualapai invite visitors to experience the splendor of the western Grand Canyon.**

**Hualapai River Runners**
www.river-runners.com
✉ Office in Hualapai Lodge in Peach Springs
P.O. Box 246, Peach Springs, AZ 86434
☎ 928/769-2219 or 888/255-9550

# North Rim

DRAMATIC VISTAS OF CHASMS AND TOWERING ROCK
pinnacles, luxuriant forests, wildflowers, and cool mountain air make
the Grand Canyon's North Rim a delight to visit. If you have seen the
canyon from the South Rim, it will look very different from here.

The southward slope of the plateau
through which the Colorado River
passes has caused tributary streams
to cut vigorously into the North
Rim and erode it far back from the
river; on the South Rim, by contrast, precipitation flows away from
the canyon, leaving the rim relatively intact. Elevations average more
than a thousand feet higher on the
North Rim and attract such heavy
snowfall that the access road is
usually closed in winter and early
spring. You can visit from about
mid-May until late October. Although a distance of only 10 miles
separates the rims, to get from one
to the other involves a five-hour
drive of more than 200 miles. Only
about one in ten canyon visitors
makes it to the North Rim, so it
is much less crowded than the
South Rim.

The **North Entrance** station
provides a park map and a North
Rim edition of *The Guide* that lists
ranger programs, hiking tips,
services, and park news. Drop in at
the **North Rim Visitor Center**
at Grand Canyon Lodge to learn
more about activities and places to
visit. Close by, an easy half-mile
round-trip walk on the paved
**Bright Angel Point Trail** takes
you to the very tip of the point.
Look into Roaring Springs Canyon
on your left for the springs blasting
out of the cliff far below, but don't
miss the equally precipitous cliffs of
The Transept on your right. Kaibab
limestone, the rock exposed here
and atop the South Rim, contains
shells of animals that lived in an
ancient sea 240 to 250 million years
ago; you can see some of them in
an outcrop just past a stone bridge.

**Grand Canyon
National Park:
North Rim**

🅰 48 D2, E2
**Visitor information**
www.nps.gov/grca
✉ P.O. Box 129, Grand
Canyon, AZ 86023
☎ 928/638-7888
💲 $$$$ per vehicle;
good at both rims
for 7 days

From the trail's end there is a dramatic vista down lengthey Bright Angel Canyon and across to the South Rim. The summits of the San Francisco Volcanic Field break the skyline. On the way back to the lodge, bear left and stroll along the **Transept Trail,** which follows the rim to North Rim Campground (3 miles round-trip). Other North Rim walks are the **Widforss Trail** (10 miles round-trip), the **Ken Patrick Trail** to Point Imperial (20 miles round-trip), and the **Uncle Jim Trail,** a popular mule ride (5 miles round-trip).

Of all the Grand Canyon trails, the **North Kaibab Trail** has some of the most dramatic scenery. The complete round-trip—28 miles from the North Rim—includes a 6,000-foot descent to the Colorado River and a strenuous climb back up. Camp at either Cottonwood or Bright Angel Campgrounds or stay at Phantom Ranch (see p. 243). Good day hikes can be made along part of the trail to **Coconino Overlook** (1.5 miles round-trip), for example, to **Supai Tunnel** (4 miles round-trip), or to

**Roaring Springs** (a strenuous 9.4-mile round-trip with a 3,050-foot elevation change).

## ACCOMMODATIONS
Grand Canyon Lodge and North Rim Campground, near Bright

**Below: Early park visitors rode mules down Bright Angel Trail, and you can too.**

Angel Point, are the only developed places to stay in this northern section of the park, so it's best to make reservations in summer. The campgrounds and dispersed camping in Kaibab National Forest (see pp. 63–64) provide another option. Just find your own spot, making sure it's not too close to paved roads or sole water sources. Bring your own shovel (for digging a latrine), water, and camping supplies.

### CAPE ROYAL & POINT IMPERIAL

Bring a picnic and spend a whole day enjoying the amazing panoramas of the **Cape Royal Scenic Drive.** You will soon see why John Wesley Powell remarked that "the canyon is a Book of Revelations in the rock-leaved Bible of geology."

From the turnoff 3 miles north of Grand Canyon Lodge, the paved road winds through meadows and forests. Turn left at the junction for **Point Imperial,** at 8,803 feet the highest overlook in the park. (The road through Fuller Canyon and on to Point Imperial was heavily affected by the Outlet Fire in 2000. You will see meadows, but much of the forested area is gone.) Views from here take in much of northeastern Arizona and the dramatic geology of the eastern Grand Canyon, where erosion and faulting have carved and tilted the rock layers into countless ridges and rock temples below. Navajo Mountain lies just across the border in Utah.

Returning to the junction and continuing toward Cape Royal (another 15 miles), you'll pass Vista Encantada, Roosevelt Point, Walhalla Overlook, and other viewpoints on the left. **Walhalla Ruins,** across the road from Walhalla Overlook, was a summer village of the ancient Pueblo people who lived in the area until about 1150. Warm air currents blowing up the canyon walls helped make agriculture possible at this 8,000-foot elevation. In winter, the villagers moved to sites such as Unkar Delta at the bottom of the canyon. Just over a mile beyond Walhalla Overlook, at a curve in the road, there is parking for the **Cliff Spring Trail.** This pretty hike (1 mile round-trip) takes you down a ravine, past an ancient ruin, to the spring.

**Cape Royal** extends far out into the Grand Canyon at one of its widest sections. You may feel as though you're on an island surrounded by a sea of rock temples and open space. A level, paved 0.6-mile trail takes you to the best

**Mount Hayden rises out of the depths below Point Imperial.**

viewpoints, while a short side trail leads out on top of **Angel's Window,** a massive natural arch. Signs at Cape Royal (elevation 7,865 feet) point out some of the features in the canyon and beyond.

## KAIBAB NATIONAL FOREST

The North Rim of the Grand Canyon extends beyond the national park to many spectacular viewpoints in Kaibab National Forest. Here you can really escape the crowds.

Although the forest roads are unpaved, some have been graded for dry-weather use by cars and small RVs. Nearly the entire forest is open for dispersed camping (except during times of fire danger), and there's always space. You can follow easy paths on the Kaibab Plateau, head down trails into the Saddle Mountain Wilderness on the east edge of the Kaibab Plateau, or descend into the Kanab Creek Wilderness on the west edge. Trails also drop into the depths of the Grand Canyon itself.

Several graded roads fan out to the east of DeMotte Park (just north of the North Rim Entrance) to reach different viewpoints on the **Eastern Kaibab Plateau.** Pick up a free map with directions to the viewpoints from the Kaibab Plateau Visitor Center at Jacob Lake or the North Kaibab Ranger District office at Fredonia. The panorama from 8,800 feet at the **East Rim Viewpoint** takes in Saddle Mountain Wilderness, the upper Grand Canyon, the Painted Desert beyond, and the Vermilion Cliffs to the north, a glowing scene at sunset and sunrise. The **Arizona Trail,** extending from the Mexican border to Utah, runs along the rim here, and other trails drop down into the canyons of Saddle Mountain Wilderness. **Dog Point,** farther north,

and **Marble Viewpoint** and **Saddle Mountain Trailhead,** to the southeast, provide additional perspectives.

A series of points along the **Western Kaibab Plateau** offers amazing panoramas into the heart of the Grand Canyon. All can be reached on spur roads from West Side Road (Forest Road 22), which runs between Arizona 67 in DeMotte Park (see above) and US 89A just east of Fredonia. **Point Sublime** (7,458 feet) is possibly the best viewpoint in the Grand Canyon. It extends so far out into the canyon that you can see both rims, rock temples, buttes—in fact, almost *everything!* You'll need a high-clearance vehicle to get over the rocks; pay close attention to maps for the drive. Camping here requires a backcountry permit.

You can reach yet more viewpoints (Swamp, Fire, Timp, and Parissawampitts, among others) farther west from West Side Road. **Rainbow Rim Trail** (18 miles one way) connects Timp and Parissawampitts Points. **Crazy Jug Point** has the best roads for cars.

You may run across turkeys *(Meleagris gallopavo)* in the forests of the North Rim.

**Kaibab National Forest**
🅰 49 E1, E2
**Visitor information**
www.fs.fed.us/r3/kai
✉ Kaibab Visitor Center, junction of Ariz. 67 & US 89A, at Jacob Lake
☎ 928/643-7298
🕐 May close in winter and some days in spring and autumn

**North Kaibab Ranger District, Kaibab National Forest**
✉ 430 S. Main St., Fredonia (P.O. Box 248, Fredonia, AZ 86022)
☎ 928/643-7395
🕐 Closed Sat.–Sun.

**Toroweap**

🅰 48 C2

**Visitor information**

✉ P.O. Box 129, Grand
Canyon, AZ 86023

☎ 928/638-7888

**From this perch near Toroweap Overlook you can see the white water of Lava Falls Rapid downstream.**

**Jumpup Point** has a nearly 360-degree panorama of Kanab Creek Wilderness, an immense landscape of rugged canyons. You'll need a high-clearance vehicle for the last few miles.

## TOROWEAP

"What a conflict of water and fire there must have been here! Just imagine a river of molten rock running down into a river of melted snow. What seething and boiling of the waters; what clouds of steam rolled into the heavens!" John Wesley Powell's colorful description shows how the volcanic landscapes around **Toroweap Overlook** on the North Rim can capture the imagination. The sheer cliffs here plunge nearly 3,000 feet into the void, and the narrow, steep canyon walls create a very different spectacle from the Grand Canyon's better-known viewpoints.

The most reliable road to Toroweap Overlook turns off Arizona 389, 7 miles west of Fredonia, close

to the state's northern boundary. A sign points the way down 61 miles of dirt road. Cautiously driven cars with good clearance can make the trip in dry weather. Watch for washouts and rough cattle guards. Take it slowly in the rocky section near the end. No supplies are available after you leave the pavement, so be sure to have water, food, supplies, and a full tank of gas. A ranger station with an emergency telephone is on the left about 6 miles before the overlook; the small campground almost a mile before the overlook sits in a scenic canyon.

On the way to Toroweap Overlook, you enter a valley flanked by the dark lava flows of the Uinkaret Mountains to the west and the light-colored sedimentary rock layers of the Kanab Plateau to the east. It's about 140 miles by road downstream from Bright Angel Point (90 river miles). **Vulcan's Throne,** a 600-foot cinder cone (formed by volcanic debris around a vent) at the lower end of the valley, is one of the youngest of approximately 60 volcanoes in the area. Eruptions from volcanoes and vents lasted from about 1.2 million to 30,000 years ago. Lava even poured into the Grand Canyon, forming dams as high as 2,000 feet, now washed away.

At Toroweap Overlook, you can peer over the edge to see the Colorado River as it flows past **Vulcan's Anvil,** an old volcanic neck rising up in the middle of the waters. Native American lands belonging to the Hualapai and the Havasupai lie opposite on the South Rim.

Don't miss the spectacle of **Lava Falls.** A few hundred yards' walk downstream along the rim, you can see the Colorado River explode into massive waves and foam in one of the Grand Canyon's fiercest rapids. ■

# River running in the Grand Canyon

Dories dance through the waves in the hands of skilled rowers.

WHETHER ON A LARGE MOTORIZED RAFT OR A KAYAK, A boat expedition is a great way to see the Grand Canyon. Whatever craft you choose, you can look forward to memorable side trips, wonderful campsites, and superb meals. It's hot in summer, but the river is always at hand to cool you off.

Most visitors who opt to see the canyon from the Colorado River take a commercial trip. A skilled crew does the hard work, allowing passengers to relax and enjoy the trip. Experienced river runners can organize their own trip, but the lengthy permit process is a formidable obstacle; read the National Park Service requirements for details. For a list of commercial outfitters or requirements for private trips, contact Grand Canyon National Park (P.O. Box 129, Grand Canyon, AZ 86023, tel 928/638-7888, www.nps.gov/grca).

Advance reservations are highly recommended, though it is sometimes possible to join a trip on short notice, especially in spring and fall or if there are just a few of you. Boat options are large motorized rafts, small oar rafts, or hard-shelled dories. Kayaks and small paddle rafts can join some raft trips. Motorized rafts travel twice as far in a day as oar-powered craft.

Nearly all trips start at Lees Ferry, just above the Grand Canyon. Some trips stop near Phantom Ranch to take on and let off hikers. Another exchange point for passengers is at Whitmore Wash in the lower canyon, where a helicopter usually ferries people in and out. Most trips end at Diamond Creek, the only road access in the canyon, but you can continue to Lake Mead and the dramatic exit from the Grand Canyon. ∎

# John Wesley Powell

Maps of the American West in the mid-1800s still showed large expanses of unexplored lands, and the one-armed Major John Wesley Powell (1834–1902) was destined to help fill in the gaps.

From early childhood, Powell's interest in natural history had taken him on field trips in his native Midwest to collect plants, animals, and minerals. His strong stance against slavery influenced his decision to enlist promptly in the Union Army when President Lincoln issued a call for volunteers at the start of the Civil War. Despite a bullet wound that resulted in the amputation of his right forearm, Major Powell persevered with his duties until the war was drawing to a close, when he left the Army to become a professor of geology at Illinois Wesleyan University in Bloomington. In 1867 he led the first of many trips to the Rocky Mountains and other areas of the West to collect specimens and carry out scientific research. His wife, Emma Dean, accompanied him and his students and became one of the first women to climb Pikes Peak. A friendly meeting with members of the Ute tribe kindled Powell's passion to study Native American customs and languages.

The idea of exploring the Green and Colorado Rivers intrigued Powell despite legends of earlier expeditions that had perished. He decided to try, selecting a hardy crew who could live off the land under the toughest conditions. On May 24, 1869, Powell set off from Green River Station, Wyoming Territory, with nine men and four boats. He knew this expedition would be an emotional ordeal when he wrote: "What falls there are, we know not; what rocks beset the channel, we know not; what walls rise over the river, we know not." Despite fear of the unknown, near-

**John Wesley Powell meets with a Paiute in the late 1800s.**

starvation, abandonment by four crew members (three never to be seen again), and raging rapids that destroyed one of the boats, the expedition emerged from the Grand Canyon and reached the mouth of the Virgin River in present-day Nevada on August 30. They had traveled more than a thousand miles, providing the first reliable reports of what lay within the canyons of the Green River and the Colorado.

Powell had hoped to accomplish far more scientific research, but loss of instruments and food along with scarcity of game had limited his work. So in the spring of 1871 he returned to the original starting point with a new crew and boats on a trip that would last a year and a half. This time the expedition had photographers and a surveyor, who helped provide a splendid record of the canyons.

Powell then moved to Washington, D.C., where he wrote scientific reports with farsighted ideas for the federal government. In 1879 he assisted in the creation of the U.S. Geological Survey and later became its director. He also pursued his interest in Native American cultures as director of the Smithsonian Institution's Bureau of Ethnology, a post he held for the rest of his life. In 1888, Powell helped found the National Geographic Society. He died in his 69th year and now lies buried with other Civil War heroes in Arlington Cemetery. ■

**Above right: The Colorado River makes a nearly complete circle around Horseshoe Bend near Page. You can hike out to this dizzying spot (see p. 71). Wide-angle lenses best capture the sweep of the river.**
**Below right: Major Powell scouted for river hazards from an armchair, which he lashed to his boat.**

# Arizona Strip

YOU CAN GLIMPSE THE ARIZONA STRIP FROM THE FEW
highways that cross it, but to really explore the land you must leave
the pavement behind. Trails and a network of back roads lead to
little-visited overlooks of the Grand Canyon, high plateaus, pine-
forested volcanoes, and prehistoric Native American sites.

Wilderness designations protect
many areas, as does the **Grand
Canyon-Parashant National
Monument,** established by President Clinton in January 2000. Experienced hikers and drivers with
high-clearance vehicles may go days
without seeing another soul. The
Bureau of Land Management
(BLM) administers most of the
backcountry except for Grand
Canyon National Park and Kaibab
National Forest. Contact the BLM

at the Interagency Visitor Center in
St. George, Utah, for information.
The BLM's Arizona Strip map helps
in navigating the back roads, most
of which require a high-clearance
vehicle and may need a four-wheel-
drive as well.

Interstate 15 follows the deep
and sheer-walled Virgin River
Gorge through the extreme north-
west corner of Arizona. **Virgin
River Canyon Recreation
Area,** just south off I-15 Exit 18, is

**Arizona Strip**

⚑ 48 B3

**Visitor information**

azstrip.az.blm.gov

✉ Bureau of Land
Management,
Interagency Visitor
Center, 345 E.
Riverside Dr., St.
George, Utah 84790

☎ 435/688-3200

🕐 Closed Sun.

a great spot for a picnic, hike, or camping; it's open year-round. Farther south, from the forested volcano of **Mount Dellenbaugh,** you get a 360-degree panorama of the Shivwits Plateau and the distant Grand Canyon. Continuing south, there are splendid vistas at the end of jeep roads to **Twin** and **Whitmore Points.** While traveling the back roads, you're likely to pass through the ghost town of **Mount Trumbull,** whose schoolhouse has been reconstructed and is worth a visit if it's open. **Whitmore Wash Trail,** the Grand Canyon's easiest rim-to-river hike, begins at the end of a rocky road south of the Mount Trumbull town site; you'll pass an exposure of columnar basalt and drop some 850 feet in about a mile to the river.

**Winsor Castle,** a fortified ranch building at **Pipe Spring National Monument,** dates from the precarious early days of ranching on the Arizona Strip. Mormons found the spring here in 1858; despite Navajo raids, they began ranching five years later. After the two groups signed a peace treaty in 1870, the Church of Jesus Christ of Latter-day Saints based a large cattle operation here. The pair of stone houses that went up took its name from the ranch's superintendent, Anson P. Winsor, who (despite the different spelling) was thought to be related to the British royal family. Gun slits and an enclosed courtyard gave Winsor Castle security, but it was never attacked. Arizona's first telegraph office opened here in 1871, connecting this isolated region with Utah and the rest of the world. So many amorous couples passed through on their way to get married in the St. George Temple that the road became known as the Honeymoon Trail.

Tension between the Church of

Early travelers and ranchers passed many a pleasant evening in the parlor of Winsor Castle, now preserved at Pipe Spring National Monument.

**Pipe Spring National Monument**
www.nps.gov/pisp
✉ 14 miles SW of Fredonia on Ariz. 389
☎ 928/643-7105
💲 $

**Sturdy stone walls at Winsor Castle offered security in the uncertain early years of ranching.**

Jesus Christ of Latter-day Saints and the federal government, primarily over the practice of polygamy, led the church to sell the ranch in 1895 to a non-Mormon. In 1923, President Warren Harding proclaimed it a national monument "as a memorial of western pioneer life."

Today you can tour Winsor Castle and the rough bunkhouses nearby. Gardening, spinning, weaving, cheese-making, and other activities in summer keep pioneer skills alive. Interpretive programs also reveal Paiute cultural traditions, such as making soap from yucca plants, wild plant foods, and brush shelters. The half-mile-loop **Rim Trail** climbs a ridge behind the ranch to an overlook, where signs tell of the region's history and geology. A gift shop sells books, maps, and Native American arts and crafts. The Paiute tribe operates a campground nearby. *(Call 928/ 643-7105 or 928/643-7245 for information.)*

Glen Canyon
National Recreation
Area
⚐ 49 E4
Visitor information
www.nps.gov/glca
✉ P.O. Box 1507,
Page, AZ 86040
☎ 928/355-2234 (Lees
Ferry), 928/608-
6404 (Carl Hayden
Visitor Center)
$ $$$

## LEES FERRY

Until Navajo Bridge spanned the Colorado River near here in 1929, a ferry provided the only direct road link between the Arizona Strip and the rest of the state. The swift, swirling waters just above the Grand Canyon had forced back explorers, among them the Spanish Dominguez–Escalante Expedition in 1776 and a Mormon party led by Jacob Hamblin in 1860. But the Mormons kept trying—they needed a route for their Utah members to reach promising new areas in Arizona. In 1871, John D. Lee answered the church's call to establish a ferry service, and he succeeded despite boat accidents and the threat of hostile Navajo. Farmers and miners came to try their hand at making a living from this remote spot but had little success.

Today, historic ranch buildings and mining relics recall the past. Visitors also come for the excellent trout fishing in the clear, cold waters released by Glen Canyon Dam. The beautiful Glen Canyon upstream can be explored on a rafting tour from Page (see p. TK) or in your own boat. National Park Service rangers look after the historic sites, trails, boat ramps, and campground at Lees Ferry and the canyon upstream. You can obtain information at the ranger station (open irregular hours), on the left 0.4 mile past the campground, or at the Carl Hayden Visitor Center at Glen Canyon Dam.

The road to Lees Ferry heads north from US 89A just west of Navajo Bridge. After about 5 miles, turn left and drive 0.2 mile to see the log cabin thought to have been built by Lee at Lonely Dell Ranch in the early 1870s. Follow signs for the **Lees Ferry Historic District** to explore old buildings and mining equipment near the ferry site.

**Navajo Bridge** has now been bypassed by a new one alongside it, but you can view the Colorado River, 470 feet below, from the old bridge. A bookstore in the visitor center *(closed in winter)* offers regional books, maps, and souvenirs. Navajo sell arts and crafts at the east end of the bridge. ∎

# Page & Glen Canyon

An aerial view reveals the otherworldly landscape surrounding Lake Powell.

A REMOTE DESERT ATOP MANSON MESA SEEMS AN unlikely location for a prosperous modern town. Page sprang into existence in 1957 when workers arrived to build Glen Canyon Dam, a 710-foot-high concrete structure that would create a 250-square-mile lake with a 2,000-mile shoreline. Today visitors find the town a handy base for discovering the beautiful canyon country all around, whether by boat on Lake Powell, by raft on the Colorado River downstream, by car, or on foot.

The **Powell Museum** introduces the land and people of this region. Its name and that of the lake honor explorer and scientist John Wesley Powell, who made two descents of the Green and Colorado Rivers (see pp. 66–67). Exhibits tell of Powell's voyages and the area's geology, tribes, pioneers, and the construction of Glen Canyon Dam. Paintings and photos convey the beauty of Antelope Canyon and other scenic places nearby.

Two dramatic viewpoints of Glen Canyon lie near Page. You can reach **"The Best Dam View"** by heading west from downtown on North Lake Powell Boulevard. Cross US 89 and continue on Scenic View Drive, then turn right to the viewpoint. Follow a short trail down to the best views.

The Colorado River makes a sharp turn at **Horseshoe Bend.** To reach it, go south 2.5 miles from Gateway Plaza on US 89, then turn right 0.2 mile past Milepost 545 to a parking area. A three-quarter-mile trail leads to the overlook.

## ANTELOPE CANYON

Many visitors are enticed by the convoluted and incredibly beautiful sandstone walls of Antelope Canyon, so narrow that only tiny beams of sunlight reach the canyon floor. You can visit two sections of the canyon on opposite sides of

**Page & Lake Powell**
🗻 49 F4
**Visitor information**
www.pagelakepowellchamber
.org
✉ Page/Lake Powell Chamber of Commerce, 644 N. Navajo Dr., Page (P.O. Box 727, Page, AZ 86040)
☎ 928/645-2741 or 888/261-7243
🕐 Closed Sat–Sun. Oct.–April

Arizona 98 southeast of Page. The more popular upper part is wider and easier to walk through. Tours operate from Page, or you can take the slightly less expensive shuttle that transports visitors up to the entrance. Most able-bodied adults and children should be able to go down the short ladders to reach the lower section. No tours are offered here; you just walk over from the parking area and climb down. Most visitors will find about an hour at either canyon sufficient. Bring a tripod if you're taking photos in the dimly lit interiors.

Antelope Canyon is a Navajo tribal park with a complex and expensive system of charges involving separate fees for the park, each section of canyon, and the upper canyon's shuttle or tours. Call first for details or ask for advice at the Powell Museum or the Page/Lake Powell Chamber of Commerce. Between December and March you'll need to call in advance and arrange to be met by a guide. Slot canyons may be just a few feet wide yet hundreds of feet deep and are deadly during flash floods, so don't

enter when storms threaten. From Page, head south on Coppermine Road or east on Arizona 98 to their junction at Big Lake Trading Post, then continue east 1 mile on Arizona 98. Parking and the ticket booth for the upper canyon are on the right; those for the lower canyon are half a mile down Antelope Point Road on the left.

## GLEN CANYON

Lake Powell in **Glen Canyon National Recreation Area** reaches far up into Utah and into seemingly countless side canyons. The sheer cliffs and rounded hills of sandstone, nearly devoid of vegetation, create scenes suggestive of another world. The yellows and reds of the slickrock contrast with the deep blues of the lake. Most of the rock you see is Navajo sandstone—ancient sand dunes turned to stone. Weather at the lake's 3,700-foot elevation tends to be hot in summer—the most popular season for boating, waterskiing, and swimming—and freezing in winter, the quietest time. Spring and autumn are usually great for explor-

**Powell Museum**
www.powellmuseum.org
✉ 6 N. Lake Powell Blvd., Page (P.O. Box 547, Page, AZ 86040)
☎ 928/645-9496 or 888/597-6873
🕐 Closed Sat.–Sun. & mid-Dec.–mid-Feb.
💲 $

**Antelope Canyon Navajo Tribal Park**
✉ P.O. Box 4803, Page, AZ 86040
☎ 928/698-2808 (call Mon.–Fri.)
💲 $$$$–$$$$$

The Colorado River comes back to life below Glen Canyon Dam. Untamed waters that once flowed warm and muddy now glide cold and clear into the Grand Canyon.

**Glen Canyon National Recreation Area & Rainbow Bridge National Monument**
www.nps.gov/glca
www.nps.gov/rabr
✉ 100 Lakeshore Dr., Page (P.O. Box 1507, Page, AZ 86040)
☎ 928/608-6404
$ $$$

**Wahweap Marina**
www.visitlakepowell.com
✉ P.O. Box 1597, Page, AZ 86040
☎ 928/645-2433 or 800/528-6154

ing the backcountry, though persistent winds can blow from February to May. If you don't have your own boat, check out the excursions and rentals at Wahweap and other marinas (see below).

Begin your visit at the **Carl Hayden Visitor Center,** named after a long-serving senator who strongly supported water development in the West. The center overlooks Glen Canyon Dam 2 miles northwest of Page. A detailed relief model of the recreation area gives an idea of the size and complexity of the canyon system. See if you can find Rainbow Bridge on it. Exhibits and slide, video, or film shows introduce the region, its wildlife, human history, recreation opportunities, and Glen Canyon Dam. One-hour tours descend into **Glen Canyon Dam** to see the generating room and other areas. **Wahweap Marina,** some 5 miles north of the dam, has the most extensive facilities on the lake, with boat tours, summer ranger programs, lodging, restaurants, an RV park, a campground, a picnic area, and a full-service marina. Wahweap

can be very crowded, especially in summer, but less developed places beckon nearby. Head out to **Lone Rock,** a primitive camping area and beach; follow US 89 from Page past the Wahweap turnoffs, cross the border into Utah, then turn right at the sign. **Antelope Point** has a paved boat ramp and nearby swimming areas; follow the directions to Antelope Canyon, then take paved Antelope Canyon Road 5 miles to its end; turn right for some small, sandy coves.

**Rainbow Bridge,** a national monument, spans a side canyon about 50 miles uplake from the dam. The graceful natural bridge—the world's largest—measures 290 feet high and 275 feet wide. The stream underneath had originally followed a sharp bend around a narrow fin of rock, erosion then carved a hole through the fin, forming the bridge. You can reach it on boat tours from Wahweap, Bullfrog, or Halls Crossing marinas. Hikers can approach overland by following trails through some of the most spectacular canyon country in the Southwest. ■

# More places to visit in Grand Canyon Country

## PARIA CANYON–VERMILION CLIFFS WILDERNESS

An exceptionally beautiful hike follows the **Paria River** through a deep gorge for 38 miles between a trailhead in southern Utah and Lees Ferry (see p. 70). Even narrower side canyons and the massive Wrather Canyon Arch invite side trips. The trip takes four to six days and requires many stream crossings. **Coyote Buttes,** on top of Paria Plateau, has swirling sandstone features; it's open for day use only. For information and permits, visit paria.az.blm.gov or contact the Bureau of Land Management at the Paria Information Station *(30 miles NW of Page on US 89 near Milepost 21, closed in winter),* the Kanab Area Office *(318 N. 100 East, Kanab, UT 84741, tel 435/644-4600),* or the Interagency Visitor Center *(345 E. Riverside Dr., St. George, UT 84790, tel 435/688-3200 or -3246).* Designated

Grand Canyon visitors first took to the skies in planes such as this Ford Trimotor at the Planes of Fame Air Museum.

in November 2000, **Vermilion Cliffs National Monument's** 293,000 acres hold a geologic treasure, including the Paria Plateau, the Vermilion Cliffs, and the sheer-walled Paria River Canyon; elevations range from 3,100 to 7,100 feet above sea level.
🅜 49 E4

## PLANES OF FAME AIR MUSEUM

Distinguished and unusual aircraft reflect the daring and accomplishments of people in aviation history. Reproductions of famous World War I planes bring that era to life. A 1928 Ford Trimotor still flies; it's thought to have been a personal aircraft of Henry Ford. An early P-51A Mustang, a Messerschmitt Bf 109G Gustav, and a Fuji Ohka 11 (a piloted suicide rocket) represent air forces of World War II. More recent fighters illustrate the dawn of the jet age. You can climb aboard the Lockheed Constellation C-121A used by Gen. Douglas MacArthur during the Korean War. Other exhibits include airplane engines, a World War II Link Trainer, and a timeline of women in aviation. The museum is at the airport in Valle, on the way to the Grand Canyon's South Rim from Flagstaff or Williams.
🅜 48 D1  ☎ 928/635-1000, www.planesoffame.org  🅢 $$

## TUSAYAN DISTRICT OF THE KAIBAB NATIONAL FOREST

Although often overlooked, the forest near the Grand Canyon's South Rim has some good hiking, mountain biking, and cross-country skiing. Get maps and information at the Tusayan Ranger Station just outside the park's South Entrance Station. **Red Butte Trail** is a 2.4-mile hike up a small mountain southeast of Tusayan. It is worth the effort for the fine panorama from the lookout tower on the 7,326-foot summit. Mountain bikers can ride three interconnected loops of the **Tusayan Bike Trails** from a trailhead on the west side of the highway 0.3 mile north of Tusayan. The **Grandview Lookout,** a few miles from the South Rim, offers an aerial perspective from the top of its 80-foot tower. This is also the starting point of the 2.2-mile **Vishnu Trail,** from which a spur trail leads to viewpoints over the Grand Canyon. Another option for hiking or mountain biking is the 9.4-mile section of the **Arizona Trail,** which follows the top of the 500-foot cliffs of the Coconino Rim.
🅜 48 D2  ✉ P.O. Box 3088, Grand Canyon, AZ 86023  ☎ 928/638-2443, www.fs.fed.us/r3/kai  ∎

For many generations, the remote, awe-inspiring landscapes of the Colorado Plateau have been home to two of the most traditional Native American tribes: the Navajo and the Hopi.

# Northeastern Arizona

**Navajo turquoise jewelry**

# Northeastern Arizona

THE LAND CATCHES THE IMAGINATION HERE AS IT DOES IN FEW OTHER places in the world. Buttes and spires march across vast desert flats of sand and rock. Deep canyons reveal strange underworlds beneath the Earth's crust. Mountains reach toward the clouds. The high plateaus of northeastern Arizona provoke awe—as well as a respect for the people who have lived in this harsh landscape.

**A Navajo girl shows off her turquoise pendant and coral necklace in Monument Valley.**

Ancient sites dot the entire region, tracing the history of cultures that developed from a simple life of hunting and gathering to societies with villages of multistory masonry buildings, irrigated fields, and complex ceremonial calendars. Migrations over the centuries have left most sites in Arizona abandoned, but the Hopi continue to live in traditional villages atop three fingerlike projections of Black Mesa. Today you can walk the dusty streets and catch glimpses of a life that has flourished in this land for more than a thousand years. Old Oraibi, dating from at least A.D. 1150, may be the oldest continuously inhabited village in the United States. About 10,000 Hopi still live on the reservation.

The Navajo, who call themselves Diné, entered the region between A.D. 1300 and 1600 and also became deeply attached to the land. These seminomadic warriors had branched off from the Athapaskan tribes of what is now western Canada. Though very different from the Hopi in language, customs, and physical appearance, the adaptable Navajo learned weaving, pottery, and farming skills from Pueblo groups such as the Hopi and picked up

GRAND CANYON COUNTRY
p. 47

4▷

3▷

2▷

△
A

NORTH-CENTRAL ARIZONA
p. 91

I▷

△
B

Lech-e
98

Bitter Springs
89

N A V A J O
6520ft
▲
Shinumo
Altar
Cedar Ridge

The Gap
N A T I O N

Willow
Springs
Tub
City

Moenko

Little Colorado

R E S E R V A T I O N

64
Cameron
89

Cedar Wash

Phoenix ★

Area of map detail

horses and livestock from the Spanish. The Navajo's habit of raiding their neighbors caused retaliatory attacks by other tribes, Spaniards, Mexicans, and Anglos. Finally, in 1863–64, the U.S. Army forced the Navajo to surrender by destroying their livestock, crops, orchards, and food caches. The Army rounded up the Navajo and marched them on The Long Walk to the bleak camp of Fort Sumner in eastern New Mexico. An attempt at enforced domestication there failed dismally, and four years later the survivors were allowed to return to their lands in Arizona.

The Long Walk had such a profound effect on the tribe that you're likely to hear references to the episode even today. Numbering about 250,000, the Navajo are now the largest tribe in the United States. At 25,000 square miles, their reservation is also the biggest: It covers most of northeastern Arizona and extends north into Utah and east into New Mexico. ■

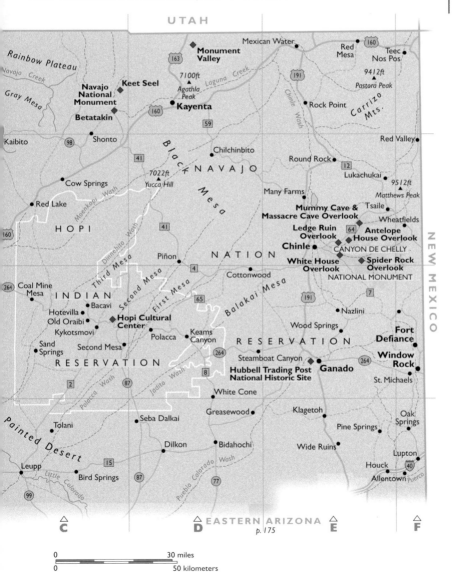

# Monument Valley

**Monument Valley
Navajo Tribal Park**

 77 D4

✉ Turnoff is 24 miles
N of Kayenta across
Utah border on US
163 (P.O. Box
360289, Monument
Valley, UT 84536)

☎ 435/727-3287 or
435/727-3353

$ $

FEW LANDSCAPES EPITOMIZE THE AMERICAN WEST MORE than Monument Valley's magnificent buttes, towering pinnacles, and lonely sand dunes. Erosion sculpted the sheer cliffs from sandstone and the gentle slopes below from shale. Volcanic eruptions in the southern part of the valley left jagged structures of black rock such as Agathla Butte. Drifting clouds, the occasional storm, and the rising and setting sun stage dramatic displays of shadow and light. The film industry has contributed to the valley's mystique: *Stagecoach,* directed by John Ford in 1938, began a long series of movies that introduced this mysterious land to the world.

The Navajo have preserved Monument Valley as a vast tribal park where you can really feel the splendor of nature. Pull up near the **visitor center** for your first gaze out across the central valley's "mittens" and other buttes that rise majestically from gently sloping pedestals. In the visitor center, check out the options for visiting the valley and see a few exhibits. A cluster of Navajo craft vendors mark the start of the 3.5-mile road to the visitor center.

You can take your own vehicle on the self-guided **Monument**

## Visiting Navajo lands

Travel here takes some extra planning because accommodations, campgrounds, and RV parks are few and generally far between. It is highly recommended that you call ahead for rooms, especially in the busy summer season. Towns surrounding the Navajo Nation provide additional (and usually less costly) options.

Be aware that the Navajo Nation—unlike the Hopi lands and the rest of Arizona—operates on daylight saving time, setting clocks ahead one hour from April through October.

The Navajo are usually agreeable to being photographed, but you should always ask first and be prepared to pay a gratuity. ■

**Freeing the spirit in the wide-open spaces of Monument Valley**

**Right: The movement of the sun and clouds across the sky conjures a show of shadow and color.**

**Valley Drive,** which drops down from the visitor center to the valley floor and makes a loop through its heart. Cyclists can ride the drive too. Enjoy a variety of sweeping vistas from overlooks and short spur roads along the way. The unpaved road is about 17 miles long and takes an hour and a half. It's normally safe for most cautiously driven cars but not for extremely low-clearance vehicles, nor for RVs over 27 feet long. Don't stop in the loose sand that sometimes blows across the road. You must stay on the designated road and not travel or hike elsewhere. No water or services are available, so you may wish to take a picnic.

### TOUR THE VALLEY

To see more of the valley, you can join one of the various vehicle, horseback, or hiking **tours** led by Navajo guides. No reservations are required—just talk with the guides to find one who offers a trip that matches your interests. Overnight excursions can be organized too; bring your own food and gear. You can arrange tours in the visitor center. The shortest trips take you by vehicle along the main drive loop in an hour and a half. Longer ones venture farther into the backcountry to visit hogans, cliff dwellings, and petroglyphs; these drives take two and a half hours or longer.

Riding stables on the way to Monument Valley and booths in the visitor center provide horseback and pack trips. Hikers must have a guide, available at the visitor center, before setting off into the valley. Nearby Goulding's Lodge and the tour operators in Kayenta also offer driving tours. Visit the old trading post at Goulding's Lodge to see the exhibits and period rooms. You can call or write the park for a list of tour operators or check www.navajonationparks.org/. ■

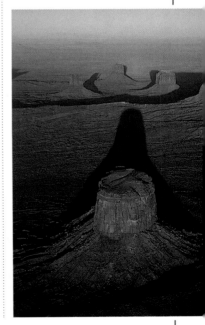

# Canyon de Chelly
# National Monument

**Canyon de Chelly
National
Monument**
⚑ 77 E3
www.nps.gov/cach
✉ P.O. Box 588, Chinle,
AZ 86503-0588
☎ 928/674-5500

SHEER CANYON WALLS UP TO 1,000 FEET HIGH SHELTER both well-preserved cliff dwellings and traditional Navajo life. The national monument centers on two large canyons—26-mile-long Canyon de Chelly (pronounced de SHAY) and its tributary, 35-mile Canyon del Muerto. Rock art and other evidence reveal that humans have sought food and shelter in these canyons for at least 4,500 years.

After about 200 B.C., the canyons' inhabitants acquired corn and the agricultural skills to supplement their diet of wild foods. Over the following centuries, the tribespeople built permanent villages with granaries, ceremonial structures, and multistoried apartments. Skilled artisans created fine baskets, pottery, and other crafts. Then, in about 1300, everyone migrated elsewhere. But some—the Hopi—remembered their old homeland, returning on pilgrimages or to look after fields of corn and other crops. Hopi visits continued over the next 400 years until the Navajo entered and settled in the canyons. Except during the four long years of captivity at Fort Sumner (see p. 77),

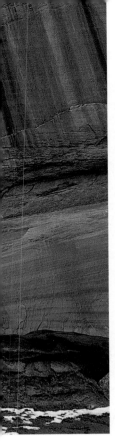

A visitor contemplates the ghosts and great sandstone walls above White House Ruin, the only site in Canyon de Chelly National Monument that you can hike to on your own.

Navajo have tended their farms, sheep, and horses here ever since.

Start your visit at the **visitor center,** near the mouth of Canyon de Chelly and just east of the town of Chinle. Museum exhibits introduce the archaic, ancient Pueblo, and Navajo cultures of the canyons. You can obtain advice on vehicle tours, horseback riding, hiking, and arranging for a guide. Check the bulletin board for upcoming interpretive programs and hikes. A picnic area and campground sit nearby in a cottonwood grove.

Two self-guided paved scenic drives begin from the visitor center, where you can buy a booklet on local geology and points of interest. Allow at least a day to do both drives to give you time to enjoy the natural beauty, admire the ancient pueblos, and hike the **White Rim Trail.** (Don't leave valuables in view when you park your vehicle.)

**South Rim Drive** leads to seven increasingly spectacular viewpoints on the rim of Canyon de Chelly in a 37-mile round-trip from the visitor center. You'll see Navajo farms and ancient pueblos of varying types and sizes. From **White House Overlook** you get a view of a cliff dwelling and a lower ruin with about 60 rooms and four kivas (ceremonial rooms). **White House Ruin Trail** descends 500 feet and crosses the valley for a close-up look at the ancient village; allow two hours for the 2.5-mile round-trip hike, and bring plenty of water. South Rim Drive ends at **Spider Rock Overlook,** where the canyon walls plummet a dizzying 1,000 feet. A grand panorama takes in the 800-foot rock spire named for Spider Woman, a Navajo deity who taught women how to weave.

**North Rim Drive** crosses the Chinle Wash near the visitor center and climbs to four vistas of Canyon

del Muerto in a 34-mile round-trip. From **Ledge Ruin Overlook,** you can see an unexcavated village with a couple of kivas. At **Antelope House Overlook,** you look almost straight down on the large pueblo and its three- and four-story tower. Navajo Fortress, a butte across the canyon, once served as a refuge. **Mummy Cave Overlook** takes in two cliff dwellings with more than 50 rooms in the larger alcove and about 20 in the west cave (to the right). **Massacre Cave Overlook** commemorates an 1805 attack by the Spanish. According to the commander's report, 115 Navajo were killed and 33 were captured.

**A Navajo pictograph in Canyon del Muerto depicts a Spanish priest (left) and cavalry.**

These two drives and White House Ruin Trail are the only self-guided excursions. All others require you to have a guide and permit, or to go on a tour; this protects the privacy of the Navajo who live and farm in the canyons. Vehicle tours wind up the sandy bottoms of both canyons on half- and full-day trips. With your own guide, you can travel almost anywhere with a high-clearance four-wheel-drive vehicle. Equestrians can bring their own animals and hire a guide or take a horseback trip from one of the stables. Hikers with a guide have exciting trail options on day or overnight trips. ∎

Navajo National
Monument
⚑ 77 C4
www.nps.gov/nava
✉ Take US 160 NE
from Tuba City for
52 miles or from
Kayenta SW for 21
miles, then turn N
for 9 miles on Ariz.
564.
☎ 928/672-2700

**Some of the well-
preserved rooms
at Betatakin have
their original
roofs.**

# Navajo National Monument

FROM HIGH IN A PINYON PINE AND JUNIPER WOODLAND,
you can gaze into a beautiful canyon and see one of Arizona's most
impressive cliff dwellings. The 135 rooms and one kiva of Betatakin,
Ledge House, lie sheltered in a massive alcove 452 feet high and 370
feet across. Ancient Pueblo people constructed and used it for only
two generations between A.D. 1260 and 1300.

The **visitor center** displays
attractive examples of pottery and
other crafts along with archaeological findings on diet, migrations,
clothing, tools, and building techniques. The **Sandal Trail** behind
the visitor center weaves through
vegetation to an overlook of
**Betatakin.** The paved path is

1 mile round-trip, with a descent
of 160 feet to the viewpoint. Take
binoculars to see details of the
pueblo. **Aspen Trail** branches off
Sandal Trail and descends into the
head of Betatakin Canyon, with a
view of the forest on the canyon
floor below. The round-trip hike is
0.8 mile, with a descent of 300 feet.

Rangers lead Betatakin hikes for
a close-up look at the pueblo. The
four-hour, 5-mile round-trip hike
goes down and then returns on a
primitive trail, strenuous because of
the trailhead's 7,300-foot elevation.
Check ahead for requirements and
arrive early; the hike is limited to
the first 25 people who sign up each
day. In summer especially, take
plenty of water, a hat, and sunscreen.

**Keet Seel,** one of the largest
and best preserved cliff dwellings in
the Southwest, has 160 rooms and
four kivas. Its residents departed
about A.D. 1300. Jars of corn left
behind in sealed rooms indicate
that the people expected to return
some day. It is easy to imagine the
houses and courtyards coming to
life again. Potsherds still lie scattered around, as the Navajo name
("Broken Pottery") suggests. A
17-mile round-trip trail, including
several stream crossings, leads to
the site, which you can hike to with
a permit; it's limited to 20 people
per day and only in the summer
season. Call three months ahead for
a permit. The trip can be done in
one day, but is most enjoyable with
an overnight near Keet Seel. ■

# Hopi Country

Bessie Namoki
fires Hopi pottery
below First Mesa.

LIFE HAS NEVER BEEN EASY FOR THE HOPI. THE FARMERS toiled in a land so dry that only the hardiest corn and other crops could be coaxed to grow. Complex social and religious obligations made many demands. Outsiders—from Spanish missionaries to federal government administrators—tried to overturn old Hopi ways. Hordes of prying anthropologists and shutter-snapping tourists besieged their villages. Yet the Hopi continue to follow their ancient traditions while making use of new technologies and opportunities.

Hopi legends tell of a long series of great migrations that eventually led them to their present-day homes atop the Hopi mesas (see pp. 84–87). Even now, clans make pilgrimages and leave *pahos* (prayer feathers) at ancestral village sites last used hundreds of years ago. Hopi social life and bonds between villages still largely revolve around the clans, which number more than 30. Each member of Hopi society has his or her own knowledge and role, depending on the person's clan, village, age group, and sex. This secrecy makes everyone important and necessary in the close-knit society. It's also the reason Hopi may be reluctant to discuss their religion with you; their knowledge may not be appropriate for a member of another clan or for a child standing nearby.

The Hopi welcome visitors to their villages and to some of their ceremonies. You'll have many opportunities to buy pottery, basketry, and silverwork (see pp. 40–42) directly from the Hopi at roadside shops and village homes—look for signs. Guides may be available to take you to rock art sites and other places of interest not normally open to visitors; ask around. Respect the privacy of residents by staying on the major streets, and never enter houses or kivas unless you are invited. To

**Hopi Mesas**
🅰 77 C2, D2

**Walpi tours, First
Mesa Tourism
Program**
✉ P.O. Box 260,
Polacca, AZ 86042
☎ 928/737-2262
🕐 Closed for
ceremonies
💲 $$

avoid offending the Hopi, take care not to hike trails without a guide, touch offerings (such as prayer feathers tied to bushes), drink alcohol, or pull out a camera. The tribe wishes visitors to receive the village life and ceremonies in their hearts—not with some gadget.

## HOPI MESAS

Sheer cliffs have long protected the Hopi mesa-top villages during times of trouble, such as those following the Pueblo Revolt against the Spanish in 1680. Although the mesas are actually southward-projecting fingers of Black Mesa, they are more commonly known as First, Second, and Third Mesas—the order in which the Spanish discovered them coming from the east.

Around 10,000 Hopi live on the reservation, and each of the 12 villages functions as a city-state with distinct ceremonial traditions. The Hopi Tribal Council does not rule the villages, but it helps with community services and acts as a liaison with state and federal governments. Arizona 264 between Window Rock and Tuba City passes near all the villages. You can also reach the reservation directly from Flagstaff on the paved Leupp Road (pronounced loop) or from Winslow via Arizona 87.

### First Mesa

If you arrive from the east, **Keams Canyon** will be the first community you encounter on the Hopi Reservation. It's an administrative town, not a village, but you may wish to stop at Keams Canyon Shopping Center for McGee's Indian Art Gallery, a café, and a

Hopi buffalo dancers brave the winter cold.

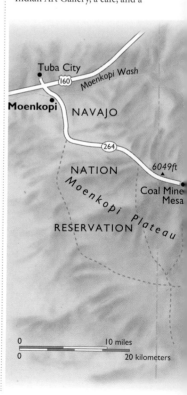

grocery store; a picnic area is across the highway. **Polacca** (pronounced po-LAH-kah), at the base of First Mesa, is a relatively new village; most residents hail from one of the three villages on the mesa. Turn up the steep 1.3-mile road to the top of the mesa for a visit to **Walpi** (WAHL-pee), one of the most inspiring places in Arizona. Park RVs, buses, and trailers in the large lot on your right partway up (near a water tank); from there you'll have to walk. First you'll come to **Hano,** which looks like a Hopi village but is actually settled by Tewa, a tribe from the Rio Grande area of New Mexico. They fled after an unsuccessful revolt against the Spanish in 1696 and sought refuge here. Hopi leaders agreed, with the condition that the Tewa serve as guardians of the

trail to the mesa. Despite three centuries of living with Hopi, Hano's residents still keep their own language.

You'll next reach **Sichomovi** (see-CHO-mo-vee), settled in the mid-1600s by people from Walpi when that village became too crowded. Stop here and register for a tour of Walpi, which lasts about one hour. With a guide, you continue across a narrow neck of land to this traditional village at the end of the mesa. You'll learn about Hopi culture and enjoy the expansive vistas. Walpi dates from about 1150, and even now its residents shun electricity and running water. Surrounded by sky, the ancient houses appear to have grown from the mesa. Bowl-shaped depressions in the rock once served to collect precious rainwater. Below, look for

**Ancient Pueblo people created wonderful animal-shaped vessels.**

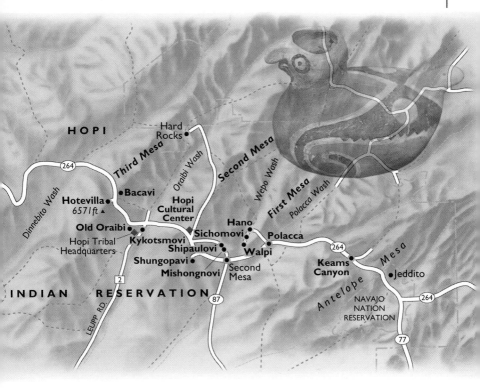

precipitous foot trails and remains of old fortifications and buildings. Villagers often sell kachina dolls and pottery.

## Second Mesa

At the junction of Arizona 264 and Arizona 87 just east of Second Mesa, you'll find a store, a café, and some arts and crafts shops. From here, two roads climb up to the three villages on Second Mesa—the main highway that passes near **Shungopavi** (shong-o-po-vee) and a narrower road to **Shipaulovi** (shih-PAW-lo-vee) and **Mishongnovi** (mih-SHONG-no-vee); both roads rejoin near the Hopi Cultural Center. Shungopavi, the largest of the three villages, was moved from a site at the base of the mesa to its present location after the Pueblo Revolt of 1680; there's an arts and crafts shop on the road into the village and a few more on the highway between here and the Hopi Cultural Center. After the Pueblo Revolt, Mishongnovi was moved up to its current site at the end of an eastward projection of the mesa, and its close neighbor

Shipaulovi was established. Both villages have an attractive setting and often open their plaza dances to the public.

The pueblo-style **Hopi Cultural Center** on the west side of Second Mesa has a good museum featuring Hopi history, culture, and art along with many historical photos of traditional life; there's a small gift shop too. At its restaurant, you can sample such Hopi foods as blue corn pancakes, paper-thin *piki* bread, *paatupsuki* (pinto beans and hominy soup), and *nöqkwivi* (lamb stew with white corn). The modern motel here, the only one on the reservation, is a good place to ask about guides and upcoming dances. Picnickers and campers can use the tables among trees just to the west. Hopi Arts & Crafts (Silvercrafts Cooperative Guild) on the other side of the campground offers a large selection.

## Third Mesa

**Old Oraibi** (o-RYE-bee), atop the mesa, has stood here for nearly 900 years, probably a longer continuous

stretch of time than any other community in the United States. It's worth a visit to absorb some of the atmosphere. A good place to park is the arts and crafts shop at the beginning of the village; more shops are back on Arizona 264 near the turnoff. Old Oraibi saw some hard times in the early 20th century. It had been one of the largest Hopi villages, with more than 800 people, until a dispute arose between two chiefs, You-ke-oma and Tawa-quap-tewa. Their factions fought it out with a push-of-war contest until one managed to push the other away. You-ke-oma's group lost and left to start a new village, Hotevilla, 4 miles away.

People from Old Oraibi also founded **Kykotsmovi** (kee-KEUTS-mo-vee) in 1890 beside a spring at the base of the mesa. To visit the Hopi tribal offices, store, and arts and crafts shop, drive south 1 mile on Indian Route 2 (Leupp Road) from Arizona 264.

**Hotevilla** (HOAT-vih-lah) had a difficult early history after its founding in 1906. Federal authori-

ties demanded that villagers move back to Old Oraibi so that the children could attend school. When most refused, the men were hauled to jail, and the schoolchildren were forced to attend a boarding school at Keams Canyon. Women and young children had to survive the winter alone in the fledgling village with little food or shelter.

**Bacavi** (BAH-kah-vee) village is another settlement that originated from the split between Hotevilla and Old Oraibi. Some of the Hotevilla people returned to the old village so their children could go to school there, but the unwelcome group found tensions unbearable and left to build its own village across the road from Hotevilla in 1909. Chief Tuba of Old Oraibi founded **Moenkopi** (The Place of Running Water) in the 1870s to take advantage of springs that could irrigate fields. The upper section of the village participates in the Hopi Tribal Council while the lower, more conservative part does not. Moenkopi is 48 miles northwest of Old Oraibi and near Tuba City. ■

**The tightly packed Hopi homes of Walpi on Third Mesa seem to grow out of the rock.**

# Kachinas:
# Spiritual world of the Hopi

Hopi life still closely follows the growing cycle of corn, as it has for the past 2,000 years. A richly detailed series of ceremonies summons kachinas—spirits, of which there are more than 500 types—to bring rain to nurture corn and other crops.

You may be fortunate enough to attend a kachina dance in a village plaza during the period when the crops most need rain, from April to early July. A long line of elaborately costumed and masked performers—men who actually *become* kachinas—chant while shaking gourd rattles and performing precise dance steps. Clowns, usually with painted horizontal stripes across their bodies, may appear and perform crazy antics. Ogre kachinas have been known to seek out naughty children and threaten to eat them, but the parents always manage to sweet-talk the ogres out of this punishment; the children usually behave much better afterward. You may see kachina dolls handed out to small girls as part of their education.

**Kachina dancers wear elaborate masks, often with a neck ruff of juniper.**

The kachina season begins with the winter solstice ceremony, when the Soyala Kachina appears. At this time, Hopi begin thinking of the upcoming growing season with wishes for fertility, moisture, and harmony with nature. They express these thoughts in kachina dances, initially mostly at night in kivas (underground ceremonial chambers), and Buffalo social dances in the plazas. In April, the kachinas appear during daytime dances on the plazas in a community prayer for rain. By the summer solstice, the kachinas have completed their task and perform the Niman (Home) Ceremony. They present the first green ears of corn and offer their last dances

for rain before returning to the San Francisco Peaks, their mountain home. During August, thoughts and ceremonies turn to the harvest and its celebration. In the Snake Dance (normally closed to the public), dancers hold snakes, often poisonous rattlesnakes, in their mouths, and these serve as messengers to the spirits. Young women perform the Butterfly Dance, also in August, followed by Women's Society Dances in autumn. November and December tend to be quiet months of prayer and meditation. Each village has its own set of dances, not all of which are performed every year.

Hopi dances usually take place on weekends; try asking a few days ahead at the Hopi Cultural Center or at shops on the reservation. Certain dances depend on astronomical observations, so even the Hopi have to wait for the go-ahead before setting a date. It's best to stand because seats and blankets are reserved. Not all dances are open to the public, but if you are turned away, remember that there is plenty more to see on the Hopi lands. If you are permitted to watch, keep in mind that these are religious ceremonies; just as in a church or synagogue, visitors should dress respectfully and not ask questions during the event. And most important of all—even if no one is around—respect the strict ban on photography and all other types of recording, such as video, sound, sketching, or note-taking. Just the sight of a camera will offend some Hopi, so it's best to stow yours in the car. ■

**Opposite: A young golden eagle receives a bath of corn pollen before being sacrificed. Bottom left and right: Hopi woodcarvers start with a cottonwood root and put thought and skill into their kachina dolls.**

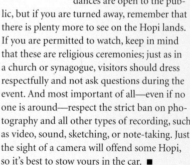

# More places to visit in northeastern Arizona

## HUBBELL TRADING POST NATIONAL HISTORIC SITE

Lorenzo Hubbell began trading with the Navajo in 1876, when they were still recovering from the trauma of The Long Walk (see p. 77). He earned the tribe's respect through his honesty, his ability to speak some of their language, and his assistance in explaining government programs. He also helped the Navajo get better prices for their rugs and silverwork by stressing the importance of high quality. Today the trading post functions much as it always has—Navajo still bring in products to trade and pick out the canned goods and other supplies they need. Visitors can choose from a great selection of Navajo rugs, jewelry, and other arts and crafts.

Hubbell's house has become a museum where you can see a wonderful collection of baskets, paintings, and rugs. In the visitor

**The rug room at Hubbell Trading Post invites you to linger over the fine examples available for purchase and to admire the framed designs on the wall, old baskets on the ceiling, and the vintage gun collection.**

center, you're likely to see a weaver at work as well as a large selection of books on Native American cultural history and the Southwest, including many for children. Scheduled tours visit Hubbell's house, and you can take a self-guided tour of the grounds and trading post. Trees shade a picnic area. The trading post is on the south side of Arizona 264, 1 mile west of Ganado between Window Rock and Keams Canyon.
🅰 77 E2  ☎ 928/755-3475, www.nps.gov/hutr

## WINDOW ROCK & VICINITY

A natural arch with a circular opening averaging 47 feet across inspired the Commissioner of Indian Affairs, John Collier, to choose this site for a Navajo administration center in the early 1930s. Today Window Rock is the capital of the Navajo Nation with a museum, zoo, parks, and shopping for arts and crafts. You can see the "rock with a hole in it" and the Navajo Nation Veterans Memorial at Window Rock Tribal Park; the turnoff is on the east side of Indian Route 12 about half a mile north of Arizona 264. On the way in you'll pass on the left the **Council Chambers** (*Tel 928/871-7160, closed Sat.–Sun.*), which has colorful murals inside and represents a great ceremonial hogan; you can visit it if not in use. The impressively large **Navajo Museum, Library, and Visitor Center** (*Tel 928/871-7371 visitor info or 928/871-7941 museum, closed Sun.*) faces east like the log hogan in front; it's on the north side of Arizona 264 in Tse Bonito Tribal Park, half a mile east of the Indian Route 12 junction. An information desk in the lobby has maps and travel advice for the Navajo Reservation. Galleries host exhibitions from the permanent collection and visiting shows. You can read more about the Navajo in the library. There's a gift shop too.

The **Navajo Nation Zoological and Botanical Park** (*Tel 928/871-6573*) offers a close-up look at wildlife of the Southwest; it's just north of the museum. **St. Michael's Historical Museum** (*Tel 928/ 871-4171, open daily in summer, visits by appt. only rest of year*), inside the original mission building, offers exhibits on the Navajo and the work of early missionaries. Head west 3 miles on Arizona 264 from the Indian Route 12 junction, then turn south at the sign.
🅰 77 F2  ∎

Nature has staged a geo-logic drama here with a cast of youthful volcanoes, a giant meteor crater, plateau uplifts, and countless canyon-carving streams. Vast conifer forests paint a great swath of green across the landscape.

# North-central Arizona

**Gold King Mine & Ghost Town, near Jerome**

# North-central Arizona

THIS DIVERSE REGION RANGES FROM SEARING DESERT TO ARIZONA'S HIGH-est summit—Humphreys Peak at 12,633 feet. The convoluted cliffs of the Mogollon Rim mark the dramatic change from the lofty Colorado Plateau in the north to the rugged hills and valleys in the south. Nature provides an endless show of color and form, from Sedona's red-rock country to the gold of the aspen forests on the San Francisco Peaks in autumn. The university town of Flagstaff offers excellent museums and galleries, as well as a handy base from which to explore the region.

Hiking is one of the best ways to enjoy the scenery, whether climbing a volcano or strolling along a canyon, and scenic drives also lead to dramatic vistas. Lakes atop the Mogollon Rim and streams flowing out through its canyons attract wildlife and pro-vide a challenge for anglers. Winter transforms the mountains with a blanket of snow, draw-ing skiers, snowboarders, and snowshoers.

Where there is year-round water in the desert, there are beaver and other wildlife, and lush growths of cottonwood, willow, and Arizona sycamore thrive. Cactuses dot the lower valleys, while higher desert areas see grasslands favored by antelope-like pronghorn or woodlands of juniper, pinyon pine, and oak. You might meet desert mule deer, white-tailed deer, black bear, coyote, fox, or rattle-snakes in the desert or in the pine forests above. Ponderosa pines cover much of the high plateaus, along with Gambel oak and

Phoenix ★

Area of map detail

4▷

**The great horned owl (Bubo virgin-ianus) has a wingspan of 45 to 60 inches.**

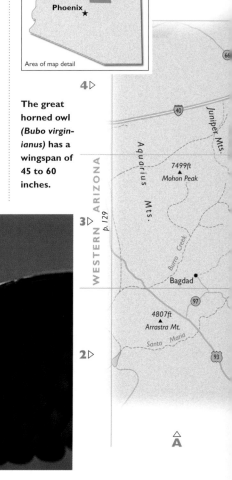

WESTERN ARIZONA

p. 129

3▷

Juniper Mts.

Aquarius Mts.

7499ft
▲
Mohon Peak

Burro Creek

Bagdad

97

4807ft
▲
Arrastra Mt.

Santa Maria

2▷

93

66

40

△
**A**

some juniper and Douglas fir. Cool forests of spruce, fir, and aspen thrive on the higher mountains. Only alpine tundra withstands the freezing temperatures and fierce winds above timberline on the San Francisco Peaks.

Ancient Pueblo people left behind many pit-house and masonry villages as they made their migrations. Yavapai and Apache followed and still live here on a few small reservations. Mining, logging, ranching, and the railroad attracted the first Anglos in the late 1800s; these industries still flavor the personalities of many towns today. ■

**Sedona's red-rock country**

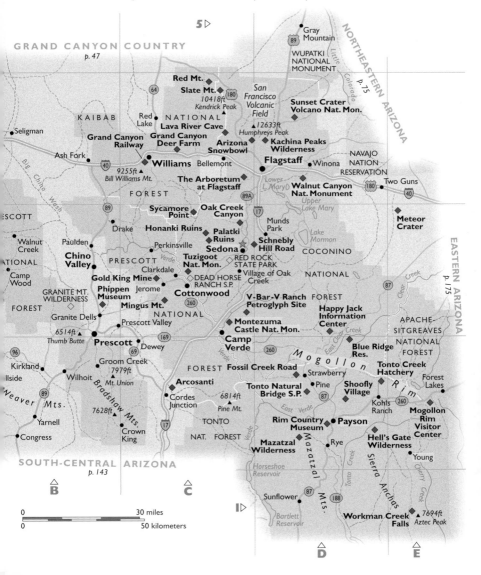

GRAND CANYON COUNTRY
p. 47

NORTHEASTERN ARIZONA
p. 75

EASTERN ARIZONA
p. 175

SOUTH-CENTRAL ARIZONA
p. 143

0    30 miles
0    50 kilometers

B    C    D    E

# Flagstaff

SET IN THE PONDEROSA PINES BELOW THE SAN FRANCISCO Peaks, Flagstaff is the largest city in the region and the home of Northern Arizona University. The town's 7,000-foot elevation gives it a mountain climate subject to winter snowstorms and summer thunderstorms, but bright sunshine is likely at any time of year. Early tribes tilled fields despite the dry climate and short growing season, then left behind villages that are now preserved in Walnut Canyon and Wupatki National Monuments. There is even an excavated pueblo right in Flagstaff.

**Flagstaff**

🗺 93 D4

**Visitor information**

www.flagstaff.az.us

✉ 1 E. Route 66, Flagstaff, AZ 86001

☎ 928/774-9541 or 800/842-7293

**Museum of Northern Arizona**

www.musnaz.org

✉ 3101 N. Fort Valley Rd. (3 miles NW of downtown Flagstaff on US 180)

☎ 928/774-5213

💲 $$

The threat of marauding tribes combined with the lack of both mineral wealth and good farmland discouraged Anglo settlers until 1876, when ranchers began raising sheep. The railroad arrived six years later, and a rough frontier town sprang up. Lumbermen set to work logging the vast forests, providing wealth for the fledgling community. Many fine old buildings from the early decades still stand downtown; look for historic markers as you walk around. The tourist office, in a 1926 railroad depot, is here, along with many restaurants, art galleries, and specialty shops. Old Route 66 still rolls through town, carrying motorists as it has since the 1920s. You can tour museums and art galleries, visit nearby archaeological sites, take in the scenery, or hike, horseback ride, and mountain bike in the surrounding area. Downhill skiing takes place at the Snowbowl on the San Francisco Peaks.

One of the finest museums in Arizona, the **Museum of Northern Arizona** portrays the land and people of the Colorado Plateau from their beginnings to the present. Illustrations and fossils show how geologic upheavals created the colorful landscapes and how the environment has changed over the millennia from oceanic to tropical to high plateau. Artifacts tell the story of early peoples as they developed from nomadic hunter-gatherers to sophisticated agricultural societies. Exhibits of modern-day tribes interpret their cultures and display superb examples of their art. In the Hopi sections, you'll see kachina dolls, pottery, basketry, silverwork, a description of their ceremonial calendar, and a full-size replica of a kiva, or room used for Hopi rituals. Navajo exhibits tell of the tribe's way of life and include jewelry, sand paintings, and richly detailed rugs. Other displays reveal the heritage of the Pai (Havasupai, Hualapai, and Paiute), New Mexican Pueblo, and Hispanic cultures. Art galleries feature changing exhibits by tribal and other Southwestern artists.

The museum is very active in research and education. Learn more by digging into the extensive library across the highway in the Research Center, attending a lecture, or signing up for a field trip or workshop.

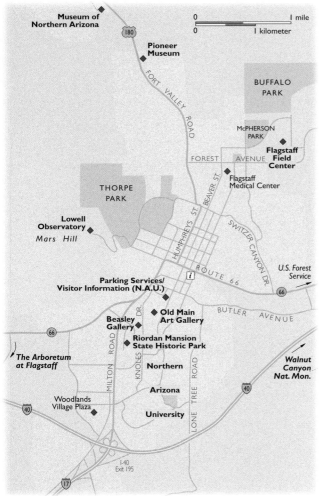

**Pioneer Museum**
- ✉ 2340 N. Fort Valley Rd. (2 miles NW of downtown on US 180)
- ☎ 928/774-6272
- 🕐 Closed Sun.
- 💲 Donation

**Riordan Mansion State Historic Park**
- ✉ 409 Riordan Rd.
- ☎ 928/779-4395
- 💲 $$

A series of summer festivals, each one dedicated to a different Southwestern culture, brings outstanding artists to show their work and demonstrate their skills. A summer-long sales exhibition, "Enduring Creations," offers masterworks of regional traditions.

The **Rio de Flag Nature Trail** descends into a little canyon beside the museum on a half-mile loop; the front desk has trail brochures for children and adults.

The **Pioneer Museum** tells of Flagstaff's settlers and their achievements. Changing exhibits illustrate the lives of ranchers, lumbermen, doctors, homemakers, astronomer Percival Lowell, and Grand Canyon photographer Emery Kolb. After completion in 1908, the stone building served for 30 years as the Coconino County Hospital, where elderly men without families could live out their days; one room from that period has been preserved. Outside, you can admire the powerful 1929 Baldwin locomotive built for the logging industry and see the restored 1908 cabin that belonged

to Ben Doney, a colorful character from the early days of Flagstaff. There's a working blacksmith shop around back in summer. You might catch the Wool Festival (shearing and other ranch skills on the first weekend of June), Independence Day Festival (pioneer craft demonstrations on the weekend nearest July 4), or Playthings of the Past (displays of old toys, dolls, games, and children's books during the winter holiday season).

A fascinating piece of early Flagstaff history is preserved at **Riordan Mansion State Historic Park.** Brothers Timothy and Michael Riordan arrived in the mid-1880s and became wealthy owners of the Arizona Lumber & Timber Company. They both married and in 1904 built this magnificent mansion south of downtown. Each family lived in one of the house's two wings, which were connected by the Rendezvous Room, complete with a billiard table. Architect Charles Whittlesey, who also designed El Tovar Hotel at the Grand Canyon, used a similar rustic style of stone and log slabs on the exterior. The interior has its original furniture, much of it in American Arts and Crafts style.

**Northern Arizona University,** just south of downtown, adds much life and culture to Flagstaff. The school began in 1899 as Northern Arizona Normal School and graduated its first class of four women teachers two years later. Visitors are welcome at the art galleries, concerts, sporting events, library, and many other facilities. A good place to start (and get a precious parking permit) is the **Parking Services/Visitor Information** office at the corner of Dupont Avenue and South Beaver Street. The 1893 Old Main building nearby on McMullen Circle has changing exhibits of contemporary art by local and regional artists in the **Old Main Art Gallery** on the first floor and a permanent collection of art and antique furniture upstairs. Paintings by Philip Curtis and Diego Rivera and sculpture by Francisco Zuniga rub shoulders with 18th-century art, furniture, silver, glassware, and prints. Farther south on Knowles Drive, the **Beasley Gallery** in the Fine and Performing Arts Building stages 30-day exhibits of work by students and faculty artists.

The large white dome of **Lowell Observatory,** atop Mars Hill just west of downtown, marks the spot where astronomer Percival Lowell searched for life on Mars. Lowell established the observatory in 1894 and installed the 24-inch Clark refractor telescope two years later. As he peered at the red planet through the eyepiece, he thought he saw canal systems that indicated an advanced civilization. That effort proved a dead end, but other observations and research here led to discoveries such as that of Pluto and the expansion of the universe.

Daytime visitors can see the telescopes used in the study of Mars and the search for Pluto, while in the evening you can look through the Clark refractor. A visitor center has multimedia programs, interactive exhibits, and equipment used by astronomers.

Scientists at the U.S. Geological Survey's **Flagstaff Field Center** played a major role in the Apollo moon landings between 1969 and 1972. Staff here still study and make discoveries about the Earth and the heavens. In Buildings 3, 4, and 6 you can see photos of the planets and their moons along with results of terrestrial studies; pick up a self-guided tour brochure in the lobby of each builiding.

About 6 miles southwest of town at the **Arboretum at Flagstaff,** you can learn about the plants of the Colorado Plateau. Gardens represent both native and introduced flora with such themes as native wildflowers, endangered species, wetlands, a butterfly garden, landscaping, vegetables, and herbs. A passive solar greenhouse protects the more fragile flora. ∎

**Pueblo pottery in the Museum of Northern Arizona**

**Flagstaff Field Center**
wwwflag.wr.usgs.gov
✉ 2255 N. Gemini Dr. (on McMillan Mesa off Cedar Ave., 1.5 miles NE of downtown)
☎ 928/556-7000
🕐 Closed Sat.–Sun.

**Arboretum at Flagstaff**
🅰 93 C4
www.thearb.org
✉ 4001 S. Woody Mountain Rd. (from S. Milton Rd, turn W 1.9 miles on Ariz. 66, then turn S 4 miles on Woody Mountain Rd.)
☎ 928/774-1442
🕐 Closed mid-Dec.–March
💲 $

The immensity of Meteor Crater drops below your feet at the observation deck outside the museum.

# Around Flagstaff

TWO REMARKABLE SITES EAST OF FLAGSTAFF ARE WELL worth a visit. The first gives insight into the lives and skills of the ancient peoples who made their dwellings in the sheer limestone cliffs of Walnut Canyon. The second is proof of the incredible impact of a meteor that fell to Earth many thousands of years ago.

**Walnut Canyon National Monument**
◭ 93 D4
www.nps.gov/waca
✉ 7 miles E of Flagstaff on I-40, then S 3 miles at Exit 204
☎ 928/526-3367
⑤ $

**Meteor Crater**
◭ 93 E3
www.meteorcrater.com
✉ 36 miles E of Flagstaff on I-40, then S 6 miles at Exit 233
☎ 928/289-2362
⑤ $$$

**Walnut Canyon National Monument** protects about 300 ancient cliff dwellings in a beautiful canyon east of Flagstaff. The tribespeople lived here from A.D. 1125 to 1250 and then moved on. A small museum in the visitor center illustrates how the inhabitants farmed, made use of wild plants and game, and traded with neighboring villages. Pottery and other artifacts show their artistry. The easy **Rim Trail** leads to canyon viewpoints, a pit house site, and a small pueblo on a three-quarter-mile loop; signs explain plant and animal life. The more exciting and strenuous **Island Trail** begins behind the visitor center and descends 240 steps for a close look at some of the cliff dwellings. On some days in summer, rangers lead hikes to a

historic cabin and cliff dwellings not on the public trails; call for the schedule.

A nickel-iron meteorite smashed into the Earth about 49,000 years ago, creating **Meteor Crater**— the world's best preserved impact crater. Measuring 4,100 feet across and 560 feet deep, it could hold 20 football fields. Museum exhibits depict the incredible forces that formed the crater. You'll also see a 1,450-pound meteorite and examples of shock-metamorphosed rock. Space exhibits honor astronauts and tell the story of the first manned flights and trips to the moon. Step outside on the viewing platforms to face the enormity of the crater. Guided hikes give you an even better feel for the crater as you follow the rim partway around. ∎

# San Francisco Volcanic Field

NORTH OF FLAGSTAFF, THE SAN FRANCISCO PEAKS SOAR 5,000 feet above the plateau to a height of 12,633 feet on Humphreys Peak—the rooftop of Arizona. They have great beauty year-round, whether covered by spring and summer greenery, autumn gold, or winter white.

The volcanic eruptions that formed these mountains began about one million to 400,000 years ago. They built up an immense volcano until the center collapsed, leaving a caldera surrounded by pieces of the crater wall. During the Pleistocene (from about 1.6 million years ago to roughly 10,000 years ago), glaciers carved deep valleys into the flanks. Surrounding the peaks, the San Francisco Volcanic Field contains hundreds of volcanic peaks, cinder cones, and lava flows across 3,000 acres. Currently the volcanoes are quiet—the most recent eruptions ended in A.D. 1280 near Sunset Crater. However, there is no reason to assume that they will al-ways be so. Periods of calm have separated eruptions all through the field's long history.

Most of the volcanoes make good day hikes, ranging from easy scrambles to the strenuous all-day climb of Humphreys Peak. Two summits are off-limits—Agassiz Peak, to safeguard its delicate tundra, and Sunset Crater, to protect the soft cinder slopes. The Peaks Ranger Station of the Coconino National Forest provides advice, maps, and trail descriptions; staffers can also suggest various camping possibilities. Be sure to take plenty of water with you on trails, as you're unlikely to find springs.

**San Francisco Volcanic Field**

🏔 93 C4, D4

**Visitor information**

www.fs.fed.us/r3/coconino

✉ Peaks Ranger Station, Coconino National Forest, 5075 N. Hwy. 89, Flagstaff, AZ 86004

☎ 928/526-0866

🕐 Closed Sat.–Sun.

**Snow covers the San Francisco Peaks—Arizona's highest—seen here from Bonito Lava Flow near Sunset Crater Volcano.**

Climbers head for the summit of Humphreys Peak (far left). On the slopes below, alpine tundra struggles for life amid the volcanic rock of the San Francisco Peaks.

## EXPLORING THE SAN FRANCISCO PEAKS

**Kachina Peaks Wilderness** encompasses much of the higher ground on the peaks. It takes its name from the Hopi spirits who reside here for part of the year, bringing rain to nurture the tribe's fields. The peaks also have a sacred role in Navajo belief as one of the cardinal directions—the west—of their lands.

Just outside the wilderness, snow lovers come in season to glide down the runs of the **Arizona Snowbowl** *(Tel 928/779-1951, www.arizonasnowbowl.com)* on the southwest side of the peaks. The Snowbowl's highest chairlift also sweeps summer visitors high up the slopes of Agassiz Peak on a **Scenic Sky Ride;** you can enjoy the views, but there's no hiking here. For cross-country skiing head for the nearby Flagstaff Nordic Center.

**Humphreys Peak Trail** begins at the Arizona Snowbowl ski area, at a height of 9,300 feet, and climbs through dense forests of aspen and conifers, which diminish in size with increasing elevation

until only hardy alpine plants are found growing among the dark volcanic rocks. This strenuous hike is 9 miles round-trip and takes about eight hours. Snow blocks the way until late June in most years and again in late September. Snow and winds can blast the summit even in summer, so good rain and wind gear are essential. Lightning can be a hazard in July and August, when you should be prepared to turn back if thunderstorms threaten. To avoid damaging the alpine vegetation, hikers above 11,400 feet should stay on trails and not make any fires or camps.

If hiking downhill appeals to you and you've arranged a vehicle shuttle, you can take the **Kachina Trail** from the lower Snowbowl parking lot to a trailhead near Schultz Pass on Schultz Pass Road. This trail winds through forests of aspen, spruce, fir, and ponderosa pine on a moderate hike of 5 miles one way with a 500-foot drop in elevation. For another way up the peaks, you can follow the 5.3-mile **Weatherford Trail** from the Schultz Pass Trailhead (8,800 feet)

to Doyle Saddle (10,800 feet). The trail continues to Fremont Saddle and on to a junction with the Humphreys Peak Trail in another 3.4 miles. A hike all the way to the summit would be a tough 20-mile round-trip. Another possibility is to go up the Weatherford Trail and down the Humphreys Peak Trail, with the option of making a side trip to the summit.

Around on the north side of the peaks, **Aubineau** and **Bear Jaw Trails** form an enjoyable 6.5-mile loop through forests, meadows, and a little canyon. A 2.1-mile section of forest road connects the upper end of the trails to make a loop. The trailhead is off unpaved Forest Road 418, which runs between US 89 and US 180.

## OTHER HIKES

**Slate Mountain,** northwest of the peaks, offers a fine panorama of the volcanic field and much of northern Arizona from its 8,215-foot summit. The climb is 5 miles round-trip with an 850-foot ascent, taking about five hours. Early visitors mistook the fine-grained, light

gray rock for slate, but it is really rhyolite—a volcanic rock. The trailhead is 27 miles northwest of Flagstaff on US 180; turn left between Mileposts 242 and 243 onto Forest Road 191 and follow it for 2 miles.

At **Red Mountain,** the thrill is walking *into* the volcano! Erosion has cut towering pinnacles and narrow canyons into the cinder slopes, making it a great place to explore. Head 33 miles northwest of Flagstaff on US 180, then turn left and go 0.3 mile on the dirt road opposite Milepost 247 to a parking area. Follow the trail 1.25 miles up the dry drainage, clambering over or around the six-foot stone dam of a former stock pond.

**Lava River Cave** leads into a volcanic underworld formed about 100,000 years ago when a lava flow began to cool and the hot core broke through, leaving this hollow tube behind. You can enter the cave through a collapse in the ceiling and explore it for 3,820 feet. Bring warm clothes and a flashlight (and a spare). The Coconino National Forest map shows the ways in. Head 14 miles northwest from Flagstaff on US 180, turn left and drive 3 miles on Forest Road 245, turn left and go 1 mile on Forest Road 171, then left about half a mile on Forest Road 171B. Another route goes 10 miles west on I-40 to the Bellemont Exit 185, turns left and runs 1 mile on the north frontage road, turns right (north) 7.5 miles on Forest Road 171, and then turns right on Forest Road 171B.

On the north edge of Flagstaff, the **Mount Elden Trail System** has many loop possibilities in a group of mountains crowned by 9,299-foot Mount Elden. The trails, which range in difficulty from easy to strenuous, are mostly for shared use by hikers, equestrians, and mountain bikers. ∎

Golden aspen contrasts with evergreens and cobalt blue skies in autumn around the San Francisco Peaks. Hart Prairie Road, northeast of Flagstaff, is a popular drive in late September and early October.

# Sunset Crater Volcano National Monument

**Sunset Crater Volcano National Monument**
www.nps.gov/sucr

🅰 93 D4
✉ Loop Road, off US 89 N of Flagstaff
☎ 928/526-0502
💲 $$ (includes Wupatki)

**Sunset Crater Volcano glows once more at day's end.**

YELLOWS AND REDS PAINT THE TOP OF SUNSET CRATER, whose smooth, dark slopes rise a thousand feet above jagged lava flows to a height of 8,029 feet. A roar of incandescent cinders gave birth to the volcano in A.D. 1064–65, kicking off a period of eruptions in the area that lasted about 200 years. The landscape still looks something like the surface of the moon.

In the visitor center, videos of volcanic eruptions, rock samples, and an operating seismograph introduce the forces that created Sunset Crater and its lava flows. Climbing the crater is now strictly forbidden to protect its soft flanks, but you can scramble up nearby **Lenox Crater** (7,240 feet), a cinder cone about 1 mile east of the visitor center. A short, stiff climb of some 280 feet leads to the rim, taking 30 to 45 minutes for the round-trip. **O'Leary Peak** (8,916 feet), north of the visitor center, has a fantastic panorama of Sunset Crater, the San Francisco Peaks, and smaller volcanoes all around. You can climb O'Leary, weather permitting, by going a quarter of a mile west from the visitor center and turning right on Forest Road 545A, an unpaved road that is 5 miles one way with some steep sections. Check with visitor center staffers to find out how much of the road can be driven. **Lava Flow Trail** begins 1.5 miles east of the visitor center and loops across the Bonita Lava Flow beside Sunset Crater. Take a trail guide and allow 30 to 60 minutes for the 1-mile walk, less for the quarter-mile paved loop that's wheelchair accessible.

From Flagstaff, head north 12 miles on US 89, then turn right 2 miles on the Loop Road to the visitor center. The 36-mile **Loop Road,** one of Arizona's most scenic drives, continues across lava and cinder fields, swings by the base of Sunset Crater, provides views of the Painted Desert to the north and east, descends to the historic pueblos at Wupatki National Monument (see p. 103), and rejoins US 89 about 26 miles north of Flagstaff. ■

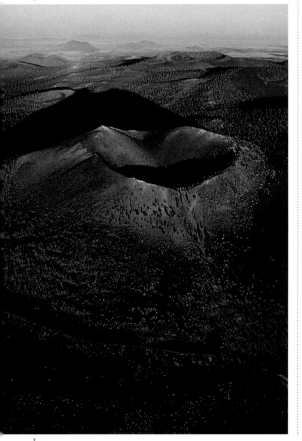

# Wupatki
# National Monument

Wupatki's dwellings sit atop a ridge overlooking the ball court in the foreground.

THE ERUPTIONS OF SUNSET CRATER IN THE 11TH AND 12TH centuries sent early tribespeople fleeing from the area, but after a few generations they returned and settled in Wupatki Basin. Pueblos with multistory stone buildings went up. Villagers maintained trade routes with regional tribes as far away as Mexico. Yet by A.D. 1250—a little over a hundred years later—the villages lay deserted.

**Wupatki Pueblo,** with up to three stories and nearly a hundred rooms, is the largest and most impressive of the pueblos (the name means "house" in Spanish) in Wupatki National Monument. Pottery, jewelry, tools, and other artifacts in the visitor center tell of the people who lived here. A brochure for the trail through the pueblo explains construction details and archaeological findings. The reconstructed ball court is the only known masonry court in the Southwest. Players probably used a rubber or stone ball during games that were open to public view. A blowhole near the ball court connects with a system of underground cracks: Air blows out, gets sucked in, or stands still, depending on the atmospheric pressure.

**Wukoki Pueblo,** though small (only three rooms are visible today), is one of the best preserved. Drive southeast a quarter of a mile from the visitor center, then turn left and go 2.6 miles. **Citadel Pueblo** stands fortress-like atop a volcanic butte 9 miles northwest of the visitor center on the Loop Road. The trail to it passes a smaller pueblo, **Nalakihu.** The well-named **Lomaki Pueblo** (Hopi for "beautiful house") overlooks a small canyon north of Citadel Pueblo. It has two stories and contained at least nine rooms. ■

**Wupatki National Monument**

🗺 93 D5

www.nps.gov/wupa

✉ Loop Road, off US 89 N of Flagstaff

☎ 928/679-2365

💲 $$ (includes Sunset Crater)

# Williams

**Williams**

📷 93 C4

**Visitor information**

www.williamschamber.com

✉ 200 W. Railroad Ave., Williams, AZ 86046

☎ 928/635-1418 or 800/863-0546

THIS SMALL COMMUNITY WEST OF FLAGSTAFF PROUDLY displays its heritage. A statue of "Old Bill" Williams, the town's namesake, stands in Monument Park on the west side of downtown. This tough trapper, guide, and trader roamed the West from 1825 until he was killed by Ute in 1849. He has been credited as a skilled shot, accomplished horse thief, prodigious drinker, and preacher of profane sermons.

**Looks like trouble: Grand Canyon Railway passengers can see some gunplay before their ride from Williams.**

Like Flagstaff, Williams was founded in the 1880s with the coming of the railroad. Steam trains still puff in and out of the station on excursions to the Grand Canyon. Local businesses thrived on Route 66 traffic right up until 1984, when the last segment of I-40 bypassed Williams. After weathering tough times, the town has spruced up its historic downtown and added some Old West entertainment. It's a fun place to visit and a handy stop on travels across northern Arizona.

The **Grand Canyon Railway** departs daily from downtown to the Grand Canyon, just 65 miles north, and back. Passengers ride restored 1923 Harriman or other coaches across the high plains and through canyons before arriving at the park's log depot near El Tovar Hotel just over two hours later. A steam locomotive leads the way in summer, with vintage diesels the rest of the year. "Train robbers" have been known to provide a little excitement on the way back as they pursue the carriages on horseback and jump aboard, but "the law" always catches up with the bandits. Whether or not you're taking the train, you can visit the station in the morning before departure to watch a Wild West show and see the railroad museum.

Children and animal lovers will enjoy hand-feeding and walking among tame deer at **Grand Canyon Deer Farm,** 8 miles east of Williams. Other regional and exotic creatures include pronghorn, bison, reindeer, wallabies, pygmy goats, potbellied pigs, talking birds, and peacocks.

Mountains, canyons, and lakes in the scenic **Kaibab National Forest** surrounding Williams offer

many recreation possibilities. Stop by the Visitor Information Center downtown for maps and details. A climb up **Bill Williams Mountain** (9,255 feet) reveals a panorama of the Grand Canyon to the north, the San Francisco Peaks and many other volcanoes to the east, Sycamore Canyon and the Verde Valley to the south, and vast rangelands to the west. Three strenuous hiking trails lead up through forests of juniper, oak, pine, aspen, fir, and spruce to a lookout on top: the 9-mile **Bill Williams Mountain Trail** on the north side, the 8.8-mile **Benham Trail** on the south and west slopes, and the 6-mile **Bixler Saddle Trail** on the west flank. With a high-clearance vehicle, you can also drive up the unpaved road.

Winter snows close the road and trails, but the small **Williams Ski Area** *(Tel 928/635-9330)* comes to life on the mountain. You can also have fun in the snow on the loops of the **Spring Valley Cross-Country Ski Trail** northeast of town and the **Oak Hill Snowplay Area** east of town.

**Keyhole Sink Trail** is an easy 1.2-mile round-trip ramble through ponderosa pines to a seasonal pool in a box canyon. It's a good spot for wildflowers in spring and summer, birds year-round, and ancient petroglyphs. Head west for 8 miles on I-40 to the Pittman Valley/Deer Farm Exit 171, exit north, then take a section of Route 66 east 2.4 miles; parking is at the Oak Hill Snowplay Area, and the trailhead is north across the road.

Four trout lakes near Williams offer relaxation and camping: **Cataract Lake** to the west, **Kaibab Lake** to the northeast, **Dogtown Lake** to the southeast, and **White Horse Lake** farther southeast. Forest roads head southeast to **Sycamore Point,** a spectacular overlook of the Sycamore Canyon Wilderness. The **Perkinsville Road** features great views of the Verde Valley on a back-road drive to Jerome. Allow about three hours one way for the trip, best done in dry weather and with a high-clearance vehicle; the first 25 miles are paved, followed by 27 miles of dirt road. ■

Steam engines of the Grand Canyon Railway pull trains from the Williams depot to the South Rim in summer, then take a rest during winter.

**Grand Canyon Railway**
www.thetrain.com
✉ Grand Canyon Blvd.
☎ 928/773-1976 (Flagstaff) or 800/843-8724
💲 $$$$$ (train excursion); show & museum free

**Grand Canyon Deer Farm**
www.deerfarm.com
✉ 6752 E. Deer Farm Rd. (I-40 Exit 171)
☎ 928/635-4073 or 800/926-3337
💲 $$

**Coffeepot Rock (on the right) and many other dramatic rock features overlook Sedona.**

# Sedona

WONDERFULLY SCULPTURED CANYON WALLS, FINS, AND great monoliths create an almost surreal setting for the Sedona area. Some people believe that powerful energies called vortexes emanate from certain natural features. Superb resorts and restaurants are among the other attractions here.

**Sedona**
🗺 93 C3
**Visitor information**
www.visitsedona.com
✉ Sedona-Oak Creek Canyon Chamber of Commerce (on N Ariz, 89A, 1 block N of Ariz. 179 junction), P.O. Box 478, Sedona, AZ 86339
☎ 928/282-7722 or 800/288-7336

The work of artists who have been inspired by Sedona and its scenery is on view on the north edge of town in **Sedona Arts Center** (*N. Ariz. 89A & Art Barn Rd., tel 928/282-3865, www.sedonaartscenter.com*) and other galleries. Even non-shoppers will be tempted by the Spanish colonial architecture, fountains, and sycamore-shaded courtyards of **Tlaquepaque** (*336 Hwy. 179, tel 928/282-4838, www.tlaq.com*). The galleries here offer Western, Native American, and other arts and crafts.

The **Sedona Heritage Museum** (*735 Jordan Rd., tel 928/282-7038, www.sedonamuseum.org*) showcases the lives of Sedona's pioneers. Many came here in the late 1800s and early 1900s to raise apples and other crops. Each room

has a different theme, such as cowboys, homemaking, farming, transportation, the U.S. Forest Service, and moviemaking. You can see the apple packing shed of the 1930 Jordan farmstead.

**Airport Mesa,** one of Sedona's vortex sites, has a great panorama of the red-rock country. Sunset is a magical time for a jeep tour, hike or horseback ride (see pp. 263–64). From the airport you can take to the skies in a biplane, a Cessna, or a helicopter. Hikers will find some short, steep trails off Airport Road. Also, enjoy the view from the **Chapel of the Holy Cross** (*Tel 928/282-4069*), set high on a sandstone ridge. To reach the chapel, drive 3 miles south of Sedona on Arizona 179, then turn left on Chapel Road. ■

# Around Sedona

THE SPECTACULAR RED-ROCK COUNTRY SURROUNDING
Sedona invites you to explore its trails, back roads, and prehistoric
sites. Except for two state parks, most of this region lies on Coconino
National Forest lands; drop by the Sedona Ranger District office or
one of the Gateway Visitor Centers for the latest information and the
Red Rock Pass, which you'll need for parking in the forest.

Southwest of town off Arizona 89A, the view of Cathedral Rock reflected in Oak Creek at **Red Rock Crossing** has long captivated photographers and has appeared in many prints and movies. Now part of a recreation area at **Crescent Moon Ranch** *(Tel 928/282-4119)*, it has picnic tables, historic irrigation canals, a working waterwheel, and natural swimming holes. From central Sedona, head west 4.2 miles on Arizona 89A, turn left and drive 1.8 miles on Upper Red Rock Loop Road, then turn left at the sign and go 0.9 mile on Chavez Ranch Road.

Farther downstream on Oak Creek, stop at **Red Rock State Park** *(Tel 928/282-6907)* to enjoy nature walks and wildlife, such as mule deer and javelina, and to have a picnic. Bird-watching is good year-round, and you can pick up a list of the species found here. Stop at the visitor center to see exhibits about the park's natural habitats. Rangers offer walks and special programs year-round. A network of trails follows Oak Creek and climbs into the hills. From Sedona, you can head west 5.5 miles on Arizona 89A, turn left and drive 3 miles on Lower Red Rock Loop Road, then turn right into the park. If you're driving from Upper Red Rock Loop Road, continue 3 miles past the Red Rock Crossing turnoff; part of the way is unpaved.

Stunning scenery unfolds as you enter the Sedona area from any direction, but for sheer drama you can't beat the approach from the east along Schnebly Hill Road. The unpaved, bumpy road, suitable only for high-clearance vehicles, turns off I-17 at Exit 320 atop the forested Mogollon Rim. About halfway along the 12-mile one-way trip, you'll reach **Schnebly Hill Vista** at the edge of the rim with a view of Sedona and its red-rock country. More views unfold as you bump your way down to Sedona and then enter a canyon. The lower end of the drive is just across the Oak Creek bridge from central Sedona on Arizona 179. Snow usually blocks the way in winter. Inquire about road conditions at the Sedona Ranger District office. ■

**Sedona Ranger
District, Coconino
National Forest**
www.fs.fed.us/r3/coconino

✉ 250 Brewer Rd.,
   Sedona (P.O. Box
   300, Sedona, AZ
   86339)

☎ 928/282-4119

🕐 Closed Sat.–Sun.

**Cooling off in the
pools of Oak
Creek in Slide
Rock State Park**

# A drive through Oak Creek Canyon

Oak Creek weaves through lush forests beneath high sandstone cliffs near Sedona in one of Arizona's most famous beauty spots. This drive through the canyon reveals marvelous vistas on every curve, with multicolored leaves adding to the magic from mid-October to mid-November. The entire distance within the canyon can be covered in less than an hour one way, but trails, picnic areas, and natural swimming holes may tempt you to linger. Try to avoid summer weekends, when heavy traffic fills up parking and camping spots.

Before you set out, pick up travel information from the local tourist and Forest Service offices in **Sedona ➊** *(Tel 928/282-7722, 800/ 288-7336, or 928/282-4119)*. Heading north on Arizona 89A, you could stop on the left at the far end of **Midgley Bridge,** a mile outside Sedona, to take in views of Wilson and Oak Creek Canyons. A little farther on, to the right, is **Grasshopper Point ➋,** a swimming hole at a bend in Oak Creek. Travelers can fish for their dinner (provided they pay for what they catch) a mile beyond here at **Rainbow Trout Farm** *(Tel 928/282-5799)*.

At **Indian Gardens ➌** you can stop at the **Oak Creek Visitor Center** for travel advice and literature. **Encinoso Picnic Area** is soon passed on the left, followed by

---

🗺 See area map p. 93
▶ Sedona
↔ 15 miles one way
🕐 40 minutes one way
▶ Oak Creek Vista

**NOT TO BE MISSED**
- Slide Rock State Park
- West Fork Oak Creek
- Oak Creek Vista

---

the turnoff to **Manzanita Campground,** along Oak Creek. The popular swimming hole at **Slide Rock State Park ➍** *(Tel 928/282-3034)* is just what the name suggests—a natural waterslide in the bed of Oak Creek! (Shorts made of heavy fabric work best.) The park also has an old apple orchard, picnic tables, bird-watching, and a short hiking trail.

About 7 miles from Sedona, **Halfway Picnic Area,** on the left, is on a sunny shelf with canyon views. Nearby **Banjo Bill Picnic Area,** also on the left, is down near the creek. **Bootlegger Campground,** a few hundred yards beyond the picnic areas, is the smallest one in the canyon and lacks water.

Definitely worth a stop, after another 1.5 miles, is **Call of the Canyon/West Fork Oak Creek Trailhead ➎,** to the left. Novelist Zane Grey took his inspiration for *Call of the Canyon* from the scenery around West Fork, a major tributary of Oak Creek. A 6-mile round-trip trail crosses a footbridge over Oak Creek, winds through the ruins of Mayhews Lodge, and then turns up West Fork. The walking is mostly easy, though you'll have to hop across rocks at the stream crossings.

**Winter can be a delightful and less busy time to explore Oak Creek Canyon.**

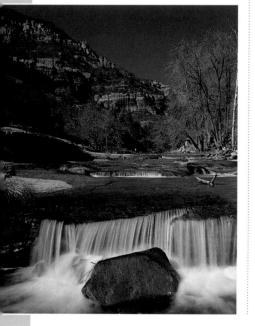

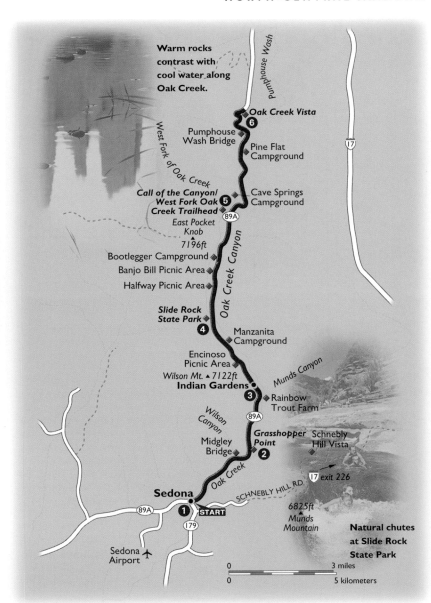

**Warm rocks contrast with cool water along Oak Creek.**

Pumphouse Wash

*West Fork of Oak Creek*

Oak Creek Vista ⑥

Pumphouse Wash Bridge

Pine Flat Campground

17

*Call of the Canyon/ West Fork Oak Creek Trailhead* ⑤

Cave Springs Campground

89A

East Pocket Knob 7196ft

Bootlegger Campground

Banjo Bill Picnic Area

Halfway Picnic Area

Oak Creek Canyon

*Slide Rock State Park* ④

Manzanita Campground

Encinoso Picnic Area

Wilson Mt. ▲ 7122ft

**Indian Gardens** ③

Munds Canyon

Rainbow Trout Farm

89A

*Wilson Canyon*

*Grasshopper Point* ②

Schnebly Hill Vista

Midgley Bridge

**Sedona** ①  **START**

Oak Creek

17 exit 226

89A

SCHNEBLY HILL RD.

179

6825ft ▲ Munds Mountain

Sedona Airport ✈

**Natural chutes at Slide Rock State Park**

| 0 | | 3 miles |
| 0 | | 5 kilometers |

A mile farther along the drive, **Cave Springs Campground** lies down a road to the left in a secluded setting beside Oak Creek. **Pine Flat Campground** is on both sides of the road after another mile, in a ponderosa pine forest. Soon Arizona 89A begins its steep climb out of the canyon to the rim, where it's worth stopping on the right at **Oak Creek Vista** ⑥ for a panorama of Pumphouse Wash just below and Oak Creek Canyon stretching into the distance. A Forest Service information booth *(closed in winter)* offers advice, maps, and books on the area.

Arizona 89A continues north another 12 miles to Flagstaff through rolling hills forested with ponderosa pines. ■

# Archaeological sites near Sedona

**Ancient ruins and rock art lie within alcoves at Palatki—typical of the wildly shaped and colored rock accessible on backcountry travels near Sedona.**

THE FOREST SERVICE, WITH THE HELP OF VOLUNTEERS, has opened several cliff dwellings and rock art sites left by ancient Pueblo people. The dirt roads to the cliff dwellings are usually passable by car in dry weather and have fine scenery along the way.

Two pueblos in a large alcove at **Palatki Ruins** housed 30 to 50 people between about A.D. 1150 and 1300. Some of the rock art on the alcove wall behind and above the ruins may represent clans. The **Red Cliffs,** a series of alcoves a short walk to the west of Palatki, hold an extensive collection of rock art. Volunteers will point out the different styles and name the time periods. A visitor center in a former ranch house lies between Palatki and the Red Cliffs. The less bumpy road to Palatki follows Arizona 89A west 9.2 miles from the center of Sedona, turns right (north) 5 miles on Forest Road 525, then continues north another 1.6 miles on Forest Road 795 to its end. Alternatively, head west 3.1 miles from Sedona on

Arizona 89A, then turn right (north) 8.5 miles on Dry Creek Road/Forest Road 152C; this curves around to the west to Forest Road 525, where you turn right, then right again on Forest Road 795.

**Honanki Ruins** may have had as many as 72 rooms housing about 120 people from about A.D. 1130 to 1280. You'll find rock art here too. From the junction of Forest Roads 525 and 795 south of Palatki, follow 525 northwest for 4 miles.

**V-Bar-V Ranch Petroglyph Site** contains more than a thousand petroglyphs in 13 panels. From Sedona drive south 15 miles on Arizona 179 to the I-17 junction, go straight for 2.4 miles and cross the Wet Beaver Creek bridge, then turn right at the sign. ■

**Sedona Ranger District, Coconino National Forest**
www.fs.fed.us/r3/coconino
✉ 250 Brewer Rd., Sedona (P.O. Box 300, Sedona, AZ 86339)
☎ 928/282-4119
🕐 Closed Sat.–Sun.

**Fort Verde State
Historic Park**
✉ 125 E. Hollamon St.
(from Main St. in
downtown, turn E
one block on
Hollamon St.)
☎ 928/567-3275
💲 $

The doctor's
quarters at Fort
Verde date from
the early 1870s.

# Camp Verde

IN EARLY 1865, KNOWING THAT THE BOOMING MINING
camps in the Prescott area would pay handsomely for fresh food, a
group of farmers decided to grow crops along the Verde River. When
raiding tribes destroyed crops and livestock, the U.S. Army built a fort
and pursued the Tonto Apache and Yavapai. Although the fort closed
in 1891, four of its adobe buildings still stand beside the old parade
ground in the modern town of Camp Verde.

Period rooms and exhibits at **Fort
Verde State Historic Park**
re-create life in the early territorial
years. Start at the administration
building to see photos and artifacts
that tell the stories of enlisted men,
officers and their families, Apache
scouts, prospectors, and settlers.
Gen. George Crook and other
commanders worked out of this
building trying to end the Indian
wars. A heliograph display shows
how the troops beamed messages
across the state with mirrors and
sunlight. The three buildings of
Officers' Row have been restored
with 1880s furnishings. Step inside
to see the quarters of the commanding officer, bachelors, and the
doctor. Reenactments take place
during Fort Verde Days on the
second Saturday of October.

The **Verde River** and nearby
wilderness areas are worth visiting
for their rugged canyon scenery and
riparian, desert, and woodland
wildlife habitats. Contact the Verde
Ranger District about running the
Verde River and exploring Cedar
Bench and Pine Mountain Wildernesses. Both this office and the Sedona Ranger District (see p. 107)
can tell you about West Clear
Creek, Wet Beaver, and Fossil
Springs Wildernesses. Experienced
kayakers and rafters can journey 59
miles down the river from Camp
Verde to Sheep Bridge above Horseshoe Reservoir, best done during
the spring run-off. ∎

**Camp Verde**
🅰 93 C3
**Visitor information**
www.campverde.org
✉ Camp Verde
Chamber of
Commerce, 385 S.
Main St. (P.O. Box
3520, Camp Verde,
AZ 86322)
☎ 928/567-9294
🕐 Closed Sat.–Sun.
(may open on Sat.
in summer)

**Verde Ranger
District, Prescott
National Forest**
www.fs.fed.us/r3/prescott
✉ 300 E. Hwy. 260
(P.O. Box 670, Camp
Verde, AZ 86322)
☎ 928/567-4121
🕐 Closed Sat.–Sun.

# Montezuma Castle
# National Monument

THIS FIVE-STORY PUEBLO SO IMPRESSED EARLY VISITORS
that they assumed it had been built by Aztec refugees from Mexico
after their overthrow by Hernán Cortés in 1521. In fact, Montezuma
Castle was constructed in the early 1100s by local ancient Pueblo
people, who also left impressive pueblos at Tuzigoot and other areas
of the Verde Valley as well as in Walnut Canyon and Wupatki (see pp.
98 and 103). Archaeologists termed the culture Sinagua (Spanish for
"without water") because of its ability to live in arid lands.

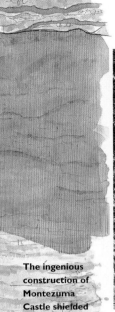

The ingenious construction of Montezuma Castle shielded its residents from the weather and invaders.

**Montezuma Castle National Monument**
93 C3
**Visitor information**
www.nps.gov/moca
From I-17 Exit 289, follow signs 2 miles E and N
928/567-3322
$

Year-round water in Beaver Creek below the village and fertile soil on a nearby terrace must have made this an attractive site for the prehistoric farming people. Wild plant foods, game, and salt deposits supplemented the staple crop of corn. The tribespeople may have learned how to build masonry villages from groups farther north and irrigation techniques from groups to the south.

**Montezuma Castle's** large alcove sheltered its residents from rain and summer heat yet let in warm rays of light in winter. Its location high in the cliffs provided a sense of security against attack. The 20 rooms inside remain remarkably well preserved, but they are too fragile for visitors to enter. The nearby less fortunate **Castle A,** which towered six stories and held 45 rooms, collapsed toward the end of its occupation. The Sinagua had abandoned the entire Verde Valley by the early 1400s.

Visitor center exhibits interpret the daily life of the Sinagua, display their artifacts, and describe the geology, plants, and wildlife of the Verde Valley. A level 0.3-mile loop trail leads to viewpoints of Montezuma Castle and the meager ruins of Castle A.

Also part of the National Monument is **Montezuma Well,** where springs rise out of a limestone sinkhole to form a lake. About 150 to 200 Sinagua lived here in small alcove dwellings and in large surface pueblos. A 0.3-mile self-guiding loop trail climbs to a viewpoint of the lake and some pueblos. Another path drops down to the lakeshore and a few rooms in a small cave. The main trail continues along the rim of the sinkhole past foundations of a pueblo and descends along the outside wall of the sinkhole. A side trail leads to a natural drainage hole where the lake water gushes at 1,100 gallons per minute into a canal built by the Sinagua and still in use today.

The lake is 11 miles northeast of Montezuma Castle. Take I-17 north to Exit 293 and follow signs for 5 miles or, near Sedona, take I-17 Exit 298, go east for half a mile, then turn south for 3 miles on an unpaved road. ∎

# Cottonwood

NAMED AFTER THE TREES THAT FLOURISH ALONG THE Verde River, Cottonwood is the focus of an area that offers an enjoyable railway trip, a large ancient pueblo, and outdoor recreation. The setting hasn't always been so green. United Verde Copper Company built the neighboring town of Clarkdale in 1912 and operated a copper smelter that smothered the valley with sulfur smoke until 1952. If you enjoy early 20th-century architecture, follow signs to Old Town Cottonwood and Clarkdale, both of which are now bypassed by Arizona 89A.

The **Clemenceau Heritage Museum** *(Willard St. & Mingus Ave., tel 928/634-2868, call for hours, donation)* in Cottonwood shows historical and craft exhibits and has a permanent model train room that illustrates seven historic Verde Valley lines.

To experience the real thing, make the four-hour round-trip along the Verde River through a scenic canyon to Perkinsville and back on the **Verde Canyon Railroad.** A guide provides background on the area's history and Native Americans and also points out wildlife, geologic features, and historical ranches. Look for bald eagles, especially during the nesting season from late November to mid-May. Starlight tours on some Saturday evenings in summer depart in the late afternoon and come back under the full moon. Follow signs for the station in Clarkdale, 2 miles northwest of Cottonwood.

**Tuzigoot National Monument,** northeast of Clarkdale, is a massive ridgetop pueblo of the Sinagua Indians, who occupied it from about A.D. 1125 to 1400. Archaeologists discovered a wealth of jewelry, stone tools, and pottery here, including offerings for 408 burials. The visitor center has many of these artifacts on display, along with findings about the farming, building, and craft skills of the Sinagua. A quarter-mile trail loops through the maze of stone walls at the site, which had perhaps 77 ground-floor and 15 second-story rooms and housed 225 people at its peak in the late 1300s.

To get a taste of the great outdoors, drive a mile north out of Cottonwood on 10th Street, following the signs to **Dead Horse Ranch State Park** *(Tel 928/634-5283)*. Activities here include hiking, mountain biking, horseback riding, regular and fly-fishing, birdwatching, picnicking, and camping beside the Verde River. ∎

**Cottonwood**

⚐ 93 C3

**Visitor information**

chamber.verdevalley.com

✉ Cottonwood Chamber of Commerce, 1010 S. Main St., Cottonwood, AZ 86326

☎ 928/634-7593

**Verde Canyon Railroad**

www.verdecanyonrr.com

✉ 300 N. Broadway, Clarkdale

☎ 928/639-0010 or 800/293-7245

🕐 Call for schedule

💲 $$$$$

**Tuzigoot National Monument**

www.nps.gov/tuzi

⚐ 93 C3

✉ Take Main St. & Broadway toward Clarkdale, then turn E 1.3 miles at sign

☎ 928/634-5564

💲 $

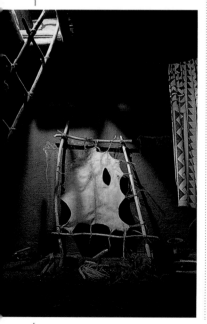

A room replica in the Tuzigoot visitor center shows how the Sinagua may have furnished their living areas.

# Jerome

A STEEP HILLSIDE HIGH ABOVE THE VERDE VALLEY SEEMS an improbable place for a town, but rich veins of copper ore lay under Cleopatra Hill. Native Americans knew of the turquoise-colored deposits and mined them for pigments and jewelry many centuries before Eugene Jerome provided the financial backing that got the mining industry going in 1883. He never visited the town named for him, missing out on its early days of boom and bust as economic cycles, fires, and Earth temblors gave it a wild ride.

Bordellos and riotous saloon life caused a New York newspaper to proclaim Jerome the "wickedest town in the West." Blasting in pit and underground mines shook the buildings so much that some started sliding downhill. The old jail, formerly on the uphill side of Hull Avenue, is now at a new address across the street!

Jerome's final bust came in 1953, when the mines shut down and residents began moving out. With the population down to 50 from its peak of 15,000 in the 1920s, Jerome seemed likely to fade away entirely. Then, in the late 1960s, artists and others began moving in for the town's unique character and low rents. Today's visitors come for the early 20th-century atmosphere, gorgeous setting, art galleries and craft shops, and three museums that tell of life in the old days.

**Jerome State Historic Park** illustrates past life in the town and its mines with photos, heirlooms, and pieces of mining equipment. The 1916 adobe mansion that houses the exhibits has great views of Jerome and the Little Daisy Mine on one side and the Verde Valley on the other. Signs at overlooks identify buildings and mining areas. Also on the grounds, you can see the *arrastre* (primitive drag-stone mill), Chilean wheels

Jerome's downtown provides many fine examples of early 20th-century architecture.

**Jerome**
🅰 93 C3
**Visitor information**
jeromechamber.com
✉ Jerome Chamber of Commerce, 310 Hull Ave. (Drawer K, Jerome, AZ 86331)
☎ 928/634-2900
🕐 Hours depend on staffing

**Jerome State Historic Park**
☎ 928/634-5381
💲 $

**Gold King Mine &
Ghost Town**
🅰 93 C3
✉ 1 mile NW of
Jerome
☎ 928/634-0053
💲 $$

The Little Daisy
Hotel—a board-
ing house for
mine workers
from 1918 to
1938—has since
been partially
rebuilt as a pri-
vate residence.

(large stone wheels that crush the
ore), and the giant stamp mill once
used to grind ore to a powder
before it could be processed. The
three-dimensional mine model
upstairs in the mansion shows the
underground geology, mine shafts,
and work areas beneath Jerome.
From Milepost 345 on Arizona 89A
in the lower part of town, turn in 1
mile at the sign.

A large flywheel, its halves
separated, is an eye-catching land-
mark for the **Jerome Historical
Society Museum** *(Main St. &
Jerome Ave., tel 928/634-5477),*
which traces Jerome's past with
paintings, photos, mining tools,
and ore samples.

For a real ghost town, visit the
**Gold King Mine & Ghost
Town.** The town of Haynes existed
from 1890 to 1914, when miners
brought out modest quantities of
gold and silver ore from its 1,200-
foot-deep shaft instead of the rich
copper ore they had hoped for. The
antique sawmill runs daily, and, for
the cost of fuel, operators will fire
up the 10,154-cubic-inch Big
Bertha engine that once powered a
mine near Bisbee (see pp. 230–31).
Before the development of the elec-
trical grid, mines had to provide
their own power and compressed
air to run the hoist, ore-transport
equipment, drills, lights, and ore-
processing machinery. You can
enter a short prospect tunnel or
visit an old schoolhouse from near-
by Prescott. Other buildings along
the dusty streets include a black-
smith shop, an assay office, and a
1930s gas station. More than a
hundred historical trucks and other
vehicles on the grounds include a
1902 Studebaker Electric; most of
them still run. To get there, turn
northwest on the Perkinsville Road
from the upper switchback in Je-
rome, drive one mile, then turn left
at the sign. You'll pass a copper
mine whence Jerome's smelter
belched poisonous gases from 1895
to 1915. Continue on the Perkins-
ville Road for great panoramas of
the Verde Valley (see p. 111).

Arizona 89A climbs above Je-
rome into the ponderosa pines of
**Mingus Mountain.** The highway
tops out at a 7,023-foot pass, where
you'll find Summit Picnic Area
during the warmer months and
Summit Snowplay in winter.
Nearby attractions include camp-
grounds, hiking trails, backcountry
drives, and the Woodchute Wilder-
ness. The Prescott National Forest
offices in Camp Verde (see p. 111)
and Prescott (see p. 120) offer maps
and information. ∎

# Prescott

*PRESCUTT*, AS THEY SAY HERE, EASILY WINS OVER VISITORS with its leafy streets and historic downtown centered on Courthouse Plaza. In 1863 the federal government chose this site for the capital of the new Arizona Territory because of its promising mineral deposits and its location far from the many Confederate sympathizers in the Tucson area.

Governor John Goodwin and his officials set up a temporary camp at Fort Whipple in Chino Valley, then moved—as did the fort—17 miles south to the present site of Prescott to be closer to the mining areas and forested land. Soldiers had to be constantly on the lookout for attacks by Tonto Apache and Yavapai as workers built the governor's mansion and other buildings. But Prescott's isolation did not appeal to all the territorial leaders, and in 1867 they moved the capital to Tucson. Ten years later they were back in Prescott; finally, in 1889, they decided that Phoenix would be the capital and departed for good.

The neatly laid-out town they left behind had taken on the appearance of a community from New England or the Midwest rather than the Spanish-flavored adobe towns of southern Arizona or the rough-and-tumble mining and logging camps in other parts of the state. Today's visitors and residents enjoy a rich cultural life, fine recreation opportunities, and an invigorating four-season climate.

At the excellent **Sharlot Hall Museum,** you can walk through Prescott's history in a series of buildings amid parklike grounds. Stop by the **Museum Center** to pick up a description of the exhibits and buildings, see temporary shows, and learn about Sharlot Hall (1870–1943). While other women contented themselves at home, Hall's love of the land and people of Arizona took her on many trips

Cutting a fast corner in the women's barrel racing event at Prescott's Frontier Days

**Prescott**
🅰 93 B3
**Visitor information**
www.prescott.org
✉ Prescott Chamber of Commerce, 117 W. Goodwin St. (P.O. Box 1147, Prescott, AZ 86302)
☎ 928/445-2000 or 800/266-7534

**Sharlot Hall Museum**
www.sharlot.org
✉ 415 W. Gurley St. (2 blocks W of Courthouse Plaza)
☎ 928/445-3122
💲 $$

**Smoki Museum**
www.smoki.com
✉ 147 N. Arizona St.
☎ 928/445-1230
🕐 Closed Nov.–
mid-April
💲 $$

**Phippen Museum**
www.phippenmuseum.org
✉ 4701 N. Hwy. 89 (6
miles N of Prescott)
☎ 928/778-1385
💲 $

**Art at the Phippen Museum captures the life and romance of the West.**

down the territory's rough roads to gather stories. Herself a pioneer, having arrived in Arizona by wagon at the age of 12 in 1882, Hall served as the first territorial historian from 1909 to 1911, working to preserve important relics of the past. She wrote stories and poems and founded this museum in 1927.

Among the museum buildings is the 1864 **Governor's Mansion.** Built of ponderosa pine logs, it may seem rustic today, but when it was new its large size and solid construction must have made it the area's most impressive structure. Governor John Goodwin and Territorial Secretary Richard McCormick moved in at opposite ends of the mansion, along with other officials and family members. Today you can see the interior furnished as it was during the early years.

In the native-stone-and-log **Sharlot Hall Building** next door, completed by the Civilian Conservation Corps in 1934, you can learn about the region's Native Americans and people of territorial Arizona. **Fort Misery,** built as a general store in 1863–64, is one of

the oldest wooden buildings in Arizona. In the 1890s, one story goes, Judge John Howard dispensed "misery" sentences to lawbreakers here. Another report says he generously took in guests but was an awful cook.

Sharlot Hall had the **Ranch House** built in 1936 "as a tribute to early ranchers." It offers living history programs. The **schoolhouse** is a replica of the territory's first public schoolhouse, built nearby in 1867.

The 1875 **Frémont House** is an early Victorian building, made of wood planking and with a restored interior. John C. Frémont, a noted explorer of the West and Arizona's fifth territorial governor, rented this house from 1878 to 1881, but he fared badly in Arizona politics and resigned under public pressure after three years in office.

Even more elegant, the 1877 **Bashford House** has some rooms restored in elaborate style, a solarium, and a gift shop. In the **Transportation Building,** you can see fine examples of how people got around in the late 19th and early 20th century. Among several gardens on the museum grounds, the **Rose Garden** honors the pioneer women of Arizona. Living history programs, talks, workshops, theater productions, music concerts, and special events take place throughout the year; call or check the website.

Inside the pueblo-style **Smoki Museum,** over on the east side of downtown, you'll find treasure in the form of Native American artistry. Excavations near Prescott uncovered much of the prehistoric jewelry, pottery, and stone implements on display. Exhibits of fine basketry, textiles, pottery, and kachina dolls represent contemporary tribes of the Southwest. Paintings and sketches by

artist Kate Cory—who lived with the Hopi from 1905 to 1912 and helped design this museum—illustrate Native American life.

Western artists reflect their feelings in works at the **Phippen Museum,** where paintings, drawings, and some bronzes represent both the Old West and contemporary life. Native American artists display their work too. George Phippen's paintings depict the life of the working cowboy, often with a humorous eye. ■

**The spartan furnishings of the Governor's Mansion recall the hard frontier life, even for high-ranking officials.**

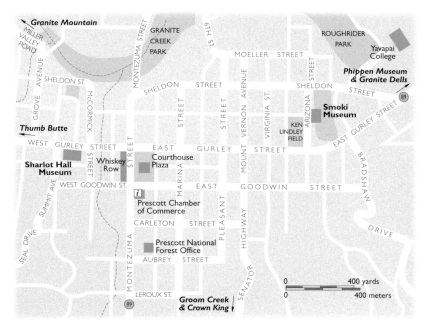

**Boulders adorn Granite Dells north of Prescott.**

# Around Prescott

PRESCOTT'S APPEAL TO VISITORS LIES NOT ONLY IN ITS historic attractions. The mile-high city is also the center of an extensive area of forested mountains, lakes, and picturesque granite boulders. Several roads out of the city lead into the great expanse of Prescott National Forest, where you will find enough trails, views, wildlife, and campgrounds to satisfy most outdoors enthusiasts.

**Prescott National Forest**
www.fs.fed.us/r3/prescott
✉ 344 S. Cortez St., Prescott, AZ 86303
☎ 928/771-4700
🕐 Closed Sat.–Sun.

Piles of smooth granite boulders line Watson Lake in **Granite Dells,** 4 miles north of Prescott on Arizona 89. **Watson Lake Park** *(Tel 928/771-5841)* on the south shore offers the easiest access as well as picnicking *(year-round)* and camping *(Fri.–Sat. May–Sept.).* **Thumb Butte** *(Tel 928/771-4700)* soars high into the sky west of Prescott. A trail loops through dense ponderosa pines up to ridges covered with pinyon pine, juniper, and oak. Here two short trails lead to vista points of Prescott and its surroundings; the 1.7-mile round-trip gains 600 feet in elevation and takes about two and a half hours. The trailhead is 3.5 miles west of downtown on Gurley Street/Thumb Butte Road.

Northwest of Prescott, **Granite Basin Lake** and **Granite Mountain Wilderness** *(Tel 928/771-4700)* also feature dramatic vistas of water, forest, stone, and sky. The lake, which lies at the foot of Granite Mountain, has a picnic area and a nearby campground and trailhead. **Granite Mountain Trail** ascends gently in 1.3 miles to Blair Pass, then turns right and switchbacks 2.5 miles to an overlook at 7,185 feet; the hike is moderate to strenuous and 8.2 miles round-trip, with a 1,600-foot elevation gain, and takes about six hours. From Prescott, head west on Gurley Street, turn right and drive for 4.3 miles on Grove Avenue/Miller Valley Road/Iron Springs Road, then turn right and drive about 5 miles on Forest Road 374.

Many scenic vistas, historical sites, and hiking trails lie south of Prescott along the **Senator Highway,** also signed as Mount Vernon Avenue in town and Forest Road 52 farther south. It twists and turns through the rugged Bradshaw Mountains to Crown King, where you can follow an old railroad grade down to I-17. In the 19th century, the "highway" connected Prescott with the Senator Mine and other mining communities. Most of these have faded away, but some of the old mines and relics of that era remain. Beyond the village of Groom Creek you'll need a high-clearance vehicle with a full tank of gas, water, and most of a day to reach I-17. Check with the Prescott National Forest office in Prescott for road conditions and opportunities for hiking and camping.

Six miles south of Prescott on the Senator Highway, the **Groom Creek School Nature Trail** offers an easy quarter-mile walk on a paved loop. Back on the Senator Highway, another half-mile through the ponderosa pines takes you to **Groom Creek Trail,** which climbs to the 7,693-foot summit of Spruce Mountain and back in a 9-mile loop. This moderate-to-strenuous, six-hour hike has good panoramas of the Prescott area, Mogollon Rim, and San Francisco Peaks, with a 1,300-foot elevation gain. Equestrians enjoy this trip and can stay with their animals near the trailhead at Groom Creek Horsecamp. Drive 3.8 miles up to the lookout and picnic area atop **Spruce Mountain** (not suited for RVs or trailers) on Forest Road 52A from a turnoff 5 miles south of Prescott; you walk the last half-mile.

Beyond Groom Creek, the Senator Highway narrows and contains some rough spots. Back on the highway, 15 miles south of Prescott, you'll pass the 1874 **Palace Station,** a former stagecoach stop between Prescott and Peck's Mine.

About 36 miles from Prescott lies **Crown King,** a small town that grew from a mining camp. The 1898 Crown King Saloon still serves food and beverages. A 1904 general store provides supplies, gas, a post office, and a phone.

From half a mile above Crown King, you can head south and east on Forest Road 52 to **Horsethief Basin Recreation Area.** Bass, catfish, and sunfish thrive in the fishing lake, while campgrounds and viewpoints beckon at the southern end of the Bradshaws. Trails continue into rugged **Castle Creek Wilderness.** Crown King Road, which has a dirt surface but is graded for vehicles, descends from Crown King to the desert below, where you can follow roads to I-17 via Cordes for those heading north or Bumble Bee for those going south. ∎

**The Crown King Saloon still does a good business. Originally built at Oro Belle, 5 miles to the southwest, it was disassembled and moved to Crown King by pack mules about 1910.**

# Arcosanti

A strange new type of city is slowly rising from the high desert of central Arizona. Architect Paolo Soleri envisions this urban laboratory as a place to think deeply about solving the problems of the world's cities through architecture. He calls his philosophy *arcology*—the joining of architecture and ecology to create a place that is both spiritually uplifting and environmentally sound.

To eliminate urban sprawl and better provide for cultural, social, and economic activities, Soleri feels, cities should grow vertically. By making greater use of the third dimension, cities would no longer need freeways. People could commute efficiently by pedestrian walk-ways or elevators, giving them more time to enjoy life. Nearby land could also be preserved in its natural state.

Born in Turin, Italy, in 1919, Soleri earned his Ph.D. from Torino Polytechnico and came to the United States in 1947 for a year and a half to study with architect Frank Lloyd Wright. Soleri's work in architecture and human ecology led to the publication in 1969 of *Arcology: The City in the Image of Man.* Construction at Arcosanti began the following year. Work progresses slowly as money is raised, but the focus is on the learning experience—the interests of Soleri and his apprentices extend beyond "bricks and mortar." Still in an early stage after three decades, Arcosanti may eventually house 7,000 people yet it would occupy only 5 percent of the land consumed by a conventional town. It could become a prototype for the world's cities.

You're welcome to see Arcosanti in action. Models, drawings, and exhibits in the visitor center illustrate Soleri's ideas. Arcosanti residents lead tours explaining some of the history and inspiration behind what you see and pointing out features such as the south-facing

**Visitor center / bakery / café**

Enjoying a meal in
the café at
Arcosanti

apses that provide shade in summer while admitting the sun in winter. A bronze foundry produces the unique wind-bells sold to help fund Arcosanti. Downstairs from the visitor center is a bakery and café. Visitors can also stay overnight; call ahead to reserve the Sky Suite or a simple, inexpensive room.

If you'd like to learn more, the visitor center sells books by Soleri. Workshops provide an opportunity to participate in a seminar and then join a hands-on program of building Arcosanti. The excellent website *(www. arcosanti.org)* offers information on the philosophies, construction, and programs offered here, or you can contact the organization *(HC 74, Box 4136, Mayer, AZ 86333, tel 928/632-7135)*. Arcosanti is 34 miles southeast of Prescott and 65 miles north of Phoenix; take I-17, Cordes Junction, Exit 262A, and follow the signs for 2.5 miles. ■

Vaults studio / housing

You can visit some of the work areas on a tour at Arcosanti. The large buildings shown in the conceptual drawing at left have yet to be constructed.

Soleri office

Sky suite

East crescent

Bronze studio / housing

Siltcast studio

Ceramics studio

# Mogollon Rim Country

BENEATH THE TOWERING CLIFFS OF THE LONG escarpment known as the Mogollon Rim, the desert gives way to cool pine forests and mountain streams. It's a place to enjoy the great outdoors. The Rim Country so entranced novelist Zane Grey that he built a cabin here in 1920 and set many of his stories in the region.

**Mogollon Rim Country**

🅰 93 D2, E2

**Visitor information**

www.rimcountrychamber .com

✉ Rim Country Regional Chamber of Commerce, 100 W. Main St. (P.O. Box 1380, Payson, AZ 85547)

☎ 928/474-4515 or 800/672-9766

### PAYSON

Named after Senator Louis Edwin Payson (who never visited the town) to repay a political favor, Payson got its start in 1881 with the arrival of gold miners and soon developed ranching and logging industries. Today, the many accommodations and restaurants make it a good base to explore the region.

The **Rim Country Museum** illustrates the history of prehistoric peoples, the Tonto Apache, and the pioneers. Exhibits depict mining, forestry, agriculture, and home life. Zane Grey memorabilia include some of his books, riding gear, guns, and posters. The museum buildings themselves reflect the past. A 1930s forest ranger's residence houses the ticket office and a gift shop. A copy of the Herron

Hotel serves as the main exhibit hall, and a 1907 forest ranger's station has forestry displays and a library. The park surrounding the museum features picnic tables, a playground, and a lake. At the Chamber of Commerce office on Beeline Highway (Arizona 87)—the main road through town—turn west 1 mile on Main Street, turn right on Green Valley Parkway, then make the first left into the museum's parking lot.

The **Mazatzal Wilderness** southwest of Payson takes in an expanse of more than 252,500 acres of rugged mountain country. The Indian name Mazatzal means "land of the deer"; you may also encounter piglike javelina (ha-vuh-LEE-nuh), black bear, and perhaps even a mountain lion. Plants such as

saguaro cactus and spiny paloverde grow in the Lower Sonoran Desert between 2,200 and 4,000 feet. In the higher regions of the Upper Sonoran Desert at 4,000 to 7,000 feet, the vegetation changes to dry grasslands and woodlands of pinyon pine and juniper; near the summits at 7,000 to 7,900 feet, it gives way to firs and ponderosa pine. The Verde River flows year-round through the western portion, but other water sources may not be reliable in summer. Fourteen trailheads provide access to the wilderness; the Payson Ranger District office of the Tonto National Forest *(Tel 928/474-7900)* has maps and hiking information.

## NORTH FROM PAYSON

Just northeast of Payson, on Tonto National Forest land, is **Shoofly Village,** which was occupied by Native Americans from about 1000 to 1250. Only scant foundations remain today, but an interpretive trail explains the site, which had plazas and some 80 rooms enclosed by a stone wall. To reach it, take Arizona 87 to the north edge of Payson, then turn right and drive for 3 miles on Houston Mesa Road.

A worthwhile detour off Arizona 87, about 11 miles from Payson, leads to **Tonto Natural Bridge State Park.** Over the millennia, mineral springs in a pretty canyon here have built up the world's largest travertine bridge. It is so big—an arch 400 feet long, 183 feet high, and up to 150 feet wide—that you can be standing atop the bridge without even realizing it. Small waterfalls sparkle brightly in the sun, supporting wildflowers and other luxuriant vegetation. Short trails, some wheelchair accessible, lead to overlooks at both ends of the bridge. Other trails descend the canyon walls, giving close views of the waterfalls and inside the bridge. The half-mile **Gowan Loop Trail** winds down from the top of the bridge to an observation deck at the canyon bottom, then climbs back out on the other canyon wall. At the observation deck, you can admire the tiny waterfall creating rainbows in the sun in front of the bridge, then walk upstream into the

**Rolling hills stretch to the distant Mazatzal Range from an overlook on the Mogollon Rim.**

**Rim Country Museum**
- ✉ 700 Green Valley Pkwy., Payson
- ☎ 928/474-3483
- 🕐 Closed Mon.–Tues.
- 💲 $

**Tonto Natural Bridge State Park**
- ✉ 11 miles N of Payson off Ariz. 87 (turn left 3 miles at the sign)
- ☎ 928/476-4202
- 💲 $$

From the bottom of the **Gowan Loop Trail**, hikers can head into the vast chamber under Tonto Natural Bridge.

vast chamber beneath the bridge. Sure-footed hikers can rock-scramble along Pine Creek through the bridge (most easily done in an upstream direction) and take **Pine Creek Trail** back to the parking area about half a mile away. **Waterfall Trail** drops partway down from the rim, passing greenery and wildflowers to reach a cave and a little waterfall in just 300 feet.

A 1927 lodge, formerly a guest ranch, now has exhibits and a gift shop. Staffers provide lodge tours and other interpretive programs. Surrounding lawns and trees make inviting picnic spots. There is no campground, but groups may be able to arrange an overnight stay in the lodge. Note that the last 1.5 miles of the approach to the canyon descend very steeply. You can park trailers or large RVs at the top of the grade if you wish. Rangers caution visitors to observe the speed limit to avoid overheating their brakes.

Back on Arizona 87, about 15 miles north of Payson you will reach the little community of Pine. The **Pine-Strawberry Museum** *(Tel 928/476-3547, closed Sun. from mid-Oct. to mid-May)* displays many pioneer exhibits in a 1917 former Mormon church. Look for a sign on your left as you head north. In another 4 miles north, you'll reach the village of Strawberry, just below the Mogollon Rim. To see the 1885 **Strawberry Schoolhouse—** Arizona's oldest—turn left at the Strawberry Lodge and drive 1.5 miles on Fossil Springs Road. The schoolhouse interior is open on summer weekends and holidays. Scenic **Fossil Springs Road** (best suited for high-clearance vehicles) continues west into the backcountry, drops steeply to Fossil Creek, then winds up into the hills and meets Arizona 260 east of Camp Verde (see p. 111). Hikers can head upstream along the creek into Fossil Creek Wilderness.

Arizona 87 sweeps up to the top of the Mogollon Rim from Strawberry, then rolls through forests of ponderosa pine to the **Happy Jack Information Center** *(Tel 928/477-2172, closed some days Nov.–April)*, half a mile before the junction with Forest Highway 3. Here staffers offer books, maps, and information on camping, hiking trails, fishing lakes, and exploring the back roads. The long, skinny **Blue Ridge Reservoir**, hemmed in by the

The views and cool, pine-scented air atop the Mogollon Rim make it a popular camping spot.

scenic walls of East Clear Creek, lies to the northeast off Arizona 87. Forest Highway 3 runs north to Flagstaff (see pp. 94–97) on a very pretty forest drive past Mormon Lake and Upper and Lower Lake Mary, with many other lakes a short drive away.

### EAST FROM PAYSON
At Kohl's Ranch Lodge, 17 miles east of Payson, turn north off Arizona 260 on Forest Road 289 for 4 miles to visit **Tonto Creek Hatchery** (*Tel 928/478-4200*). An interpretive walk takes you past outdoor raceways (long, water-filled tanks) and lets you peer through windows into the hatchery rooms. Exhibits describe the life cycle of the rainbow and other trout species that grow up here.

The show pond is full of huge adult trout. You can feed them, too; buy feed at the dispenser.

After the hatchery turnoff, Arizona 260 climbs steadily up the Mogollon Rim. At the top, look on the right for the **Mogollon Rim Visitor Center** (*closed in winter*), which has exhibits and information on recreation in the area. Expansive views unfold behind the visitor center across countless forested mountains below the Mogollon Rim. A series of lakes nearby offers fishing, boating, and camping in cool mountain air. Try to come midweek in summer if possible, because weekends tend to be crowded. Forest Road 300 turns off opposite the visitor center and parallels the Mogollon Rim all the way to Arizona 87 to the northwest,

**Payson Ranger District, Tonto National Forest**
www.fs.fed.us/r3/tonto
✉ 1009 E. Hwy. 260, Payson, AZ 85541
☎ 928/474-7900
🕐 Closed Sat.–Sun.

**Black Mesa Ranger Station, Apache-Sitgreaves National Forest**
www.fs.fed.us/r3/asnf
✉ 55 miles east of Payson on Ariz. 260 (P.O. Box 968, Overgaard, AZ 85933)
☎ 928/535-4481
🕐 Closed Sat.–Sun. (but may open Sat. May–Dec.)

**Getting airborne—bronc riding at the Payson Rodeo**

passing vista points, hiking trails, and campgrounds, and coming close to three lakes. **Rim Lakes Vista Trail** is an easy 3-mile one-way hike along the rim between Rim and Mogollon Campgrounds, both off Forest Road 300. **Forest Lakes Touring Center** *(Tel 928/535-4047)*, 6 miles east of the visitor center, offers cross-country ski trails in winter and fishing-boat and canoe rentals in summer. You can obtain recreation information year-round at **Black Mesa Ranger Station,** on Arizona 260 between Mileposts 307 and 308, some 25 miles west of the Mogollon Rim Visitor Center.

### YOUNG

Sometimes called "Arizona's last cow town," Young lies in Pleasant

**Pleasant Valley Ranger District, Tonto National Forest**
www.fs.fed.us/r3/tonto
✉ P.O. Box 450, Young, AZ 85554
☎ 928/462-4300
🕐 Closed Sat.–Sun. except possibly in summer

Valley, southeast of Payson. North of Young in the late 1800s, a range war played out between the cattlemen of the Graham clan and the sheepmen of the Tewksburys. The law proved powerless to stop the bloodshed as the feud raged on, killing at least 30 people in a five-year span. Five of the Graham victims lie buried at the Young Baptist Church cemetery. Author Zane

Grey based his novel *To the Last Man* (1922) on these events.

An exceptionally scenic drive on Young Road connects Young with the Mogollon Rim to the north and the Roosevelt Lake area to the south, with some great hiking, camping, and backcountry drives along the way. Sections of the drive in Young and at the south end are paved, but much of the road is gravel, and it is passable by cars in dry weather. Young offers a small motel as well as some rustic cafés and rental cabins. For information on the area, including the Sierra Ancha and Hell's Gate Wildernesses, contact the Pleasant Valley Ranger District office of the Tonto National Forest.

The north turnoff for Young is 33 miles east of Payson on Arizona 260 near Milepost 284, where you turn south on Forest Road 512 and drive 24 miles to Young. Only the last four miles is paved. Side roads lead to Colcord Lookout (7,513 feet), Canyon Creek Hatchery, historic sites of the Pleasant Valley War, and campgrounds.

South of Young, Arizona 288 weaves through the meadows and forests of the Sierra Ancha and descends to the Salt River. The drive ends 47 miles from town at the Arizona 188 junction between Roosevelt Lake and Globe; the last 13 miles is paved. About halfway (between Mileposts 285 and 284), the road crosses Workman Creek. Forest Road 487 turns east here past several primitive campsites, climbs steeply (may be too rough for cars) to the top of 200-foot Workman Creek Falls, 3.2 miles from the highway, and continues up Forest Road 487 another 3.7 miles to the top of Aztec Peak (7,694 feet). A 250-yard walk downstream on Workman Creek from the highway leads to the "tubs," or natural swimming holes. ■

The Colorado River defines Arizona's western boundary and forms the region's main attraction. From 19th-century steamboats to 21st-century agriculture and water sports, the river has been the lifeblood of the people.

# Western Arizona

**Romance of Route 66**

# Western Arizona

THE COLORADO RIVER'S GENTLE CURRENT AND MANY VAST LAKES HAVE made it a magnet for visitors. Some explore backwaters in canoes or fishing boats, while others raft Black Canyon below Hoover Dam, skim the open waters, or cruise in houseboats. Many come here simply to relax by the shore. Skies are normally sunny year-round, encouraging visitors to flee northern climes in winter to enjoy pleasant daytime temperatures in the 60s and 70s—ideal for camping, fishing, hiking, and exploring the backcountry. The recreation scene heats up with summer temperatures. Towns here often make national highs at well over 100°F, but waterskiing, swimming, and zipping across the water feel great.

Small mountain ranges, seemingly lifeless from a distance, break up the desert plains. A closer look reveals hardy and adaptable life sheltered within the rocky terrain. You might see desert bighorn sheep, mule deer, coyote, desert tortoise, and Gambel's quail. The Kofas, reaching 4,877 feet, harbor California fan palms. Farther north, mountains such as the Hualapais (8,417 feet) are biological islands supporting forests of ponderosa pine, pinyon pine, oak, and some aspen and fir.

Native American groups migrated in and out of this region, depending on food availability and tribal wars. Simple huts of brush and mud gave shelter, the river watered their crops, and the surrounding desert provided game and wild plants. The Cocopah wound up in the lowermost part of the Colorado drainage, the Quechan upstream, and the Mohave farther upriver. The Maricopa once lived here too, but warfare forced them up the Gila River to central Arizona in the mid-1800s. The

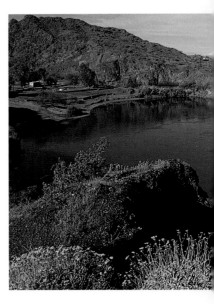

Chemehuevi, a nomadic Paiute group, joined the river tribes in the early 1800s, as did some Navajo and Hopi beginning in 1945. Many now farm or work in casinos and live on reservations. You can visit tribal museums near Parker (see p. 140) and Yuma (see pp. 141–42).

The Spanish had explored the lower Colorado River as early as 1540, but they did not attempt to settle until 1780, when fears arose of Russian expansion down the California coast. The Spanish decided to open an overland route to California and built two missions near present-day Yuma. Abuses by the

**One of the Yuma Weavers & Spinners displays her skills at Yuma Crossing State Park.**

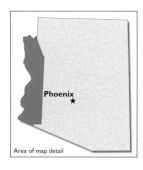

Phoenix ★

Area of map detail

**The Colorado River glides below an overlook in River Island State Park.**

colonizers led to a revolt by the Quechan and destruction of the missions within a year. Spanish troops ransomed the survivors and withdrew from the area. American mountain men began crossing the region in the early 1800s, followed by government explorers and forty-niners bound for California. The development of western Arizona began with the establishment of an Army camp at Yuma Crossing in 1851 and the advent of steamboats, better roads, and discoveries of valuable minerals. ■

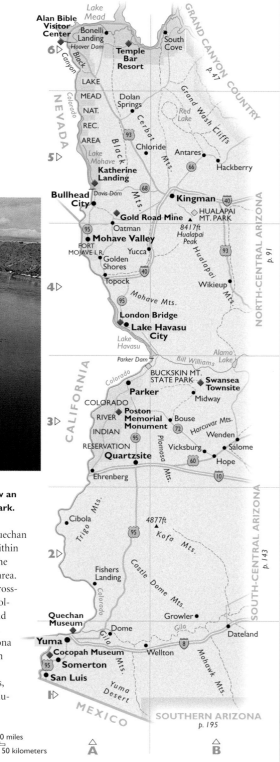

Lake Mead
Alan Bible Visitor Center
Bonelli Landing
South Cove
Hoover Dam
**GRAND CANYON COUNTRY** p. 47
6
**Temple Bar Resort**
Black Canyon
LAKE
MEAD
Dolan Springs
Grand Wash Cliffs
Red Lake
NAT.
93
REC.
Chloride
Antares
AREA
66
Hackberry
NEVADA
Colorado
5
Lake Mohave
Black Mts.
**Katherine Landing**
68
● **Kingman** 40
Davis Dam
**Bullhead City**
HUALAPAI MT. PARK
**Gold Road Mine**
Oatman
95
8417ft
Hualapai Peak
**Mohave Valley**
FORT MOJAVE I.R.
Yucca
93
Golden Shores
40
Topock
Wikieup
4
Hualapai Mts.
95
Mohave Mts.
**London Bridge**
**Lake Havasu City**
Lake Havasu
Alamo Lake
Parker Dam
Bill Williams
**BUCKSKIN MT. STATE PARK**
Colorado
**Swansea Townsite**
**Parker**
Midway
COLORADO
**Poston Memorial Monument**
Bouse
72
Harcuvar Mts.
RIVER
Wenden
INDIAN
95
Vicksburg
Sálome
RESERVATION
60
Hope
**Quartzsite**
10
Plomosa Mts.
CALIFORNIA
Ehrenberg
NORTH-CENTRAL ARIZONA p. 91
Cerbat Mts.

Cibola
Trigo Mts.
4877ft
95
Kofa Mts.
2
Fishers Landing
Castle Dome Mts.
Colorado
Growler
**Quechan Museum**
Gila
Dateland
Dome
8
**Yuma** ●
Gila
**Cocopah Museum**
Wellton
**Somerton**
95
Mohawk Mts.
● **San Luis**
Yuma Desert
1
MEXICO
SOUTH-CENTRAL ARIZONA p. 143
**SOUTHERN ARIZONA** p. 195

0 ____ 30 miles
0 ____ 50 kilometers
A   B

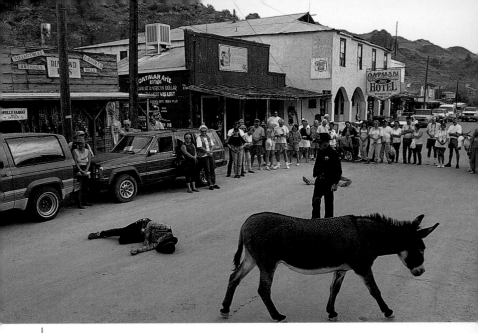

# Kingman

LEWIS KINGMAN WORKED ON THE SURVEY FOR THE
Atlantic and Pacific Railroad, which opened the high desert country
of northwestern Arizona in the 1880s to mining, ranching, and trade.
He also gave his name to this town, today a good base for retracing
historic Route 66, visiting ghost towns, and driving up into the cool
Hualapai and Cerbat Mountains.

**Kingman**

⚑ 131 B5

**Visitor information**

www.arizonaguide.com/visit
kingman

✉ Powerhouse Visitor
Center, 120 W. Andy
Devine Ave. (P.O.
Box 1150, Kingman,
AZ 86402)

☎ 928/753-6106 or
866/427-7866

**Mohave Museum of
History and Arts**

www.citlink.net/citlink/m/
mocohist/museum

✉ 400 W. Beale St.

☎ 928/753-3195

💲 $

For an introduction to Kingman,
visit the **Powerhouse Visitor
Center,** downtown in a huge
1907 building once used for power
generation. Here you will find photo exhibits, the Route 66 Museum,
a theater, model railroad, soda
fountain, and shops. Wide-ranging
exhibits in the **Mohave Museum
of History and Arts** show this
region and its people from earliest
times to the present. The Hualapai
Indian Room has a full-size
wickiup brush shelter, cradleboard,
baskets, and pottery. In the auditorium, paintings of the U.S. presidents and their wives hang from the
walls. Photos illustrate the building
of the Hoover Dam, and a video
depicts ranchers talking about their
lifestyle. The Andy Devine exhibit

tells the story of the town's favorite
son, who acted in many movies and
TV shows. Additional mining,
ranching, and railroad gear is outside in back. The museum has a
research library and sells regional
books and Native American crafts.

The **Bonelli House** (430 E.
Spring St. & N. 5th St., tel 928/753-
1413, closed Tues.–Wed., donation),
built of native tufa stone, reflects
the tastes and way of life of a
prominent Kingman family in the
early 20th century.

The forests and scenic views of
**Hualapai Mountain Park** draw
visitors to the high country south
of Kingman for hiking, picnicking,
camping, or stays in rustic cabins.
Elevations range from 5,000 feet
near the entrance to 8,417 feet at

the summit of this county park. The mountains take their name from the Hualapai (meaning "pine tree people"), who lived here until they were relocated north near the Grand Canyon in the 1870s.

Offices at the park and in Bull-head City have checklists of birds and other animals that you might see and information on hiking trails to overlooks and the summits of Aspen and Hayden Peaks. The park is open all year, though winter snow may require chains or four-wheel-drive. A 14-mile paved road provides easy access; take any of the three I-40 Kingman exits to the junction of Andy Devine Avenue and Stockton Hill Road, then turn southeast on Hualapai Mountain Road.

Gold discovered in the western foothills of the Black Mountains in 1904 created the boomtown of **Oatman,** 31 miles southwest of Kingman. Four roads lead here, the two most scenic being old sections of Route 66—southwest over the Black Mountains from I-40 Mc-Connico Exit 44 (near Kingman) or north from I-40 Topock Exit 1 (take the Oatman Highway at Golden Shores).

At its peak, Oatman had 12,000 citizens, seven hotels, 20 saloons, and a stock exchange. The bust came in the 1930s, but the town hung on as a stop on Route 66 for a while, then as a tourist destination. Many of the old buildings survive, including the two-story **Oatman Hotel** *(Tel 928/768-4408),* where Clark Gable and Carole Lombard honeymooned in 1939. You can go upstairs and see their room or rent one of the others down the hall.

Another Oatman attraction will likely find *you:* Burros—descendants of those used by prospectors—wander down the street, hoping to be fed. It's best not to,

however, because they can bite. Saloons and shops provide other diversions in town.

To see where gold fever started, head east 2.5 miles on Route 66 up into the Black Mountains and take a tour of **Gold Road Mine** *( Tel 928/768-1600, www.goldroad-mine.com).* A guide provides a hard hat and drives you in a "getman" vehicle, rather like a truck, up to the original entrance, where an easy walk of about an hour will take you to see the workings inside. You'll get the history of the mine and a miner's perspective of how the facility operated, then an ore sample to take home. Longer tours can be arranged by reservation. ∎

**Hualapai Mountain Park**

✉ 14 miles SE of Kingman. Mohave County Parks, P.O. Box 2078, Bullhead City, AZ 86430

☎ 928/754-7273 or 877/757-0915 (cabin & group area reservations)

**Get a feel for the life of a miner on a tour of the Gold Road Mine.**

# Route 66

The "Mother Road," as writer John Steinbeck called it, beckons us to previous eras when the asphalt led to the promised land of California, when every motel and restaurant had its own identity, and when driving could be a romantic adventure. Route 66 once ran from Chicago to Los Angeles in an unbroken 2,400-mile path, carrying generations of Americans to new homes and dreams.

Those times seemed to end in October 1984, when the last stretch of I-40 was paved at Williams, bypassing the old road forever. Songwriter Bobby Troup sang his "Get your kicks on Route 66" one last time in a sentimental ceremony to mark the passing of US 66 as a highway. Not everyone shed tears—gone were the long lines of traffic funneling down the narrow two-lane road.

Yet Route 66 still runs across the Arizona countryside, still goes through the old downtowns, and still passes some of the old cafés and motor courts used

by early motorists. The highway can be lonely, giving its travelers a chance to contemplate the scenery and the past. Short segments in eastern and central Arizona worthwhile for history or scenery include Holbrook (I-40 Exits 285 and 289), Winslow (I-40 Exits 252 and 257), Flagstaff (I-40 Exits 191 and 204), Coconino National Forest (I-40 Exits 171 and 178), Williams (I-40 Exits 161 and 165), and Ash Fork (I-40 Exits 144 and 146).

The longest continuous stretch of Route 66 twists across 158 miles of western Arizona from a desolate junction east of Seligman (I-40 Exit 139) to near the California border (I-40 Exit 1). Take the I-40 Crookton Road Exit 139 for a gently undulating ride to Seligman, where you can drop into the colorful Degadillo's Snow Cap for a soda or burger and perhaps a joke or two. Vast chambers of Grand Canyon Caverns lie underground off Route 66 northwest of Seligman. A detour to the north via Indian Route 18 leads to Hualapai Hilltop on the Havasupai Indian Reservation, where a hiking trail descends to beautiful waterfalls and pools (see

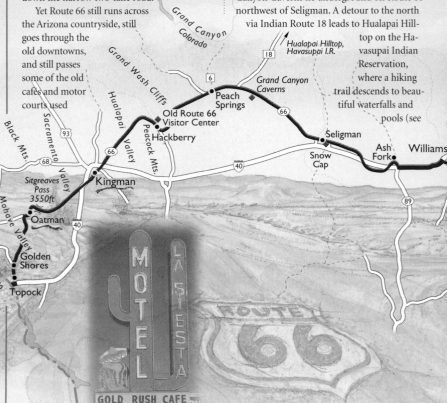

0    30 miles

0    50 kilometers

**Drop into a roadside saloon for a beer, a game of pool, or an earful of a local band.**

pp. 58–59). On the Hualapai Indian Reservation, you can take back roads into the depths of the Grand Canyon or to overlooks on the rim (see pp. 64–65). The road skirts the south end of the Grand Wash Cliffs—the escarpment that marks the lower end of the Grand Canyon to the north—and then passes the Old Route 66 Visitor Center and

General Store opposite the Hackberry turnoff. Stop at this homestead and former gas station to see its vintage cars, signs, and other Route 66 memorabilia.

After curving past the north end of the Peacock Mountains, Route 66 sweeps across the Hualapai Valley to Kingman, where it becomes Andy Devine Avenue through downtown. The road crosses the Sacramento Valley, climbs over the Black Mountains at 3,550-foot-high Sitgreaves Pass, and descends through Oatman, an old mining town (see p. 133). After a run southwest across the Mohave Valley, the old road meets I-40 Exit 1 near the Colorado River. ■

180

12633ft
Humphreys
Peak

Parks
Flagstaff
Winona
17

Two Guns
99
40
Winslow
87
Little Colorado

Joseph City
40
Holbrook
77

# Lake Mead
# National Recreation Area

**Lake Mead National
Recreation Area**
131 A5, A6
**Visitor information**
www.nps.gov/lame
Alan Bible Visitor
Center, Lake Mead
National Recreation
Area, 601 Nevada
Hwy., Boulder City,
NV (near junction of
US 93 and Nev.
166)
702/293-8990
$$

STRADDLING THE STATE BOUNDARY BETWEEN ARIZONA and Nevada are two giant reservoirs, Lake Mead and Lake Mohave, which together form the centerpiece of this National Recreation Area. With the section of the Colorado River that connects them in Black Canyon, they provide many opportunities for leisure pursuits. Small beaches and coves along the shores beckon boaters, and you can rent boats at the marinas and pick up supplies. Adventurous travelers can explore jeep roads and hike backcountry that rarely sees a soul.

**Lake Mead** reaches into the lower Grand Canyon, where the raging rapids fade into a smooth current. The water then glides beneath towering cliffs and emerges abruptly at the Grand Wash Cliffs into a broad desert valley.

Another major tributary, the Virgin River, feeds the lake's Overton Arm from the north. These two arms give 110-mile-long Lake Mead its roughly Y shape. Hoover Dam holds back the reservoir—at 247 square miles, it is the largest in the United States. **Temple Bar Resort** is the only developed area on the Arizona shores.

**Alan Bible Visitor Center** overlooks Lake Mead from the Nevada shore. It is near Boulder City, just 4 miles from Hoover Dam. A video program and exhibits tell of the area's natural and human history. Handouts include maps, places to visit, announcements of interpretive programs, and lists of plants and animals. The botanical garden outside identifies local species. The **Historic Railway Trail** begins nearby and goes through huge tunnels once used to haul penstock (water) pipes and heavy equipment toward the dam; the trail is 2.6 miles one way.

Having your own boat opens up many places to explore in Black Canyon on the Colorado River below Hoover Dam.

**Hoover Dam Visitor Center**

www.hooverdam.usbr.com

☎ 702/294-3523

💲 $. Free with Regular ($$) or Hard Hat ($$$$) tours

**Bureau of Reclamation**

www.hooverdam.usbr.com

✉ Attn.: Canoe Launch Permits, P.O. Box 60400, Boulder City, NV 89006

☎ 702/294-3524

**Hoover Dam,** an engineering and artistic landmark completed in 1935, attracts one million visitors a year. Exhibits in the visitor center on the Nevada side illustrate the construction of the dam. A theater program provides background on its history and the importance of water. Regular tours leave frequently for a look at the dam's generators, a 30-foot-diameter pipe, and tailraces; the tours last about 35 minutes on a half-mile walk that is accessible to wheelchairs. Hard-hat tours proceed at a brisker pace and cover many areas not on the regular tours in a walk of about 1.5 miles lasting 60 to 75 minutes (no wheelchairs).

On your own, admire the graceful curves of the dam and its art deco embellishments. Flanking the flagpole, the pair of bronze "Winged Figures of the Republic" by Norwegian-born Oskar Hansen (1882–1971) reflect American ideals: what Hansen described as "…the immutable calm of intellectual resolution, and the enormous power of trained physical strength, equally enthroned in placid triumph of scientific accomplishment." Hansen also made the surrounding star map of more than 200 brass disks that show how the sky looked on September 30, 1935, when President Franklin Roosevelt dedicated the dam. This date is also enshrined in a Wheel of Time below the flagpole; markers represent the building of the last great pyramid, the birth of Christ, and the building of Hoover Dam. Hansen designed the terrazzo floor below the flagpole and the bas-reliefs on the Nevada and Arizona elevator towers atop the dam. The five Nevada bas-reliefs represent the benefits of the dam—flood control, navigation, irrigation, water storage, and power. The Arizona reliefs depict "the visages of those Indian tribes who have inhabited mountains and plains from ages distant." The easiest parking at the dam, for cars only, is a covered lot near the visitor center. Outdoor lots on the Arizona side have free parking and areas for RVs and trailers.

Rafts, canoes, and kayaks float the Colorado River through **Black Canyon,** beginning from just below Hoover Dam. **Black Canyon River Raft Tours** operates trips to Willow Beach (see Travelwise, p. 264). Besides the canyon scenery, boaters can enjoy a flooded cave, hot waterfalls, hot springs, historical sites, and sightings of bighorn sheep.

**Lake Mohave** stretches 67 miles upstream from Davis Dam but has a maximum width of only 4 miles. The dam, completed in 1953, has overlooks but no tours. Reach it by driving several miles north from either Bullhead City or Laughlin. **Katherine Landing,** 6 miles north of Bullhead City, is the largest resort on the Arizona side. ■

Hot springs in Black Canyon entice boaters and hikers.

**Lake Havasu City**

**M** 131 A4

**Visitor information**

www.golakehavasu.com

✉ Lake Havasu Tourism Bureau, 314 London Bridge Rd., Lake Havasu City

☎ 928/453-3344 or 800/242-8278

🕐 Closed Sat.–Sun. (tourist office in English Village is open daily)

# Lake Havasu City ✕

THE BLUE WATERS OF LAKE HAVASU PROVIDE A STRIKING setting for the town and its famous London Bridge. People come to ride fast watercraft, waterski, sail, and fish on the vast lake.

Founded on the east shore of Lake Havasu by chain-saw manufacturer Robert McCulloch in 1963, this town features a remarkable center-piece: **London Bridge** (see box below). English architecture, food, and shopping add to the ambience. Parks and beaches near each end of the bridge make ideal spots for a stroll, picnic, or swim. Admire the bridge from **English Village;** turn west onto London Bridge Road

from Arizona 95 and make the first left into the parking lot. You'll find a tourist office *(Tel 928/855-5655)* here, along with a bit of re-created London. Tour boats and rental boats dock nearby. You can walk south along the shore to **Rotary Community Park.** Drive across the bridge on McCulloch Boulevard and turn in at either of the first two lefts to parking and **London Bridge Beach.** ■

**Timeworn stones of London Bridge bask in the warm sunshine at Lake Havasu City.**

**Bureau of Land Management**

www.az.blm.gov

✉ 2610 Sweetwater Ave., Lake Havasu City

☎ 928/505-1200 or 888/213-2582

🕐 Closed Sat.–Sun.

## London Bridge

Lake Havasu City might have been just an ordinary town had not its founder Robert McCulloch and town planner C. V. Wood, Jr., decided to buy London Bridge. A part of the London landscape for 137 years, the old bridge had been slowly sinking into the River Thames. No longer able to carry heavy city traffic, it was replaced and went on the auction block in 1967. Robert McCulloch bought it the following year for $2,460,000—shipping and handling not included. He had to spend another seven million dollars to have its 10,276 blocks shipped to Long Beach, California, via the Panama Canal, trucked to Lake Havasu City, and reassembled there. On September 23, 1968, the Lord Mayor of London, Sir Gilbert Inglefield, laid the cornerstone, just as a predecessor had done on the other side of the Atlantic in 1825. At first the bridge spanned dry land at the base of Pittsburgh Point; a mile-long channel dug beneath it later turned the point into an island. The bridge was dedicated on October 10, 1971. ■

# Parker Strip

LAKE MOOVALYA, HELD BACK BY THE HEADGATE ROCK dam just above Parker, is better known as the Parker Strip. Resorts and parks line its shores and the Colorado River for 11 miles upstream.

Parker originally served as a trade center for the Colorado River Indian Reservation and nearby mines. Today the town is a center for agriculture and visitors who come to enjoy life on the water. Most of the Arizona development lies along Riverside Drive (Business 95), which turns off Arizona 95 several miles north of Parker and rejoins the highway at Buckskin Mountain State Park.

A **scenic drive** takes in the river and the surrounding rugged mountains on a 32-mile loop along both shores. Start by crossing the bridge at Parker, then follow Parker Dam Road north along the California shore to Parker Dam, cross the dam, and return to Parker on Arizona 95 and Business 95. Only the top third of **Parker Dam,** which holds back Lake Havasu, is visible because its builders had to

**Parker**

⛰ 131 A3

**Visitor information**
www.coloradoriverinfo.com/
parker

✉ Parker Chamber of
Commerce, 1217
California Ave. (P.O.
Box 627, Parker, AZ
85344)

☎ 928/669-2174

🕐 Closed Sat.–Sun.

**Tomb of camel driver Hadji Ali in Quartzsite. In 1856–57 the U.S. Army tried using camels out West.**

World War II Japanese relocation camps (see below).

The **Poston Memorial Monument,** 13 miles south of the museum on the Parker-Ehrenberg road, commemorates the 17,867 people of Japanese ancestry who endured confinement at three camps nearby from May 1942 to November 1945. Most of the buildings have given way to farmland, but you can still see a large adobe auditorium in the distance across the road; it and other sites lie on private land. Look for a broken column beside the road, where you'll find the monument's information kiosk and inscriptions.

Nowhere do snowbirds descend on the desert in greater profusion than at the little town of **Quartzsite** during the winter months. Thousands of RVers stay in vast campgrounds in the surrounding desert to socialize, soak up sunshine, and attend gem and mineral shows and swapfests. The town is 35 miles south of Parker on Arizona 95 at its junction with I-10 (Exits 17 and 19). **Tyson's Well Stage Station** (*just E of Ariz. 95 jct. downtown, tel 928/927-5229, closed Mon.–Tues. & April–Oct., donation*) dates from 1866–67 and now houses historical exhibits. The **Hadji Ali Monument** in the cemetery on the west of town marks the resting place of a Syrian camel driver who came to this country to help the Army conduct a camel experiment in 1856–57. The hardy beasts showed promise as pack animals, but the Army abandoned the project during the Civil War. Hadji Ali stayed on in the Southwest, becaming a prospector.

**Swansea Townsite,** about 30 miles east of Parker, is one of Arizona's best preserved ghost towns. Ruins of a 1910 brick smelter, store, office, housing, and other structures still stand. ■

**Snowbirds flock to western Arizona in winter to socialize and attend outdoor events, such as this Quartzsite Pow-wow Gem & Mineral Show.**

**Quartzsite**
🅰 131 A3
**Visitor information**
www.quartzsitechamber.com
✉ One block north of I-10 Exit 17 Quartzsite Chamber of Commerce, P.O. Box 85, Quartzsite, AZ 85346
☎ 928/927-5600
🕐 Closed Sat.–Sun. in winter, shorter schedule the rest of the year

dig 235 feet below the riverbed to secure the foundations. You can park at overlooks on each end.

Facilities at **La Paz County Park** (*8 miles N of Parker at 7350 Riverside Dr., tel 928/667-2069*) include a swimming beach, picnicking, and camping; across the road is **Emerald Canyon Golf Course** (*Tel 928/667-3366*). **Buckskin Mountain State Park** (*11 miles N of Parker on Ariz. 95, tel 928/667-3231*) lies on a bend in the river with a swimming beach, picnicking, camping, boat ramp, hiking, a seasonal store, and snack bar. **River Island State Park** (*12.5 miles N of Parker on Ariz. 95, tel 928/667-3386*) provides similar facilities but no hookups or store.

Members of the Mohave, Chemehuevi, Hopi, and Navajo tribes live south of Parker on the Colorado River Indian Reservation. Find out more about the four tribes at the **Colorado River Indian Tribes (CRIT) Museum** (*2 miles SW of Parker at 2nd Ave. and Mohave Rd., tel 928/669-1335, closed noon–1 & Sat.–Sun.*). Look for exhibits on early peoples and on

# Yuma

THIS SITE, CLOSE TO ARIZONA'S SOUTHWESTERN CORNER, has long been valued as the best place to cross the lower Colorado. Native Americans, the Spanish, and early settlers left a rich heritage that you can explore at historic sites and museums. Recreation on the Colorado River and its lakes, along with shopping in nearby Mexico, makes Yuma a popular destination today.

In winter, the warm sunshine draws an estimated 80,000 snowbirds, more than doubling the town's population. An attractive pedestrian mall on a downtown section of Main Street comprises restaurants, shops, and the colorful **Lute's Casino,** a 1940s gambling hall that is now a popular spot for pool, dominoes, video games, and fast food.

Exhibits and period rooms in the **Century House Museum**

downtown give a feel for the region's Native Americans, explorers, soldiers, missionaries, miners, riverboat captains, and early settlers. The house, one of the oldest in town, dates from the 1870s. Subtropical vegetation and exotic birds thrive in a garden in back. The Adobe Annex next door sells local crafts and a good selection of historical books. The Garden Café, a pleasant spot farther back and next

The 1922 St. Thomas Mission stands on Indian Hill across the Colorado River.

**Yuma**
🅰 131 A1
**Visitor information**
www.visityuma.com
✉ Yuma Convention and Visitors Bureau, 377 S. Main St. (P.O. Box 11059, Yuma, AZ 85366)
☎ 928/783-0071 or 800/293-0071
🕐 Closed Sat. p.m., & Sun. May–Sept.

**Century House Museum**

- ✉ 240 S. Madison Ave.
- ☎ 928/782-1841
- 🕐 Closed Sun.–Mon.
- 💲 $

**Yuma Territorial Prison State Historic Park**

- ✉ Giss Pkwy. & Prison Hill Rd. (Take Prison Hill Rd. from Giss Pkwy. near I-8 Exit 1)
- ☎ 928/783-4771
- 💲 $

**Walk through the iron gates at Yuma Territorial Prison State Historic Park.**

to the museum's gardens, serves breakfast and lunch.

In 1875 the territorial legislature awarded Yuma the funds to build a major prison. The hostile desert and the treacherous currents of the Colorado and Gila Rivers discouraged escape attempts. For 33 years, 29 women and about 3,000 men gazed through iron bars here. By 1909 the site proved too small, so the last prisoners were shipped to new quarters in Florence. The prison is now the **Yuma Territorial Prison State Historic Park.** Step into the cells and imagine what life here must have been like. In the museum, photos and stories of the inmates and guards recount escape attempts, riots, and daily life. Outside, you can climb the main watchtower, visit the graveyard, and walk down to the riverbank.

**Yuma Crossing State Historic Park**

- ✉ 201 N. 4th Ave. (just before the Colorado River bridge)
- ☎ 928/329-0471
- 🕐 Closed Tues.–Wed. May–Oct.
- 💲 $

**Yuma Crossing State Historic Park** vividly illustrates the importance of this site for early travelers. Buildings from the 19th-century Yuma Quartermaster Depot still stand, including the restored commanding officer's quarters, which dates from 1859. An office in the quartermaster depot looks as it did during the Indian wars from 1864 to 1883,

when the depot supplied vital goods to posts all over the Southwest. Steamboats tied up nearby with cargo from ships docked at Port Isabel, near the mouth of the Colorado River. The goods then traveled farther upstream by steamboat or overland on mule-drawn wagons to Army posts.

A 1907 Southern Pacific locomotive symbolizes the arrival of the railroad and the end of the steamboat era. A section of the plank road used by early motorists to traverse the sand dunes west of Yuma dates from 1916, while a 1931 Model A truck represents the vehicles used by Dust Bowl victims of the 1930s.

The **Yuma Valley Railway** *(1st St. and 2nd Ave., tel 928/783-3456, closed June–Sept. & Mon.–Fri. Oct.–May)* heads out along the banks of the Colorado River on a half-day narrated tour about the area's Cocopah Native American lands, canals, farming, and wildlife. A vintage diesel pulls a 1922 Pullman coach from the station behind City Hall.

Two museums operated by local Native American tribes offer historical and cultural exhibits. Call before you go to check opening times.

The **Quechan Museum** *(Tel 760/572-0661, closed Sun.)* lies across the river from Yuma in an 1855 building of Fort Yuma. Take Fourth Avenue or I-8 to Winterhaven, turn right on S24, and follow the signs.

To reach **Cocopah Museum** *(Tel 928/627-1992, closed Sat.–Sun.)*, head south 13 miles on US 95 to Somerton; continue 1 mile farther, turn right and go 1 mile on Avenue G; turn left and drive about 2 miles on 15th Street, turn right after the railroad tracks, then take the next right, following signs for "West Cocopah Indian Reservation" and "Tribal Headquarters." ■

Phoenix—the geographic, governmental, and business heart of Arizona—has an intensity unmatched in the rest of the state. Visitors enjoy the city's culture, recreational facilities, and amazing number of luxurious resorts.

# South-central Arizona

**Giant cowboy belt buckle**

# South-central Arizona

PHOENIX LIES IN THE BROAD SALT RIVER VALLEY, WHOSE WATERS, DIVERTED by canals farther upstream, nourish both people and crops. You are likely to hear the area called the Valley of the Sun for its warm climate and average of 300 sunny days a year.

An early farming culture called the Hohokam began settling along the green shores of the Salt and nearby Gila Rivers about A.D. 1. They dug canals to channel water to their fields of corn, beans, squash, cotton, and other crops. Wild plants, small game, and fish rounded out their diet. Residents lived in year-round villages of mud-walled, partly underground pit houses and later also in houses of adobe above the ground. The Hohokam created beautiful pottery and jewelry, played in ball courts, and built large platform mounds for ceremonial purposes. About 1450, less than a century before the Spanish arrived in the region, the Hohokam culture collapsed. Legends of the modern-day Pima and Tohono

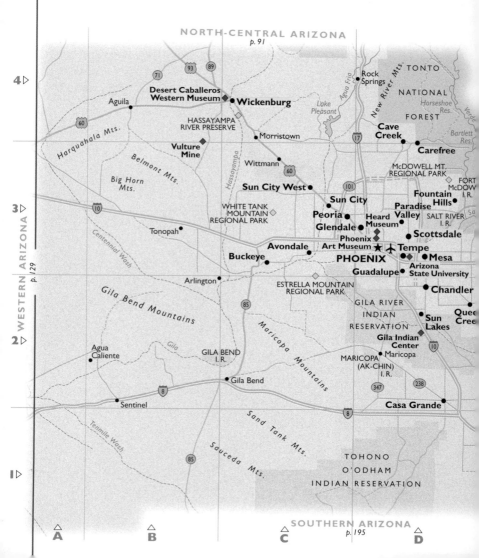

O'odham in southern Arizona trace their ancestry back to the Hohokam.

Apache tribes later roamed the Salt River Valley, preventing European settlement until the U.S. Army constructed Camp McDowell in 1865. Two years later, Jack Swilling, a prospector and former Confederate soldier, got some miners together and dug out the old Hohokam canals to irrigate fields of wheat and barley. More farmers arrived and a town began to take shape. Darrel Duppa, an adventurer known for his ability to speak five languages fluently (all at once when drunk, it is said), proclaimed it "Phoenix," a city that would rise from the ancient Hohokam ruins just as the mythical Egyptian bird arose from its own ashes.

By 1889, the young town had secured the state capital and had grown to become the political, business, and agricultural center of Ari-

**Downtown Phoenix hosts a lively cultural and sporting scene.**

zona Territory. World War II brought the rapid growth of aviation and other critical industries, boosting the population and the economy. Newcomers liked the area and stayed on—just as many, including retirees and snowbirds, have continued to do down to the present.

Phoenix's neighbors in the Salt River Valley include Tempe (home of Arizona State University) to the southeast, Scottsdale (renowned for its superb resorts and art galleries) to the northeast, Mesa (Arizona's third largest city and home of the Mormons' Arizona Temple) farther east, and Glendale (the state's antique capital and fourth largest city) to the northwest. ■

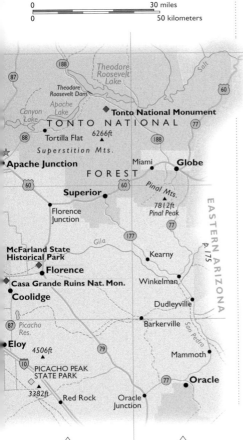

Area of map detail

# Downtown Phoenix

FORMERLY STAID DOWNTOWN PHOENIX HAS BECOME A
lively place thanks to a building boom that began in the 1990s, adding
new museums, sports stadiums, entertainment venues, and skyscrapers. Head downtown for a look at both the past and the future of
Arizona's largest city with a population of close to 1.3 million.

**Phoenix**
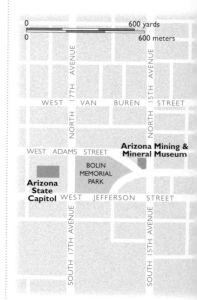 144 D3
**Visitor information**
www.phoenixcvb.com
✉ Greater Phoenix
Convention &
Visitors Bureau, 50
N. 2nd St., Phoenix
☎ 602/254-6500 or
877/225-5749
🕐 Closed Sat.–Sun.

**Arizona State
Capitol**
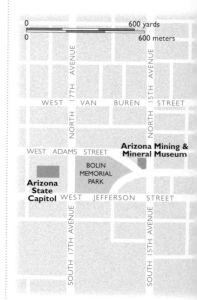 Map p. 146 & inside
back cover C2
www.lib.az.us
✉ 1700 W. Washington
St.
☎ 602/542-4675

**Arizona Mining &
Mineral Museum**
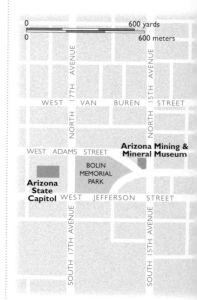 Map p. 146
www.admmr.state.az.us
✉ 1502 Washington
St. at 15th Ave.
☎ 602/255-3791
🕐 Closed Sun. & state
holidays

**Arizona Science
Center**
www.azscience.org
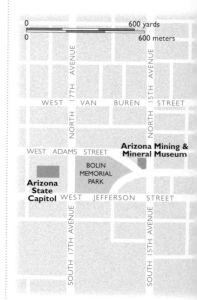 Map p. 147
✉ 600 E. Washington
St.
☎ 602/716-2000
💲 $$

A view west down Washington
Street takes in the shiny copper
dome of the **Arizona State
Capitol.** Dating from 1900, the
building has been well restored to
the time when Arizona made the
transition from a territory to a state
12 years later. Guided tours begin
at 10 a.m. and 2 p.m., or you can
go around on your own. Details
to look for include the 16-foot
"Winged Victory" wind vane atop
the dome and a state seal inlaid in
the floor of the rotunda. Step into
the old offices and senate and house
chambers to get a sense of history.
A lifelike figure of George Wiley
Paul Hunt presides in the governor's office. (Hunt, Arizona's first
governor upon statehood, served
seven terms.)

Other rooms contain exhibits
illuminating Arizona's people and
events. Artifacts from the U.S.S.
*Arizona,* including its silver service,
illustrate life aboard the battleship
before its destruction at Pearl Harbor on December 7, 1941; there is
also a piece of the battered ship
itself. To dig deeper into the state's
history, go to the research library in
Room 300, where you can see a set
of 1937 murals, "Pageant of Arizona Progress." Outside in front, the
many monuments in the Wesley
Bolin Memorial Plaza include an
anchor and a signal mast from the
*Arizona.* (There's free parking on
the north side of the plaza; turn in
from Adams Street.)

Glittering gold and silver plus
colorful copper drew many of
Arizona's pioneers. The **Arizona**

**Mining & Mineral Museum**
displays beautiful specimens, along
with some of the tools used by early
miners. Fossils reveal the history
of life from cyanobacteria more
than one billion years old to the
dinosaurs and other more recent
creatures. Housed in a striking
Moorish-style building, the museum is also a good place to learn of
upcoming rock and mineral shows
and to shop for rock-hounding
books, minerals, and jewelry. (Free
parking is available behind the
museum.)

The **Arizona Hall of Fame**
*(1101 W. Washington St., tel
602/255-2110, closed Sat.–Sun.)*
tells the stories of those who played

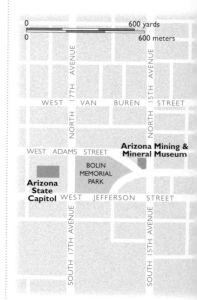

a major role in the state's development. The permanent Arizona Women's Hall of Fame is accompanied by changing exhibits displayed in a building opened in 1908 as a Carnegie public library. (Park across the street beside the 1893 Victorian Evans House; parking for people with disabilities is behind the hall off Jefferson Street.)

The galleries of **Museo Chicano** *(147 E. Adams St., tel 602/257-5536, closed Sun.–Mon.)* concentrate on the colorful and energetic art of Latin America, especially Chicano and Mexican cultures. Exhibits change several times a year.

You can view the last remaining residential block of the original township at the **Heritage & Science Park.** Here, in addition to some of Phoenix's earliest buildings, you will find the **Phoenix Museum of History** and the **Arizona Science Center.** (Park in the covered lot on the grounds at the southeast

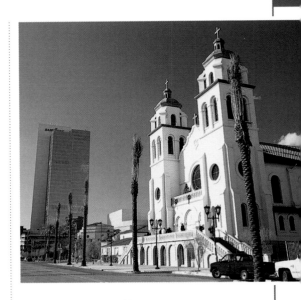

corner of Monroe and Fifth Streets; museums and businesses validate parking.)

The elegant 1895 **Rosson House** is the centerpiece of a group of venerable residences and shops. Not until the railroad ar-

**St. Mary's Basilica on East Monroe Street, completed in 1914, recalls a time before downtown filled with skyscrapers.**

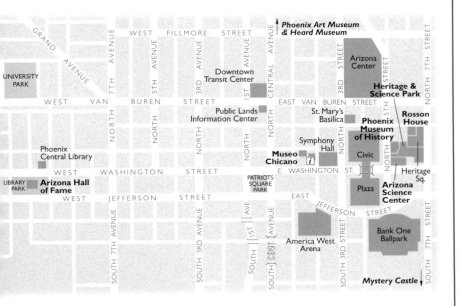

**Rosson House marks Phoenix's transition in the late 1800s to the dynamic business and political center of Arizona.**

**Rosson House**

- Map p. 147
- Heritage & Science Park
- 602/262-5070
- Closed Mon.–Tues. & possibly Aug.
- $

**Phoenix Museum of History**

- Map p. 147
- 105 N. 5th St.
- 602/253-2734
- $$

rived in 1887, bringing wood for construction and for firing brick kilns, did wood-frame and brick houses become practical. Before then, residents had to live in simple adobe houses not much different from those of the early Hohokam. Tours of the Victorian-style Rosson House tell the story of its construction and its residents.

Neighboring buildings date from the beginning of the 20th century. The 1901 Stevens House contains the **Arizona Doll & Toy Museum** *(Tel 602/253-9337, closed Mon. & Aug.)*. The **Bouvier-Teeter House** (1899) is now the Teeter House Tea Room *(Tel 602/252-4682, closed Mon. & Aug.)*. The **Baird Machine Shop** (1929) and **Thomas House** (1909) next door house the Pizzeria Bianco *(Tel 602/258-8300, closed Mon. & first two weeks Sept.)*.

The **Phoenix Museum of History** illustrates the work, play, and challenges of the city's early residents. Highlights include a general store, a Native American curio shop, a tent house for tuberculosis patients, a steam locomotive

used in mining, a collection of printing presses, and an ostrich farm exhibit. Motorcyclists will be amazed to see how far their machines have evolved since the days when the diminutive 1883 steam engine on display here powered a high-wheeler bicycle.

"Have fun with science," suggests the Arizona Science Center, where you can choose from several hundred hands-on experiments. The staff offers daily presentations and frequently adds new exhibits to explore such fields as networks, the body, the environment, optics, forces, movement, and aerospace. Art shows and visiting exhibits illustrate the beauty of science. Radio hams at station W7ASC show how to "work the world." A planetarium features star shows. Spectacular movies play in a giant-screen theater.

The interactive Water Works fountain performs different tricks when you touch one of the sensors that have been installed around it. Finally, the Awesome Atoms Science Store offers a large selection of educational toys and projects. ■

# Phoenix Art Museum

BEAUTIFUL AND THOUGHT-PROVOKING ART FROM MANY ages and places appears in the spacious galleries here. Most of the temporary exhibits reside in nearby galleries on the ground floor, along with the Art of Asia Galleries.

**Phoenix Art Museum**
www.phxart.org
- 144 D3 & inside back cover D2
- 1625 N. Central Ave.
- 602/257-1222
- Closed Mon.
- $$

The **Asian Collection** displays outstanding Chinese ceramics, cloisonné, bronzes, and paintings, as well as artwork from Japan, Tibet, India, and Southeast Asia.

**"Art of Our Time"** ranges from early 20th-century pioneers of modern art to artists of today. Look for Picasso's "Female Bather with Raised Arms" (1929), Thiebaud's "Four Ice Cream Cones" (1964), and Burkhardt's "Lime Pit" (1990).

The **Western Collection** covers the explorations of Arizona: through the 1800s with artists such as Remington, Russell, Bierstadt, and Moran, and up to the present.

Nearby, don't miss the **Thorne Miniature Rooms,** which replicate historic European and American interiors at a scale of 1 to 12.

In the **Latin American Collection** you'll find portraits from Spanish colonial times, religious art, and decorative arts as well as 20th-century Mexican pieces by artists such as Diego Rivera.

The museum's **American Collection,** dating from 1790 to 1930, reflects three themes: American People, Americans Abroad, and the American Landscape.

In the three galleries of the **European Collection,** look for "Salome with the Head of St. John the Baptist" by Dolci; "Madame Victoire" by Vigée-Le Brun; and "The Kiss" by Rodin.

The **Fashion Design Collection** illustrates European and American trends, with an emphasis on 20th-century American designers. Interactive tools and exercises in the **Art-Works Gallery** give children a chance to explore art. ■

**Inside the Phoenix Art Museum**

# Heard Museum

**Heard Museum**
www.heard.org

⛰ 144 D2 & inside back cover D2

✉ 2301 N. Central Ave.

☎ 602/252-8848 (recorded information & events) or 602/252-8840 (administration)

💲 $$

**Hoop dancing at the Heard Museum**

OUTSTANDING EXHIBITS ON THE NATIVE AMERICAN TRIBES and lands of the Southwest are on tap at this museum. The galleries in the Spanish colonial-style building take you from prehistoric times to the present. Courtyards with fountains and sculptures add to the enjoyment of wandering through the museum.

Native Americans express their thoughts and music in the audio-visual program "Our Voices, Our Land." Exhibits of jewelry, tools, pottery, weaving, and basketry all help tell the story of how the tribes adapted and interacted with the land. You'll pass copies of an Apache wickiup, a Navajo hogan, and a Hopi corn-grinding room. A stun-ning exhibition of kachina dolls (see pp. 88–89), many from the collection of Senator Barry Goldwater, hints at the complexity of Hopi religious and ceremonial beliefs. Contemporary Native American artists express their feelings in a variety of subjects, media, and forms.

Visitors of all ages will find something of interest. Families and small children can do projects in galleries set aside for them. You can take a docent-led tour, rent an audio program, or study in the large research library.

Special programs are an integral part of the museum's offerings. On Saturdays there are music or dance performances, artists' demonstrations, or workshops; call or check the website for the schedule. Three major festivals take place annually. The **World Championship Hoop Dance** on the first weekend in February hosts top dancers for amazing feats of agility. The **Guild Indian Fair and Market** on the first weekend in March attracts nearly 500 of the finest Native American artists; it also offers entertainment and food. **Celebration of Basketweaving** runs on the first weekend in December.

The museum shop, an attraction in itself, has top-quality jewelry, art, crafts, kachina dolls, and books. (For free parking, turn east at the sign off Central Avenue.)

In northern Scottsdale, you can visit the museum's branch, the **Heard Museum North Shop and Gallery** (*34505 N. Scottsdale Rd., tel 480/488-9817*). ∎

# North Phoenix

TWO ATTRACTIONS IN THE NORTHERN PART OF THE CITY throw light on the people who lived in Arizona during two very different periods of the area's long and intriguing history: its earliest beginnings and the 19th century.

A superb group of more than 1,500 petroglyphs is the focus of **Deer Valley Rock Art Center.** Tribes carved the symbols into boulders to mark periods of migration and residence between about 5000 B.C. and A.D. 1450. Modern-day tribes still feel a connection with the ancient designs and hold them sacred.

Visitor center exhibits and a video introduce the rock art from the perspectives of archaeologists, Native Americans, and physical scientists. Petroglyphs cover volcanic boulders near the end of a level quarter-mile walk. Bring binoculars (or rent them here) to see the details—visitors are not permitted to climb onto the rocks. The gift shop sells jewelry inspired by the rock art, clothing, reproductions, and books. To reach the center, take I-17 Deer Valley Road Exit 217B (about 18 miles north of downtown) and go west 2.5 miles, bearing right at the fork.

At the **Pioneer Arizona Living History Museum,** visitors can stroll through a town of some 30 buildings from the state's early years—a vivid portrayal of what life was like for Arizonans between the mid-1800s and statehood in 1912. The buildings are either originals that have been moved here or reconstructions from photographs or plans. Residences include the home of John Sears, one of the first wood-framed houses in Phoenix. A miner's cabin and ranch buildings recall the rough living conditions in remote corners of the state. Other buildings include the opera house, church,

bank, and shops. Costumed interpreters often work in the blacksmith shop or the one-room schoolhouse. Horses and other animals bring life to the farms; to recapture that authentic feel, take a ride on a pony, horse, or wagon.

Call to find out the times of special events, such as melodramas, barn dances, and historical reenactments. The biggest celebration takes place on the weekend nearest February 14—the anniversary of both Pioneer Arizona and the state itself. Pioneer Restaurant *(Tel 623/465-5681)* serves meals and has a magnificent 1861 bar. Pioneer Arizona is just west of I-17 Pioneer Road Exit 225, about 26 miles north of downtown. ∎

**Prehistoric peoples recorded their life events on boulders at Deer Valley Rock Art Center.**

# Wickenburg

IN 1863 THE PROMISE OF GOLD ATTRACTED GERMAN immigrant Henry Wickenburg to the scenic hills of the Sonoran Desert, where he struck it rich. The rush was on at the Vulture Mine, but water was needed for processing, so miners hauled the ore 14 miles northeast to a site beside the Hassayampa River. Three years later the riverside mining camp had grown to become Arizona's third largest town—and nearly won the right to be its state capital.

Wickenburg lies 58 miles northwest of downtown Phoenix via US 60 (Grand Ave.). Today, it has a Western atmosphere where you can explore a ghost town, ride the range, and stay at guest ranches (see pp. 000–00). A walking tour *(details available from the Wickenburg Chamber of Commerce, in the 1895 Santa Fe Depot)* takes in many old buildings and monuments downtown including the Jail Tree, a 200-year-old mesquite to which 19th-century outlaws were chained.

The **Desert Caballeros Western Museum** reveals the beauty of the land and the spirit of the people through its range of artistic, natural, and historical exhibits. Dioramas illustrate Henry Wickenburg's discovery of gold and the frenzied activity that followed. Downstairs, you can walk into a street scene with period rooms from the early town.

Southwestern *caballeros* (horsemen) are one major theme of the museum: The "Spirit of the Cowboy" collection displays old and modern cowboy gear along with rodeo, movie, and parade memorabilia. Valuable ores and precious stones gleam in the **Mineral Room,** while the **Native American Room** exhibits tribal artistry in the form of stone carvings, pottery, basketry, and kachina dolls. Paintings and sculpture by outstanding Western artists such as Frederic Remington and Charles Russell are the focus of the **Western Art Galleries.** The small park in back features "Thanks for the Rain," a life-size bronze sculpture by Joe Beeler, along with some picnic tables.

The riverbed in town is usually dry, but the river resurfaces for a 5-mile section downstream in the **Hassayampa River Preserve** (Hassayampa is Apache for "river that runs upside down"). Managed by the Arizona Chapter of the Nature Conservancy, several trails loop through the lush vegetation down to the river's edge and to spring-fed Palm Lake. More than 230 species of bird live, visit, or nest

**Wickenburg**

▲ 144 C4

**Visitor information**

www.wickenburgchamber.com

✉ Wickenburg Chamber of Commerce, 216 N. Frontier St.

☎ 928/684-5479

🕐 Closed Sun. & sometimes Sat.

**Desert Caballeros Western Museum**

www.westernmuseum.org

✉ 21 N. Frontier St.

☎ 928/684-2272

💲 $$

**Left: An old head frame at the Vulture Mine**

**Cowboys work the range near Wickenburg.**

**Hassayampa River Preserve**

www.tncarizona.org

✉ 49614 Hwy. 60 (3 miles SE of Wickenburg on US 60)

☎ 928/684-2772

🕐 Closed Mon.–Tues. year-round & Mon.–Thurs. May–Sept.

💲 $$

in the 333-acre preserve. The huge trees provide perches for raptors such as the zone-tailed and black hawks, which fly in from Mexico to breed. Marshy Palm Lake attracts great blue heron, white-faced ibis, pied-billed grebe, and others to this desert oasis. The riverbank is a good place to see mule deer and javelina, plus tracks of mountain lion, bobcat, and ring-tailed cat.

The 1860s four-room adobe that houses the visitor center has seen use as a ranch, a stagecoach way station, and one of the state's first guest ranches. Today it is worth a stop to see the displays on local wildlife, including the rare Goodding willow-Fremont cotton-wood forest found here. Natural history enthusiasts should stop at the Hassayampa Bookstore.

The **Vulture Mine** *(Tel 602/ 859-2743, closed Aug. & Mon.–Fri. June–July)* is a rare example of a mine and ghost town that have been neither destroyed nor dressed up for tourists. A self-guided tour (wear good walking shoes) takes you along dusty roads to the old head frame, where a mine shaft plunges more than 2,000 feet into the earth. It's not safe to enter the shafts, but above ground you can see the ball mill, power plant, assay office, blacksmith shop, and apart-ments and mess hall. For safety, stay on the marked trail, keeping an eye peeled for rattlesnakes.

Head west out of town for 2.5 miles on Wickenburg Way, then turn south and drive 12 miles on paved Vulture Mine Road; the en-trance is on your right. ■

**Visitors can enter reconstructed Hohokam dwellings at Pueblo Grande Museum & Archaeological Park .**

# East Phoenix

SEVERAL MAJOR SIGHTS LIE IN AND AROUND PAPAGO PARK on the east edge of Phoenix. The beautiful landscape of rounded hills and thriving desert vegetation led to its protection as a national monument. Today it's a city park with the Desert Botanical Garden, Phoenix Zoo, picnicking, easy hiking and biking trails, and ballfields.

**Pueblo Grande Museum & Archaeological Park**
www.pueblogrande.com
- Inside back cover D2
- 4619 E. Washington St. (5 miles E of downtown)
- 602/495-0900
- $; free on Sun.

**Phoenix Zoo**
www.phoenixzoo.org
- Inside back cover D2
- 455 N. Galvin Pkwy. (in central Papago Park)
- 602/273-1341
- $$ (Safari Train $)

The **Pueblo Grande Museum & Archaeological Park** reveals the life of Hohokam farmers (see pp. 144–45) through the ruins of a major village and excellent exhibits, including beautiful ceramics and jewelry. A map of an intricate canal network shows how the Hohokam brought water to their fields in the desert, and you'll see some of the tools they used to tend their waterways and crops. A model of Pueblo Grande (Great Town) shows how the complex may have looked. The Hohokam began construction of a large platform mound atop a terrace overlooking the Salt River about 1150. Rooms for residential or religious use sat on top. Possible solstice markings suggest that the tribe had a calendar to guide the planting and harvesting of crops.

Signs along a short trail to the top of the mound describe the layout and construction details. The trail also leads to a reconstructed pit house and adobe compound, then to a depression thought to have been a ball court. Visitors can watch a video illustrating how life may have been for the Hohokam. Children can take part in archaeology projects in the museum, and the shop sells books and Native American crafts. Ask the staff for information on hikes, tours, and special events.

A visit to the **Phoenix Zoo** brings you into contact with the exotic wildlife of the tropical rain forest, savanna, wetland, desert hills, and temperate woodland. Natural-looking enclosures are used instead of cages when possi-

## Desert Botanical Garden

www.dbg.org

◩ Inside back cover D2

✉ 1201 N. Galvin Pkwy. (in northern Papago Park)

☎ 480/941-1225 (general information) or 480/481-8134 (garden activities; wildflower hotline March–mid-April)

⑤ $$

## Hall of Flame

www.hallofflame.org

◩ Map p. 147 & inside back cover D2

✉ 6101 E. Van Buren St. (S of Papago Park)

☎ 602/275-3473

⑤ $$

## Arizona Historical Society Museum

www.tempe.gov/ahs

◩ IBC D2

✉ 1300 N. College Ave. (SE corner of Papago Park)

☎ 480/929-0292

**Wondrous displays of cactuses line the paths at Desert Botanical Garden.**

ble. Animals explore new scents and even get to forage for or chase after their food in behavioral enrichment programs. Rarely seen animals of Arizona, such as the gila monster and the black-footed ferret, are here too. A Safari Train with narration offers a good introduction. On the Children's Trail, young visitors can touch sculptures and pet tame animals. Schedules list the day's animal encounters, feeding times, and zookeeper talks. In summer, gates open at 7 a.m. to enable visitors to beat the heat. The zoo has snack bars and a large gift shop.

Find out what it takes to be a cactus at the **Desert Botanical Garden,** a great setting to enjoy and learn about desert plants of Arizona and the world. The Desert Discovery Trail makes a 0.3-mile loop past thousands of plants, including more than half the world's cactus species. Short trails lead off to the Cactus House and the Succulent House. The Plants and People of the Sonoran Desert Trail interprets how Native Americans relied on the desert's resources. The Sonoran Desert Nature Trail shows the relationships between plants and wildlife, while the Center for Desert Living Trail leads to a residence whose architecture, gardens, and landscaping have been specially designed for the desert, as explained by a video program and exhibits. On the Wildflower Trail in front of the gift shop, you can see plants from the four deserts in the United States. The garden also has a café, research library, and special programs.

The **Hall of Flame** displays an amazingly large and well-preserved collection of fire-fighting equipment from all over the world. Hand- and steam-powered pumpers along with horse-drawn apparatus in the first gallery date back to the 18th and 19th centuries, while motorized trucks line up in the second gallery. Exhibits and videos commemorate the bravery of firefighters. A gift shop carries books and souvenirs with a fire-fighting theme.

The **Arizona Historical Society Museum** brings to life central Arizona's 20th-century years. Enter the spacious courtyard and follow the sound of rushing water to the outdoor exhibit about Roosevelt Dam, with displays of some of its stone blocks and construction machinery. Inside the museum, a wide-screen video, "Traces on the Land," introduces Arizona's people and geography. Realistic scenes and interactive exhibits take you through the territorial years, agricultural accomplishments, transportation, military communities, and Phoenix's postwar boom. The museum also has visiting exhibits, a research library, special events, guided tours *(by appointment),* and a gift shop. ∎

Mystery Castle—a dream that became a reality—is open for tours south of Phoenix.

# West & South Phoenix

AN EXCEPTIONALLY FINE COLLECTION OF WILDLIFE FROM the far corners of the world lies out in the western Valley of the Sun. To the south, Mystery Castle is a fanciful home built by a loving father.

## Wildlife World Zoo

www.wildlifeworld.com

⊠ Inside back cover B3

✉ Northern Ave. & 165th Ave. (Take I-10 W 18 miles to Cotton Lane Exit 124, then go 6 miles N on 303 Loop or Cotton Lane)

☎ 623/935-9453

$ $$$

## Mystery Castle

⊠ Inside back cover D2

✉ 800 E. Mineral Rd. (7 miles S of downtown)

☎ 602/268-1581

🕐 Closed Mon.–Wed. & July–Sept.

$ $$

Many beautiful and exotic creatures live at the **Wildlife World Zoo,** established in 1974 as a breeding farm for rare species. The impressive bird collections include ostriches (all five of the world's species), raptors, parrots, waterfowl, and a walk-through aviary. Among the African animals are lion, rhinoceros, giraffe, zebra, and African wild dog. Oryx and other graceful antelope roam their enclosures. South America is represented by llamas, tapirs, and maned wolves. Monkeys perform their customary antics, and tigers in regular and white colorations prowl their territories. There is also an aquarium, a reptile house, and small mammal buildings.

You can get a closer look at small animals in the wildlife-encounter shows, and feedings take place daily. Children also enjoy the Safari Train ride and petting area. The zoo has a snack bar and gift shop.

Not every little girl gets the castle of her dreams, but Mary Lou Gulley was different. As a child in Washington State, she would cry when the tide washed away her sand castles—she wanted a real one to live in! Her father, Boyce Luther Gulley, believing himself near death's door, disappeared in 1930. Unknown to his family, he had gone to the desert of Arizona and set to work on his daughter's vision. The result was **Mystery Castle.** Not until 1945 did Mary Lou discover his secret, but her father had died just before sending for his family. Now Mary Lou and her assistants lead 30-minute tours through this remarkable assemblage of folk art. Call ahead to check hours. ■

# Phoenix parks

THE CITY PARKS OFFER PLENTY OF ROOM TO ROAM, AS well as a variety of scenery from grass and shady trees to the rugged landscapes and flora of the desert.

On the north side of downtown, monuments honor Phoenix's eight sister cities in **Margaret T. Hance Park.** The park's **Musoan ("Dream for the Future") Tea House** *(Tel 602/262-6412)* offers guided tours on Sunday afternoons and tea ceremonies (by reservation) on the second Saturday of the month from October through May. **Phoenix Street Railway** *(Tel 602/254-0307 or 277-6627)* runs tours in the park on Saturdays during the winter months.

In **Encanto Park,** 2 miles northwest of downtown, concerts are often held in the evenings from April through October. In the south half are picnic areas, playgrounds, a swimming pool, and courts for tennis, racquetball, volleyball, and basketball. **Enchanted Island** *(Tel 602/254-1200; parking north of En-*

*canto Blvd. between 7th and 15th Aves.)* runs a carousel, a train, and other rides on weekends and some weekdays. Farther north, you can rent boats or fish on a small lake. A driving range and two golf courses are located in the park's north end.

Rock hills overlook a desert oasis at **Papago Park** in east Phoenix. Visitors and locals come to picnic, fish, and take easy hikes to the Hole in the Rock or former governor George W. P. Hunt's tomb.

Head northeast of downtown to **Squaw Peak Park** *(Tel 602/262-6696)* or **Camelback Mountain** *(Echo Canyon Recreation Area, tel 602/256-3220)* for challenging hikes to each summit and great views. **South Mountain Park** *(Tel 602/495-0222),* 7 miles south of downtown, has a paved road to the summit, passing viewpoints on the way up. ∎

**Encanto Park offers many recreational facilities in an oasis near downtown Phoenix.**

**Visitor information**
www.ci.phoenix.az.us

✉ Parks, Recreation, & Library Dept., 200 W. Washington St., 16th Floor, Phoenix, AZ 85003

☎ 602/262-6862

**Encanto Park office**
✉ 2700 N. 15th Ave.
☎ 602/261-8991

**Papago Park**
🅰 Inside back cover D2
✉ Take the Phoenix Zoo turnoff from Galvin Pkwy., then turn left to the recreation area
☎ 602/256-3220

Maricopa County parks offer scenic pathways through the Sonoran Desert, including the horseback trail above in Estrella Mountain Park.

# Maricopa County parks

IN THE SCENIC DESERT AREAS ON THE EDGES OF THE Valley of the Sun are several parks where you can experience the great outdoors without traveling too far from Phoenix. All have picnic areas, campgrounds, and extensive recreation facilities. Lake Pleasant is the place for boating, fishing, or just relaxing by the water. The other parks have excellent trails for hiking, mountain biking, and horseback riding. You're likely to see many birds and other wildlife, especially in the early morning and evening. Rangers lead hikes, present educational programs, and host competitive activities on weekends during the cooler winter months; call or check the website for details. Maps and descriptions are available from the main office, but staff here may not have detailed firsthand knowledge of all the parks.

Spanish explorers named the rugged mountains 26 miles southwest of Phoenix in **Estrella Mountain Regional Park** (*Tel 623/932-3811*) for their star-shaped drainages. Trails lead off into the desert foothills and interconnect to make a variety of loops. Families like the park's huge grassy area with its ballfields, playgrounds, and picnic tables. You can also play on the nearby 18-hole **Estrella Mountain Golf Course** (*Tel 623/932-3714*) or catch an event at

a rodeo arena. To reach the park, take I-10 to Estrella Parkway Exit 126, go south 5 miles, then turn left half a mile.

The extensive trail system in **White Tank Mountain Regional Park** (*Tel 623/935-6056 program information; 623/935-2505 Ramada and group campground reservations*), approximately 30 miles to the west of Phoenix, winds up canyons and climbs atop high ridges. The mountains get their name from water-filled depressions

**Maricopa County parks**

🅰 144 C2

**Visitor information**

www.maricopa.gov

✉ 411 N. Central Ave., Suite 470, Phoenix, AZ 85004

☎ 602/506-2930

🕐 Office closed Sat.–Sun.

💲 $–$$ (day-use fee),; $$–$$$ (camping)

that flash floods have carved in the white granite bedrock. You can see one of these tanks in a shady canyon at the end of Waterfall Trail, an easy round-trip of about 2 miles; look for petroglyphs on boulders along the way. The waterfall puts on a show only after wet periods.

**Goat Camp, Ford Canyon,** and **Mesquite Canyon Trails** all lead high into the mountains, where they meet. If you plan to head into the backcountry, rangers recommend that you see them for trail advisories; overnight trips require a permit. You'll pass a visitor center on the right inside the park. The picnic areas and campground offer views of the mountains to the west and the vast Valley of the Sun to the east; sunset and sunrise here are magical. To reach the park, take I-10 to Cotton Lane Exit 124, go north 7 miles to Olive Avenue, then turn east to the entrance.

**Lake Pleasant Regional Park** *(Tel 928/501-1702)* attracts boaters, anglers, and campers to recreation areas on the west shore of a 10,000-acre reservoir 30 miles northwest of Phoenix. Follow signs to Waddell Dam Overlook for the visitor center, a gift shop, and a panorama. Nearby are a ten-lane boat ramp, a marina, picnic areas, and two campgrounds. Reach Lake Pleasant from I-17 Exit 223; head west 11.5 miles on Arizona 74, turn right and drive 2.2 miles on Castle Hot Springs Road, then turn right into the park.

Trails loop through the rocky hills of an old mining area at **Cave Creek Recreation Area** *(Tel 623/465-0431),* 32 miles north of Phoenix. Equestrians enjoy rides here, and there is a horse staging area. For this park, take I-17 to Exit 223, turn east and go 7 miles on Carefree Highway, then take a left and drive 1.6 miles on 32nd Street.

Enjoying a family picnic above Lake Pleasant.

Many trails wend their way across the foothills and lower slopes in **McDowell Mountain Regional Park** *(Tel 480/471-0173),* 25 miles northeast of Phoenix. The 1995 Rio Fire burned two-thirds of the park, and the desert is still recovering. To reach the park, take Shea Boulevard or Arizona 87 to Fountain Hills, then turn north and drive about 5 miles to the entrance. Stop to admire one of the world's largest fountains in a park on Saguaro Boulevard; water jets 560 feet into the sky in a 15-minute show that begins on the hour from 9 a.m. to 9 p.m.

High cliffs of greenish volcanic ash deposits called tuff overlook **Usery Mountain Recreation Area** *(Tel 480/984-0032),* 25 miles east of Phoenix. Trails loop around the central area, while the moderate 3.2-mile Wind Cave Trail climbs to caves in the cliffs of Pass Mountain. The rugged Pass Mountain Trail goes 7.1 miles around the mountain. From the Superstition Freeway in Mesa, take Ellsworth Road/Usery Pass Road north about 7 miles to the entrance. ■

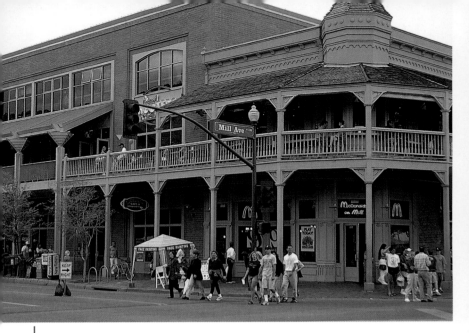

# Tempe

IN 1872, CHARLES HAYDEN CHOSE THIS SITE ON THE SALT River's south bank for his trading post and later a ferry and a flour mill. Darrel Duppa, who had given Phoenix its name, dropped by Hayden's ferry one day and remarked that the area reminded him of the Vale of Tempe in Thessaly, Greece. The name stuck. In 1885, Arizona Teachers College was established in the farming settlement, just southeast of Phoenix, and later became Arizona State University.

Downtown Tempe (tem-PEE) centers on Mill Avenue, lined with restaurants, nightspots, and specialty shops. Historic buildings include Hayden's early 1870s house (now La Casa Vieja Restaurant) at First Street and Mill Avenue, and commercial buildings dating from the late 1800s, such as the Hackett House/Tempe Bakery at 95 West Fourth Street, as well as three on South Mill Avenue: Hotel Casa Loma at 398; the Laird & Dines Building at 501; the Tempe Hardware Building at 520. Tempe Town Lake offers shoreline parks and boating in a stretch of the Salt River just north of downtown. Tempe Convention & Visitors Bureau is a good place to begin a visit.

The **Tempe Historical Museum** *(809 E. Southern Ave., tel 480/350-5100, closed Fri., www.tempe.gov/museum)* portrays the people and times from the Hohokam up to the present day. A 40-foot model of the Salt River and its canals shows how late 19th-century Tempe residents made the desert bloom.

A visit to the 1892 **Niels Petersen House** gives insight into the lives of early settlers. Tours explain the house's evolution from a Queen Anne-Victorian style to a 1930s bungalow appearance. You'll also learn about the house's residents, such as Danish immigrant Neils Petersen, who developed the area's farming potential. ∎

# Arizona State University

FROM A FOUR-ROOM REDBRICK BUILDING SET ON 20 ACRES of cow pasture, ASU has become the state's biggest university (about 49,700 full-time and part-time students) with a beautifully landscaped 700-acre main campus. Highlights include the Nelson Fine Arts Center, smaller museums, cultural activities, and sporting events. The domed visitor center on the southeast corner of the campus offers maps, a self-guided walking tour, an arboretum, events, and state travel literature. There is free parking here. Guided tours lasting about an hour leave from the Student Services Building *(Tel 480/965-2604)* Monday through Friday. Keep an eye (and ear) out for students zipping by on scooters, bikes, and in-line skates.

The **Nelson Fine Arts Center,** built in gray-purple stucco, recalls the color of a nearby hill. This complex of geometric buildings interspersed with terraces and plazas echoes a Hopi pueblo, yet it is unique in its interpretation. Inside, the spacious galleries of the **ASU Art Museum** display visiting shows and works from the permanent collection of American art, American and European prints, and Latin American, contemporary, and ceramic art. The institution also seeks out underrecognized artists and offers new ways to explore the world of art. Outdoor terraces display sculpture. The gift shop sells many fine handicrafts and books. The Nelson center also includes a theater, dance laboratory, and performance spaces. To visit the center, turn east from Mill Avenue onto Tenth Street and look for parking at the meters or in the nearby lot at Tenth and Myrtle.

A short walk from the Nelson center, at **Northlight Gallery** *(Tyler Mall, tel 480/965-6517, closed Fri.–Sun. & summer)* in Matthews

## ASU Art Museum at Nelson Fine Arts Center

asuartmuseum.asu.edu

 10th St. at Mill Ave.

☎ 480/965-2787 (museum) or 480/965-6447 (box office)

🕐 Closed Mon.

Expect anything and everything at the ASU Art Museum—including the earthenware-with-terra-sigillata "Rabbit Head" (1990) by Deborah G. Masuoka.

Hall, the photographic exhibits are selected from historical and contemporary collections.

MFA (Master of Fine Arts) students exhibit their work in the **Harry Wood Art Gallery** *(Forest Mall, tel 480/965-3468, closed Sat.–Sun.)* in the School of Arts Building. Drawings and scale models illustrate the newest architectural designs in the **Gallery of Design** *(Forest Mall, tel 480/965-8169, closed Sat.–Sun.)*, part of the College of Architecture and Environmental Design.

**The Museum of Anthropology** *(Cady Mall, tel 480/965-6213, closed Sat.–Sun.)* interprets both Hohokam and contemporary Native American cultures along with exhibits on archaeological techniques and concepts of anthropology.

The university's scientific exhibits are equally varied, ranging from live rattlesnakes and other reptiles at the **Life Sciences Center** *(Tyler Mall, tel 480/965-3571, closed Sat.–Sun.)* to visitors from outer space in the **Center for Meteorite Studies** *(Palm Walk, tel 480/965-6511, closed Sat.–Sun.)*, located in Room C-139 and adjacent hallways of the Physical Sciences Building. In the same building, star shows run some days in the **ASU Planetarium** *(Palm Walk, tel 480/965-6891)*. On a more terrestrial theme, a range of equipment including a Foucault pendulum and a seismograph keeps tabs on Earth in the **Geology Museum** *(Palm Walk, tel 480/965-7065, closed Sat.–Sun.)*, also in the Physical Sciences Building (F wing). Other exhibits here display rocks, minerals, and fossils along with explanations of geologic processes.

The distinctive circular 3,000-seat **Gammage Auditorium**

*(Mill Ave. & Apache Blvd., tel 480/965-3434 box office, 480/965-4050 tour information)* hosts many performances and events. Named after a former ASU president and dedicated in 1964, it is the last major public building designed by architect Frank Lloyd Wright. Half-hour tours run from Monday to Friday between October and mid-May.

The **Memorial Union** *(Cady & Orange Malls, tel 480/965-5728)* is the social center of ASU. Here you will find an information desk, an art gallery *(closed Sat.–Sun.)*, fast-food eateries, a cafeteria, a movie theater, and bowling lanes. The **ASU Bookstore** lies east of the Memorial Union. Also nearby is the **Hayden Library** *(Cady Mall, tel 480/965-5902, www.asu.edu/lib)*, which houses the main collection plus holdings on Arizona, Chicano Studies, East Asia, and federal documents.

The **Daniel E. Noble Science Library** *(Tyler Mall, tel 480/965-7607)* serves the nearby science and engineering departments. Hikers can plan their trips using topographical maps, while inventors can check their ideas in the U.S. Patents and Trademark Depository Library.

Enthusiastic followers of the school's Sun Devils attend football games at the 74,000-seat **Sun Devil Stadium,** basketball games at the 14,000-seat **University Activity Center,** and baseball games at the 8,000-seat **Packard Stadium;** all three facilities are located in the northern part of the campus. The **Sports Hall of Fame** *(closed Sat.–Sun.)* displays trophies and photos of ASU's sporting past in the University Activity Center, where you will also find the Sun Devils Athletic Ticket Office *(Tel 480/965-2381, www.thesundevils.com)*. ∎

# Scottsdale

CAPT. WINFIELD SCOTT HOMESTEADED HERE, JUST TO THE northeast of Phoenix, in the 1880s, proclaiming the land "unequaled in greater fertility or richer promise." Perhaps he would be impressed if he could see the luxurious resorts, art galleries, fine restaurants, cultural events, and attractive landscaping that are Scottsdale today.

Experience the genius of Frank Lloyd Wright at Taliesin West.

## DOWNTOWN

The Scottsdale Mall is home to the Scottsdale Historical Museum, the Scottsdale Museum of Contemporary Art, a tourist office, and a library, all connected by paths in a beautiful park. Porch-fronted shops of Old Town Scottsdale, on the west side of the mall, sell Western and Native American arts and crafts.

The area's cotton fields and dairy farms have disappeared, but just east of the intersection of Brown Avenue and Main Street you can still step into the Little Red Schoolhouse, now the **Scottsdale Historical Museum,** to get a feel for the old days. Photographs, artifacts, and period furniture depict the community's development since the little school opened

in 1909, when its two classrooms could hold all the town's children.

In complete contrast, the exhibits at the **Scottsdale Museum of Contemporary Art,** just a short walk to the southeast, entertain and challenge with the latest concepts in art, architecture, and design. The shows change every two or three months. The galleries are housed in the Scottsdale Center for the Arts and the adjacent Gerard L. Cafesjian Pavilion, which opened in February 1999. There is also a sculpture garden outside. Performances and special events often take place in the center's theater, cinema, and amphitheater. Both the center and the pavilion have large gift shops, often with art related to current exhibits.

**Scottsdale**
🅰 144 D3
**Visitor information**
www.scottsdalecvb.com
✉ Scottsdale Convention and Visitors Bureau, 7343 Scottsdale Mall, Scottsdale, AZ 85251
☎ 480/945-8481 or 800/877-1117

**Scottsdale Historical Museum**
✉ 7333 E. Scottsdale Mall
☎ 480/945-4499
🕐 Closed Mon.–Tues. & July–Aug.

**Scottsdale Museum of Contemporary Art**

www.scottsdalearts.org

✉ 7374 E. 2nd St.

☎ 480/994-ARTS

🕐 Closed Mon.

💲 $$. Free & open until 9 p.m. on Thurs.

**McCormick-Stillman Railroad Park**

✉ 7301 E. Indian Bend Rd. (SE corner of Indian Bend & Scottsdale Rds.)

☎ 480/312-2312

💲 $ (train & carousel rides)

Best of friends: Calvin the tiger with Gerry at Out of Africa Wildlife Park

## FARTHER AFIELD

Railfans will enjoy exploring the 30-acre **McCormick-Stillman Railroad Park.** You can hop aboard the ⁵/₁₂-scale Paradise and Pacific Railroad for a 1-mile loop through the grassy grounds. It's modeled after narrow-gauge trains of Colorado and has both diesel and steam locomotives to pull the passenger-carrying gondolas and other cars. You'll also see a standard-gauge, Mogul-type Baldwin steam locomotive, a variety of railroad cars, and seasonal museum exhibits. The Stillman Station, a copy of the depot at Clifton, sells tickets and gifts. Two historic depots house model train equipment, memorabilia, and souvenirs; they also serve snacks. Another snack bar is in a caboose.

Model railroad clubs meet in the park on Sunday afternoons, when you can view their layouts and working steam locomotive models. Other attractions include a 1950 carousel, playgrounds, covered picnic tables, and a small xeriscape arboretum.

Architecture and the desert meet at **Taliesin West,** a masterpiece by architect Frank Lloyd Wright. In 1937 he began work on the site as a winter home for both his family and his apprentices, where they could learn from nature and from one another. Apprentices still live here in tents and simple shelters, just as they did more than 60 years ago. Wright instilled in his students ideas of how to "grow" building designs from the inside out, rather than relying on facts and figures. Wright died in 1959, but his school continues to train architects today, most of whom stay for three to five years.

Site tours show how Wright's architecture looks fresh and different from every angle. The one-hour **Panorama Tour** introduces his

work with photos, a video, models, and a walk through some of the grounds and buildings; tours begin frequently during the day *(no reservations needed).*

The 90-minute **Insights Tour** covers the same ground but adds a visit to Wright's spacious living room; tours leave only a few times daily, but no reservations are not required.

For architecture enthusiasts, the **Behind the Scenes Tour** is the most detailed and exciting. It includes a meeting with Wright associates and takes in areas not on the other tours. Call for times and make a reservation. Seasonal tours include desert walks, visits to the apprentice shelters, and twilight tours. The Taliesin West Bookstore carries an extensive selection of related books and arts and crafts.

The 600-acre site rests on the McDowell Mountain foothills 13 miles northeast of central Scottsdale. Go north 7 miles on 101 (Pima Freeway) or Pima Road, turn right 5 miles on Cactus Road to the entrance across Frank Lloyd Wright Boulevard, then continue 1 mile on Taliesin Drive.

Big cats and other wildlife in the **Out of Africa Wildlife Park** roam within near-natural enclosures. The animals reveal their behavior and personalities during wildlife encounter demonstrations by the knowledgeable staff. For the popular **Tiger Splash,** staffers get into a pool and coax tigers to join them and play with "prey" toys. Various shows are staged during the day, so arrive early to make the most of your visit. On summer weekdays *(closed Mon. & Tues.),* the park does not open until late afternoon; on summer weekends it opens at 9:30 a.m. Between shows, you can wander among the exhibits, which have wildlife from Arizona and around the world. The

Re-creating the
Old West at
Rawhide

**Taliesin West**
www.franklloydwright.org
✉ 12621 Frank Lloyd
Wright Blvd.
☎ 480/860-2700
$ $$$$–$$$$$

**Out of Africa
Wildlife Park**
www.outofafricapark.com
✉ Beeline Hwy. (Ariz.
87) & Fort Mc-
Dowell Rd.
☎ 480/837-7779
(recording) or 837-
6683 (office)
🕐 Closed Mon. year-
round; closed Mon.
& Tues. June–Sept.)
$ $$$

**Artist Douglas
Miley shows his
technique.**

park is 18 miles northeast of downtown Scottsdale; take Shea Boulevard to Beeline Highway (Arizona
87), continue east 2 miles, then turn
right on Fort McDowell Road.

**Rawhide Wild West Town**
*(23023 N. Scottsdale Rd., tel 480/
502-5600 or 800/527-1880,
www.rawhide.com)* re-creates an
1880s Old West town in northern
Scottsdale. Lots of activities take
place in and around some 25
reconstructed buildings of the
period: stunt action shows, Native
American performances, live music,
stagecoach rides, train trips, burro
rides, and arcade games. Shops sell
sweets and Western gear, and the
Rawhide Steakhouse serves dinner
from a long list of dishes.

Visitors have a choice of entry
passes; the more expensive one
includes a package of rides and theater performances. Rawhide opens
at 5 p.m. (earlier on weekends during the cooler months). To reach it,
head north about 13 miles on
Scottsdale Road from downtown.

The **Heard Museum North**
*(34505 N. Scottsdale Rd., tel
480/488-9817)* provides a taste of
the Heard Museum in downtown
Phoenix (see p. 150) with Native
American exhibits and a gift shop
in El Pedregal Festival Marketplace
at the corner of Scottsdale Road
and Carefree Highway in the north
of Scottsdale. ■

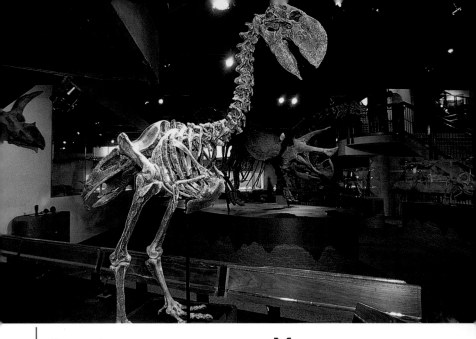

# Mesa

ARIZONA'S THIRD LARGEST CITY AFTER PHOENIX AND
Tucson, Mesa spreads across a low plateau on the east side of the
Valley of the Sun. The tablelike site inspired the Spanish name. After
arriving here in 1878, Mormon settlers built a small fort and irrigated their fields with a reworked Hohokam canal system.

**Mesa**
🅽 144 D3
**Visitor information**
www.mesacvb.com
✉ Mesa Convention &
 Visitors Bureau,
 120 N. Center St.
☎ 480/827-4700 or
 800/283-6372
🕐 Closed Sat.–Sun.

**Mesa Southwest
Museum**
www.ci.mesa.az.us
✉ 53 N. Macdonald St.
 (corner of
 Macdonald & 1st
 St.)
☎ 480/644-2230
🕐 Closed Mon.
💲 $$

Uncover some of the mysteries of
the past at the **Mesa Southwest
Museum,** where dinosaurs pose in
ancient landscapes, prehistoric Na-
tive American villages look only re-
cently abandoned, the Guevavi
Mission exhibit represents Spanish
influence, and the Lost Dutchman
Mine relates legends of gold. The
mineral and astronomy halls show
wonders of the natural world. An
orientation theater introduces the
displays, and changing exhibits
offer perspectives on the area. You
can visit the hands-on Discovery
Resource Center or try projects
scattered around the museum.

Two blocks away is the 1896
**Sirrine House** *(160 N. Center St.,
tel 480/644-2760),* one of Mesa's
finest early residences. Tours run on
weekends from October to March.

Visitors are welcome to see
the gardens and exhibits of the
**Arizona Mormon Temple.** In
the visitor center videos and di-
oramas explain the beliefs of the
Mormon Church, more formally
known as the Church of Jesus
Christ of Latter-day Saints. The
temple, completed in 1927, con-
tains elements of classical Greek
architecture. Eight friezes on the
top corners of the exterior depict
church members, most traveling to
unite with others. Religious cere-
monies are held inside the temple
itself, so it is not open for tours. A
big Easter Pageant takes place the
week before Easter. Music programs
and 600,000 lights brighten the
Christmas season. To trace family
roots, head across the street to
check out the introductory video

*Sentimental Journey is the pride and joy of the Arizona Wing of the Confederate Air Force.*

**Arizona Mormon Temple**
www.lds.org
✉ 525 E. Main St.
☎ 480/964-7164

**Champlin Fighter Aircraft Museum**
www.champlinfighter.com
✉ 4636 Fighter Aces Dr., off McKellips Rd. (7 miles NE of downtown)
☎ 480/830-4540
$ $$

**Confederate Air Force–Arizona Wing**
www.arizonawingcaf.org
✉ 2017 N. Greenfield Rd. (turn N on Greenfield Rd. from McKellips Rd. at the SW corner of Falcon Field)
☎ 480/924-1940
$ $$

and other resources at the **Mesa Family History Center** *(41 S. Hobson Rd., tel 480/964-1200).*

You can still see three sections of the Hohokam canals later used by pioneers at the **Park of the Canals** *(1710 N. Horne Rd.)* about 2 miles north of downtown; the park also has a desert botanical garden. Farther north, the **Mesa Historical Museum** *(2345 N. Horne Rd., tel 480/835-7358, closed Sun.–Mon. & June–Aug.)* portrays the life of early settlers. Antique farm equipment sits outside the museum building, a former schoolhouse dating from 1913.

The **Champlin Fighter Aircraft Museum** tells the remarkable stories of fliers from World War I, World War II, and the jet age. The museum is at Falcon Field—originally a secret training base for British airmen during World War II. Videos and artwork show fighter pilots and aircraft in action. The unique collection of more than 30 aircraft includes reproductions of the Rumpler Taube—the world's first plane to fly in combat—and the Fokker Dr-1 triplane, most

famously flown by Manfred von Richthofen, the "Red Baron." Planes such as the P-51D Mustang, Supermarine Spitfire Mk IX, and Messerschmitt 109E represent World War II. In the jet hangar, tiny MiGs and an F86 Sabre stand near an imposing F4 Phantom. Aircraft mechanics keep the planes in flying condition in the restoration area, which you can view. Docents conduct tours, or you can explore the exhibits on your own. (Although the collection has been acquired by the Museum of Flight in Seattle it will remain open in its current location until mid- to late 2002.)

Rare military aircraft undergo restoration and take to the skies at the **Confederate Air Force–Arizona Wing.** The B-17G named *Sentimental Journey* is said to be the most authentically restored model flying today. To experience a flight in the B-17 or another vintage aircraft, call to schedule a warbird ride. Among the exhibits are radio and navigational equipment, engines, flying gear, and historical photos. ■

# Apache Trail loop drive

To nature lover and U.S. president Theodore Roosevelt, "The Apache Trail combines the grandeur of the Alps, the glory of the Rockies, the magnificence of the Grand Canyon and then adds an indefinable something that none of the others have. To me, it is the most awe-inspiring and most sublimely beautiful panorama nature has ever created."

Today the Apache Trail remains one of Arizona's most scenic drives. Twisting over jagged ridges and plunging into sheer-walled canyons, it steers its wild course along the northern flanks of the Superstition Mountains, linking the Valley of the Sun and Theodore Roosevelt Lake. Native Americans walked the trail for hundreds of years until the late 1800s, when workers upgraded it to a horse trail. The decision to build Theodore Roosevelt Dam required engineers to carve out a road to bring in construction equipment. That task took

nearly two years, and the road opened in 1905.

Though designated a state highway (Arizona 88), much of the road is still unpaved, demanding cautious driving. It is normally fine for cars and smaller RVs, but large trailers are not recommended. By combining Arizona 88, Arizona 188, and US 60 via Globe-Miami, travelers can follow a 200-mile loop around the Superstition Mountains with great views all the way. The loop can be driven in a long day, but two or more days allow for a more leisurely journey, with stops to see the sights

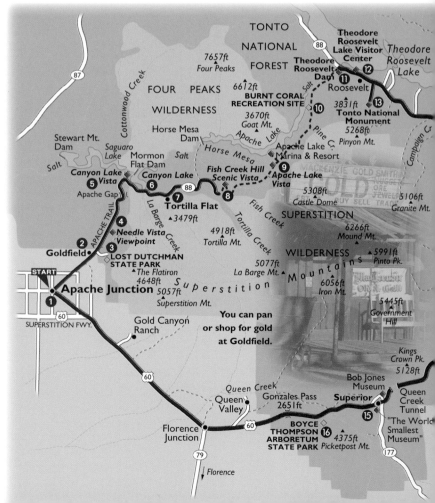

and tackle some hikes. There are many camp-grounds on the way, and Apache Junction and Globe-Miami offer a large selection of motels and restaurants. The drive lies within three districts of Tonto National Forest; the Super-visor's Office *(2324 E. McDowell Rd., Phoenix, AZ 85006, tel 602/225-5200, closed Sat.–Sun., www.fs.fed.us/r3/tonto)* has maps and general information.

**Apache Junction ❶** is a convenient starting point and a good place to stock up on

gas and supplies. Head northeast on Arizona 88 to **Goldfield ❷** *(Tel 480/983-0333),* which sprang into existence when prospectors dis-covered gold in the mid-1890s. The attractions here are manifold; they include the **Superstition/Lost Dutchman Museum** *(Tel 480/983-4888);* a tour in a replica of the nearby **Mammoth Mine;** a narrated ride on the 1.5-mile **Superstition Scenic Railway** around the site; horseback riding *(Tel 480/ 982-0133),* hiking, and back-road tours *(Tel 480/982-7661);* and the Mammoth Steakhouse and Saloon *(Tel 480/983-6402).*

In **Lost Dutchman State Park ❸** *(Tel 480/982-4485)* you can hike, picnic, and camp at the base of the Superstition Mountains; during the cooler months, campers will have to arrive early to find a spot. **Needle Vista Viewpoint ❹** affords a view of the 4,535-

---

| | See area map p. 145 |
|---|---|
| ▶ | Apache Junction |
| ↔ | 200 miles |
| ⏲ | About 6 hours plus stops |
| ▶ | Apache Junction |

**NOT TO BE MISSED**
- Needle Vista Viewpoint
- Tonto National Monument
- Besh-Ba-Gowah at Globe
- Boyce Thompson Arboretum State Park

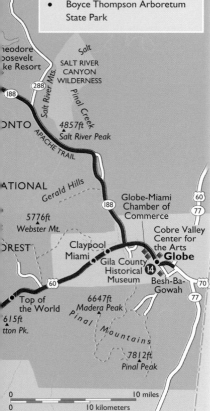

**The reconstructed ghost town of Goldfield stages activities that appeal to families.**

**Riding in the Superstition Mountains**

foot-high pinnacle that figures in so many lost-mine legends. **Canyon Lake Vista ❺** takes in this large reservoir on the Salt River. **Canyon Lake ❻** has a marina *(Tel 602/944-6504)* with boat rentals, a restaurant, and a

campground. Budget about 90 minutes for a narrated lake tour aboard the *Dolly Steamboat (Tel 480/827-9144).*

**Tortilla Flat ❼** looks like an Old West movie set; step inside for the restaurant, curio shop, and country store. Across the highway, **Tortilla Campground** *(Tel 480/610-3300, closed May–Sept.)* is popular with RVers. The pavement runs out 23 miles from Apache Junction, after which it's another 2 miles to **Fish Creek Hill Scenic Vista ❽**—a good place to get a feel for the rugged beauty of this land. The descent of **Fish Creek Hill,** a 1,500-foot drop over 3 miles, is the most challenging section to drive. You can take in a panorama of the second largest reservoir on this drive at **Apache Lake Vista ❾.** A road here leads down to Apache Lake Marina & Resort *(Tel 928/467-2511)*, where you'll find a motel, an RV campground, a restaurant, boat rentals, and a store. Facilities at **Burnt Corral Recreation Site ❿** on Apache Lake include camping, a picnic site, boat ramp, and beach.

The road climbs Apache Lake Gorge to **Theodore Roosevelt Dam ⓫** and two overlooks. Engineers had doubts about the masonry dam's ability to survive a moderate earthquake or major flood, so they encased it in concrete and raised the level to increase storage capacity. Theodore Roosevelt Lake covers about 19,199 acres when full and is the largest of the four Salt River reservoirs. The very helpful **Roosevelt Lake Visitor Center ⓬** *(Tel 928/467-3200)* houses exhibits and an information desk and sells relevant books and maps.

**Tonto National Monument ⓭** *(Tel 928/467-2241, www.nps.gov/tont)* protects two cliff dwellings constructed by the Native American tribe known as the Salado in the hills overlooking the Salt River nearly 700 years ago. A video and exhibits in the visitor center show how the tribe lived. You'll also see examples of their pottery, tools, and cotton textiles. A self-guided paved trail behind the visitor center climbs 350 feet to the 19-room Lower Cliff Dwelling; allow an hour for the 1-mile round-trip. You can visit the Upper Cliff Dwelling only on ranger-led tours that

**Paper currency papers the walls of the restaurant at Tortilla Flat.**

run on certain days from November through April. If your travel plans allow you to make a reservation, the 3-mile hike (with a 600-foot climb) pays off with a visit to a large and very well-preserved 40-room pueblo.

Continue on Arizona 188 to Globe-Miami at the road's end. Turn left to detour to **Globe ⑭,** with its well-preserved early 20th-century downtown, extensive visitor facilities, and forest roads leading up into the Pinal Mountains. On the way into town, on the right, you'll pass the **Globe-Miami Chamber of Commerce** *(1360 N. Broad St., tel 928/425-4495 or 800/804-5623, may close Sat.–Sun.)* and the **Gila County Historical Museum** *(1330 N. Broad St., tel 928/425-7385, closed Sun.)* next door. Downtown, the **Cobre Valley Center for the Arts** *(101 N. Broad St., tel 928/ 425-0884)* displays a large collection of local art. The Salado lived in the large 200-room pueblo of **Besh-Ba-Gowah** *(Tel 928/425-0320)* between 1225 and 1450. A good museum introduces the Salado and the partially reconstructed site. To reach it, head downtown, continue to the end of South Broad Street, turn right across the bridge onto Jess Hayes Street and continue about 1 mile, then turn right up the hill and follow the road around the site to the entrance.

The Globe-Miami area's long history of copper mining is evident as you drive through

**A short hike through the desert from the visitor center at Tonto National Monument takes you into the world of the prehistoric Salado.**

the towns and continue west on US 60 to complete the Apache Trail loop. After some rugged hill and canyon country, the road drops into the old mining town of **Superior ⑮.** A sign on the highway indicates **"The World's Smallest Museum,"** while the **Bob Jones Museum** *(Main St. & Neary, closed Mon.–Tues.),* in the former home of Arizona's sixth governor, stands downtown; both display historical exhibits.

Continue 3 miles west from Superior to **Boyce Thompson Arboretum State Park ⑯** *(Tel 520/689-2811).* Here, the largest (323 acres) and oldest (1920s) arboretum in Arizona displays collections of plants from the Southwest and around the world. Spring heralds a floral explosion of colors. Birds and other wildlife come to the desert oases at Ayer Lake and Queen Creek. The visitor center sells books, seeds, and plants.

An easy drive on US 60 leads back to Apache Junction, or you can turn south to visit the historic town of Florence and Casa Grande Ruins National Monument, a Hohokam great house (see p. 173). ■

# Florence

TIME SEEMS TO HAVE BYPASSED THIS OLD TOWN, FOUNDED in 1866 near a ford on the Gila River. Even the 1891 Pinal County courthouse "clock" remains stuck at 11:44; funds ran out before a real clock could be installed, so workers simply painted on the hands. More than 150 buildings on the National Register of Historic Places line the porch-fronted Main Street and nearby lanes. Museums and visitor centers offer a "Historic Florence Walking Tour" handout.

The 1878 adobe building in **Mc-Farland State Historic Park** on the north side of town has seen use as Pinal County's first courthouse, sheriff's office, jail, and hospital. Exhibits illustrate these periods and tell of Florence's notable and notorious historical figures.

JAN. 6, 1880  –  OCT. 12, 1940
IN MEMORY OF
TOM MIX
WHOSE SPIRIT LEFT HIS BODY ON THIS SPOT
AND WHOSE CHARACTERIZATION AND PORTRAYAL
IN LIFE SERVED TO BETTER FIX MEMORIES OF
THE OLD WEST IN THE MINDS OF LIVING MEN

Photos of the POW camp depict the experiences of some of the 13,000 German and Italian prisoners who spent time here during World War II. A building out back houses exhibits and the library of Pinal County attorney Ernest McFarland (1894–1984), who went on to become a U.S. senator, Arizona governor, and chief justice of the state supreme court.

On the south side of town, the **Pinal County Historical Museum** begins with pottery and stone tools of early cultures, then portrays the lives of pioneers. An 1880 opera coach reveals a glimpse of olden-day elegance, while the mining and household items show day-to-day existence. News clippings of silent-screen hero Tom Mix relate his fatal car accident south of town. Hangman's nooses frame photos of their victims; among the prison exhibits you'll encounter massive prison registers and a gas chamber chair. Step out the back door to see a blacksmith shop, farm equipment, mining gear, and a homesteader's shack.

The Pima and Maricopa run the **Gila Indian Center** *(Tel 480/963-3981)* on their land west of Florence. Exhibits in the museum interpret the archaeology and culture of Arizona's Native Americans, and you can buy jewelry, baskets, pottery, Hopi kachina dolls, and Navajo rugs in the shop. It's just off I-10 Exit 175, 26 miles southeast of Phoenix. ■

**Florence**

◬ 145 E2

**Visitor information**

florenceaz.org

✉ Florence Visitors Center, 291 N. Bailey St. at 8th St. (P.O. Box 929, Florence, AZ 85232)

☎ 520/868-9433 or 800/437-9433

🕐 Closed Sat.–Sun.


www.co.pinal.az.us

✉ Pinal County Visitor Center, 330 E. Butte Ave. (P.O. Box 967, Florence, AZ 85232)

☎ 520/868-4331 or 888/469-0175

🕐 Closed Sat.–Sun.

**McFarland State Historic Park**

✉ Main & Ruggles Sts.

☎ 520/868-5216

🕐 Closed Tues.–Wed.

💲 $

**Pinal County Historical Museum**

✉ 715 S. Main St.

☎ 520/868-4382

🕐 Closed Mon. & mid-July–end Aug.

💲 Donation

**Fans of movie hero Tom Mix mourned the actor after he died in a car accident here on October 12, 1940. His monument is 17 miles south of Florence on the west side of Arizona 79.**

# Casa Grande Ruins National Monument

THE MASSIVE AND MYSTERIOUS GREAT HOUSE BUILT BY the Hohokam looms over the desert flats near the Gila River. It dates from the early 1300s, toward the end of the culture's existence.

You can try to solve the riddle of this enigmatic Hohokam building (c. 1300) or simply take in its impressive dimensions as you inspect its details.

Archaeologists have speculated that the ruin might have been a combination temple, palace, and storehouse. Openings in the walls appear to correspond with solar and lunar events. From the roof the Hohokam could survey their extensive canal system, used for watering crops. Layers of mud (3,000 tons in all) made from caliche—a desert subsoil whose high lime content helps it dry to concrete-like hardness—constitute the walls, which measure four feet six inches thick at the base, then taper to one foot nine inches near the top. A five-foot base gives the building even greater prominence and a height equivalent to a modern four-story building.

Interior walls divide the space into five chambers. Logs once supported floors and ceilings that gave the central section three stories and the rest two for a total of 11 rooms. In 1697, Spanish priest Father Kino recorded that the building had burned; no wood is in place today. Near the ruins look for the foundations of a surrounding wall and remnants of some of the more than 60 rooms inside the compound.

Rangers lead tours, or you can make a self-guided visit. Signs identify desert plants, and museum exhibits tell of the Hohokam's farming techniques, trade routes, and history. Beautiful pottery and shell jewelry reflect their artistry.

Casa Grande's entrance is 1 mile north of Coolidge. From Florence, head west 9 miles on Arizona 287, then turn left and drive half a mile on Arizona 87. From I-10, take any of the Coolidge exits. ∎

**Casa Grande Ruins National Monument**
www.nps.gov/cagr
🄰 145 E2
✉ Junction of Ariz. 87 & Ariz. 287
☎ 520/723-3172
🅂 $

# Picacho Peak State Park

THE VOLCANIC SPIRE HERE HAS SERVED AS A LANDMARK
for travelers from the earliest tribes to 21st-century motorists. Anglos
picked up the Spanish name, which simply means "peak," without
comprehending it, resulting in its current bilingual pleonasm of
"Peak Peak." Sonoran plants such as saguaro, ocotillo, and paloverde
cover the rocky hillsides. Winter rains often usher in spectacular
springtime displays of such bright flowers as Mexican poppies.

You can walk easy loops at the base
of the peak or climb 1,500 feet on a
steep and challenging trail to the
3,374-foot summit, a 4-mile round-
trip of four or five hours. Historic
markers across the road from the
entrance station commemorate the
Battle of Picacho Pass, considered
to be the westernmost significant
action in the Civil War (see box
below). A "Civil War in the Southwest" reenactment takes place on
the second weekend of March. Two
campgrounds and day-use areas
provide a pleasant break from
travels on busy I-10. ∎

## Battle of Picacho Pass

During the Civil War, the Confederacy made plans to forge
a link across Arizona to southern
California, creating a coast-to-
coast Rebel nation. In January
1862, Confederate general Henry
Sibley and his Texas army marched
to Santa Fe, where he ordered
Capt. Sherod Hunter and 54
cavalry troops farther west to
occupy Tucson. This Hunter did
on February 28, 1862.

The California plans unraveled
when Union loyalists gained full
control there, then sent 2,000 volunteers of the California Column
marching east to Yuma Crossing.

The two sides skirmished at
Stanwix, about 80 miles east of
Yuma Crossing, where Hunter's
forces wounded one of the
Californians before retreating to
Tucson. En route, Hunter posted a
sergeant and nine enlisted men
at Picacho Pass. Union troops under Lt. James Barrett showed up
there a few days later, on April 15.
When the shooting stopped, Barrett and two privates lay mortally
wounded. Knowing that a much
larger Union column was on its
way, the Confederates withdrew to
the Rio Grande, never to return.
The battle for Arizona was over. ∎

Beautiful forests cover the eastern part of Arizona—the rainbow-hued logs of Petrified Forest National Park in the north, the tall conifers of the White Mountains in the center, and the isolated groves on the sky islands in the south.

# Eastern Arizona

**Hitting the jackpot in an Apache reservation casino**

# Eastern Arizona

THE LUSH FORESTS AND MEADOWS THAT SPREAD ACROSS THE WHITE Mountains and the Mogollon Rim will surprise anyone who thinks of Arizona as primarily desert. Here mountains and plateaus formed by geologic upheavals provide a vivid account of the Earth's history.

Rock layers in Petrified Forest National Park tell not only of giant trees but also of primitive plants, giant amphibians, and fierce reptiles in a land far warmer and wetter than today's. Volcanoes on the Colorado Plateau spewed forth lava and cinders, forming lofty summits such as Baldy Peak, the state's second highest at 11,403 feet. Farther south, great blocks of the Earth's crust were thrust upward, creating the Pinaleno Mountains and other sky islands; these remnants of cool-climate forests are now surrounded by desert.

Early tribes left behind masonry pueblos and even one made of petrified wood in Petrified Forest National Park. Around the 16th century, Apache moved in from the east and managed to hold on to their homelands in what are now the White Mountain Apache and San Carlos Apache Indian Reservations. Tribal members maintain traditional beliefs, such as the training of medicine men and coming-of-age Sunrise Dances for young women. Cultural centers and recreation areas are open to the public on both reservations.

The arrival of the railroad in the early 1880s opened eastern Arizona to cattle companies, which ran huge herds across the vast grasslands. Winslow and Holbrook became important ranching centers; indeed, they retain much of their Old West character today. Spanish explorers under Francisco Vásquez de Coronado never discovered the gold and cop-

**The vast meadow of Terry Flat lies below Escudilla Mountain near the northern end of the Coronado Trail.**

per that lay along their trek through the mountains in 1540, but later Mexican and American prospectors found the deposits. You can watch copper miners at work in the enormous open-pit Morenci Mine.

Discover the outdoor pleasures of eastern Arizona—hiking and skiing in the mountains, fishing in the streams and lakes, rafting and kayaking the rivers, and driving through the majestic scenery. The Coronado Trail takes in some of the state's most awe-inspiring views and forests. Another great drive descends into the immense Salt River Canyon and up the other side. Or you can ascend a sky island on the Swift Trail in the Pinaleno Mountains. ■

**At Blue Mesa in the Petrified Forest, clay hills of the Chinle Formation give up fossils of ancient animals and forests.**

Phoenix ★

Area of map detail

NORTHEASTERN ARIZONA
p. 75

NORTH-CENTRAL ARIZONA
p. 91

SOUTH-CENTRAL ARIZONA
p. 143

N E W   M E X I C O

LITTLE PAINTED DESERT
COUNTY PARK

PETRIFIED

Chambers

Sanders

NAVAJO   NATION

RESERVATION

191

40

Puerco

61

87

Homolovi Ruins
State Park

Joseph
City

Painted Desert
Visitor Center

FOREST

NATIONAL

Winslow

Sun Valley

PARK

87

McHOOD
PARK

Little Colorado

Rock
Station

Holbrook

Rainbow
Forest Museum

377

77

Silver Creek

Little Colorado

180

ZUNI
I. R.

191

Clear Creek

Chevelon Canyon

Snowflake

St. Johns

APACHE-

SITGREAVES

Heber

Taylor

Concho

NATIONAL

Overgaard

Shumway

61

LYMAN LAKE
STATE PARK

260

FOREST

Pintail
Lake

60

Casa
Malpais

Mogollon   Rim

FOOL HOLLOW
REC. AREA

Show Low

WHITE   MOUNTAIN

Lakeside

Big
Springs

Pinetop

Springerville

Horseshoe
Lake

260

Eager

Cibecue

77

Hon-Dah

Sunrise
Lake

Greer

10912ft
Escudilla Mt.

60

Carrizo

73

Hawley
Lake

11403ft

APACHE

Baldy
Peak

White   Mountains

APACHE-

Alpine

Salt River
Canyon

60

Kinishba
Ruins

Whiteriver

Salt

White

Fort Apache

RESERVATION

180

SITGREAVES

Black

Hannagan
Meadow

NATIONAL

Blue

SAN   CARLOS

San Carlos

Natanes   Mts.

8786ft
Rose Peak

FOREST

San
Carlos

APACHE

Point of Pines

191

Blue

Apache
Gold Hotel-
Casino-Resort

Apache Cultural
Center

RESERVATION

San Carlos
Lake

Bonita Creek

Eagle Creek

San Francisco

Morenci
Mine

Gila

Coolidge
Dam

70

Gila   Mountains

191

Morenci

Clifton

Bylas

8282ft

Gila

78

Aravaipa
Canyon
Wilderness

Santa Teresa Mts.

Pima

Thatcher

191

Gila

75

77

Klondyke

10086ft
Webb Peak

Discovery
Park

Safford

Duncan

Peloncillo Mts.

Galiuro Mts.

10720ft
Mt. Graham

Lebanon

70

366

CORONADO

Pinaleno Mts.

10028ft
Heliograph Peak

NATIONAL

FOREST

Bonita

CORONADO
NAT.

266

7663ft

FOREST

0                              30 miles
0                    50 kilometers

A                              B                              C

SOUTHERN ARIZONA
p. 195

# Winslow

NAMED AFTER RAILROAD PRESIDENT EDWARD WINSLOW, this town began life as a rail terminal in 1882 and soon prospered with livestock and trade. Route 66 brought America to Winslow's downtown after 1926. Aviator Charles Lindbergh not only designed the airport here but made the inaugural flight from it in 1930. Also in that year, the Santa Fe Railroad opened a railroad resort hotel, La Posada. Winslow had become an important Arizona city and could look forward to a bright future.

Instead, the good times began to unravel. Newer airplanes no longer needed to stop here, travelers had little use for passenger trains or their hotels, and I-40 bypassed Route 66. Tumbleweeds soon seemed to outnumber tourists.

Recently, however, visitors have rediscovered the romance of Route 66 in the historic buildings downtown, and La Posada Hotel once again welcomes guests.

A 1921 commercial building just off Route 66 downtown houses the **Old Trails Museum,** where displays include pottery and other artifacts from the nearby Homolovi pueblos and memorabilia of ranching, territorial doctors, drugstores, Route 66, and La Posada's Harvey Girls. These were single women recruited by the Fred Harvey Company to staff its hotels and restaurants in the West. The model of Brigham City shows the Mormon settlement built in 1876 just north of present-day Winslow, along the Little Colorado River; it had to be abandoned in 1881 when the river proved too tough to tame.

Architect Mary Colter didn't just design **La Posada Hotel** *(303 E. 2nd St., tel 928/289-4366, www.laposada.org);* she constructed a story around it as the grand hacienda of an 18th-century Spanish don. The hotel that helped put Winslow on the map has been painstakingly and lavishly renovated, and you can now enjoy a self-guided tour (see p. 256). More recently, Winslow's name came to the world's attention in the lyrics of the Eagles' 1972 ballad "Take it Easy" ("Well I'm a-standin' on a corner in Winslow, Arizona…"). The song inspired a little park at

**Winslow**

⚠ 177 A6

**Visitor information**

winslowarizona.org

✉ Winslow Chamber of Commerce, 300 W. North Rd., Winslow, AZ 86047 (just north of I-40 Exit 253)

☎ 928/289-2434

**Left: "Whispering Giant," honoring Native Americans, welcomes visitors to the Winslow Chamber of Commerce. Hungarian-born Peter "Wolf" Toth presented a different statue to each of the 50 states; this one dates from 1980.**

the corner of Route 66 (Second Avenue) and Kinsley, where a statue of a guitarist stands in front of a large mural illustrating the girl in a flatbed Ford from the song.

For a scenic place to stop for a picnic or walk, try **Little Painted Desert County Park,** 15 miles north of town off Arizona 87, on the way to the Navajo and Hopi Indian Reservations. **McHood Park** *(Tel 928/289-3411)* offers picnicking, swimming, fishing, and boating at Clear Creek Lake, southeast of town. Boaters can head 2.5 miles up a pretty canyon. From downtown go south for 1.2 miles on Arizona 87, then turn left and drive 4.3 miles on Arizona 99.

Ancient Pueblo people lived in the Winslow area from A.D. 600 to 1400, first in small pit house villages, then in large masonry and adobe pueblos. **Homolovi Ruins State Park** now protects these sites. The pueblos are neither as picturesque nor as well preserved as those in Walnut Canyon (see p. 98) or Wupatki (see p. 103) to the west, but they are far larger. You can get a feel for what a major ruin looks like

before it has been extensively excavated. Exhibits in the visitor center tell of the people who lived here and their connection with the Hopi, who trace some of their clans to Homolovi. Decorated pottery shows the artistry of the ancient people. **Homolovi II,** on a mesa 3.1 miles north of the visitor center, is the largest and most impressive of the sites. More than 1,200 rooms sheltered as many as 3,000 people between 1250 and 1400. The pueblo probably served as a major trade center and a staging ground for migrations to the north. A 0.25-mile trail with interpretive signs loops through the ruins. **Homolovi I** contained more than a thousand rooms; it is 1.5 miles south of the visitor center, then a short walk. You can visit two other sites, too; ask at the visitor center.

Only the cemetery is left at the townsite of **Sunset,** where Mormon pioneers settled in 1876 and stayed 12 years, trying to irrigate crops with the silt-laden Little Colorado River. The cemetery is a half-mile round-trip walk from the visitor center. ■

**Handmade furniture and artwork decorate the ballroom of La Posada Hotel.**

**Old Trails Museum**
- ✉ 212 Kinsley Ave.
- ☎ 928/289-5861
- 🕐 Closed Sun.–Mon. year-round, & Wed. Nov.–Feb.
- 💲 Donation

**Homolovi Ruins State Park**
- ✉ From I-40 Exit 257, go N 1.3 miles on Ariz. 87, turn left & drive 2.1 miles to visitor center
- ☎ 928/289-4106
- 💲 $$ per vehicle

# Holbrook

**Holbrook**
🅰 177 B5
**Visitor information**
azjournal.com
✉ Holbrook Chamber
of Commerce, Old
County Courthouse,
100 E. Arizona St.,
Holbrook, AZ 86025
☎ 928/524-6558 or
800/524-2459

WITHIN A FEW YEARS OF THE RAILROAD'S ARRIVAL HERE in 1881, Eastern investors had set up the nearby Aztec Land and Cattle Company, better known as the Hashknife outfit for the shape of its brand. It became the third largest such company in the United States, with more than 40,000 head of cattle. Hashknife cowboys would gallop through town, guns blazing, having a good time. Sheriffs had to be tough, and good shots, to work here. Today Holbrook, named for a railroad chief engineer, has quieted down, but it has preserved some of its Old West and Route 66 heritage.

**Vintage cars enhance the atmosphere of the Wigwam Motel, a Route 66 icon that still welcomes guests to its cozy interiors.**

Inside the 1898 courthouse the **Navajo County Museum** (*100 E. Arizona St.*) shows how Native Americans, pioneers, ranchers, soldiers, and businesspeople lived and worked. Head upstairs to see the restored courtroom, with its high stamped-metal ceiling, and the law library. No one escaped from the old jail in the dungeonlike basement. The Holbrook Chamber of Commerce, also in the courthouse, provides local and statewide tourist information, including a tour map.

The white stucco tepees of the **Wigwam Motel** (*811 W. Hopi Blvd., tel 928/524-3048*) date from the late 1940s and are still open for business (see p. 255).

Of the five Mormon farming settlements established along the Little Colorado River in the 1870s, only **Joseph City** has survived. You can detour through the little community, the oldest Anglo settlement in Navajo County, 11 miles west of Holbrook between I-40 Exits 274 and 277. ■

# Petrified Forest National Park

A rainbow mirrors the colors of wood turned to stone at Petrified Forest National Park.

THE GENTLE HILLS OF THE PAINTED DESERT CONTAIN A landscape frozen in time for 225 million years. Layers of soft rock, tinted in grays, whites, oranges, and reds, have worn down over the millennia to reveal colored petrified wood and animal fossils.

Floods of that long-ago time carried fallen trees onto a plain, where minerals in the water gradually replaced the wood cells, filling the spaces between them with brilliant quartz and jasper crystals. Fossils from other plants and animals have enabled scientists to piece together a picture of the Triassic Period. Towering pinelike trees grew, along with ferns and palmlike cycads. Massive phytosaurs, resembling today's crocodiles, and large fish-eating amphibians prowled the streams and marshes. A diminutive six-inch shark searched for food in these waters too. Herds of *placerias*—reptiles weighing two to three tons—roamed the land. Small dinosaurs scampered about, ancestors of their giant Jurassic cousins.

In the late 1800s, when people began hauling off the wood and dynamiting logs for crystals, conservationists pushed for a bill to protect the area. Theodore Roosevelt signed the bill in 1906.

Nomadic groups passed through the area about 10,000 years ago and foraged for wild foods. Some later settled, farmed, and built masonry pueblos, but all departed about A.D. 1400. The early Native Americans left behind petroglyphs and potsherds.

The natural landscape is still recovering from overgrazing begun in the late 1800s, but you're apt to see birds, lizards, and perhaps the speedy, antelope-like pronghorn. After sufficient rains, wildflowers blossom from March to May. ■

**Petrified Forest National Park**
www.nps.gov/pefo
177 B5, B6
S Entrance: 19 miles E of Holbrook on US 180
N Entrance: 24 miles NE of Holbrook off I-40 Exit 31
928/524-6228
$$$ per vehicle

# Petrified Forest National Park drive

A 28-mile park road connects the petrified wood areas, archaeological sites, and Painted Desert viewpoints. You could easily spend most of a day here, walking the short trails and stopping at most of the overlooks.

**The well-named Newspaper Rock at Petrified Forest National Park has many stories to tell. Use your imagination!**

Each end of the park has a visitor center with exhibits. You may wish to bring a picnic, since restaurants crop up only at the beginning and end of the drive. The road is open year-round during park hours, but it closes at night and is also closed on Christmas. Dress for the temperature extremes (swings of up to 40°F between day and night) and bright sunshine of the high desert. No accommodations or campgrounds exist within the park.

If you're driving across the state on I-40, you'll save time and distance by starting at the park's south entrance on an eastbound trip and at its north entrance on a westbound one. Otherwise, you may wish to start at the south entrance, as described here, to be sure of having enough time to see the petrified wood, which is concentrated at this end, and then to enjoy the afternoon light over the Painted Desert near the north end of the drive. Hikers can explore wilderness areas of the park. Talk with a ranger for suggestions and to obtain the permit required for overnight trips.

Just inside the south entrance, 19 miles east of Holbrook on US 180, the **Rainbow Forest Museum** ➊ displays skeletons of the strange animals that once lived here and

samples of petrified wood from different types of tree. Staff at the information desk/bookstore proffer suggestions and literature on exploring the park. A "Conscience Wood" exhibit displays stolen pieces returned with remorseful stories and apologies. The **Giant Logs Trail,** behind the museum, follows a half-mile loop among monster-size logs. A bit farther down the drive, the **Long Logs Trail** ➋ provides another close look at massive logs, some more than 100 feet long, on a half-mile loop. At a trail fork, you can turn off for a half-mile round-trip to **Agate House,** a seven-room prehistoric pueblo constructed entirely of petrified wood. The **Crystal Forest Trail** ➌ leads past some of the prettiest and most abundant petrified wood on a half-mile loop. From **Jasper Forest** overlook you get a view of petrified wood that has eroded from hillsides below. A Hashknife cowboy (named after the shape of the brand of the Aztec Land and Cattle Company) once successfully rode his horse across **Agate Bridge**—a petrified log spanning a gully—on a ten-dollar bet. A side road climbs atop **Blue Mesa** ➍ for views of the surrounding badlands; you can descend into the badlands on a one-mile interpretive trail.

Back on the main road, the cone-shaped hills called **The Tepees** stand out, with the

---

🅰 See area map p. 177
► Rainbow Forest Museum
🔄 28 miles
🕐 45 minutes to all day
► Painted Desert Visitor Center

**NOT TO BE MISSED**
- Rainbow Forest Museum & Giant Logs Trail
- Long Logs Trail & Agate House
- Crystal Forest Trail
- Puerco Pueblo
- Painted Desert viewpoints
- Painted Desert Inn

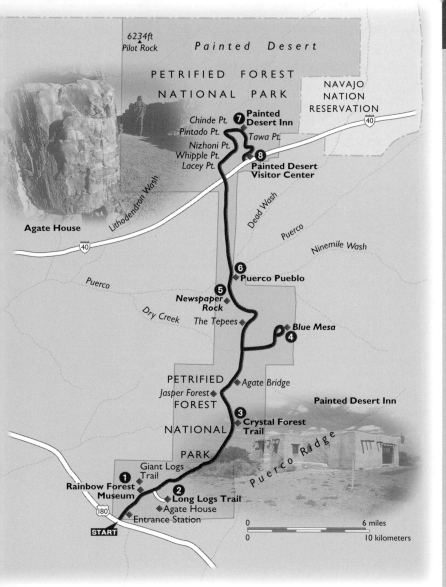

6234ft
Pilot Rock

Painted Desert

PETRIFIED FOREST
NATIONAL PARK

NAVAJO
NATION
RESERVATION

Chinde Pt.
Pintado Pt.
Nizhoni Pt.
Whipple Pt.
Lacey Pt.

**7** Painted Desert Inn

Tawa Pt.

**8** Painted Desert Visitor Center

Lithodendron Wash

Agate House

Dead Wash

Puerco

Ninemile Wash

Puerco

**6** Puerco Pueblo

**5** Newspaper Rock

Dry Creek

The Tepees

**4** Blue Mesa

Agate Bridge

PETRIFIED FOREST

Jasper Forest

Painted Desert Inn

**3** Crystal Forest Trail

NATIONAL

Puerco Ridge

PARK

Giant Logs Trail

**1** Rainbow Forest Museum

**2** Long Logs Trail

Agate House

Entrance Station

START

0          6 miles
0          10 kilometers

minerals in the rock forming bands of colors. Petroglyphs on giant boulders at **Newspaper Rock 5** show animal, human, and geometric designs left by early Native American tribes. About a hundred rooms surround the plaza of **Puerco Pueblo 6**. A kiva (underground chamber) near the northwest corner indicates that ceremonial life played an important role here.

Each of the **viewpoints** at the north end of the drive provides a different panorama of the Painted Desert, whose stark landscape,

nearly devoid of vegetation, reveals its multicolored rock layers. **Painted Desert Inn 7**, built as a traveler's stop with Indian labor and local materials, opened at Kachina Point in 1924. It later expanded into a pueblo-style building with picture windows and Hopi murals. Today you can step inside to see the murals and other historical exhibits. A rim trail goes to Tawa Point, half a mile away. The **Painted Desert Visitor Center 8**, just off I-40 Exit 311 (24 miles northeast of Holbrook), is near the north entrance. ∎

# South to the Mogollon Rim

AS YOU TRAVEL SOUTH ALONG ARIZ. 77 FROM HOLBROOK, the high-desert grasslands yield to sparse pinyon pine and juniper woodlands, then to tall stands of ponderosa pine near the Mogollon Rim. Along the way, there is pioneer history aplenty in Snowflake and outdoor recreation in Show Low and Pinetop-Lakeside.

**Snowflake's** Mormon pioneers had a little fun in the naming of their town, which honors its first leader, Erastus Snow, and a traveling church official, William Flake. Many buildings dating from the early decades of Snowflake, founded in 1878, still stand; some have become museums. The 1893 **John Freeman House** (Closed Sun.) at the corner of Main (Arizona 77) and First North Streets contains period rooms. The Snowflake-Taylor Chamber of Commerce provides a map and information on other places to see.

A poker game gave **Show Low** its name. When two ranch partners found their 100,000-acre spread too small for the two of them in 1870, they decided to play a game of seven-up until one was able to "show low" by drawing the winning card—a deuce of clubs—and taking the ranch. The small **Show Low Historical Society Museum** (541 E. Deuce of Clubs, tel 928/532-7115, closed Sat.–Sun., open by appt. only in winter) displays Native American and pioneer exhibits.

**Pintail Lake** attracts waterfowl and other wildlife 3.5 miles north of town on Arizona 77; turn east at the sign between Mileposts 345 and 346. For swimming, boating, picnicking, and camping, head for **Fool Hollow Recreation Area** (Tel 928/537-3680), just northwest of Show Low off Arizona 260, and **Show Low Lake** (Tel 928/537-4126), 5 miles south of town off Arizona 260.

On the **Mogollon Rim Interpretive Trail** (Tel 928/368-5111) you get a fine view of forested hills stretching to the horizon; the level, self-guided loop is about 1 mile; the first 0.3 mile is paved. The trailhead is just west off Arizona 260; drive 5.5 miles south from Show Low and turn right, or go 3 miles north from the Lakeside Ranger Station and turn left.

**Pinetop-Lakeside's** name describes the pretty countryside here. Staffers at the Lakeside Ranger Station on Arizona 260 can tell you about the lakes, hiking, and camping in the area. ■

**Boaters brave the wild waters of the Salt River.**

**Snowflake**
🏔 177 B5
**Visitor information**
✉ Snowflake-Taylor Chamber of Commerce, 110 N. Main St., Snowflake, AZ 85937
☎ 928/536-4331
🕐 Closed Sun.

**Show Low**
🏔 177 B4
**Visitor information**
www.showlowchamberof commerce.com
✉ Show Low Chamber of Commerce, 951 W. Deuce of Clubs (P.O. Box 1083, Show Low, AZ 85902)
☎ 928/537-2326 or 888/746-9569

**Pinetop**
🏔 177 B4
**Visitor information**
www.pinetoplakeside.cc
✉ Pinetop-Lakeside Chamber of Commerce, P.O. Box 4220, Pinetop, AZ 85935
☎ 928/367-4290 or 800/573-4031
🕐 Closed Sat.–Sun. except in summer

**Lakeside Ranger Station**
www.fs.fed.us/r3/asnf
✉ Rte. 3, Box B-50, Lakeside, AZ 85929
☎ 928/368-5111
🕐 Closed Sat.–Sun.

# White Mountain Apache Reservation

SOME OF ARIZONA'S PRETTIEST COUNTRY BELONGS TO THE White Mountain Apache. Their land of forests, lakes, canyons, and mountains lies between the Mogollon Rim to the north and the Salt River and its Black River tributary to the south. You'll need a tribal permit, sold at stores on and near the reservation, for recreational activities and for driving on unpaved roads.

**Hon-Dah,** Apache for "be my guest," is a large tourist complex 3 miles south of Pinetop-Lakeside at the junction of Arizona 260 and Arizona 73. In addition to a hotel, restaurants, a casino, and an RV park, there is the Hon-Dah Ski and Outdoor Sport store—the best source of recreation information, permits, guides, and supplies on the reservation.

Most of the recreational areas lie in the high country east of Hon-Dah. The 260-acre **Hawley Lake,** at an elevation of 8,300 feet, has a resort *(Tel 928/335-7511, closed in winter)* with cabins, a lodge, an RV park, campground, boat rentals,

and store; it's 11.3 miles east of Hon-Dah on Arizona 260, then south 11 miles on Arizona 473. **Horseshoe Lake** covers 121 acres at an elevation of 8,100 feet. Facilities include a campground, summertime store, and boat rentals *(Tel 928/521-2613)*; head 13.5 miles east from Hon-Dah on Arizona 260, then turn south 1 mile at the sign. **Sunrise Lake,** the largest lake at 891 acres, lies in the northeast corner of the reservation at 9,300 feet. **Sunrise Park Resort** *(Tel 928/735-7669 or 800/772-7669, www.sunriseskipark.com)* features both winter and summer activities. A lodge overlooks the lake, a store

The Salt River separates the lands of the White Mountain Apache to the north from the San Carlos Apache to the south. To enter this magnificent canyon, take a drive along US 60/Arizona 77 between Show Low and Globe.

**White Mountain Apache Reservation**

⊠ 177 A3 & A4, B3 & B4

**Visitor information**
www.wmatoutdoors.com

✉ Hon-Dah Ski & Outdoor Sport, P.O. Box 3250, Pinetop, AZ 85935

☎ 928/369-7669 or 877/226-4868

carries recreation permits and supplies, and there's also a marina and ski area. Visitors can ride a lift to the heights on weekends from the end of May to mid-October.

**Whiteriver,** the main administration town, lies 19 miles south of Hon-Dah. The tribal Game and Fish Department *(Tel 928/338-4385, closed Sat.–Sun.)* provides recreation information and permits. Southwest of the town, signposted off Arizona 73, lies historic **Fort Apache,** with buildings from the frontier days. Drop by the **Apache Cultural Center** *(Tel 928/338-4625, closed Sat. except in summer & Sun., www.wmat.nsn.us)* on the grounds of the fort to see exhibits on the Apache way of life and displays of their arts and crafts. Fort Apache's oldest structure, the commanding officer's building, dates from 1871. Step inside for the tribal tourist office *(Tel 928/338-1230, closed Sat.–Sun.)* and to see the historical exhibits that illustrate the life of the Apache, their work as scouts, and the way they adapted to the Army's presence. When the cavalry rode into the White River

Valley in 1869, troops found peaceful bands of Apache farmers in a gardenlike setting. The Army established a camp here the following year as a base to keep an eye on local Indians while pursuing renegade groups nearby.

**Kinishba Ruins,** about 5 miles away, consist of two large pueblos built and enlarged between A.D. 1232 and 1320. Archaeologists found a variety of pottery and jewelry when they excavated and partly reconstructed the site in the 1930s. Evidence suggests that groups from the Little Colorado, central Gila, and Salt Rivers converged here. Check with the cultural center first before visiting the ruins.

Farther southwest, the highway (US 60/Arizona 77) drops into the spectacular **Salt River Canyon,** 3 miles wide and 1,410 feet deep. Pullouts allow you to stop and admire the views. To see more of the canyon, obtain a recreation permit from the store north of the bridge, then drive the dirt roads downstream along the north shore. In spring, rafters put in for excursions on the Salt River. ■

**Exhibits at the Apache Cultural Center provide a look into Apache beliefs and artistry.**

# San Carlos
# Apache Reservation

SOUTH FROM THE SALT AND BLACK RIVERS, THE LANDSCAPE
gradually changes from one extreme to the other. Cool mountain
forests give way to dry woodlands and grasslands, which in turn are
replaced farther south by a cactus-studded desert.

The administrative town of San
Carlos is the largest community
on the reservation, but it lacks
charm. You can get information
and buy permits at the San Carlos
Recreation and Wildlife Department, on Moon Base Road just
north of US 70, about 1.5 miles east
of the Arizona 170 junction. Other
sources for permits include the San
Carlos Lake Store and businesses in
towns off the reservation. No permit is required for the paved roads,
such as the drive to San Carlos
Lake, but travel on unpaved roads
requires one, as do recreation
activities.

Exhibits in the **San Carlos
Apache Cultural Center**
*(Tel 928/475-2894)* tell the tribe's
history from an Apache perspective.
Here you'll learn about Apache
spiritual beginnings, cultural traditions, migrations across the Southwest, confinement to reservations
in the 19th century, contemporary
life, and aspirations for the future.
A gift shop sells local art and
crafts. The cultural center is located
on the north side of US 70 near
Milepost 272, just east of the Arizona 170 junction.

You can stay, eat, gamble, and
play golf at the **Apache Gold
Hotel-Casino-Resort** *(Tel
928/425-7800 or 800/272-2438,
www.apachegoldcasinoresort.com)*
on US 70 just 7 miles east of Globe.
**San Carlos Lake** on the Gila
River attracts visitors year-round.
Covering 19,500 acres when full,
the lake is the largest within the

state—23 miles long and approximately 2 miles wide. The 880-foot-
high **Coolidge Dam,** dedicated
in 1930 by President Calvin Coolidge, is worth a stop for the view of
the dam and canyon. Paved roads to
the lake branch off US 70 south
of the Arizona 170 junction and
near Bylas.

The San Carlos Store, 9.5 miles
south of US 70 and 2 miles north of
the dam, carries supplies, permits,
and gas; it also offers a small park
for recreational vehicles. A
paved road leads 1 mile from
the store to Soda Canyon Point
Campground and a marina with
boat rentals. ■

**San Carlos Apache
Reservation**

◪ 177 A2 & A3, B2 &
B3

**Visitor information**

✉ San Carlos
Recreation &
Wildlife Dept., P.O.
Box 97, San Carlos,
AZ 85550

☎ 928/475-2343

🕐 Closed Sun.

**In a photo from
the 1800s, Amos
Gustina of Bylas,
a tiny reservation
community, holds
the violin now on
display in the San
Carlos Apache
Cultural Center.**

# The Apache

**An Apache woman dresses up for an 1898 portrait.**

Calling themselves Indeh (the people), the Apache share an Athapascan heritage with the Navajo. The ancestors of both tribes may have crossed the Bering Strait land bridge about 6,000 years ago and eventually migrated to the Great Plains, then to the Southwest. By the end of the 16th century, loose groups had settled in what is now Arizona—the Navajo in the Four Corners region, the Western Apache in the central and eastern mountains, and the Chiricahua Apache in the southeastern mountains.

incompatible groups together on the same reservation caused friction, sparking escapes by bands who terrorized the Southwest. The Chiricahua Apache met a particularly sad fate. Unlike the Navajo, who had been allowed to return to their homeland after deportation, the Chiricahua were forced from their lands, never to return. The Western Apache fared best, retaining extensive homelands in eastern Arizona and smaller lands in central Arizona.

Today the Apache live and work like most other Arizo-

The early Apache lived a nomadic life with few possessions. The men hunted and the women foraged for wild plants. Small conical huts covered with animal skins provided shelter. Later, the tribespeople learned from their Navajo or pueblo neighbors how to cultivate corn, beans, and squash to supplement their diet. Horses, acquired from raids on the Spanish and later on Mexican and Anglo soldiers and settlers, gave the Apache great speed and range, which they used with skill to raid other tribes, the Spanish, and the Anglos.

So proficient were Apache warriors that they nearly always prevailed in conflicts. Their tenacity at holding onto their lands forestalled Anglo settlement long after other tribes had made peace. Only with the surrender of Geronimo in 1886 did travelers and settlers feel safe in the region. Much of the credit for the eventual success of the U.S. Army has to be given to the Apache scouts. These men voluntarily enlisted with the Army, using their traditional warrior and tracking skills to hunt down renegade bands of Apache. In exchange, the scouts received pay, horses and other valuables, and experience with a new way of life.

The federal government committed many blunders through dishonest or misguided dealings with the Apache. Attempts to force

nans, yet many of the tribe still speak Apache and follow traditional ways. Boys may train under medicine men to learn the prayers, rituals, and medicinal plants used for healing ceremonies and other rites. Young women may mark their passage to adulthood with the Sunrise Dance, a difficult ordeal that lasts four days. Apache spirit dancers, also known as crown dancers, wear masks and crowns of sticks in Sunrise Dances and other religious ceremonies as representatives of the *gaan*—friendly mountain spirits who bless and protect the Apache. Staffers at cultural centers can tell you of dances open to the public, as well as rodeos and other events.

The Apache weave very fine baskets—one of the few articles suited to an itinerant lifestyle. Women make beautiful buckskin clothing, worn at Sunrise Dances. Artists and craftspeople create paintings, crown dancer figures, and beadwork, which you'll find in galleries and cultural center gift shops. ■

**Above: Young Apache women still undergo the coming-of-age Sunrise Ceremonies. Below: Apache leader Geronimo (1829–1909), on the right, with some of his braves at his surrender, September 4, 1886.**

# Safford

FARMERS HAVE LONG TILLED THE SOIL OF THE GILA RIVER
Valley—Mogollon, Hohokam, and Salado in early times and, from
the 1870s till the present, Anglo colonists. Fields of cotton, together
with some wheat, barley, and other crops, now cover the bottomland.
The town of Safford, named for the third territorial governor, makes
a pleasant base for exploring nearby mountain and wilderness areas.

**Safford**
A 177 B1
**Visitor information**
www.graham-chamber.com
✉ Graham County
Chamber of
Commerce, 1111
Thatcher Blvd.,
Safford, AZ 85546
☎ 928/428-2511 or
888/837-1841

**Discovery Park**
www.discoverypark.com
✉ 1651 Discovery
Park Blvd.
☎ 928/428-6260
🕐 Closed Sun.–Mon.
💲 $$

Some of the wonders of the uni-
verse are unveiled at **Discovery
Park.** Gaze at an image of nearby
Mount Graham projected by a
camera obscura, or see the heavens
at night through a 20-inch tele-
scope once used on Kitt Peak. The
Polaris Space Flight Simulator takes
you on a wild ride through the
solar system. A narrated train ride
loops through the desert with in-
formation on the area's history, ge-
ology, vegetation, and wildlife. A
wildlife sanctuary contains a variety
of habitats with trails and viewing
blinds. Three new buildings—the
Mining Museum, the Agricultural
Museum, and the Tunnel of Time
(prehistory and history)—are
scheduled to open soon. Tours of
the Mount Graham International

Observatory depart some days from
mid-May to mid-November. From
US 70 on the west side of town,
turn south on 20th Avenue to its
end; or, from US 191 south of
town, turn west on Discovery Park
Boulevard and go to its end at 20th
Avenue, then turn left.

Journey back in time at the
**Graham County Historical
Society Museum** in Thatcher,
just northwest of Safford (*US 70 &
4th Ave., tel 928/348-0470, closed
Sun. & Wed.–Fri.*). Rooms in a 1917
school illustrate early history, pio-
neer life, ranching, farming, school
spirit, and community pride.

All that cotton in the Safford
area comes to **ginning mills** dur-
ing the October to December har-
vest. You can tour one by calling

ahead to the Safford Valley Cotton Growers Co-op *(Tel 928/428-0714)*, just off US 191 in Safford or to the Glenbar Gin *(Tel 928/485-9255)*, just west of Pima.

For dramatic views of the mountain ranges and valleys, hiking, picnicking, and camping, it's hard to beat the **Swift Trail** (Arizona 366), a scenic drive that climbs onto the long ridge of the Pinaleno Mountains, southwest of Safford. Start from US 191, about 7 miles south of Safford, or drive 26 miles north from I-10 Exit 352 to the start. The first 21 miles of the trail are paved, followed by a 14-mile gravel section that is open from mid-April to mid-November.

The Pinalenos are crowned by **Mount Graham** (10,720 feet), its summit towering more than 7,000 feet above the surrounding desert. On the way up, the cactus and mesquite of the upper Sonoran Desert change to conifer forests of ponderosa pine, Douglas and white fir, aspen, and Engelmann spruce. The summit has been closed to the public to protect the Mount Graham red squirrel, a subspecies that lives only in the Pinalenos. Construction of new buildings at the nearby Mount Graham International Observatory faced bitter opposition (since partly resolved) from conservationists and from Apache, who feared loss of access to this sacred area. You can visit the observatory on tours from Discovery Park.

**Heliograph Peak** (10,028 feet), near the east end of the mountains, and **Webb Peak** (10,086 feet), farther west, provide panoramas of southeastern Arizona. You'll normally need to walk the last 2.2 miles of unpaved road to Heliograph; likewise, you can hike the 1-mile (one way) **Webb Peak Trail** or walk the last 1.7 miles of road to Webb. Contact the Safford Ranger District for recreation information.

You must obtain a permit in advance to enter **Aravaipa Canyon Wilderness,** even for day hikes. The 11-mile canyon has a trailhead at each end. Contact the Bureau of Land Management office in Safford for directions. ■

**Safford Ranger District, Coronado National Forest**
www.fs.fed.us/r3/coronado
504 5th Ave., Safford (P.O. Box 709, Safford, AZ 85548)
928/428-4150
Closed Sat.–Sun.

**Bureau of Land Management**
safford.az.blm.gov
711 14th Ave., Safford, AZ 85546
928/348-4400
Closed Sat.–Sun.

**Cottonwood trees and other lush vegetation stand in welcome contrast to the dry, rocky cliffs of Aravaipa Canyon.**

# A drive on the Coronado Trail

The paved highway that retraces Francisco Vásquez de Coronado's epic journey in 1540 provides one of the greatest driving adventures in the West, with wonderful panoramas and beautiful alpine country along the way. Many back roads, camping areas, hiking trails, mountain streams, and lakes lie near the drive, which is equally scenic in both directions. Directions here are given from the south, starting in Clifton.

With some 460 curves in the section between Morenci and Alpine, this is not a trip for those in a hurry. Although you could travel the 123 miles in four hours nonstop, the scenery calls for a more leisurely pace. Hannagan Meadow and Alpine offer accommodations, and you'll find plenty of campgrounds. The Apache-Sitgreaves National Forest *(Tel 928/333-4301, www.fs.fed.us/r3/asnf)* is steward for most of the land along the way. It's best to stock up on food and gas before setting out. Snow can close the section between Morenci and Hannagan Meadow from mid-December to mid-March, when cross-country skiers come out to enjoy the winter landscape.

**Clifton** ❶ bears several reminders of its mining past. Stop by the Greenlee Chamber of Commerce *(Tel 928/865-3313, closed Sat.–Sun.)*, in a 1913 train depot beside US 191, for information and to see the Copper Head locomotive and old jail across the highway. Turn left up Chase Creek Street, lined with early 20th-century buildings, for exhibits on the area and its mines at **Greenlee Historical Museum** *(317 Chase Creek St., tel 928/865-3115, call for hours)*.

US 191 switchbacks northwest up to the modern mining town of **Morenci,** where you may be able to go on a tour of the copper mine run by Phelps Dodge *(Tel 928/865-1180 or 800/882-1291, closed Sun., www.phelps dodge.com)*. Continuing higher, you'll reach an overlook on the right for the open-pit **Morenci Mine** ❷. At 3 miles wide and 6 miles long, it's one of the world's largest man-made holes. Past the mining operation, the highway enters the forest and ascends higher into the mountains. **Cherry Lodge Picnic Area,** 20 miles from Clifton on the left between Mileposts 178 and 179, is a pleasant spot to rest; a campground lies across the highway. **Rose Peak** ❸ has a great panorama from a fire lookout on its 8,786-foot sum-

mit; you can hike up a 1-mile trail *(one way)* or drive the rough 1.4-mile road near Milepost 207 *(high-clearance vehicle needed)*.

The highway climbs up the Mogollon Rim to **Blue Vista** ❹, a 9,184-foot-high overlook from which you can see countless ridges and mountains, including Mount Graham, 70 miles southwest in the Pinalenos; the turnoff is on the left near Milepost 225. Splendid forests of spruce, fir, and aspen blanket either side of the highway in the **Hannagan Meadow** ❺ area, 73 miles from Clifton. There's a year-round lodge *(Tel 928/339-4370, www .hannaganmeadow.com)*, plus campgrounds, trails, and cross-country skiing nearby.

Another 22 miles north takes you to the town of **Alpine** *(928/339-4330, www.alpine-az.com)*, where you'll find lodging, restaurants, and supplies. **Escudilla Mountain** (10,912 feet), a bit farther north still, is Arizona's third highest summit and a wilderness area. As US 191/180 drops to the high-desert area around Springerville, on the left you'll pass **Nelson Reservoir,** a 60-acre lake popular for boating and fishing. **Springerville** ❻ marks the end of the trail; the staff at the **Round Valley Chamber of Commerce** *(318 E. Main St., tel 928/333-2123, www.springerville.com)* can recommend things to see and do in the area. (See p. 194 for the principal sights.) ∎

---

🔼 See area map p. 177
▶ Clifton
🔁 123 miles
🕐 4 hours plus stops
▶ Springerville

**NOT TO BE MISSED**
- Clifton
- Morenci Mine
- Blue Vista
- Hannagan Meadow

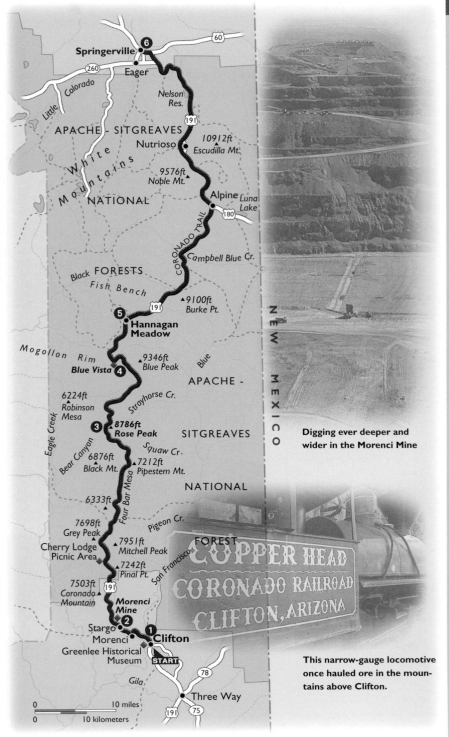

Digging ever deeper and
wider in the Morenci Mine

This narrow-gauge locomotive
once hauled ore in the mountains above Clifton.

COPPER HEAD
CORONADO RAILROAD
CLIFTON, ARIZONA

## More places to visit in eastern Arizona

### CASA MALPAIS

Just north of Springerville, this prehistoric pueblo (whose Spanish name means "House of the Badlands") boasts some unusual features. The Mogollon culture built it between A.D. 1260 and 1440 at the edge of a lava flow—and on top of more than a hundred underground cracks that once served as ritual and burial chambers. (Sacred to modern pueblo tribes, the rooms are not open to the public.) A **Great Kiva** (ceremonial chamber) covering 62 feet by 55 feet (possibly roofed) and an enclosure that may have been an astronomical observatory reinforce the view that this pueblo was a major trade and ceremonial center. The main ruin stood two and three stories high, with more than 120 rooms. Look for rock art and the unusual masonry stairways; normally wood ladders were used. You may enter the site only on tours, which take about 1.5

**Rock art at the end of the Ultimate Petroglyph Trail, Lyman Lake State Park**

hours, with 1.5 miles of walking and a climb of 250 feet. Visitors are asked to call ahead for tour times, then meet at the **Casa Malpais Museum** in Springerville before continuing to the site.
🅰 177 C4  ✉ museum, 318 E. Main St., Springerville ☎ 928/333-5375, www.casamalpais.com 💲 $$ (museum free)

### GREER

Evergreen and aspen forests surround this village, set in a pretty valley at an elevation of 8,500 feet in the White Mountains. It's a popular summer retreat and a winter recreation center. Trails and fishing lakes lie close at hand. When the snow arrives, people set off on cross-country skis or head for the slopes of nearby Sunrise Ski Area. Luxurious lodges, rustic cabins, and campgrounds afford places to stay. Mormons settled here in 1879 and later named their community for one of its pioneers.

Two extraordinary residents, author James Willard Schultz (1859–1947) and his artist son "Lone Wolf" (1882–1970), lived in a cabin that has since become the **Butterfly Lodge Museum** (Cty. Rd. 1126; turn E from Ariz. 373 0.5 mile S of the Circle B Market, tel 928/735-7514, closed Mon–Thurs. & autumn– spring, $). Inside, you can learn about the elder Schultz, who married a Blackfoot woman, explored the West, and wrote 37 adventure stories, and see works by his son, who portrayed the West in paintings and sculpture. To reach Greer, head west 16 miles from Springerville on Arizona 260, then turn south and drive for 5 miles on Arizona 373.
🅰 177 C4  **Visitor information**
✉ 318 E. Main St., Springerville (P.O. Box 31, Springerville, AZ 85938)
☎ 928/333-2123, www.az-tourist.com
🕐 Closed Sun.

### LYMAN LAKE STATE PARK

Junipers and other high-desert vegetation surround a 1,500-acre lake fed by the Little Colorado River. People come to Lyman Lake for boating, swimming, picnicking, and camping. Short trails lead across a peninsula to petroglyph panels. On summer weekends, rangers conduct tours to another petroglyph site and to Rattlesnake Point Pueblo; reservations are recommended. A store rents boats and sells groceries from April through October. Look for bison roaming near the park's entrance.
🅰 177 C4  ✉ 18 miles N of Springerville on US 191/180 (between Mileposts 380 and 381)
☎ 928/337-4441 💲 $$ vehicle fee ■

Native American, Spanish, Mexican, and Anglo heritages have created a rich tapestry of culture and art in this region. The Sonoran Desert and sky islands harbor an exceptional diversity of birds and other wildlife.

# Southern Arizona

Prickly pear cactus

# Southern Arizona

SOUTHERN ARIZONA'S MANY HISTORIC SIGHTS AND PLACES OF NATURAL splendor make it an especially enjoyable region to visit. The variety of scenic beauty extends to many levels—underground in Kartchner Caverns and Colossal Cave, above ground in desert and mountain settings, and in the heavens with astronomy exhibits and observatories. Across the region, rugged mountains thrust high above the desert. Isolated cool-climate forests cover the four highest ranges, all with peaks above 9,000 feet: the Santa Catalinas, the Santa Ritas, the Huachucas, and the Chiricahuas. The canyons and summits of these "sky islands" provide homes for a profusion of plants and animals.

The stately saguaro cactuses of the Sonoran Desert cover much of southern Arizona's landscape, along with a profusion of other unusual plants. Although rainfall may be scant—just 11 inches annually in Tucson, for example—it occurs during two seasons only, with winter and summer showers. The resulting greenery may come as a surprise. Wildflowers stage a colorful show in spring, especially when winter rains have been plentiful. So remarkable are the plants and wildlife of the Sonoran Desert that Saguaro National Park and Organ Pipe Cactus National Monument were created to protect them.

The Hohokam settled along the rivers, channeling water to their fields of corn, beans, squash, and cotton. For reasons still unknown,

the Hohokam's sophisticated culture collapsed between A.D. 1300 and 1450. Their descendants likely became the modern O'odham (AH-tomb), who carried on with a simpler farming existence along rivers as the Akimel O'odham (also known as Pima) or at springs

**A winter storm in the mountains frosts an elusive mountain lion.**

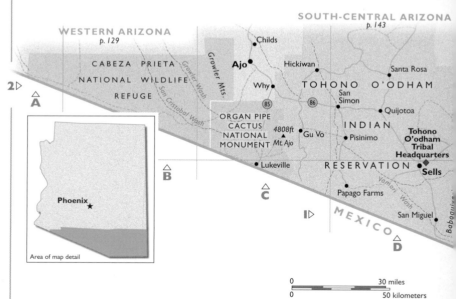

in the Sonoran Desert as the Tohono O'odham (formerly called Papago).

Spanish explorers had entered the region on unsuccessful quests for gold as early as 1539, but no attempt at a permanent Spanish presence was made until Jesuit priest Eusebio Francisco Kino arrived as a missionary in 1691. His efforts led to the founding of missions such as San Xavier del Bac, where the O'odham still worship. Presidios (fortified towns) at Tucson, Tubac, and elsewhere provided some security, but neither the Spanish

**Chilis, ocotillo branches, and pottery form a Southwestern motif at a shop in Tubac.**

nor their Mexican successors managed to subjugate the Apache, who periodically terrorized both Indian and European settlements.

Americans poured in during the late 1800s and struck silver in places such as Tombstone, famed for its shootout at the OK Corral. Vast copper deposits, still mined today, proved more valuable in the long term, giving Arizona its nickname: the Copper State. ■

*Viewed from "A" Mountain, Tucson catches the last of the day's sun.*

# Tucson

TUCSON CLAIMS TO BE THE OLDEST CONTINUOUSLY inhabited settlement in the United States. Hohokam farmers had arrived here by the first century A.D. Their Akimel O'odham successors called their village, at the foot of Sentinel Peak, Stjukshon (spring at the foot of a black mountain). Spanish soldiers arrived in 1775 and built a presidio, adapting the name to Tucson. The settlement became a Mexican village and finally the second largest city in Arizona, with more than 700,000 residents.

**Tucson**

🅰 197 E2

**Visitor information**

www.visittucson.org

✉ Tucson Visitors Center, 110 S. Church Ave., Tucson, AZ 85701

☎ 520/624-1817 or 800/638-8350

**University of Arizona Visitor Center**

🅰 201 C2

www.arizona.edu

✉ 1 block W on University Blvd. from Campbell Ave.

☎ 520/621-5130

🕐 Closed Sat. p.m. (all day in summer) & Sun.

Visitors to Tucson can explore the town for quite a while before they run out of things to do. Plenty of memorable places to visit lie in the city or within an hour's drive. Nature is never far away, from alpine forests to the Sonoran Desert's saguaro cactuses and other intriguing plants. The 9,157-foot-high Mount Lemmon of the Santa Catalinas stands just to the north, offering scenic drives, challenging hiking trails, and the United States' southernmost ski area.

In the city itself, the Old Pueblo retains its rich and lengthy heritage. Visitors can step into old adobe buildings for a glimpse of the past, join in the lively arts scene, or ex-

plore the frontiers of science: Tucson reaches for the stars with its claim to be the "astronomy capital of the world."

The **University of Arizona,** east of downtown, opened in 1891 with 32 students housed and taught in a single building, now known as Old Main. The students number around 35,000 today, and the university has some excellent museums and a lively cultural life. The visitor center, on the east side of the campus, offers maps, tours, and listings of things to see and do. (Signs direct you to visitor parking around the edges of campus—the central area is closed to motor traffic.)

North across University Boule-

some evenings, the public gets a chance to use the facility's 16-inch telescope.

The **Arizona State Museum** (*Tel 520/621-6302, www.statemuseum.arizona.edu*), a great place to learn about Arizona's Native Americans, is on the west side of campus near University Boulevard and Park Avenue. Take time to experience the outstanding "Paths of Life: American Indians of the Southwest" exhibit; it conveys the cultural traditions and contemporary lifestyles of ten Native American peoples of Arizona and northern Mexico. Temporary exhibits appear, too. A gift shop sells books and Native American crafts.

The **Arizona Historical Society Museum** (*949 E. 2nd St., tel 520/628-5774, w3.arizona.edu/~azhist*) brings the territorial years to life. Although not part of the university, it lies just west, across Park Avenue from the campus. (Park in the garage one block west on Second Street.)

vard from the visitor center, the **Flandrau Science Center and Planetarium** (*Tel 520/621-7827, www.flandrau.org*) presents hands-on science exhibits, astronomy programs in the planetarium, and glittering mineral displays. On

**A gently sloping pathway winds past works in the Tucson Museum of Art.**

Next door, the 1866 adobe **Stevens-Duffield House** displays Precolumbian, Spanish colonial, and folk art; and also has a restaurant. If you walk to the street in front of the Stevens House and turn right, you'll reach the **Corbett House,** a Mission Revival bungalow dating from 1906–07; step inside to see the Arts and Crafts furnishings.

Return to the courtyard in front of the museum and walk east to **La**

**Richly detailed art from Spanish times fills the Tucson Museum of Art & Historic Block.**

The **University of Arizona Art Museum** *(Tel 520/621-7567, closed Sat., artmuseum.arizona.edu),* part of the Fine Arts Center in the northwestern part of the campus, features Renaissance, later European, American, and contemporary art. Student and visiting shows appear too. (Visitor parking is north across Speedway.)

The **Center for Creative Photography** *(Tel 520/621-7968, www.creativephotography.org),* just southeast of the art museum, showcases of some of the world's greatest photographers, among them Richard Avedon, Ansel Adams, and Paul Strand. The center has a research library and small gift shop.

Galleries in the main building of the downtown **Tucson Museum of Art & Historic Block** display modern and contemporary art along with visiting exhibits. To the west, across a courtyard with a 150-year-old olive tree, is the **Goodman Pavilion of Western Art.** Among the permanent and visiting collections here, you'll find paintings of landscapes and cowboy life along with bronzes.

**Tucson Museum of Art & Historic Block**

🅐 201 C2

www.tucsonarts.com

✉ 140 N. Main Ave.

☎ 520/624-2333

💲 $$

**Casa Cordova,** an adobe dating from about 1848; restored rooms illustrate life in the mid- and late 1800s, along with some historical exhibits and the seasonal El Nacimiento, an elaborate tableau of biblical and Mexican scenes, usually on display from November to March.

Regional and exotic flora appear in an array of beautiful settings, including a tropical greenhouse, in **Tucson Botanical Gardens.** You'll find something of interest,

from cactuses and succulents to an exhibit of Native American crops or a xeriscape (dry) garden. If you bring children with you, don't miss the children's discovery garden. Themed areas feature gardens devoted to irises, wildflowers, and plants to attract butterflies. Pick up a self-guiding brochure; a tour is offered most days, except in summer. The gardens organize seasonal events and sales, and there's a library and gift shop. ∎

**Tucson Botanical Gardens**

🅰 201 D2

www.tucsonbotanical.org

✉ 2150 N. Alvernon Way

☎ 520/326-9686 or 520/326-9255 (recording)

💲 $$

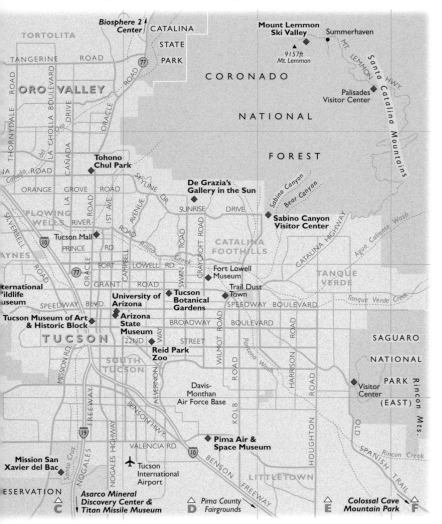

# Tucson historical walking tour

This walk gives insight into the lives of Spaniards, Mexicans, and Anglos in early Tucson. Beginning in El Presidio Historic District, the site of the 1775 presidio, the tour then loops south to the Barrio Histórico District. Guided tours are scheduled at the Tucson Museum of Art and the Sosa-Carillo-Frémont House Museum.

Start the walk at the **Tucson Museum of Art & Historic Block ①** at 140 North Main Avenue (see p. 200). You can park in the museum's lot west across Main (the entrance is on Paseo Redondo) or in one of the other parking lots nearby. The museum doesn't open until 10 a.m. (noon on Sundays), so you may prefer to wait until the end of your walk to go inside.

**Old Town Artisans,** in an 1862 adobe across Meyer, carries Southwestern arts and crafts. From the northwest corner of the historic block, cross Washington to the **Sam Hughes House.** Hughes came to Tucson for his health, then became an important businessman and developer. He moved into the house in 1864 and expanded it considerably to accommodate his 15 children. (It is not open to the public.)

North one block and across Main, the 1900 **Steinfeld Mansion,** with its Spanish mission-style architecture of brick and stucco, shows how the wealthy lived in Tucson at the beginning of the 20th century. French stone-

mason Jules le Flein came to Tucson in the 1890s to work on the St. Augustine Cathedral; then, in 1900, he built his house on Court Avenue—now **El Charro** Mexican Restaurant, founded by Flein's daughter Monica in 1922—of dark stone from Sentinel Peak. The adobe **Stork's Nest,** one block south, served as Tucson's first maternity ward.

Continue south on Court, turn left on Alameda, then go right on Church to the domed 1928 **Pima County Courthouse ②,** a colorful mix of Moorish, Spanish, and Southwestern architecture. A small exhibit of the original presidio wall lies inside the Assessor-Treasurer office (turn left from the front courtyard). Two blocks farther south on Church, you can take a break at the small **Veinte de Agosto Park,** which commemorates the founding of the presidio on August 20, 1775. An equestrian statue of General Francisco "Pancho" Villa stands in the center. You may wish to stop by the **Tucson Visitors Center** across Broadway in La Placita Village.

From the park, head east one block on Broadway past the **Charles O. Brown House,** now El Centro Cultural de Las Americas, built on Jackson in 1858 and extended to Broadway between 1868 and 1877. Around the corner and two blocks south on Stone, you'll reach the 1896 **St. Augustine Cathedral ❸,** remodeled in the late 1920s with an attractive sandstone facade styled after the Cathedral of Querétaro in Mexico. Look for Southwestern elements along with religious designs.

Turn right after the Police Station (check out the John Dillinger exhibits in the lobby) onto Cushing and pass the **Montijo House,** built by a Mexican ranching family in the 1860s, then re-modeled in Victorian style in the 1890s. Joseph Ferrin ran a store in the late 1800s in what is now the **Cushing Street Bar & Grill.** Next door and around the corner on Meyer is the **America West**

Opposite: The tiled dome of Pima County Courthouse adds color to downtown.

**Gallery,** home to rancher Francisco Carillo in the 1860s; you can go inside to see the collection of exotic antiques from around the world and primitive art. **Teatro Carmen,** across the street, opened in 1915 as a Spanish-language theater. A block west on Simpson is a **Tortilla Factory,** where you can watch tortillas being made in the morning.

**El Tiradito ❹,** or the Wishing Shrine, marks the grave of young Juan Oliveras. He was caught having an affair with his mother-in-law, and his father-in-law killed him in 1880. On account of his sins, Juan couldn't be buried in consecrated ground, so people laid him to rest here, lit candles, and prayed for his

◪ See area map p. 201
► Tucson Museum of
Art & Historic Block
◖ 3.3 miles
◷ Half a day
► Tucson Museum of
Art & Historic Block

**NOT TO BE MISSED**

• Tucson Museum of
Art & Historic Block
• Pima County
Courthouse
• St. Augustine
Cathedral
• El Tiradito
• Sosa-Carillo-
Frémont House

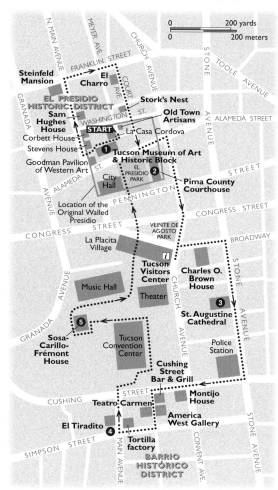

soul. A custom developed that if a candle lit on the grave burned down to its base, the candle lighter's wish would be granted.

Follow the sidewalk around the Exhibit Hall and Arena of the Tucson Convention Center to the **Sosa-Carillo-Frémont House** ❺ *(151 S. Granada Ave., tel 520/622-0956, closed Sun.–Tues.).* The Carillo family built this adobe residence around 1880 on land purchased from the Sosas, then rented it in 1881 to the fifth territorial governor, John C. Frémont. From the Frémont House, walk up the steps alongside the Music Hall to a small park, then turn left (north) through La Placita Village, a group of modern shops and offices styled to look like a Mexican village. Continue across two footbridges to **El Presidio Park,** where Spanish soldiers drilled and held fiestas two centuries ago. From here, the Tucson Museum of Art & Historic Block is just a short stroll north. ∎

**Left: Check out the details on the sandstone facade of St. Augustine Cathedral before stepping inside to see the stained glass and other artwork. Below: The big rodeo parade of La Fiesta de los Vaqueros relies entirely on muscle power.**

## More places to visit in Tucson

### DE GRAZIA'S GALLERY IN THE SUN

Arizona artist Ettore "Ted" De Grazia died in 1982, but his gallery remains open as a museum. Born in the Morenci mining district, De Grazia was fascinated by the colors and cultures of the Southwest. Though best known for his paintings, he used a variety of other media and even wrote some books. Wander through the many rooms to see how De Grazia explored different themes and techniques. Don't miss the 1950s open-roofed Mission in the Sun. Local artists exhibit in the Little Gallery from November through April. From downtown, head east 4 miles on Broadway; turn left and go 6 miles north on Swan Road. ⚒ 201 D3 ✉ 6300 N. Swan Rd. ☎ 520/299-9191 or 800/545-2185

### REID PARK ZOO

Come here to meet both the big African animals and some lesser known creatures, such as anteaters. The South American loop has a

The adobe Mission in the Sun is dedicated to Our Lady of Guadalupe.

walk-in aviary among its dozen exhibits. Vegetation from many lands provides natural habitats. From downtown, go east 3.5 miles on 22nd Street; the entrance is between Country Club Road and Alvernon Way. ⚒ 201 D2 ☎ 520/791-4022 $ $$

### TOHONO CHUL PARK

As its Tohono O'odham name (meaning Desert Corner) suggests, here you can enjoy the desert in the city. Nature trails weave through 48 acres, where you're likely to see birds and other wildlife. A variety of plants grow in themed gardens, including an ethno-botanical garden, a hummingbird garden, and one for children. A wall beside the demonstration garden explains the geology of the Santa Catalinas. Art shows in the Exhibit House reflect Southwestern and Mexican themes. From the junction of Oracle and Ina Roads in northwest Tucson, head west one block on Ina, then turn north (right) at the first light. ⚒ 201 C3 ✉ 7366 N. Paseo del Norte ☎ 520/575-8468 (recording), 520/742-6455 (office), www.tohonochulpark.org $ Donation ∎

# West from Tucson

**International
Wildlife Museum**

🅰 201 C2

www.thewildlifemuseum.org

✉ 4800 W. Gates
Pass Rd. (The
section between
Tucson and the
museum is fine for
large vehicles.)

☎ 520/617-1439
(recording) or
520/629-0100
(office)

💲 $$

A SCENIC DRIVE WEST FROM TUCSON OVER GATES PASS
(cars only—not suitable for RVs or vehicles with trailers) makes a
fine start to a day trip that takes in the rugged Tucson Mountains and
the following attractions, including the outstanding Arizona–Sonora
Desert Museum (see pp. 209–210).

Closest to the city, 5 miles west of
I-10 on Gates Pass Road, is the
**International Wildlife
Museum.** Taxidermists have
prepared and mounted mammals,
birds, and insects of more than 400
species, displayed here in dioramas
and natural-looking settings. A
30-foot "mountain" forms the
centerpiece for the wild sheep and
goats. Dazzling butterflies and
beetles show the beauty of the
insect world. A nocturnal exhibit

re-creates life on a desert evening.
You can also see and learn about
unusual wildlife, such as rare
birds-of-paradise from Papua New
Guinea and passenger pigeons,
once abundant in the United States
but now extinct. Whatever your
age, try out the touch and
interactive exhibits.

Unless you have a large rig, head
west on Gates Pass Road over the
pass, where a scenic overlook on the
right is worth a stop. About 11

miles from Tucson, turn left on Kinney Road, then left again in less than a mile for **Old Tucson Studios,** which replicates the town's Wild West years. The site started out as a movie set for the Columbia Pictures film *Arizona* in 1939 and has hosted hundreds of movie and television features since. Adobe and frontier buildings line the dusty streets, where visitors come to watch gunfighters in blazing battles. Enjoy the hilarious entertainment in the **Grand Palace Saloon,** a large theater with stage shows. Then settle down to watch movie clips in the **Arizona Theater** or listen to Southwestern tales in the **Storytellers Theater.** Take a stagecoach or trail ride, hop on a carousel, visit the petting zoo, and experience the **Iron Door Mine.** A narrated train ride around Old

Tucson is a good introduction to the site's history and layout. Special events take place, such as haunted evenings around Halloween.

If you continue northwest about 5 miles on Kinney Road from the junction with Gates Pass Road, you will come to **Saguaro National Park (West),** where the Red Hills Visitor Center introduces you to Sonoran Desert life and various activities here. The nearby **Cactus Garden Trail** identifies plants along a short path. The half-mile **Desert Discovery Nature Trail,** northwest of the visitor center, loops through cactuses on a bajada—the gentle slope between mountain and plain favored by desert plants. Both trails are paved and wheelchair accessible.

Other trails pass through nearby washes and hills, including 4,687-

**A cyclist speeds down from Gates Pass into the Avra Valley, home to Old Tucson, the Arizona–Sonora Desert Museum, and Saguaro National Park West.**

## The saguaro cactus

The giant of the cactus world starts out small and takes its time. The babies develop from a pinhead-size black seed, require protective shade, and may reach only a quarter of an inch in their first year. Most don't make it; as seedlings they are vulnerable to birds, rodents, and other foraging animals. They produce their first flowers and fruit at about 30 years, when they are just a few feet high. Arms may begin to appear around age 75. The largest specimens can have half a dozen arms or more, weigh eight tons, tower 50 feet high , and live more than 150 years.

White blossoms appear on evenings in late spring, then fade the following day. Both Tohono O'odham and wildlife savor the red fruit, which ripens in June and July. ∎

Blessed with a bit of cloud and some luck, you may be treated to a flaming Arizona sunset.

foot Wasson Peak; ask for a map and descriptions at the visitor center. The 6-mile **Bajada Loop Drive** begins at the visitor center and winds through scenic countryside past saguaro cactuses, picnic areas, overlooks, and trailheads; 6 miles are graded dirt road. On the drive, you can hike the 0.8-mile round-trip **Valley View Trail** through washes and up a ridge for a panorama of the Avra Valley. Farther along, **Signal Hill Petroglyphs Trail** (a quarter-mile round-trip) ascends from Signal Hill Picnic Area to a rock art site. ∎

**Old Tucson Studios**
www.oldtucson.com
- 200 B2
- 201 S. Kinney Rd.
- 520/883-0100
- $$$$

**Saguaro National Park West**
www.nps.gov/sagu
- 200 B3
- 2700 N. Kinney Rd.
- 520/733-5158
- $$

# Arizona–Sonora Desert Museum

THE EXCELLENT EXHIBITS HERE—IN A MIX OF ZOO, natural history museum, and botanical garden—help reveal the life of the Sonoran Desert. The range of flora and wildlife comes not just from Arizona but also from the Mexican state of Sonora and the Gulf of California. There's a lot to see both indoors and out on the 21-acre grounds; you may decide to stay longer than you'd intended!

**Arizona–Sonora Desert Museum**
www.desertmuseum.org
🏔 200 B2
✉ 2021 N. Kinney Rd. (14 miles W of I-10 on Speedway Boulevard/Gates Pass Rd.; large vehicles use Ajo Way and Kinney Road from I-19)
☎ 520/883-2702
💲 $$$

The orientation room, just past the entrance, introduces the Sonoran Desert and the museum's many exhibits. You can check listings for the day's wildlife demonstrations, bird walks, interpretive tours, and talks. Docents on the grounds offer informal presentations.

Natural-looking enclosures and environments provide homes for most of the wildlife. A cave reproduction in the **Earth Sciences** area contains amazingly realistic chambers filled with stalactites and stalagmites, along with salamanders and other cave life; the mineral gallery nearby displays superb specimens. Vegetation in the **Mountain Woodland** area creates the setting for mountain lion, black bear, Mexican wolf, white-tailed deer, and other large animals found at elevations between 4,000 and 7,000 feet. Both upper and lower levels give views of the feline species in the dens of **Cat Canyon,** while prairie dogs socialize in their colony at the **Desert Grassland** area. Reptiles include strikingly beautiful rattlesnakes and Gila monsters. Tarantulas, scorpions, and other arthropods put in appearances too.

**A docent introduces a tarantula to visitors at the Arizona–Sonora Desert Museum.**

**Hummingbirds buzz around the Arizona–Sonora Desert Museum in search of their favorite flowers.**

Coyote and javelina roam the **Arizona Upland** area (spot the nearly invisible fencing that keeps them in). In the **Riparian Corridor,** underwater viewing ports let visitors look at otters playing and beavers working in their pools and streams. Coati, with their pointed snouts and long tails, explore their streamside habitat nearby, while desert bighorn sheep display balancing skills as they scramble up rocky ledges.

In the **Life Underground** exhibit, nocturnal animals and insects find protection from the desert's temperature extremes. A walk-in aviary lets you get close to desert birds. Look carefully—they are well camouflaged. You can join hummingbirds in another walk-in aviary. Back near the park entrance, amphibians and endangered fish such as the Colorado squawfish and Gila topminnow have a home.

More than 1,200 species of desert plants add to the beauty of the grounds, including the many members of the cactus family identified in the **Cactus Garden.** Small gardens demonstrate flora used by different types of pollinators.

You will also enjoy expansive views across the Avra Valley to Kitt Peak (6,875 feet), home to important astronomical observatories (see p. 219), and the sacred Baboquivari Peak (7,730 feet), both on the Tohono O'odham Indian Reservation. The Gallery at the Desert Museum hosts changing art exhibitions.

An early start is recommended to enjoy the cool of the morning, see the animals at their most active, and have enough time for a visit. A hat, sunscreen, and good walking shoes will be appreciated (the trails total nearly 2 miles).

On summer Saturdays from June through September, the museum stays open late so that you can experience desert life in the evening. (The exception is the aviaries, which remain off-limits in the evening so the birds can roost undisturbed.) There is a choice of restaurants and snack bars, but for a picnic you must head outside the museum, perhaps to nearby Tucson Mountain Park. ■

# North from Tucson

SO GREAT IS THE RANGE OF VEGETATION AND CLIMATE along the way that a trip into the Santa Catalina Mountains has been likened to a drive from Mexico to Canada. The cool forests of fir and aspen on the north-facing slopes above 8,000 feet seem a world away from the saguaro of the desert below.

On the south side of the **Santa Catalina Mountains,** water dances down the streambed of **Sabino Canyon,** bringing life and color to the desert. Come to admire the sparkling pools, lush greenery, wildlife, and rugged canyon scenery. Just outside the **Sabino Canyon Visitor Center** *(Tel 520/749-8700)* the quarter-mile-loop Bajada Nature Trail identifies desert plants. Shuttle buses *(Tel 520/749-2861, $$)* make frequent narrated trips from here through the canyon. No cars are permitted in the canyon, and cyclists can ride only in early morning and evening hours on certain days.

## CATALINA HIGHWAY

The journey from Tucson up the paved, 25-mile-long Catalina Highway/Sky Island Byway takes about an hour—more if you stop to enjoy the many mountain panoramas en route. Palisades Visitor Center at mile 19.9 is open most weekends and on some weekdays, and the village of Summerhaven offers several places to stay and eat.

The chairlift at **Mount Lemmon Ski Valley** *(Tel 520/ 576-1400)* takes skiers up the slopes in winter, sightseers in the summer. From about May to October you can hike to the summit of **Mount Lemmon** (9,157 feet) from Mount Lemmon Ski Valley or nearby trailheads in about 1.5 miles one way. Ask someone to point out one of the trailheads, or take the lift up

and walk down. A network of trails leads to ridges and canyons from many trailheads; expect to encounter steep and strenuous hiking on most of these.

## CATALINA STATE PARK

You can explore the western foothills of the Santa Catalinas in **Catalina State Park,** 14 miles north of downtown Tucson off Arizona 77. Hiking trails, picnic areas, and campgrounds help you make the most of the desert and mountain scenery, and there are great opportunities to see wildlife, such as javelina, desert mule deer, Gambel's quail, and red-tailed hawk, on the nature trail and the

**Santa Catalina Ranger District Coronado National Forest**
www.fs.fed.us/r3/coronado/scrd
✉ 5700 N. Sabino Canyon Rd., Tucson, AZ 85750 (13 miles NE of downtown Tucson)
☎ 520/749-8700
⑤ $$ (Sabino Canyon/Catalina Hwy.)

**Catalina State Park**
⚠ 201 D4
✉ 11570 N. Oracle Rd.
☎ 520/628-5798
⑤ $$ (day-use fee)

**Windy Point in the Santa Catalinas**

Science and art dovetail in the beautiful geometry of the Biosphere 2 Center.

**Biosphere 2 Center**
www.bio2.edu
🅜 201 D4
✉ Ariz. 77 near mile marker 96.5
☎ 520/825-1289 or 800/828-2462
💲 $$$

birding trail (each 1 mile). Romero Ruins Interpretive Trail climbs a ridge on a loop measuring about one-third of a mile to reach the ruins of a Hohokam village and the site of a mid-19th-century ranch.

### BIOSPHERE 2 CENTER
Farther north off Arizona 77, experience the natural world in a different way at the **Biosphere 2 Center.** Aimed at increasing humankind's understanding of how our home planet—that is, Biosphere 1—operates, scientists and engineers have constructed the world's largest greenhouse; it covers more than three acres. Inside the sealed structure are five biomes, or self-sustaining ecosystems: rain forest, desert, savanna, marsh, and ocean.

The first crew—four women and four men—entered Biosphere 2 through an air lock on September 26, 1991. Their mission was to work and conduct scientific research for two years in the facility's self-contained environment. The team enjoyed access to a garden and livestock as well as a computer center

and living quarters. Two giant "lungs" outside allowed the greenhouse to breathe by compensating for changes in atmospheric pressure. Enthusiasts saw it as a step toward rescuing humans from impending ecological ruination. The Biospherians lasted out the two years, but various problems occurred and little scientific work was accomplished. In 1996, Columbia University took over the project and redirected the operation toward research.

First, take in the introductory multimedia show and exhibits in the visitor center. Then join a guided tour or set off on your own, passing the prototype and walking through demonstration laboratories before reaching Biosphere 2. Glass-paneled walls soar upward, supported by a geometric maze of interior trusses. You can peer into the biomes, learn about current research, visit exhibit areas, and see where the Biospherians once lived and worked. Biosphere 2 also offers a behind-the-scenes Under the Glass tour, astronomy programs, dining, and accommodations. ■

# East from Tucson

TAKE THE OLD SPANISH TRAIL OUT OF TUCSON TO SEE THE magnificent cactuses in the other half of Saguaro National Park, in the foothills of the Rincon Mountains. Aviation enthusiasts can head out on I-10 and trace the history of flight at the Pima Air and Space Museum. If you have time, continue out of town a few more miles to experience the subterranean wonders of Colossal Cave.

The saguaros in **Saguaro National Park East,** the larger and older section of the park (see pp. 207–208), tend to be very young or very old. Before these lands were protected, woodcutters and grazing cattle had trampled young plants and removed the necessary nursery trees that would have shaded them. Find out more about the ecology, geology, plants, and wildlife of the Sonoran Desert at the visitor center just inside the park entrance. The Cactus Garden just outside identifies a variety of plants. To see more of the park, drive or bike the Cactus Forest Drive, a scenic 8-mile loop. After driving 2.2 miles from the visitor center, you can turn left to Mica View Picnic Area, named for 8,666-foot Mica Mountain, visible

to the east. In another 0.3 mile on the drive, you'll reach the start of the Desert Ecology Trail, a paved quarter-mile loop that explains how plants and wildlife interact and adapt. Freeman Homestead Nature Trail begins near the end of the drive. On this 1-mile loop through giant saguaro and a mesquite woodland, signs tell of homesteading in the desert.

A 128-mile trail network weaves across the desert, up ridges, and through the canyons of the Rincon Mountains. Trails also climb to the heights from adjacent Coronado National Forest. You can camp at designated sites *(backcountry permit available at visitor center).* Rangers can advise on trail conditions for both hikers and equestrians.

Douglas Spring Trail in Saguaro National Park East gives commanding views of Tucson and the Santa Catalina Mountains.

**Saguaro National Park East**
www.nps.gov/sagu
🅰 201 E2
✉ 3693 S. Old Spanish Trail
☎ 520/733-5153
💲 $$

**Aircraft at the Pima Air & Space Museum range in time from a full-size copy of the Wright brothers' 1903 Wright Flyer to a Lear jet.**

**Colossal Cave Mountain Park**
www.colossalcave.com
⬛ 201 F1
✉ 22 miles SE of Tucson off Old Spanish Trail, or 7 miles N from I-10 Exit 279
☎ 520/647-7275
💲 $ (park entry), $$ (cave tour)

Continuing southeast for 12 miles from Saguaro will bring you to **Colossal Cave Mountain Park.** Although water once seeped through limestone cracks to create the cave's stalactites, stalagmites, flowstone, helictites, and boxwork (flat crystals that form little enclosures open on one side), the interior is now dry and a very pleasant 70°F year-round. Regular tours leave frequently and last 45 to 55 minutes, with about half a mile of walking. You'll be descending, then climbing six-and-a-half stories on steps, though at a leisurely pace. Your guide will tell of the local geology, the history of the cave, and a story of outlaws who once hid out here and may have left $60,000 in gold concealed somewhere. In the mid-1930s the Civilian Conserva-

tion Corps constructed the stone buildings and overlook near the cave entrance and the flagstone paths inside the cave. Ladder Tours take you off the normal route with helmets and flashlights to explore seldom-seen sections of the cave; call ahead to make a reservation.

**La Posta Quemada,** also in Colossal Cave Mountain Park, is a 120-year-old working ranch with a museum, hiking trails, horseback riding *(Tel 520/647-3450)*, research library, and café. Exhibits describe the cave's formation, its resident life, and some of the prehistoric artifacts found inside. Historical displays explain the area's history and ranch life. A per-vehicle fee collected at the park entrance covers the ranch, picnicking, and camping; you must arrive before

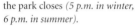

the park closes *(5 p.m. in winter, 6 p.m. in summer).*

More than 250 historic aircraft spread over 75 acres at the **Pima Air & Space Museum** illustrate the spectacular advances in aviation. Rare and unusual planes can be seen here, too. A narrated tram ride circles the grounds and introduces the aircraft; you can hop on and off at stops along its route.

Inside the entrance, a full-size reproduction of the 1903 Wright Flyer marks the beginning of the story of controlled flight. Most planes come from the military's World War II years and the jet age that followed. Civilian, helicopter, and space exhibits round out the collection. You'll see famous fighters and gleaming B-17, B-24, and B-29 bombers from the World

War II era, along with memorabilia and photos of the men who flew them. Jet aircraft illustrate the evolution from early models to the F100 series and thence to the amazingly fast SR-71 Blackbird, one of which flew coast to coast in less than an hour. Huge transports and B-52 bombers impress with their size. You can tour a VC-118A/DC-6A presidential plane used by Presidents John F. Kennedy and Lyndon B. Johnson.

Narrated **AMARC (Aerospace Maintenance and Regeneration Center) Tours** take you by bus to see the long rows of planes and helicopters in the vast aircraft storage area at nearby Davis-Monthan Air Force Base. The tours begin at the museum on weekdays and last about an hour. ■

**Peering into the depths at Crystal Forest on a tour of Colossal Cave**

**Pima Air & Space Museum**
www.pimaair.org
🅰 201 D1
✉ 6000 E. Valencia Rd. (12 miles SE of downtown; 2 miles E from I-10 Exit 267)
☎ 520/574-0462
💲 $$, $ (tram)

# Adaptation in the Desert

The Sonoran Desert covers much of central and southern Arizona, extending beyond the state's boundaries into southeastern California, the western half of the Mexican state of Sonora, and most of Baja California. It is unique among North American deserts in having two rainy seasons. Although the coastal range of California blocks most Pacific Ocean storms, some winter ones have enough strength to arrive as gentle showers. No mountains obstruct the way from the south, so when moisture blows in from the Gulf of California during late summer, rain can fall in heavy, spotty bursts.

Plants have developed many tricks to survive heat and droughts. Many annuals and ephemerals produce tough seeds that can wait years for seasonal rain. When it comes, they quickly complete their cycle—growth, bloom, and seed—before wilting away. For some species, the entire process takes just a matter of weeks. Their flowering can turn the desert into an explosion of color. Perennials survive by remaining dormant during droughts. The whiplike ocotillo, for example, takes advantage

of irregular rains by leafing out and blooming, then reentering dormancy within a period of a few weeks—a cycle that can be repeated five times in a year.

To help reduce water loss, leaves on desert shrubs and trees are often tiny. Phreatophytes such as the mesquite tree seek out water underground with extremely long roots; 80-foot lengths have been recorded. Cactuses and similar plants soak up water from a shallow root system and transfer it to their expandable tissue in preparation for dry spells. Spines provide shade and reflect heat; an absence of leaves and the presence of a thick, waxy skin also help cactuses retain fluids. The creosote bush can thrive where few other plants grow; its tiny leaf pores close during the day to retain moisture and open at night to capture it. Its unpleasant smell and taste repel most browsing animals, and its double root system—shallow for rainfall, deep for ground water—is ideal for changing conditions.

Organ pipe cactus

Rattlesnake

Javelina

Gila monster

Paloverde

Ocotillo

Cactus wren

Kangaroo rat

Coyote

Teddybear cholla

Roadrunner

Like plants, desert animals have adapted to cope with baking heat and shortage of water. Most simply avoid the intense summer sun. Birds may fly on to cooler climates after breeding in late winter or early spring. Some reptiles, rodents, bats, and larger animals such as foxes and skunks spend the day in underground burrows or dens. Many are nocturnal. Diurnal mammals, such as the round-tailed ground squirrel, may pass the summer and winter in a state of torpor. Lizards manage during the day by scampering from one piece of shade to the next. The huge ears of jackrabbits cool their blood quickly as they rest in shady places. The well-adapted kangaroo rat doesn't need to drink water because it metabolizes dry seeds. Insects obtain all the water they need from plants. In turn they provide food and fluids for birds, mammals, reptiles, and even other insects. ■

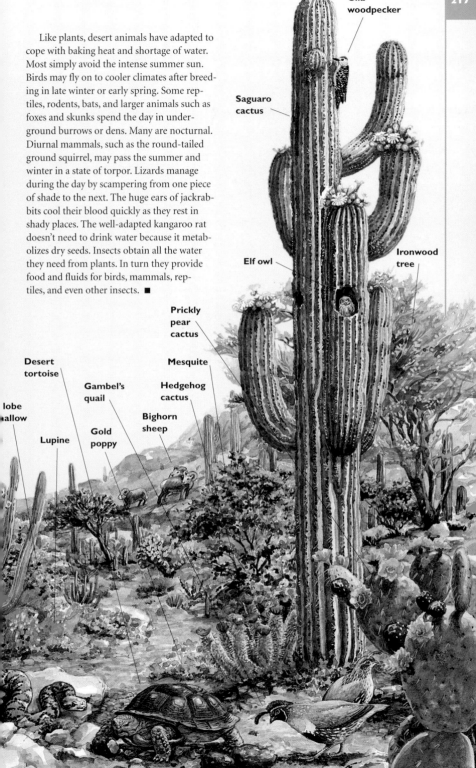

Gila woodpecker

Saguaro cactus

Elf owl

Ironwood tree

Prickly pear cactus

Desert tortoise

Mesquite

Gambel's quail

Hedgehog cactus

lobe mallow

Lupine

Gold poppy

Bighorn sheep

# South from Tucson

TWO DIFFERENT 20TH-CENTURY TECHNOLOGIES ARE THE
focus of a trip south out of Tucson on I-19. On a journey that begins
with mining machinery and ends at the former site of an apocalyp-
tic nuclear warhead, contemplative travelers can reflect on the nature
of progress.

**Asarco Mineral
Discovery Center**
www.mineraldiscovery.com
- 🅰 197 E2
- ✉ 12 miles S of town
  off I-19 Exit 80
- ☎ 520/625-7513
  (recording)
- 🕐 Closed Sun.–Mon.
- 💲 $$ (tour), museum
  free

**Titan Missile
Museum**
www.pimaair.org
- 🅰 197 E1
- ✉ 25 miles S of
  Tucson; follow signs
  off I-19 to Duval
  Mine Rd.
- ☎ 520/625-7736
- 💲 $$

Copper ore comes out of large
open-pit and underground ex-
cavations among the terraced white
hills southwest of Tucson. To learn
more about the mining industry or
see the mine in action, stop by the
**Asarco Mineral Discovery
Center.** Exhibits and short videos
illustrate the uses of copper and
how miners find and extract it.
Tours take you to the edge of the
Mission Mine pit, a quarter mile
deep and up to two miles across,
where giant cranes load 320-ton
trucks. Next you enter the mill to
see the machinery that grinds and
concentrates the ore to 28 percent
copper.

Although the formerly top-
secret site has been deactivated, you
may feel apprehension on entering
the **Titan Missile Museum.**

From 1963 to 1982, a fully fueled
missile with a nuclear warhead
stood ready for launch in seconds.
A tour begins with a video introduction that shows crews at work
and a missile roaring into the sky.
You then head outside to see fuel-
ing and other support equipment,
the massive silo cover, rocket engines, and the Titan II missile.
Wearing a hard hat, you descend
the metal stairs, pass through blast
doors, and enter a control room
where your guide runs through the
launch sequence. A cable-filled
corridor leads to the silo for a close
look at the missile. A visit may fill
you with awe at the technology
employed as well as horror at the
devastation a launch most certainly
would have wreaked. Reservations
are recommended. ∎

# Tohono O'odham Indian Reservation & Kitt Peak

IN THE HEART OF THE SONORAN DESERT SOUTHWEST OF Tucson and far from any life-sustaining rivers, the Tohono O'odham (tah-HO-no AH-tomb) have lived for centuries. Their name (as you would expect) means "Desert People." For visitors, Kitt Peak and Mission San Xavier del Bac (see p. 222) are the biggest attractions.

The O'odham know the land and its springs so well they can garden and harvest wild foods in an environment other people would find uninhabitable. They live in settlements scattered across a huge reservation. Sells is the main town and site of the **Tohono O'odham Tribal Headquarters.**

Two dozen telescopes dot the summit of **Kitt Peak** (6,875 feet). You can drive up the paved road and take a guided or self-guided tour. A video and exhibits illustrate the nature of light and explain how astronomers are using it and other spectra to unravel the mysteries of the cosmos.

Three of Kitt Peak's largest telescopes have viewing galleries—the slanted, partly underground McMath-Pierce Solar, the 2.1-meter (84 inch), and the huge Mayall 4-meter (158 inch). If you stop at the picnic area to the left 1.5 miles before the summit, you'll see the larger of two radio telescopes; a sign explains how it is used. Stargazing programs in the evenings use the 16-inch telescope beside the visitor center to observe and learn about objects in the heavens. An Advanced Observing Program is offered for amateur astronomers too. Make reservations and dress *very* warmly.

Bring drinks, food, and gas, as they aren't available here. The summit is 10° to 20°F cooler than Tucson, so take warm clothes. ∎

**Kitt Peak**
🅰 197 E2

**National Optical Astronomy Observatories**
www.noao.edu
☎ 520/318-8200 (recording), 520/318-8726 (visitor center)
💲 Donation ($$$$$ for stargazing program)

# Organ Pipe Cactus National Monument

THE ROUGH-HEWN MOUNTAINS AND GENTLE VALLEYS here along the Mexican border support a wonderfully diverse display of Sonoran Desert plants. Far from any major city, this land has a feel of remoteness and solitude.

A warm climate allows organ pipe cactus, elephant trees, and other rare flora to flourish. You can easily recognize organ pipe cactus by its 5 to 20 branches curving up from a point near the ground. It can grow as high as 23 feet and is second in size only to the saguaro in the United States.

Start at the visitor center for an excellent introduction to the area. Naturalist programs take place at the main campground. A paved nature trail by the visitor center identifies common desert plants. Two hiking trails begin from the campground: The **Desert View Nature Trail,** a 1.2-mile loop, goes through a wash and up a ridge for views, and the 4.5-mile round-trip **Victoria Mine Trail** leads to a historical mine. Evenings and early mornings are best for seeing wildlife. Use a flashlight at night, when rattlesnakes and Gila monsters will most likely be about.

There is also a small primitive campground, but you'll need to get a permit from the visitor center. Five miles south of the visitor center in Lukeville, you'll find a motel, RV park, café, and store.

Two unpaved scenic drives loop through the desert; the visitor center sells an informative guide to each drive.

Highlights of the 53-mile **Puerto Blanco Drive** include Quitobaquito Oasis and the rare desert plants of Senita Basin. The drive takes about half a day; bring drinks and perhaps a picnic. **Red Tanks Tinaja Trail** (1.2 miles round-trip) begins at mile 3.7 along the drive and winds through desert vegetation to natural pools in a wash. **Dripping Springs Mine Trail** (4 miles round-trip) starts at mile 11.9 and climbs over a little pass to an early 20th-century mining area. The drive continues past Golden Bell Mine on the left at mile 17 and Bonita Well (used by ranchers to water their cattle) on the right at mile 18.3. At mile 23.9, turn right 0.4 mile for Quitobaquito Oasis. A short trail leads to the spring and a pond. (Don't leave valuables in cars parked here or anywhere else near the border.) At mile 33.3,

**Organ Pipe Cactus National Monument**
www.nps.gov/orpi
🄰 196 C2
✉ 120 miles W of Tucson on Ariz. 86, then 22 miles S on Ariz. 85
☎ 520/387-6849
💲 $$

**Left: In early spring you might be lucky to see the desert floor carpeted with Mexican gold poppies or other wildflowers.**

turn left for the 4-mile spur road to Senita Basin, home of the elephant tree (with its short, stout, tapered trunks) and senita cactus (a columnar cactus with whiskerlike tufts). Hikers can follow old mining roads on the 2.25-mile **Senita Basin Loop,** which begins at road's end.

Across the highway from the visitor center, the 21-mile **Ajo Mountain Drive** provides a close look at the flora and geology in the foothills of the range crowned by Mount Ajo (4,808 feet). Allow about two hours of driving time through the rugged countryside. ■

**Evening primrose and sand verbena briefly color the harsh terrain of Cabeza Prieta National Wildlife Refuge.**

## El Camino del Diablo

Native Americans, Spanish missionaries and explorers, and California gold-seeking forty-niners used the Devil's Highway, which connected the town of Caborca in Sonora, Mexico, with the Colorado River 250 miles away. This route avoided hostile tribes farther north, but conditions could be brutal, especially in summer.

Inexperienced travelers died when they ran out of water between the infrequent springs in some of the Sonoran Desert's driest regions. Bring a map or atlas of the area and you can retrace the heart of this route with a 4WD vehicle, supplies for remote travel, and a permit from the Cabeza Prieta National Wildlife Refuge office in Ajo. ■

**Cabeza Prieta National Wildlife Refuge**
southwest.fws.gov
✉ 1611 N. 2nd Ave., Ajo, AZ 85321
☎ 520/387-6483
🕐 Office closed Sat.–Sun.

The faith of Fran-
ciscan mission-
aries and local
O'odham created
this masterpiece
from desert soil.

# Mission San Xavier del Bac

THE "WHITE DOVE OF THE DESERT," AS THIS CHURCH IS known, has called to pilgrims and other devout followers for more than 200 years. Jesuit priest and explorer Eusebio Francisco Kino trekked across the harsh landscape from Mexico in 1692 to minister to Indians at the farming village of Bac. Kino named the mission he founded after his patron saint, a Jesuit missionary in Asia.

A chapel served early converts, but the mission community often lacked a resident priest. O'odham revolts in 1734 and 1751 damaged the mission, and raiding Apache caused hardships. The Franciscans began to build the present adobe church in the late 1770s. Artists from Mexico filled the interior with statues of saints, elaborate orna-mentation, and murals, creating a folk-art style. Luxuries were out of the question, so painters textured the main altar to resemble marble and drew chandeliers on the upper walls. Workers never completed the east bell tower and other parts of the church.

Padre Kino would be pleased to see the results of his faith after more than three centuries. The mission is one of the few that has served its original purpose from Spanish times to the present. O'odham, Hispanic, and Anglo worshipers join for the Sunday Masses and other ceremonies. Unless a service is taking place, you are welcome to enter and admire the richly detailed interior. A recorded message tells of the church's history, identifies statues, and explains the symbolism.

The **mission museum** on the east side of the church illustrates the early history and life of the mission; it also displays furnishings, vestments, and art. A walk around the grounds takes you to a former mortuary chapel to the west and up to a copy of the Grotto of Lourdes in a small hill to the east. ■

**Mission San Xavier
del Bac**

⚠ 197 E2

✉ 10 miles S of
downtown Tucson;
follow signs from
I-19 Exit 92

☎ 520/294-2624

$ Donation

# Santa Rita Mountains

THE FORESTED SLOPES OF MOUNT WRIGHTSON (9,453 feet) tower high above the desert 38 miles south of Tucson. Spring-fed Madera Canyon is famed among birders, especially from mid-March to mid-September; more than 240 species, including many hummingbirds, have been identified here. Sightings of the elegant trogon, a colorful parrotlike bird from Mexico, are eagerly sought.

Elegant trogons such as this female arrive from Mexico in late spring to breed in the sycamore-wooded canyons of southeastern Arizona.

Desert grasslands and shrubs give way to mesquite groves, then oak, juniper, cottonwood, and Arizona sycamore along the paved road into **Madera Canyon.** Short paved loops on the right near the entrance offer an easy walk and wheelchair access from Proctor Parking Area and Whitehouse Picnic Area. The road forks and ends 2 miles up Madera Canyon at Roundup Picnic Area; take the left fork to trailheads for **Old Baldy, Super,** and **Vault Mine Trails,** or the right fork for the upper end of the **Nature Trail.** Interpretive signs line the trail as it descends to the Amphi-theater trailhead in 2.7 miles one way. You could continue hiking along the creek to Proctor Parking Area in 4.4 miles total one way.

For more of a challenge, you can hike into the surrounding Mount Wrightson Wilderness. The 5.5-mile **Bog Springs Loop** is popular. It starts from Madera Picnic Area, about halfway up the canyon, and gains 1,600 feet in elevation.

The strenuous trek to the summit of Mount Wrightson can be done as a long day hike. Both the steep Old Baldy Trail (5.4 miles one way) and the more gentle Super Trail (8.1 miles one way) depart from Roundup Picnic Area.

From March to November, **Whipple Observatory** offers six-hour tours of the telescopes and superb views atop Mount Hopkins (8,550 feet), just southwest of Mount Wrightson. Call in advance to make reservations. ∎

**Whipple Observatory Visitor Center**
cfa-www.harvard.edu/flwo
▲ 197 E1
✉ 11.5 miles SE of I-19 Exit 56
☎ 520/670-5707
🕐 Closed Sat.–Sun.
💲 $$ (tour), visitor center free

# Tubac

**Tubac**
⚠ 197 E1
**Visitor information**
www.tubacaz.com
✉ Tubac Chamber of
Commerce, P.O.
Box 1866, Tubac,
AZ 85646
☎ 520/398-2704

**Tubac Center of
the Arts**
www.tubacarts.org
✉ 9 Plaza Rd.
☎ 520/398-2371
🕐 Closed Mon. & mid-
May—early Sept.
💲 Donation

**Tubac Presidio
State Historic Park**
✉ Burruel St. &
Tubac Rd.
☎ 520/398-2252
💲 $

**Tubac Presidio
State Historic Park**

NOW KNOWN AS AN ARTISTS' COLONY, WITH THE MOTTO the "Place Where Art and History Meet," Tubac goes back to 1752, when the Spanish built the Tubac presidio (fort). This was the first European settlement in what is now Arizona.

American prospectors and adventurers, hearing tales of old Spanish mines, streamed in after the United States bought southern Arizona from Mexico in the Gadsden Purchase of 1854 and hit rich silver ore. Tubac boomed, but the good times came to an abrupt halt in the early 1860s when troops stationed there headed east to fight the Civil War.

The town began its transformation into the Tubac of today when an art school opened in 1948. About a hundred studios and galleries now display such work as paintings, prints, glassware, ceramics, wood carvings, jewelry, and batiks.

**Tubac Center of the Arts** exhibits work by local, regional, and national artists. Staffers organize a performing arts series, children's programs, lectures, and workshops.

**Tubac Presidio State Historic Park** recounts the history of the people who lived in Tubac during various periods. You can enter an underground excavation to see a foundation and part of a wall of an early building. Models and artifacts illustrate how the town developed. The printing press used in 1859 for the first newspaper in what is now Arizona is here (you can buy a reproduction of the first issue). Other sights include the 1885 schoolhouse and 1920s church, both successors to ones built in the 1700s, and the state park itself—Arizona's first, opened in 1959. ∎

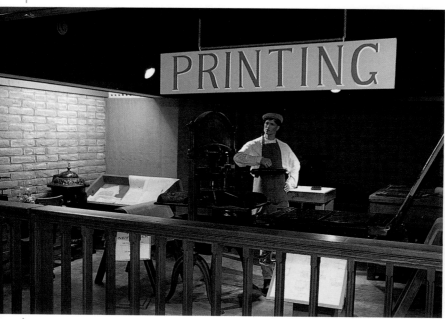

# Tumacácori
# National Historical Park

A museum model shows how the church at Tumacácori once looked. Compare this scene with the present-day interior.

THE GREAT ADOBE RUIN OF TUMACÁCORI TESTIFIES TO the devotion and difficulties of early O'odham and Spanish residents. A basic shade ramada served as a church when Father Kino first visited the O'odham here in 1691. Mission work continued over the following century, but the present church was not begun until 1800.

Franciscan father Narcisco Gutierrez intended to build a structure as splendid as San Xavier del Bac (see p. 222), but work had not quite finished 22 years later when the Mexican government took over from Spain and cut the funding. Mexican missionaries assisted from time to time, but Apache raids eventually made life too difficult. The last residents packed up in 1848 and moved north to San Xavier del Bac.

Tumacácori fell into ruin before it received protection as a national monument in 1908. The museum displays some of the original santos—wooden statues of saints. A video introduces life in the mission, and exhibits illustrate the architecture and history. The mission was far more than just the church, as you will see from the model and self-guided tour of the grounds. Walk through the church's baptistry, sanctuary, and sacristy and continue outside to the cemetery and its mortuary chapel, then to a granary, courtyard, lime kiln, ruins of the priests' quarters, and the foundations of an earlier church.

For a hike with a sense of history, take the **Juan Bautista de Anza National Historic Trail.** It follows the Santa Cruz River 4.5 miles one way to Tubac, crossing the river twice. The trail is named for the captain who led colonists to California in 1775–76 and founded San Francisco. ■

**Tumacácori National Historical Park**
www.nps.gov/tuma
🅰 197 E1
✉ 48 miles S of Tucson near I-19 Exit 29
☎ 520/398-2341
💲 $

# Huachuca Mountains

MILLER PEAK TOPS THIS RANGE OF CANYONS AND ALPINE forests southeast of Tucson. Scenic drives climb partway into the heights, but only trails continue to the 9,466-foot summit in Miller Peak Wilderness. Two sites commemorate the region's history: Fort Huachuca (wa-CHOO-ka) Museum, near the north end of the mountains, and Coronado National Memorial, at the south end.

## FORT HUACHUCA

Of the U.S. Army forts established during the Indian wars, only **Fort Huachuca** continues its service as a military base. In 1877, Capt. Samuel Marmaduke Whitside chose the site for its commanding view of the San Pedro Valley and for the abundance of timber, game, and water in the mountains. It served as the advance headquarters in the campaign to capture the formidable Apache leader Geronimo. When the Apache were finally subdued in 1886, the fort took up the job of patrolling the Mexican border. Today, the Army tests electronics and other gear and runs an intelligence

school at the fort. **Brown Parade Field,** with officers' houses on one side and barracks on the other, dates back to the 1880s.

The two buildings of **Fort Huachuca Museum** display a large collection of photos, Native American and Army memorabilia, period rooms, and dioramas. The "Black Experience" relates the exploits of the Buffalo Soldiers. Nearby, the **Army Intelligence Museum** *(Tel 520/533-1127, call for hours)* illustrates the Army's history and techniques of spying. From the main gate in the town of Sierra Vista, follow signs west for about 2.5 miles.

**Huachuca Mountains**
🗺 197 F1
**Visitor information**
www.visitsierravista.com
✉ Sierra Vista Convention & Visitors Bureau, 21 E. Wilcox Dr., Sierra Vista, AZ 85635
☎ 520/417-6960 or 800/288-3861
🕐 Closed Sun.

**Fort Huachuca Museum**
🗺 197 F1
✉ Hungerford Ave. & Grierson Ave.
☎ 520/533-5736 (recording) or 520/533-3638 (office)
💲 Donation

**Sierra Vista Ranger Station, Coronado National Forest**
www.fs.fed.us/r3/coronado
✉ 5990 S. Hwy. 92, Hereford, AZ 85615
☎ 520/378-0311
🕐 Closed Sat.–Sun.

Dubbed "Buffalo soldiers" by Native Americans, black soldiers at Fort Huachuca earned respect for their discipline and hard work.

The Nature Conservancy looks after **Ramsey Canyon Preserve,** a 300-acre wildlife sanctuary on the east side of the Huachucas. As many as 14 hummingbird species visit from spring to early autumn. It's also a great spot to see other birds and wildlife. More than 400 plant species grow here. Start at the visitor center and follow **Hamburg Trail** for a mile one way up the canyon to an overlook. It is possible to continue hiking on trails in Coronado National Forest (bring water).

**Carr Canyon Road** ascends 7.8 miles up the east side of the Huachucas to spectacular overlooks of the San Pedro Valley and to alpine meadows and cool forests at an elevation of 7,200 feet. **Reef Historic Trail** passes near old mine and mill sites in a 0.75-mile loop from the far end of Reef Townsite Campground; signs explain the area's mining history. The drive begins 7.5 miles south of Sierra Vista on Arizona 92 between mileposts 328 and 329. Only the first mile is paved, but cars can usually make the trip if the road is dry.

The Sierra Vista Ranger Station, half a mile north on Arizona 92 from the Carr Canyon turnoff, has recreation information.

## CORONADO NATIONAL MEMORIAL

Although Francisco Vásquez de Coronado failed in his quest to find gold in 1540, he's recognized at the **Coronado National Memorial** as the leader of the first major European expedition in the Southwest. A video and exhibits at the visitor center tell of his journey. You can also learn about wildlife and flora here and on the nature walk outside. **Coronado Cave Trail** leads to an undeveloped limestone cave in a 1.5-mile round-trip hike. Bring two flashlights and obtain a free permit from a ranger. You can also hike the 3-mile **Joe's Canyon Trail** (1,345-foot elevation gain) west to Montezuma Pass (or drive there on an unpaved road) for a sweeping panorama of mountains and valleys in Arizona and Mexico. For the best views, hike the 0.75-mile round-trip trail from the pass to 6,864-foot Coronado Peak. ■

The southern Huachuca Mountains and the distant Santa Ritas fill the view from Coronado Peak.

**Ramsey Canyon Preserve**
www.tncarizona.org
✉ 6 miles S from Sierra Vista on Ariz. 92, then right 3.5 miles on Ramsey Canyon Rd.
☎ 520/378-2785
$ $$ (No RVs or trailers in visitor center parking area)

**Coronado National Memorial**
www.nps.gov/coro
✉ 14 miles S from Sierra Vista on Ariz. 92, then 4.5 miles S & E on Coronado Memorial Blvd.
☎ 520/366-5515

# Tombstone

TOMBSTONE IS THE REAL THING—A WILD WEST MINING town that survived booms, busts, and some of the territory's most notorious gunslingers. Stroll down the boardwalks past 19th-century saloons, ride a stage, and watch a reenactment of the Shootout at the O.K. Corral. The old town lies 70 miles southeast of Tucson.

**Tombstone**

🅰 197 G1

**Visitor information**

www.tombstone.org

✉ Tombstone Visitor Center, Allen & 4th Sts., Tombstone (P.O. Box 1314, Tombstone, AZ 85638)

☎ 520/457-3929 (visitor center), 888/457-3929 (Chamber of Commerce)

**After a botched robbery in which innocent people died, John Heath was strung up from a telegraph pole.**

When prospector Ed Shieffelin ventured out this way in 1877, Army troops told him that his own tombstone was the only thing he'd find in the rattlesnake-ridden country, inhabited by hostile Apache. Shieffelin traveled alone and staked his first silver claim as Tombstone. The town sprang up just two years later and grew to be one of Arizona's most important.

Hard-working miners and prospectors found their entertainment here; it was said that saloons and gambling halls made up two of every three buildings. Law and order didn't come easily at first as Apache, defending their land, and crooks, along with political corruption, gave the place its notoriety. Fires twice raged through Tombstone, but it was flooding of the mines in 1886 that nearly undid the town. Somehow the "Town Too Tough to Die" hung on, though it ceased to be a county seat and much of its population moved on. Many buildings from the early days still stand on or near Allen Street. Desperadoes and lawmen fight blazing gun battles in historical reenactments; ask at the visitor center for a schedule and locations. Stagecoaches on Allen Street offer short narrated tours.

Exhibits at **Tombstone Courthouse State Historic Park** (3rd & Toughnut Sts., tel 520/ 457-3311) introduce the Native Americans, prospectors, pioneers, cattlemen, lawmen, and women who lived here. A card table and a roulette wheel recall saloon life.

Historical displays tell of the fateful day, October 26, 1881, when Doc Holliday and the Earps, seeking to enforce the law, shot it out with the free-spirited Clanton cowboys near the O.K. Corral. Mining exhibits show how ore was dug out and assayed. Upstairs are the former Cochise County Attorney's office and the courtroom where many trials took place. A gallows outside the 1882 redbrick courthouse spelled the end of the road for some.

Over on Allen, between Third and Fourth Streets, you can step into the **O.K. Corral** to see lifesize statues that depict the famous gunfight. A daily reenactment takes place nearby. Other sights include a reconstructed photographer's studio, old stables, carriages, and a cozy shack from the red-light district. At **Historama** next door, movies and animated scenes illustrate major events in Tombstone's history. The 1879 **Crystal Palace Saloon** serves beverages in its beautifully restored interior at the corner of Allen and Fifth Streets.

Ed Schieffelin allegedly suggested the name for the town's newspaper. Drop into the **office of the Epitaph,** on Fifth around the corner from the Crystal Palace, to pick up a copy of your own *Epitaph*.

Doors never closed during the first eight years at the 1881 **Bird Cage Theatre.** The marvelously preserved interior of this combined dance hall, theater, saloon, brothel, and gambling house retains its stage, gambling tables, and rare circus posters.

"A Bird in a Gilded Cage," the hit song about ladies of the night written at the theater (above) in the early 1880s, may have inspired the name. Right: Prostitutes scouted for customers from the cribs above, then drew the curtains when plying their trade.

The gift of a rose plant to a homesick bride in 1885 has grown so much that it shades an 8,000-square-foot courtyard at the **Rose Tree Museum** *(Fourth & Toughnut Streets)*. The museum also has pioneer exhibits and period rooms. The 1882 **St. Paul's Episcopal Church** at Third and Safford Streets is Arizona's oldest Protestant church. You can usually take a look inside and see the two ship's lamps and stained-glass windows.

Grave markers on **Boot Hill,** just off the highway on the north edge of town, tell about life in early Tombstone. Ed Schieffelin request-

ed a different kind of burial: "It is my wish, if convenient, to be buried in the dress of a prospector, my old pick and canteen with me, on top of the granite hills about three miles westerly from the city of Tombstone, Arizona, and that a monument such as prospectors build when locating a mining claim be built over my grave…under no circumstances do I want to be buried in a graveyard or cemetery." Tombstone's first prospector now rests under the **Schieffelin Monument,** in a lonely spot 2.3 miles west of town on Allen Street. ■

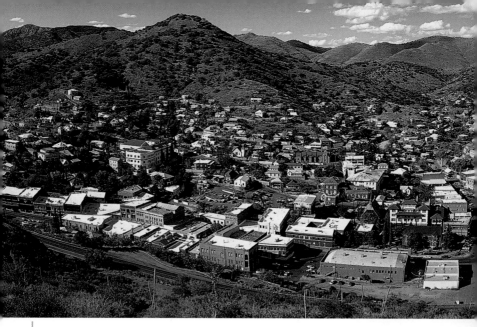

**In this view from above the Queen Mine, mineral-rich hills squeeze downtown Bisbee into narrow canyons.**

# Bisbee

TUCKED INTO CANYONS OF THE MULE MOUNTAINS 24 miles south of Tombstone, Bisbee still has much of its early 20th-century character. It rode the wave of copper mining, meeting the needs of the new electrical industries and leaving a legacy of splendid Victorian houses and substantial commercial buildings.

**Bisbee**

◪ 197 G1

**Visitor information**

www.bisbeearizona.com

✉ Bisbee Chamber of Commerce, 31 Subway St. (P.O. Box BA, Bisbee, AZ 85603)

☎ 520/432-5421 or 866/224-7233

The history of Bisbee really began more than a hundred million years ago, when molten rock deep within the Earth expelled enormous quantities of steam and hot water. The acidic, mineral-rich solutions gradually replaced overlying limestone with copper-iron sulfides. Early prospectors, hoping to find silver, were disappointed, but some established copper claims nonetheless.

In 1880, Judge DeWitt Bisbee and some San Francisco financiers bought the rights, though the judge never visited the town named for him. The city grew rich and built up a fine business district. The miners fared less well: When they went on strike in 1917, more than 1,000 were rounded up at gunpoint and shipped out of the state in boxcars. Working conditions improved,

but copper prices ruled the town's economy. Work in the Lavender Pit east of town ceased in 1974, and underground mining ended the following year. Vast quantities of ore remain and may be excavated if copper prices go high enough.

Bisbee's Victorian architecture and setting have made it a popular place for artists, retirees, and visitors. Shops and galleries display jewelry—some containing beautiful copper minerals—plus paintings, ceramics, and other work. A 5,300-foot elevation gives the town a pleasant climate most of the year.

More than 2,000 miles of mine tunnels run through the Bisbee district. The **Queen Mine Tour** furnishes you with a yellow slicker, hard hat, and lamp as you ride mine cars into the workings. This

mine, with 143 miles of passage-
ways on seven levels, operated for
60 years until it closed in 1943.
Bring a jacket or sweater; the mine
temperature is only 47°F. The guide
will explain the mine's history and
how the miners used their drilling,
blasting, and ore-loading skills in
the stope (work area) and tunnels.
Tours last 60 to 75 minutes and
depart from the large Queen Mine
Building south across the highway
from downtown Bisbee. A surface
tour of 60 to 75 minutes starts here
and visits areas near the Lavender
Pit normally closed to the public.

For a feeling of life in Bisbee's
early years, drop by the **Bisbee
Mining & Historical Museum**
in the 1897 Phelps Dodge General
Office Building downtown. Exhibits
illustrate the town's development,
mining, and local ranching. You'll
see some of the 300-plus copper
compounds from the area, many
sparkling with bright greens or
deep blues. The elegant general
manager's office reveals the luxury
enjoyed by top company officials.
An affiliate of the Smithsonian
Institution, the museum opens its
research library to those wishing to
delve deeper into history.

Community and family heirlooms are on display in the **Bisbee
Restoration Museum** *(37 Main
Street, closed Sun.–Mon.)*, a former
department store. Fifty watering
holes in the canyon known as
**Brewery Gulch** served the miners until Prohibition turned off the
spigots. The **Stock Exchange
Bar** upstairs in the 1905 Muheim
Block at 15 Brewery Avenue still has
the original trading board. Between
1898 and 1915, Swiss immigrant
and entrepreneur Joseph Muheim
Senior built what is now the
**Muheim Heritage House**
*(207B Youngblood Hill, tel 520/432-
7698, call for hours)*. Tours tell of
family life and of Muheim's many
businesses in town. Walk up Brewery Avenue, then climb stairs up the
hillside to the house.

A pullout on the highway just
southeast of town overlooks the
**Lavender Pit,** a hole 1,000 feet
deep, 0.75 mile wide, and 1.5 miles
long. Digging began in 1951 and
removed 380 million tons of ore
and rock over the next 23 years. ∎

**Togged in slickers,
hard hats, and
lamps, visitors
prepare to enter
the portal of
Queen Mine.**

**Queen Mine Tour**
✉ 478 N. Dart Rd.
☎ 520/432-2071 or
866/432-2071
💲 $$$ (underground
tour), $$ (surface
tour)

**Bisbee Mining &
Historical Museum**
✉ 5 Copper Queen
Plaza
☎ 520/432-7071
💲 $$

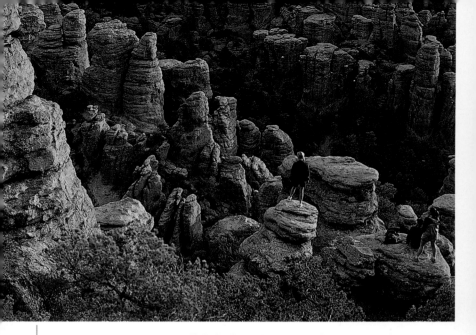

A maze of fanciful rocks near the end of Bonita Canyon Drive, Chiricahua National Monument

# Chiricahua Mountains

IN THE SOUTHEAST CORNER OF ARIZONA, THE DRAMATIC rock spires and cliffs of the huge sky island of the Chiricahuas (CHEER-ee-KAH-wahs) shelter a variety of wildlife, including javelina, coatimundi, skunks, white-tailed deer, bear, and mountain lions.

**Chiricahua National Monument**
www.nps.gov/chir
- 197 G2
- 120 miles SE of Tucson via I-10, Ariz. 186, & Ariz. 181
- 520/824-3560
- $$ (entry), $ (Faraway Ranch guided tour)

**Douglas Ranger Station, Coronado National Forest**
www.fs.fed.us/r3/coronado
- 197 G1
- 3081 N. Leslie Canyon Rd., Douglas, AZ 85607
- 520/364-3468
- Closed Sat.–Sun.

Hiking trails in **Chiricahua National Monument** take you into a maze of pinnacles and balanced rocks. The 8-mile paved **Bonita Canyon Drive** curves up to Massai Point (6,870 feet) for views, a geology exhibit, and a short nature trail. **Echo Canyon Trail** begins nearby on a 3.5-mile loop through some spectacular scenery.

Rangers offer tours inside the ranch house at **Faraway Ranch** most days. They tell of the Erickson family, who lived on the ranch for 91 years until 1979. From the 1920s on, the Ericksons ran a guest ranch and promoted the scenery, which led to National Monument status for these rock formations.

An unpaved mountain road (usually closed in winter) crosses the Chiricahuas between Chiricahua National Monument and **Cave Creek Canyon,** on the eastern flanks, where birdwatchers come to see the elegant trogon and some 330 other species. Between the two is Onion Saddle (7,600 feet), where you can turn south up another road to a campground and trailhead among tall pines at Rustler Park (8,400 feet). The **Crest Trail** heads south from here into the Chiricahua Wilderness and to the range's highest summit— **Chiricahua Peak** (9,796 feet)— in 5.25 miles one way. An alternative hike from Rustler Park is to follow the Crest Trail south 2.5 miles to just inside the wilderness boundary, then turn east about 1.8 miles on the **Centrella Trail** to **Centrella Point** (9,320 feet). From here a stunning panorama extends over the Cave Creek Canyon area and into New Mexico. ∎

# Kartchner Caverns State Park

IN 1974, WHEN CAVE EXPLORERS RANDY TUFTS AND GARY Tenen discovered this beautiful limestone cave on the east side of the Whetstone Mountains, they dared not publicize their find until the site's protection could be guaranteed. That occurred in 1988, when Kartchner Caverns became Arizona's 25th state park.

Kartchner Caverns
State Park

197 F1

www.pr.state.az.us

Off Ariz. 90, 8 miles
S of I-10 Exit 302
or 19 miles N of
Sierra Vista

520/586-4100
(information),
520/586-2283 (tour
reservations)

$$$

**The Kubla Khan formation emerges from the darkness as the lights switch on.**

Speleotherms (cave features) continue to grow drop by drop in this living cave as they have done for the past 200,000 years. Nearly every type of feature known to exist can be found in the cave, including a few that were first seen here, such as the "turnip shield" and the "bird's-nest" needle quartz formations. A multimedia show in the **Discovery Center** recounts how the explorers found and entered the cave. Exhibits illustrate the formation of the cave and its features. A copy of the 21-foot soda straw hangs inside. Other exhibits reveal the mysteries of the cave's animal life and include a life-size model of the 80,000-year-old Shasta ground sloth, whose skeleton was discovered by cave researchers.

Advance reservations are highly recommended for the popular cave tour. A tram takes you up a hill to the cave entrance, where you pass through an air lock that maintains the 99 percent humidity needed for growth of the cave formations. The easy, 0.75-mile paved trail is wheelchair accessible. Temperatures average a comfortable 68°F. Your guide will identify the many types of cave features seen on the one-hour tour.

The rich colors of the features come from hematite, manganese, and organic matter that have seeped in through the ceiling. For many visitors the highlight is Kubla Khan, an ornate 58-foot column in the Throne Room, one of the largest and most heavily decorated rooms in the cave.

Above ground you can wander in the hummingbird garden, hike the 2.4-mile **Foothills Loop Trail,** or head out on the 4.2-mile **Guindani Trail Loop** in adjacent Coronado National Forest. ■

# More places to visit in southern Arizona

### AMERIND FOUNDATION

You might not expect to find an outstanding museum in the middle of the rocky desert far from any town, but the Amerind is a jewel worth seeking out. Since 1937, when it was established by amateur archaeologist William Fulton, the foundation has devoted itself to studies of American Indian cultures—hence its name, a contraction of the two words. Set among the massive boulders of Texas Canyon, the Spanish-colonial revival buildings house an outstanding collection of artifacts, mostly from the Southwest and Mexico, which help interpret the past and preserve contemporary Native American traditions.

The Amerind Art Gallery nearby displays paintings and sculptures by American artists of the 19th and 20th centuries. The Museum Store sells Native American art, crafts, jewelry,

**This building at Fort Bowie held the sutler's store, where soldiers and their wives did their shopping.**

and books. Take I-10 Dragoon Exit 318, head southeast for 1 mile, then turn left and drive for 0.75 mile at the sign.

🅰 197 G2  ✉ 64 miles E of Tucson, off I-10 between Benson and Willcox
☎ 520/586-3666, www.amerind.org
🕐 Closed Mon.–Tues. June–Aug. 💲 $

### FORT BOWIE NATIONAL HISTORIC SITE

Ruins mark the site of an Army fort that guarded the strategic Apache Pass during the Indian wars. It began as a primitive camp in 1862 after Apache ambushed troops and later became a center in the campaigns against renegade Apache. After their leader Geronimo surrendered in 1886, the fort was little used, and the Army abandoned it in 1894. A self-guided 3-mile round-trip walk passes the ruin of a station used by Butterfield's Overland Mail Company from 1858 to 1861, the post cemetery, the site of the Battle of Apache Pass, and Apache Spring. The walk also takes you near ruins of the first fort, as well as the larger second fort, where you'll find a small visitor center.

🅰 197 G2  ✉ On Apache Pass Road (all but the last 0.8 mile is paved), 12 miles S of Bowie
☎ 520/847-2500, www.nps.gov/fobo

### REX ALLEN ARIZONA COWBOY MUSEUM

Rex Allen's (1920–1999) talent for playing the guitar and singing took him from his family's homestead near Willcox into the recording business. Allen went on to star in the 1950 film *Arizona Cowboy* and in other movies and television shows. Here, in an early 1890s building on the original main street of Willcox, you can see his sequined cowboy suits, guitars, saddles, movie posters, and a buggy used in the television series *Frontier Doctor.* A park across the street features his statue and a memorial to his horse, Koko. A few doors north of the museum, the Apache leader Geronimo once shopped at the 1880 **Willcox Commercial Store,** Arizona's oldest commercial building still selling clothes and other goods at its original location. South and around the corner at 127 E. Maley Street, the **Chiricahua Regional Museum & Research Center** *(Tel 520/384-3971, closed Sun.)* has displays on the area's land and people. The 1880 **Southern Pacific Depot,** south on Railroad Avenue, has been restored; step into its lobby to see some exhibits.

🅰 197 G2  ✉ 150 N. Railroad Ave., Willcox
☎ 520/384-4583 💲 $ ■

# Travelwise

**Hot-air balloon over
Monument Valley**

# TRAVELWISE INFORMATION

## PLANNING YOUR TRIP

### WHEN TO GO

You can enjoy a visit to Arizona in any month of the year. Sunshine prevails year-round, but to avoid extremes of temperature, simply adjust your elevation, according to season, between the cooler mountains and plateaus of the north and the warmer deserts to the south. Summer is the time to head to the high country, where the world's largest ponderosa pine forest extends across much of the state; highs typically run in the 70s and 80s. At the same time the deserts get so hot that you'll feel you're in an oven. Highs in the low 100s are common and can exceed 110°F, leaving visitors wondering how people survived in this part of the U.S. before air-conditioning. (Some of the museums and pioneer houses explain how Native Americans and early settlers coped.)

Thunderstorms rumble over Arizona's landscape in late summer, drenching some areas while leaving adjacent ones dry; that's when drivers and backcountry travelers need to watch for flash floods. Another series of storms, more gentle this time, arrives in winter, bringing ski resorts to life in the mountains and awakening desert plants. "Snowbirds"—visitors from the northern states and provinces—flock to the desert then to enjoy delightful weather with highs in the 60s and 70s.

If you migrate to the high country in summer and the low in winter, you'll find not only more comfortable temperatures, but also more festivals and events. But don't forget that other people do the same, so you will need to make room reservations. In spring and autumn you can enjoy visiting the entire state, with lower prices and greater availability of accommodations.

### FESTIVALS

**JANUARY**

**Fiesta Bowl Game** Sun Devil Stadium, Tempe, early Jan., tel 480/350-0900 (information) or 800/635-5748 (ticket office), www.tostitosfiestabowl.com. Holiday celebrations (see December, p. 238) culminate with this football classic.

**Scottsdale Celebration of Fine Art** Scottsdale, mid-Jan. to late March, tel 480/443-7695, www.celebrateart.com. More than 100 artists, many of whom can be seen at work, gather for this giant exhibition. It takes place off Scottsdale Road, a mile north of Bell Road.

**Phoenix Open Golf Tournament** Scottsdale, last full week, tel 602/870-4431. PGA players compete in this celebrated event.

**Tucson Open** Tucson, Jan. or Feb., tel 520/571-0400 or 800/882-7660, www.tucsonopen.pgatour.com. Top pros play in this PGA tournament.

**FEBRUARY**

**Parada del Sol Parade and Rodeo** Scottsdale, early Feb., tel 480/945-8481 or 800/877-1117, www.scottsdalecvb.com. The world's longest horse-drawn parade is accompanied by a big rodeo and a street dance.

**Tucson Gem & Mineral Show** Tucson, 2nd weekend, tel 520/322-5773, www.tgms.org. The world's biggest gem and mineral show runs Thursday through Sunday with displays, programs, and sales.

**Flagstaff Winterfest** Flagstaff, tel 928/774-9541 or 800/842-7293. Flagstaff celebrates the winter season with a parade, ski competitions, sled-dog races, family games, and cultural events.

**M.C.A.S. Air Show** Yuma, tel 928/783-0071 or 800/293-0071. Pilots and skydivers take to the air above the Marine Corps Air Station.

**La Fiesta de los Vaqueros** Tucson, late Feb., tel 520/741-2233, www.tucsonrodeo.com. Cowpunchers and their fans gather for rodeo action. The Tucson Rodeo Parade is said to be the longest nonmotorized one in the world.

**MARCH**

**Sedona International Film Festival** Sedona, 1st weekend, tel 928/282-0747, www.sedonafilmfestival.com. Movie enthusiasts gather to see new movies and to attend a workshop.

**Heard Museum Guild Indian Fair & Market** Phoenix, 1st full weekend, tel 602/252-8840, www.heard.org. Native American groups present dances and demonstrations along with food and exhibit arts and crafts.

**Scottsdale Arts Festival** Scottsdale, 2nd weekend, tel 480/994-2787. Art exhibitions and performances, along with children's activities, take place on the Scottsdale Mall.

**St. Patrick's Day Parade** Sedona, March 17 (or nearest Saturday), tel 928/204-2390, www.sedonamainstreet.com. Fans of the Irish bring out the green.

**Midnight at the Oasis Car Show** Yuma, tel 928/783-0071 or 800/293-0071. Beautiful and unusual vehicles on display. Bands give concerts.

**Cactus League Spring Training** Phoenix area and Tucson, tel 480/827-4700 or 800/283-6372, www.mesacvb.com. Baseball fans watch major-league teams warm up for the season in a series of practice and exhibition games.

**Fourth Avenue Street Fair** Tucson, late March, tel 520/624-5004, www.avefun.com. Entertainers, craftspeople, artists, and food create a festival atmosphere. The event repeats in early December.

**Cox Communications Air &**

**Motor Show Spectacular**
Mesa, March or April, tel
480/774-9355 or 480/827-4700,
www.coxairshow.com. Pilots of
military and civilian aircraft show
their skill in the skies. Ground
displays and monster truck
activities are offered too.

**APRIL**
**Arizona Book Festival**
Phoenix, 1st Sat. in April, tel 602/
257-0335, www.azbookfestival.
org. You can meet over 100
authors, listen to them read
their works, and see publishers'
latest books.
**Sunday on Central** Phoenix,
early April, tel 602/262-6862.
Musicians and dancers entertain
in this big street fair.
**Easter Pageant** Mesa, week
preceding Easter, tel 480/964-
7164, www.easterpageant.org.
This popular event takes place at
the Mormon Church's Arizona
Temple.
**Maricopa County Fair**
Phoenix, tel 602/252-0717,
www.maricopacountyfair.org.
Entertainment, carnival rides,
animals, and exhibits draw
crowds to this big event.
**Tucson International
Mariachi Conference** Tucson,
mid to late April, tel 520/624-
1817 or 800/638-8350. Bands
play this traditional form of
Mexican music to appreciative
audiences.
**Pima County Fair** Tucson,
late April, tel 520/762-9100,
www.pimafair.com. The fair has
seemingly countless fun things to
see and do, including circus
events, concerts, carnival rides,
exhibits, and livestock shows.
**Summer Rodeo Series**
Williams, April or May to mid-
August, tel 928/635-9592.
Working cowboys show their
skills on Friday and Saturday
nights.

**MAY**
**Cinco de Mayo** Tucson,
weekend closest to 5th, tel
520/624-1817 or 800/638-8350.
Folk dancers, musicians, artists,
and food vendors commemorate
Mexico's 1862 victory over the

French.
**Chamber Music Sedona**
Sedona, early May, tel 928/204-
2415, www.chambermusic
sedona.org. Musicians gather
from all over the world for this
10-day event. Additional
concerts take place over the
autumn-winter season.
**Bill Williams Rendezvous**
Williams, Memorial Day
weekend, tel 928/635-4061 or
800/863-0546. The Bill Williams
Buckskinners set up an 1800s-
style fur-trade era encampment
for a black-powder shoot, crafts,
and competitions. Everyone
celebrates with a parade, a
street dance, and an arts and
crafts show.
**Phippen Western Art Show
& Sale** Prescott, Memorial Day
weekend, tel 928/778-1385.
About 150 artists come to
Courthouse Plaza for a juried
fine arts show.

**JUNE**
**Sharlot Hall Folk Arts Fair**
Prescott, 1st weekend, tel
928/445-3122, www.sharlot.org.
Costumed actors bring the territorial years to life demonstrat-
ing blacksmithing, woodworking,
churning, spinning, weaving, cowboy cooking, and entertainment.
**Sedona Taste** Sedona, Sun.
before Father's Day, tel 928/282-
7822. Top chefs prepare samples
of food and serve fine wines.
**Pine Country Pro Rodeo**
Flagstaff, 3rd weekend, tel
928/774-9541 or 800/842-7293,
www.pinecountryprorodeo.com.
Top rodeo cowboys provide
plenty of thrills.
**Shakespeare Sedona** Sedona,
June–July, tel 928/821-4391
www.shakespearesedona.com.
The Bard's plays are performed
under the open sky.

**JULY**
**July 4 Celebration** Page, tel
928/645-2741 or 888/261-7243.
Fireworks burst above Glen
Canyon Dam after a parade and
other festivities.
**Prescott Frontier Days**
Prescott, July 4 week, tel
928/445-3103 or 800/358-1888,

www.worldsoldestrodeo.com.
Cowboys have been celebrating
Independence Day with rodeos
here since 1888. The action with
professional rodeo cowboys
begins in late June and lasts
through the July 4 holiday.
Prescott Frontier Days Parade—
one of the biggest in the state—
rolls through downtown on the
Saturday nearest July 4. Other
festivities include dances, a
concert, a Whiskey Row Boot
Race, fun runs, a golf tournament, a rodeo queen coronation,
and fireworks.
**July 4 Celebration** Flagstaff, tel
928/774-9541 or 800/842-7293.
A parade, an arts and crafts
show, Pioneer Days Festival,
and fireworks celebrate both
Independence Day and the
legendary naming of Flagstaff.
Coconino County Horse Races
run on the weekend of July 4.
**Arizona Highland & Celtic
Festival** Flagstaff, 3rd Sat., tel
928/774-9541 or 800/842-7293.
The celebration relives the
heritage of Brittany, Cornwall,
Ireland, the Isle of Man, Scotland,
and Wales. You'll see bagpipers,
dances, athletic demonstrations,
and food.
**White Mountain Native
American Art Festival &
Indian Market** Pinetop-
Lakeside, 3rd weekend, tel
928/367-4290 or 800/573-4031,
www.pinetoplakeside.cc. Tribes
from across the Southwest
gather for dances, music, arts
and crafts displays, and food.
**Arizona Cardinals Training
Camp** Flagstaff, late July to mid-
Aug., tel 928/523-2273, 928/774-
9541, or 800/842-7293,
www.azcardinals.com.
Most practice sessions of this
NFL team at Northern Arizona
University are open to visitors.

**AUGUST**
**Summerfest** Flagstaff, 1st full
weekend, tel 928/774-9541 or
800/842-7293. A big arts and
crafts festival at Fort Tuthill
south of town.
**White Mountain Bluegrass
Music Festival** Pinetop-
Lakeside, 2nd weekend, tel

928/367-4290 or 800/573-4031, www.pinetoplakeside.cc. Musicians play lively music among the pines.
**Payson Rodeo** Payson, 3rd weekend, tel 928/474-9440. Local rodeo fans claim this is the world's oldest continuous rodeo—since 1884. A parade and dance accompany the professional rodeo thrills.
**Arizona Cowboy Poets Gathering** Prescott, 3rd weekend, tel 928/445-3122, www.sharlot.org. Stories, poems, and songs recall life in the saddle.

## SEPTEMBER
**Navajo Nation Fair** Window Rock, early Sept., tel 928/871-6478 or 928/871-6702, www.navajoland.com. Navajo and visitors gather for a rodeo, powwow, the Miss Navajo Pageant, a carnival, and exhibits.
**Coconino County Fair** Flagstaff, Labor Day weekend, tel 928/774-5139. The large fair features livestock, entertainment, exhibits, a carnival, and a demolition derby.
**Grand Canyon Music Festival** Grand Canyon Village, tel 928/638-9215 or 800/997-8285, www.grandcanyonmusic fest.org. Classical music and some jazz waft over the South Rim in a series of concerts.
**Jazz on the Rocks Festival** Sedona, 3rd weekend, tel 928/282-1985, www.sedona jazz.com. Some of the great names in jazz perform for large audiences.
**Apache County Fair** St. Johns, 3rd weekend after Labor Day, tel 928/337-2000. Entertainment, livestock shows, horse racing, and exhibits.
**Flagstaff Festival of Science** Flagstaff, late Sept., tel 928/774-9541 or 800/842-7293. The ten-day festival celebrates the excitement of science with talks by top scientists, interactive exhibits, and field trips.

## OCTOBER
**Air Affaire** Page, 1st weekend, tel 928/645-9373. Air-show

pilots thrill and entertain.
**Kingman Air & Auto Show** Kingman, 1st weekend, tel 928/753-6106, www.kingman airshow.com. Pilots display acrobatic skills in the sky while racing cars compete on the ground.
**Andy Devine Days** Kingman, 2nd weekend, tel 928/753-6106, www.kingmanchamber.org. A parade, PRCA rodeo, and other festivities honor Kingman's favorite son.
**Fort Verde Days** Camp Verde, 2nd weekend, tel 928/567-0535. The cavalry of the Old West returns to parade and drill. Other festivities include a barbecue, roping events, arts and crafts show, games, and dance.
**Helldorado Days** Tombstone, 3rd weekend, tel 520/457-3929 or 888/457-3929, www.cityoftombstone.com. Three days of shootouts, parades, dances, and other entertainment celebrate Tombstone's rip-roaring 1880s heritage.
**Apache Jii Day** Globe, 4th Sat., tel 928/425-4495 or 800/804-5623. Apache and other tribes celebrate with dances, crafts, and food.
**London Bridge Days** Lake Havasu City, late Oct., tel 928/855-4115, www.golakehavasu.com. A Grand Parade, entertainment, and food celebrate the famous bridge's dedication.

## NOVEMBER
**Yuma Colorado River Crossing Balloon Festival** Yuma, tel 928/783-0071 or 800/293-0071. Hot-air balloons fill the skies.

## DECEMBER
**Wahweap Festival of Lights** Page, 1st Sat., tel 928/645-2741 or 888/261-7243. Decorated boats cruise to the dam and back to Wahweap.
**Christmas City** Prescott, Nov.–Dec., tel 928/445-2000 or 800/266-7534. Its Christmas parade, courthouse lighting, music,

and exhibits have earned Prescott the epithet "Arizona's Christmas City."
**Fourth Avenue Street Fair** Tucson, early Dec., tel 520/624-5004, www.avefun.com. Artists and craftspeople display their work while entertainers and food booths provide diversions.
**Festival of Lights** Sedona, 2nd Sat., tel 928/282-4838, www.tlaq.com. Thousands of luminaria light up the grounds of Tlaquepaque while musicians and choirs celebrate the holiday season.
**Fiesta Bowl Parade** Phoenix area, late Dec., tel 480/350-0900 (information) or 800/635-5748 (ticket office), www.tostitosfiesta bowl.com. A parade, the National Band Championship, a block party, and sporting events lead up to the big game (see also January, p. 236).

## WHAT TO TAKE

Because of low humidity, temperatures can swing drastically at any time of year, so dressing in layers is the best way to adapt. Comfortable clothes and sturdy walking shoes will add to your enjoyment. Arizonans tend to dress informally. Only a handful of restaurants in the state expect men to wear ties, and a few western-style restaurants even prohibit them, as is sometimes evident from the snipped-off ends tacked onto the ceiling! The bola tie, a cord held by a clasp typically made of silver with inlaid minerals, is the preferred neckwear; bolas are sold at many jewelry and gift shops.

A hat and sunblock will fend off the dazzling sun. You're unlikely to encounter biting insects, but a few canyons have them in summer, when repellent comes in handy.

## FURTHER READING
Both city sights and outdoors are covered in several regularly revised, comprehensive state or regional guidebooks. More spe-

cialized guides for hikers include *100 Hikes in Arizona* (1994) by Scott S. Warren (also the author of *Exploring Arizona's Wild Areas*, 1996), *Hiking the Grand Canyon National Park* (1997) by Ron Adkison, and *Sedona Hikes* (1997) by Richard and Sherry Mangum. For descriptions and maps of great bike rides, try *Mountain Biking Arizona* (1998) by Sarah Bennett.

Bill Weir's compact *Grand Canyon Handbook* (revised regularly) and the illustrated *Grand Canyon Country: Its Majesty and Its Lore* (1997) by Seymour L. Fishbein concentrate on the state's most famous attraction. *A Field Guide to the Grand Canyon* (1996) by Stephen Whitney identifies the plant and animal life. Natural history buffs should take a look at Barbara Kingsolver's *High Tide in Tucson* and Gary Paul Nabhan's *The Desert Smells Llke Rain: A Naturalist in Papago Indian Country*.

Ancient cultures and their legacy are described and pictured in *Those Who Came Before: Southwestern Archaeology in the National Park System* (1994) by Robert and Florence Lister, while the story of Arizona's people from Paleolithic times to the present is told in *Arizona: A History* (1995) by Thomas E. Sheridan. John Wesley Powell's account of his epic 19th-century boat trips through the Grand Canyon, *The Exploration of the Colorado River and its Canyons* (1895) is widely available in reprints. A different first-hand account of frontier Arizona is *Vanished Arizona* (1911) by Martha Summerhayes. *Arizona Ghost Towns and Mining Camps* (1995) by Philip Varney will help you find and appreciate these old communities.

Aspects of Native American cultures are explored in *Left Handed Son of Old Man Hat: A Navajo Autobiography* (1938) recorded by Walter Dyk and available in reprints, and also in the illustrated *The Enduring Navajo* (1994) by Laura Gilpin, *Hopi* (1982) by Susanne and Jake Page, and *Art of the Hopi* (1998) by Jerry and Lois Essary Jacka.

Stories about life in Arizona include the many novels of Zane Grey and the more recent *Doc Holliday's Woman* (1995) by Jane Candia Coleman and *In Search of Snow* (1994) by Luis Urrea.

# GETTING AROUND

## AIRPORTS

Sky Harbor International Airport, conveniently located for Phoenix, Tempe, and Scottsdale, provides the most connections to the rest of the country and beyond (tel 602/273-3300, www.phxskyharbor.com). Commuter flights radiate out from here. The major carriers also serve Tucson International Airport in the southeastern part of the state (tel 520/573-8000, www.tucsonairport.org). Flights to and from Tucson airport may cost more, so shop around. Both airports are well served by rental car agencies, taxis, and local buses. Grand Canyon's airport (tel 928/638-2446) is the next busiest, though most of the flights here are in smaller aircraft and originate in Las Vegas, Nevada.

## CAR TRAVEL

Most people find their own vehicle the handiest way of getting around Arizona. Public transport is generally useful only between the cities and within the Phoenix and Tucson urban areas. Additionally, the Grand Canyon National Park has shuttle services on the south rim to alleviate traffic congestion.

Many rental-car agencies compete for your business; you may be able to rent an RV or a 4WD vehicle as well. Advance reserva-

tions will usually secure the lowest rate. You'll need insurance, but check to see if your personal policy or your credit card will provide sufficient coverage before paying extra. Major agencies include:

**Alamo** Tel 800/462-5266, www.goalamo.com
**Avis** Tel 800/331-1212, www.avis.com
**Budget** Tel 800/527-0700, www.drivebudget.com
**Dollar** Tel 800/800-4000, www.dollarcar.com
**Hertz** Tel 800/654-3131, www.hertz.com
**Thrifty** Tel 800/367-2277, www.thrifty.com.

## TRAINS

Amtrak runs two luxury trains across the state, connecting Los Angeles with New Orleans, Chicago, and other points to the east (tel 800/872-7245, www.amtrak.com). The *Southwest Chief* goes through the north of the state and runs daily in each direction via Kingman, Williams Junction, Flagstaff, and Winslow. The *Sunset Limited* goes across southern Arizona only three times weekly in each direction via Yuma, Tucson, and Benson.

## BUSES

Greyhound has several routes in Arizona and connects with smaller bus companies (tel 800/231-2222, www.greyhound.com). Nava-Hopi Tours (tel 800/892-8687, www.navahopitours.com) connects the Grand Canyon with Flagstaff and Phoenix (at the Metrocenter and at the airport).

## OTHER OPTIONS

Day and overnight tours take in some of the state's scenic and historic destinations from major cities. Senior citizens can check out Elderhostel's many educational offerings in Arizona, tel 617/426-7788 or 877/426-8056, www.elderhostel.org.

# PRACTICAL ADVICE

## MAPS

Statewide maps are widely available at tourist offices and bookstores. The *Arizona Road & Recreation Atlas* (published by Benchmark Maps) shows much greater detail than most and has back roads, shaded relief, public land designations, GPS grids, and recreation information. Each of Arizona's national forests has one or more maps that will help in navigating back roads and in finding trailheads and other points of interest. The Bureau of Land Management has a good map of the Arizona Strip in the far north; it's recommended if you plan to explore the backcountry there. Hikers have a choice of topographic map scales, of which the 1:24,000 (7.5-minute) series has the most detail.

## SAFETY

Arizona has a low crime rate. You're unlikely to have problems if you're aware of natural hazards and take care with your gear. Even the downtowns of the big cities are considered safe at night, but avoid run-down areas nearby on foot after dark.

Flash floods can sometimes obstruct highways after storms; just wait for the water to go down, which normally happens quite quickly. Dust storms can block visibility so badly that it is best to pull off the road (turn off lights so as not to confuse other drivers).

## TAXES & TIPPING

A sales tax of between 7 and 10 percent is added to the bill at most motels, hotels, resorts, commercial campgrounds, restaurants, shops, and some attractions. Tax is not usually added to prices at federal, state, or Native American sites and campgrounds. Taxi drivers, hairdressers, bartenders, and waiters who provide table service expect a tip of 15 to 20 percent.

## TIME

"What time is it?" bewildered travelers often ask in northeastern Arizona. To avoid mixups, remember that the state is on mountain standard time all year, except for the Navajo Reservation, which goes on daylight saving time—add one hour April to October—to conform with its Utah and New Mexico sections. The Hopi Reservation, completely within Arizona and surrounded by the Navajo Reservation, stays on standard time year-round along with the rest of the state.

## TRAVELERS WITH DISABILITIES

Airlines, ground transport, newer motels and hotels, restaurants, parks, and public buildings often have facilities for people with mobility difficulties. You can call ahead with your special needs. Tourist offices may have advice and literature too. Access-Able Travel Source (P.O. Box 1796, Wheat Ridge, CO 80034, tel 303/232-2979, fax 303/239-8486, www.access-able.com) provides information to help people with disabilities enjoy worry-free journeys.

## VISITOR INFORMATION

The Arizona Office of Tourism at 2702 N. Third St., 4th floor, Suite 4015, Phoenix, AZ 85004, tel 602/230-7733 or 888/520-3434, fax 602/240-5475, e-mail travel-info@azot.com is a good place to start. It's open Mon.–Fri., 8 a.m.–5 p.m. Information is also available at local tourist offices and at the Painted Cliffs Welcome Center just off I-40 Exit 359 near the New Mexico border.

## WEBSITES

The Arizona Office of Tourism's excellent website (www.arizona guide.com) contains travel information and links to many visitor bureaus and chamber of commerce sites. For the Grand Canyon, try Grand Canyon National Park's official site at www.nps.gov/grca and the Grand Canyon Chamber of Commerce's site at www.thecanyon.com.

Other useful sites include: www.flagstaffarizona.org www.phoenix.cvb.com www.visittucson.org and, for hiking, www.gorp.com.

# EMERGENCIES

## EMERGENCY PHONE NUMBER

Dial 911 (or the number posted on the telephone) for police, ambulance, or fire emergencies.

## HEALTH

For nonemergency medical care, a doctor's office or a clinic will have lower costs than a hospital emergency room.

## LOST PROPERTY

Numbers to report missing credit cards or traveler's checks:
**Credit cards**
American Express, tel 800/528-4800
Diners Club, tel 800/234-6377
Discover, tel 800/347-2683
MasterCard, tel 800/826-2181
Visa, tel 800/336-8472
**Traveler's checks**
American Express, tel 800/221-7282
Citicorp, tel 800/645-6556
MasterCard, tel 800/223-9920
Thomas Cook, tel 800/223-7373
Visa, tel 800/227-6811.

# HOTELS & RESTAURANTS

Accommodations in Arizona range from world-famous resorts and guest ranches with excellent recreation facilities in spectacular settings, through an abundance of good-value motels, both mid-range and bargain-priced, to youth hostels. The accommodations described here lie close to the attractions listed in this book or are destinations in themselves.

## ACCOMMODATIONS

Peak times—when it's best to make reservations—are late winter and early spring in the desert areas and summer weekends in the high country. It's a good idea to call ahead for Grand Canyon accommodations any time of year. Across the state, weekends and holidays tend to be busiest and often cost more. Off-season is bargain time, when you can find great prices at motels and check into a resort for as little as half the peak-season rate.

Nearly all places provide non-smoking rooms. Smaller inns and bed-and-breakfasts often prohibit smoking or restrict it to outdoors. All accommodations and restaurants provide parking lots or valet parking for their guests, except Phantom Ranch in the Grand Canyon or Havasupai Lodge in Havasu Canyon, which are reached on foot or by mule.

### Hotels & motels

The major chains have become very popular—you're likely to find your favorites in the cities and larger towns. Chains include:
Best Western, tel 800/528-1234, www.bestwestern.com
Comfort Inn, tel 800/228-5150, www.comfortinn.com
Days Inn, tel 800/329-7466, www.daysinn.com
Econo Lodge, tel 800/553-2666, www.econolodge.com
Hilton, tel 800/445-8667, www.hilton.com
Holiday Inn and Holiday Inn Express, tel 800/465-4329, www.holiday-inn.com
Marriott Hotels, tel 800/228-9290, www.marriott.com
Motel 6, tel 800/466-8356, www.motel6.com
Radisson, tel 800/333-3333, www.radisson.com
Ramada Inn, tel 800/272-6232, www.ramada.com,
Rodeway Inn, tel 800/228-2000, www.rodeway.com
Super 8, tel 800/800-8000, www.super8.com.

Historic hotels will take you back to earlier times. The grand hotels, well worth a visit to the lobby even if you're staying elsewhere, include El Tovar on the Grand Canyon's South Rim, Grand Canyon Lodge on the North Rim, La Posada in Winslow, the Hassayampa Inn at Prescott, the Copper Queen Hotel in Bisbee, and the Gadsden Hotel in Douglas. More modest historic hotels have lots of character too, such as the Weatherford in Flagstaff and the Congress in Tucson, but loud music coming from the bands downstairs can make sleep difficult at these two!

Older motels, long since bypassed by interstates and freeways, can be fine and often go for a bargain price. They're numerous on segments of Route 66, in towns across northern Arizona, and on the old highways through cities in the rest of the state. The key to happiness in these independents is to check the room before handing over your money—not all places will give refunds if you change your mind. Guests staying at family-owned motels not only save money but also help preserve these disappearing pieces of Americana.

### Bed-and-breakfasts

Hosts offer a personal service and comfortable rooms both in the cities and out in the countryside. Because a B&B reflects the owner's personality, it's worth asking about the establishment's policies and features. Reservation agencies can be a big help in matching you with a proprietor who has similar interests. The agencies also know of small bed-and-breakfasts that have no advertising or listings elsewhere. Mi Casa Su Casa, P.O. Box 950, Tempe, AZ 85280-0950, tel 480/990-0682 or 800/456-0682, www.azres.com, has many places statewide and beyond. Arizona Trails Bed & Breakfast Reservation Service, P.O. Box 18998, Fountain Hills, AZ 85269-8998, tel 480/837-4284 or 888/799-4284, www.arizona trails.com, also offers listings statewide and beyond. Arizona Association of Bed & Breakfast Inns, P.O. Box 22086, Flagstaff, AZ 86002-2086, tel 800/284-2589, www.arizona-bed-breakfast.com, provides information about its members.

### Guest ranches

Staying on a ranch gives you the opportunity to view the scenery from horseback. Guest ranches provide a mix of Old West atmosphere and resort comforts. The Arizona Dude Ranch Association, P.O. Box 603, Cortaro, AZ 85652, www.azdra.com, will tell you about the guest ranch experience and who their members are.

### Hostels

Popular with budget travelers of all ages, hostels can be great places to meet people from around the world. Accommodations are shared (usually separate men's and women's sleeping rooms) and most places have a kitchen, TV lounge, and recreation facilities. In Arizona, you will find hostels at Tuba City, Flagstaff, Williams, Sedona, Phoenix, and Tucson. A hostel card available from Hostelling International or international affiliates, will give lower rates at both Tuba City and Phoenix. Hostelling International cards can be purchased at the Phoenix hostel, Metcalf House, 1026 N. Ninth St., Phoenix, AZ 85006, tel 602/254-9803 or from the national office, Hostelling International, 733 15th St., Suite

840, Washington, D.C. 20005, tel 202/783-6161, www.hiayh.org. *Hostels U.S.A.*, published by Globe Pequot Press, has detailed descriptions and ratings. Online, try www.hostels.com.

### Campgrounds

By pitching a tent or parking an RV, you can be in the midst of some of the most beautiful places in Arizona. You have thousands of choices. The commercial campgrounds offer the most amenities—hookups, showers, laundromats, and recreation facilities. Arizona State Park campgrounds tend to be the best deal—they have most of the services of a commercial campground plus some great locations near lakes, mountains, or other features. National Forest, National Park Service, and Indian campgrounds tend to have just the basics—a picnic table, a place to park, and a toilet or outhouse; water may be available, but only occasionally will showers be nearby.

Dispersed camping is an option on much of the National Forest, Bureau of Land Management, and National Recreation Area lands. This takes a bit more work—you have to check regulations, bring water, carry a shovel for burying wastes, and find a suitable spot away from towns, highways, developed recreation areas, and sole water sources (used by wildlife and stock). Check for fire restrictions—you may need a campfire permit. During dry periods, smoking, campfires, and even entry to certain areas of forests may be prohibited. The benefits of dispersed camping can be tranquility rarely experienced in established campgrounds, cost savings, and the freedom to come and go as you please.

### Credit cards

Abbreviations used are: AE (American Express), DC (Diners Club), MC (Mastercard), and V (Visa).

### RESTAURANTS

Chefs at major resorts and independent restaurants strive to provide an excellent dining experience for their guests. It is always a good idea to call ahead to resort and other fine-dining restaurants for dinner reservations and to check on dress codes. Arizonans enjoy ethnic food, too, and you'll rarely be far from a Mexican or Chinese restaurant. Other cuisines abound in the larger cities, especially those with universities.
L = lunch   D = dinner

The hotels and restaurants listed here have been grouped first accordiing to their region, then listed alphabetically within their price category. For disabled access, it is best to check with the establishment to verify the extent of their facilities.

### GRAND CANYON VILLAGE (SOUTH RIM)

**Reservations.** You can make reservations for all lodging inside the park on the South and North Rims through Grand Canyon National Park Lodges, 14001 E. Iliff Ave., Suite 600, Aurora, CO 80014, tel 303/297-2757 (advance reservations), 928/638-2631 (same- and next-day reservations South Rim and Phantom Ranch, fax 303/297-3175, www.grandcanyonlodges.com), 928/638-2611 (same- and next-day reservations North Rim), or www.amfac.com (all areas).

## SOMETHING SPECIAL

### 🏨 EL TOVAR HOTEL
**$$$$$**

Since the doors opened in 1905, El Tovar has offered its guests the finest accommodations and dining in the park. The lobby's cathedral ceiling, handmade furniture, fireplace, and

## PRICES

### HOTELS
An indication of the cost of a double room is given by $ signs.

| | |
|---|---|
| $$$$$ | Over $280 |
| $$$$ | $200–$280 |
| $$$ | $120–$200 |
| $$ | $80–$120 |
| $ | Under $80 |

### RESTAURANTS
An indication of the cost of a three-course dinner without drinks is given by $ signs.

| | |
|---|---|
| $$$$$ | Over $80 |
| $$$$ | $50–$80 |
| $$$ | $35–$50 |
| $$ | $20–$35 |
| $ | Under $20 |

pine-log walls greet you as you enter this rustic, yet elegant lodge. Rooms—no two alike—range from small to spacious; all have private baths. Four suites have canyon views.
**$$$–$$$$$**
RESERVATIONS SEE ABOVE
ℹ 78  🅿  ♿  All major cards

### 🏨 BRIGHT ANGEL LODGE
**$–$$$$**
RESERVATIONS SEE ABOVE
Some of the cabins around this rustic lodge have canyon views and fireplaces. The early 1890s Buckey O'Neill Suite cabin is one of the oldest buildings in the park. Basic rooms inside the lodge have shared facilities. This popular spot on the rim near the Bright Angel Trailhead offers a snack bar, mule rides desk, and two restaurants. Some tables in the informal restaurant have canyon views. The Arizona Room opens for dinner with steaks, chicken, ribs, fish, and vegetarian entrées. No reservations.
ℹ 89  🅿  All major cards

## THUNDERBIRD & KACHINA LODGES
**$$$**
RESERVATIONS SEE P. 242
The contemporary design of these lodges doesn't fit in with the historic log-and-stone buildings nearby on the rim, but they do offer comfortable rooms in a very convenient location. The second-story canyon-side rooms have views, yet cost only a bit more than those on the back.
🛏 104 🅿 All major cards

## MASWIK LODGE
**$$-$$$**
RESERVATIONS SEE P. 242
Back in the woods from the rim, guests have a choice of small cabins or two types of motel rooms. There's a cafeteria, too.
🛏 278 🅿 All major cards

## YAVAPAI LODGE
**$$-$$$**
RESERVATIONS SEE P. 242
Largest of the lodges within the park, Yavapai has two types of motel rooms and a cafeteria. It's a mile east of Bright Angel Lodge and set back from the rim.
🛏 358 🅿 All major cards

## EL TOVAR
**$$**
TEL 928/638-2631
Canyon views complement the fine service and food in the restaurant of the El Tovar Hotel (see p. 242). The menu offers both American and Continental cuisine. Dinner reservations are required and can be made up to six months in advance.
🍴 250 🅿 🅢 All major cards

## INNER GORGE

## PHANTOM RANCH
**$$**
RESERVATIONS SEE P. 242
You can hike or ride a mule down to these rustic stone cabins near the sparkling Bright Angel Creek at the bottom of the Grand Canyon. Dormitory beds ($) are available too. Evaporative coolers fend off the summer heat. The ranch-style dining room offers breakfast, box lunches, and a choice of stew, vegetarian, or steak dinners. During the day it sells snacks.
🛏 13 All major cards

## TUSAYAN

Nine miles south of Grand Canyon Village, this busy tourist village has many places to stay, a selection of restaurants, IMAX theater, and a nearby airport.

## BEST WESTERN GRAND CANYON SQUIRE INN
**$$$-$$$$**
TEL 928/638-2681 or 800/622-6966
FAX 928/638-2782
www.grandcanyonsquire.com
The inn offers large modern rooms, two dining rooms, a sports bar, and many amenities—bowling, tennis, pool, whirlpool, sauna, exercise room, and a video arcade. The Coronado Room offers fine dining nightly, and the main dining room offers all meals.
🛏 250 🅿 🛗 🅢 🏊 🏥 All major cards

## GRAND CANYON QUALITY INN & SUITES
**$$$-$$$$**
TEL 928/638-2673 or 800/228-5151
FAX 928/638-9537
Distinct southwest style with earth tones decorates the spacious rooms, most with patios or balconies. The suites have living areas. An attractive, large atrium houses a Wintergarten Lounge with trees and flowers as well as the restaurant. There are indoor and outdoor spas, and an outdoor pool.
🛏 232 🅿 🛗 🅢 🏊 🏥 All major cards

## GRAND HOTEL
**$$$**
TEL 928/638-3333 or 888/634-7263
FAX 928/638-3131
The rustic stone-and-timber exterior encloses an indoor pool and spa, and comfortable hotel rooms with Native American art setting the theme. Some rooms have balconies; those on the back have a forest view. Native American dancers and cowboy singers entertain in the Canyon Star restaurant
🛏 121 🅿 🛗 🅢 🏊 🏥 All major cards

## NORTH RIM

## GRAND CANYON LODGE
Motel rooms and three types of cabin have a wonderful location amid the ponderosa pines. The splendid main lodge features a soaring roof with huge windows facing the sublime immensity of the Grand Canyon. Amenities include a mule rides desk, a sunroom, an auditorium, a snack bar, post office, and saloon. Diners at the Lodge have a rim-side seat and the memorable dinners (reservations required) offer a choice of steak, prime rib, salmon, chicken, pork, and pasta dishes. Grand Canyon Lodge provides the only accommodations within the park on the North Rim, so reserve well in advance.
**$$**
RESERVATIONS SEE P. 242
🛏 209 🅿 🕐 Closed mid-Oct.–mid-May All major cards

## KAIBAB LODGE
**$$-$$$**
ARIZ. 67
TEL 928/638-2389 IN SEASON,

**HOTELS & RESTAURANTS**

928/526-0924 or 800/525-0924
OFF-SEASON
FAX 928/638-9864 IN SEASON,
928/527-9398 OFF-SEASON
www.canyoneers.com
Rustic cabins with wooden
floors nestle in an aspen and
pine forest beside a meadow
in the Kaibab National Forest.
The main lodge's great room
has high beamed ceilings and
a beautiful stone hearth. The
restaurant serves breakfast
and dinner. The Lodge is
located 18.5 miles north of
Bright Angel Point and 26
miles south of Jacob Lake.
[i] 29 [P] [⊕] Closed
Nov. I–mid-May [MC, V

🏨 **JACOB LAKE INN**
**$$**
JUNCTION OF US 89A &
ARIZ. 67
TEL 928/643-7232
FAX 928/643-7235
www.jacoblake.com
Accommodations at this
inn, situated in the Kaibab
National Forest, consist of 27
cabins (summer only) and 12
motel rooms.
[i] 39 [P] [All major
cards

**PAGE**

🏨 **COURTYARD BY
MARRIOTT**
**$$$$**
600 CLUBHOUSE DR.
TEL 928/645-5000 or
800/851-3855
FAX 928/645-5004
Spacious accommodations,
views of Lake Powell from
some rooms, and the adjacent
Lake Powell National Golf
Course make this hotel a top
choice for many.
[i] 153 [P] [⊕] [All major cards

🏨 **WAHWEAP LODGE**
**$$$$**
100 LAKESHORE DR.
TEL 928/645-2433 or
800/528-6154
FAX 928/645-1031
www.visitlakepowell.com
On the shore of Lake Powell,

the lodge offers boat tours
of the lake, and a variety of
boat rentals. Half the rooms
overlook the water (best
views in the west wing). The
restaurant's curved glass wall
provides diners with a pan-
orama of Lake Powell.
[i] 375 [P] [All major cards

🏨 **BEST WESTERN
ARIZONA INN**
**$$**
716 RIM VIEW DR.
TEL 928/645-2466 or
800/826-2718
FAX 928/645-2053
Half of the rooms of this
modern motel have a grand
panorama of Lake Powell;
other rooms are slightly
cheaper. There's a restaurant/
steakhouse next door.
[i] 103 [P] [All major cards

🏨 **LU LU'S SLEEP EZZE
MOTEL**
**$–$$**
105 8TH AVE. & ELM
TEL 928/608-0273 or
800/553-6211
E-MAIL mldiehl@yahoo.com
This little motel lies in Page's
"historic district," a quiet
avenue lined with apartments
dating from the time of the
construction of Glen Canyon
Dam. Rooms have been
attractively renovated.
[i] 8 [P] [MC, V

🍴 **KEN'S OLD WEST
RESTAURANT**
**$–$$**
718 VISTA AVE.
TEL 928/645-5160
This cowboy steakhouse
serves dinners of steak, prime
rib, chicken, and seafood. A
Western band performs here
on many nights.
[🪑] 285 [P] [⊕] Closed Sun.
& Mon. in winter [All
major cards

🍴 **BELLA NAPOLI**
**$**
810 N. NAVAJO DR.
TEL 928/645-2706

Fine Italian cuisine is served
for dinner with inside and
patio seating.
[🪑] 100 [P] [⊕] Call [AE, MC, V

**PEACH SPRINGS**

🏨 **HUALAPAI LODGE**
**$$**
ROUTE 66
TEL 928/769-2230 or
888/255-9550
FAX 928/769-2372
www.hualapaitours.com
The modern lodge is a good
base for visiting the western
Grand Canyon. You can
arrange river trips here and
obtain information on visiting
spectacular overlooks or
taking the drive into the
bottom of the canyon. Peach
Springs is at the midpoint on
the longest remaining section
of old Route 66.
[i] 60 [P] [All
major cards

**NORTHEASTERN
ARIZONA**

**CAMERON**

🏨 **CAMERON TRADING
🍴 POST MOTEL**
**$$–$$$$**
TEL 928/679-2231 or
800/338-7385
FAX 928/679-2350
www.camerontradingpost.com
Southwestern decor enhances
the rooms at this trading post
beside the Little Colorado
River. It's a popular stop
between the Canyon's South
and North Rims, and with
visitors to Navajo and Hopi
lands. Excellent restaurant.
[i] 66 [P] [All major
cards

**CANYON DE CHELLY &
CHINLE**

🏨 **HOLIDAY INN**
🍴 **$$$**
TEL 928/674-5000 or
800/HOLIDAY
FAX 928/674-8264
Most of the rooms have a

balcony or patio and face a cottonwood-shaded courtyard and pool. It's located near the mouth of Canyon de Chelly on the road from Chinle. A full-service restaurant prepares American and Navajo cuisine (lunch Mon.–Fri. only). Navajo food is based largely on fried bread, which can be served with toppings of meat, beans, lettuce, tomato or other vegetables, and cheese, rather like a pizza.
🛏 108 🅿 ❄ 🏊 🏋
🔑 All major cards

### 🏨 THUNDERBIRD LODGE
**$$–$$$**
TEL 928/674-5841 or 800/679-2473
FAX 928/674-5844
www.tbirdlodge.com
Cottonwood trees and lawns surround the lodge buildings near the mouth of Canyon de Chelly. Rooms have Navajo art and decor. The original 1896 trading post is now a cafeteria that serves American and Navajo food. Canyon tours depart from the lodge.
🛏 73 🅿 ❄ 🔑 All major cards

## KAYENTA

### 🏨 HAMPTON INN
**$$–$$$**
US 160
TEL 928/697-3170 or 800/426-7866
FAX 928/697-3189
Large rooms are decorated with Southwestern art and motifs. The restaurant serves a continental breakfast to guests only and then is open for lunch and dinner. Kayenta is a handy base for exploring Monument Valley and Navajo National Monument.
🛏 73 🅿 🔄 ❄ 🏊
🔑 All major cards

## MANY FARMS

### 🏨 MANY FARMS INN
**$**
MANY FARMS HIGH SCHOOL

TEL 928/781-6362 (BEST TO CALL ON A WEEKDAY)
Students run this inn as a training project. Rooms have one or two beds and shared baths. There's nothing to see in Many Farms, but it is a convenient stop between Monument Valley and Canyon de Chelly.
🛏 30 🅿 ❄

## MONUMENT VALLEY, UTAH

### 🏨 GOULDING'S LODGE
The modern rooms each have a private balcony from which you can gaze out across the expansive scenery. The lodge also offers historic exhibits in the original trading post, an audiovisual program, and Monument Valley tours. The restaurant prepares American dishes and some Navajo items. Goulding's is just north of the Arizona border on US 163, then west 1.5 miles.
**$$$–$$$$**
TEL 435/727-3231 or 800/874-0902
FAX 435/727-3344
www.gouldings.com
🛏 62 🅿 ❄ 🏊 🏋
🔑 All major cards

## SECOND MESA

### 🏨🍴 HOPI CULTURAL CENTER INN
**$$$**
TEL 928/734-2401
FAX 928/734-6651
Modern rooms provide the only accommodations on the Hopi reservation. Sample authentic Hopi food, such as *paatupsuki* (pinto beans and hominy soup) and *tsili' ngava* (pinto beans and ground beef in a chili sauce). For breakfast, try the blue corn pancakes. American favorites too.
🛏 33 🅿 ❄ 🔑 All major cards

## WINDOW ROCK

### 🏨 NAVAJOLAND DAYS INN
**$$**
392 W. HWY. 264
TEL 928/871-5690 or 800/325-2525
FAX 928/871-5699
An indoor pool and spa are features of this motel in St. Michaels, 3.4 miles west of Window Rock.
🛏 92 🅿 ❄ 🏊 🏋
🔑 All major cards

### 🏨 NAVAJO NATION INN
**$$**
48 W. HWY. 264
TEL 928/871-4108 or 800/662-6189
FAX 928/871-5466
Rooms have Navajo decor, and the restaurant serves Navajo and American food.
🛏 56 🅿 ❄ 🔑 All major cards

## COTTONWOOD

### 🏨 BEST WESTERN COTTONWOOD INN
**$$–$$$**
993 S. MAIN ST. (JCT. OF ARIZ. 89A & ARIZ. 260)
TEL 928/634-5575 or 800/350-0025
FAX 928/634-5576
This comfortable motel has a central location and a restaurant that serves all meals.
🛏 77 🅿 ❄ 🏊 🏋 🔑 All major cards

### 🍴 BLUEGRASS CAFE
**$–$$**
315 S. MAIN ST.
TEL 928/639-3620
The kitchen turns out American favorites such as steak, chicken, seafood, and pasta.
🍴 52 🅿 🕐 Closed Mon. ❄ 🔑 DC, MC, V

HOTELS & RESTAURANTS

## 🍴 BLAZIN' M RANCH CHUCKWAGON
$
OFF 10TH ST.
TEL 928/634-0334 or
800/937-8643
www.blazinm.com
A supper of cowboy food is followed by a show with cowboy songs and skits. There's a choice of beef, chicken, or vegetarian main course. It's great fun and popular with children. Reserve, especially for the veggie dinner.
🪑 260  🅿  🕐 Closed
Sun.–Tues., all Jan. & Aug.
💳 AE, MC, V

### FLAGSTAFF

## 🏨 INN AT 410
Each of the rooms in this beautifully restored Craftsman-style bungalow has a different theme and most have fireplaces. Gourmet breakfasts.
$$$–$$$$
410 N. LEROUX ST.
TEL 928/774-0088 or
800/774-2008
FAX 928/774-6354
www.inn410.com
🛏9  🅿  🕐 Closed 2 weeks after New Year  💳
💳 MC, V

## 🏨 LITTLE AMERICA
$$$
2515 E. BUTLER AVE.
TEL 928/779-7900 or
800/352-4386
FAX 928/779-7983
www.flagstaff.littleamerica.com
Rooms and suites have balconies at this large hotel just off I-40. The Western Gold Room offers American and Continental cuisine.
🛏246  🅿  💳  🏊  🍽
💳 All major cards

## 🏨 RADISSON WOODLANDS HOTEL
$$$
1175 W. ROUTE 66
TEL 928/773-8888 or
800/333-3333
FAX 928/773-0597
In perhaps the most elegant hotel in Flagstaff, you'll find many amenities, including two good restaurants, the Sakura with Japanese cuisine and the Woodlands Café.
🛏 183  🅿  💳  🏊  🍽
💳 All major cards

## 🏨 SLED DOG INN
$$–$$$$
10155 MOUNTAINAIRE RD.
TEL 928/525-6212 or
800/754-0664
FAX 928/525-1855
www.sleddoginn.com
Located beside a meadow in the ponderosa pines south of Flagstaff, the inn offers a hot tub, sauna, and winter dog sledding. A full breakfast is served family-style.
🛏 10  🅿  💳  💳 AE, MC, V

## 🏨 ARIZONA MOUNTAIN INN
$$–$$$
4200 LAKE MARY RD.
TEL 928/774-8959 or
800/239-5236
FAX 928/774-8837
www.arizonamountaininn.com
Bed-and-breakfast suites and rustic cabins set amid ponderosa pines south of town.
🛏 20  🅿  💳 All major cards

## 🏨 HOTEL MONTE VISTA
$–$$$
100 N. SAN FRANCISCO ST.
TEL 928/779-6971 or
800/545-3068
FAX 928/779-2904
www.hotelmontevista.com
In the heart of town, this 1927 hotel has been restored to its original grandeur. Rooms and suites come in many sizes and prices.
🛏 46  🅿  💳  💳 AE, MC, V

## 🍴 CHEZ MARC BISTRO
$$
503 N. HUMPHREYS ST.
TEL 928/774-1343

Country French cuisine with fine service in a restored 1911 house close to downtown.
🪑 70  🅿  🕐 Closed L Mon.–Wed. and fall–spring
💳  💳 All major cards

## 🍴 COTTAGE PLACE
$$
126 W. COTTAGE AVE.
TEL 928/774-8431
www.cottageplace.com
This elegant restaurant serves Continental cuisine in a 1909 bungalow on the south side of downtown.
🪑 35  🅿  🕐 Closed Mon.
💳  💳 AE, MC, V

## 🍴 HORSEMEN LODGE
$–$$
8500 N. HWY. 89
TEL 928/526-2655
Join the locals at this popular dinner spot, 3 miles north of the Flagstaff Mall, for steak, ribs, chicken, trout, and seafood.
🪑 200  🅿  🕐 Closed Sun. (also Mon. in winter)  💳
💳 AE, MC, V

## 🍴 DELHI PALACE
$
2700 S. WOODLAND VILLAGE BLVD.
TEL 928/556-0019
Tasty north-Indian cuisine

provides an adventure in delicate spices. At lunchtime there's a buffet option.

🍴 70 🅿 🅢 🅢 All major cards

### 🍴 DOWN UNDER
$
6 E. ASPEN AVE. & LEROUX
TEL 928/774-6677
www.DownUnderNZ.com
Chefs here specialize in New Zealand food. The restaurant is at Heritage Square.
🍴 50 🅢 🅢 All major cards

### 🍴 GALAXY DINER
$
931 W. ROUTE 66
TEL 928/774-2466
This fun diner has photos of movie stars, and 1950s decor. The honest American food includes great breakfasts and serious desserts.
🍴 195 🅿 🅢 🅢 All major cards

### 🍴 PASTO
$
19 E. ASPEN AVE.
TEL 928/779-1937
Italian cuisine is served in a casual fine-dining setting.
🍴 60 🅢 🕒 Closed L 🅢 AE, MC, V

## JEROME

### 🏨 JEROME GRAND HOTEL
Opened in 1927 as the United Verde Hospital and renovated as a hotel in 1996, this imposing landmark offers six categories of rooms. Its mile-high perch above the Verde Valley provides stunning views. Enjoy them from The Asylum (closed Mon.) while dining on New American cuisine. Bands entertain on some weekends.'
$$–$$$$
200 HILL ST.
TEL 928/634-8200 or
888/817-6786;
RESTAURANT TEL 928/639-3197
FAX 928/639-0299

www.jeromegrandhotel.net
🛏 22 🅿 ⬍ 🅢 🅢 AE, MC, V

## PAYSON

### 🏨 MAJESTIC MOUNTAIN INN
$$–$$$
602 E. HWY. 260
TEL 928/474-0185 or
800/408-2442
FAX 928/472-6097
The modern mountain-lodge architecture makes this an enjoyable place to stay. You have a choice of standard, deluxe, and luxury rooms.
🛏 50 🅿 🅢 🅢 🅢 All major cards

### 🏨 CHRISTOPHER CREEK LODGE
$$
23 MILES E OF PAYSON ON ARIZ. 260
TEL 928/478-4300
Motel rooms and cabins in woods beside the creek.
🛏 24 🅿 🅢 MC, V

## PRESCOTT

### 🏨 HASSAYAMPA INN
Since opening its doors in 1927 as Prescott's finest hotel, the Hassayampa has continued to be one of the top places in town to stay. The elegant lobby with its painted ceiling and the attractive rooms and suites recall the era of the grand hotel.
$$$–$$$$
122 E. GURLEY ST.
TEL 928/778-9434 or
800/322-1927
FAX 928/445-8590
www.hassayampainn.com
🛏 68 🅿 ⬍ 🅢 🅢 All major cards

### 🏨 HOTEL VENDOME
$$$–$$$$
230 S. CORTEZ ST.
TEL 928/776-0900 or
888/468-3583

FAX 928/771-0395
www.vendomehotel.com
This beautifully restored small inn dates from 1917. It lies on a quiet street just one block from Courthouse Plaza and boasts rooms that have floral linens and antique fixtures.
🛏 20 🅿 🅢 🅢 All major cards

### 🏨 HOTEL ST. MICHAEL
$$
205 W. GURLEY ST.
TEL 928/776-1999 or
800/678-3757
FAX 928/776-7318
On the corner of Gurley and Montezuma, you're right on Whiskey Row in this 1900 hotel! This block of Montezuma became known as "Whiskey Row" because of the many saloons here. Some are still in business (see the Palace, below). Rooms in the hotel come in many sizes. Café St. Michael is a popular spot for a coffee or a snack.
🛏 72 ⬍ 🅢 🅢 AE, MC, V

### 🍴 MURPHY'S
$$–$$$
201 N. CORTEZ ST.
TEL 928/445-4044
The high-ceilinged dining room in an 1890 mercantile building provides a great setting for steak, prime rib, mesquite-broiled seafood, and other offerings.
🍴 205 🅢 🅢 All major cards

### 🍴 PEACOCK ROOM
$$
122 E. GURLEY ST.
TEL 928/778-9434
The dining room of the Hassayampa Hotel has a 1920s elegance for American and Continental choices.
🍴 50 🅿 🅢 🅢 All major cards

### 🍴 ROSE
$$
234 S. CORTEZ ST.
TEL 928/777-8308
Chef Linda Rose's northern

Italian food includes dishes prepared with marsala wine, sun-dried cherries, or brandy sauce. othe delights include sautéed, char-broiled, or pan-seared seafood along with pasta dishes tossed with fresh herbs or prepared in traditional sauces.
🪑 44 🅿 🕒 Closed Mon.–Tues. 💲 💳 All major cards

### 🍴 PALACE
$–$$
120 S. MONTEZUMA ST.
TEL 928/541-1996
www.historicpalace.com
Thirsty patrons have strolled up to the magnificently ornate Brunswick bar for 120 years. They even carried the bar across the street to safety during the 1900 fire. The dining room offers an Old West atmosphere for steaks, prime ribs, pasta, and seafood dinners with a distinct Southwestern-style. Entrées are prepared with glazes such as honey, Dijon mustard, or Merlot, or marinated and served with staples like baked or mashed potatoes, salads, or Arizona rice.
🪑 140 💲 💳 AE, MC, V

## SEDONA

### 🏨 ENCHANTMENT
### 🍴 RESORT
Enchantment's magical red-rock setting west of Sedona charms its guests. Hiking and the many resort activities can keep you busy by day, followed by fine dining and star-gazing in the evening. Native American cultures influence the adobe-style casitas, resort activities, and spa treatments. The two restaurants offer superb food and spectacular canyon views from both indoor and patio tables. The spa not only provides many types of therapies and activities, but also has accommodations and a restaurant on its grounds. Camp Coyote

organizes activities for children.
$$$$$
525 BOYNTON CANYON RD.
TEL 928/282-2900 or
800/826-4180
FAX 928/282-9249
www.enchantmentresort.com
🛏 222 🅿 💲 ☎ 🌊
📺 💳 All major cards

### 🏨 LOS ABRIGADOS RESORT & SPA
$$$$$
160 PORTAL LANE
TEL 928/282-1777 or
800/521-3131
FAX 928/282-2614
www.ilxresorts.com
Luxurious suites, many with fireplaces and whirlpool spas, lie among landscaped grounds beside Oak Creek. Sedona Spa provides invigorating treatments and fitness classes. Restaurants prepare Italian and grilled food.
🛏 172 🅿 🍴 💲 🌊
📺 💳 All major cards

### 🏨 JUNIPINE RESORT
$$$$–$$$$$
8 MILES N ON HWY. 89A
TEL 928/282-3375 or
800/742-7463
FAX 928/282-7402
www.junipine.com
In the midst of Oak Creek Canyon, each "creek house" has two bedrooms, two baths, a kitchen, and two fireplaces. You can also rent them as one-bedroom, one-bath units. The Junipine Café & Grill serves Southwestern and Continental cuisine.
🛏 32 🅿 💳 All major cards

### 🏨 L'AUBERGE DE SEDONA
A romantic getaway, this French-style country inn has an idyllic setting under sycamores beside Oak Creek. One- and two-bedroom cottages have canopied beds, fireplaces, and private decks. Lodge rooms also have canopied beds and

French decor. Above on the hillside, rooms in The Orchards offer views from patios or balconies; top-floor rooms have fireplaces. L'Auberge Restaurant is one of the finest in Arizona (see p. 249).
$$$$–$$$$$
301 L'AUBERGE LANE
TEL 928/282-1661 or
800/272-6777
FAX 928/282-1064
www.lauberge.com
🛏 100 🅿 💲 🌊 💳 All major cards

### 🏨 APPLE ORCHARD INN
$$$–$$$$$
656 JORDAN RD.
TEL 928/282-5328 or
800/663-6968
FAX 928/204-0044
www.appleorchardbb.com
Each of the luxurious guest rooms has a different Old West theme. Guests also enjoy a gourmet breakfast, a cooling pool, and a spa.
🛏 7 🅿 💲 🌊 💳 AE, MC, V

### 🏨 RADISSON POCO
### 🍴 DIABLO RESORT
$$$–$$$$$
1752 S. HWY. 179
TEL 928/282-7333 or
800/528-4275
FAX 928/282-9712
www.pocodiablo.com
Modern rooms, some with fireplaces and spas, overlook landscaped grounds beside Oak Creek. Guests enjoy tennis courts, a nine-hole golf course, and T. Carl's restaurant (Southwestern cuisine).
🛏 137 🅿 💲 🌊 💳 📺 💳 All major cards

### 🏨 BEST WESTERN ARROYO ROBLE HOTEL & CREEKSIDE VILLAS
$$$–$$$$
400 N. HWY. 89A
TEL 928/282-4001 or
800/773-3662
FAX 928/282-4001
www.bestwesternsedona.com
The five-story main building

has good views from most of its rooms. You can also stay down beside Oak Creek in a two-bedroom villa. All rooms and villas have a private balcony or patio.

🛈 67 🖀 🕄 🎐 🌊 📺 🕃 All major cards

### 🏨 SKY RANCH LODGE
**$$–$$$$**
1105 AIRPORT RD.
TEL 928/282-6400 or
888/708-6400
FAX 928/282-7682
www.skyranchlodge.com
You'll find one of the best views in town here atop Airport Mesa. The lodge has a variety of rooms and cottages, priced according to the view and the extra amenities such as fireplaces, decks, and kitchenettes.

🛈 94 🅿 🕄 🌊 🕃 AE, MC, V

### 🍴 L'AUBERGE
**$$$**
L'AUBERGE DE SEDONA
301 L'AUBERGE LANE
TEL 928/282-1667
Elegant surroundings set the stage for magnificent French dishes, including the popular six-course prix-fixe dinner option. Breakfast and Sunday brunch are served.

🍴 100 🅿 🕄 🕃 All major cards

### 🍴 RENÉ AT TLAQUEPAQUE
**$$–$$$**
336 HWY. 179
TEL 928/282-9225
Great American and Continental lunches and dinners are served daily in a French Provincial atmosphere.

🍴 90 🅿 🕄 🕃 MC, V

### 🍴 YAVAPAI RESTAURANT
**$$–$$$**
525 BOYNTON CANYON RD.
TEL 928/282-2900
Panoramic views of Boynton Canyon accompany the Southwest-inspired cuisine, which you can enjoy for breakfast (buffet available),

lunch, and dinner. The nearby Tii Gavo (Havasupai for "Gathering Place") offers lighter fare. Both have patios.

🍴 140 🅿 🕄 🕃 All major cards

### 🍴 COWBOY CLUB
**$$**
241 N. HWY. 89A
TEL 928/282-4200
Western decor accentuates the "high desert cuisine." Roast venison seasoned with apricot chutney, grilled fish, and vegetarian items are available. Open nightly, the Silver Saddle Dining Room features an upscale "rustic and romantic" experience.

🍴 120 🅿 🕄 🕃 AE, MC, V

### 🍴 DAHL & DILUCA RISTORANTE ITALIANO
**$–$$**
2321 W. HWY. 89A
TEL 928/282-5219
Chefs prepare Roman cuisine nightly with tasty offerings such as penne pasta with spicy sausage in marinara sauce or prawns sautéed with mushrooms, garlic, and tomatoes.

🍴 90 🅿 🕄 🕃 All major cards

### 🍴 SEDONA AIRPORT RESTAURANT
**$**
AIRPORT MESA
TEL 928/282-3576
Small planes taking off and landing provide entertainment while diners enjoy entrées such as sizzling vegetable fajitas or roast pork with apricot glaze. Breakfast also served.

🍴 81 🅿 🕄 🕃 MC, V

## WILLIAMS

### 🏨 FRAY MARCOS HOTEL
**$$$**
235 N. GRAND CANYON BLVD.
TEL 928/635-4010 or
800/843-8723
FAX 928/635-2180

www.thetrain.com
This modern hotel blends in with the adjacent 1908 Williams Depot, where the Grand Canyon Railway trains depart for the Grand Canyon. The large lobby and spacious rooms have a Southwest decor. Spenser's Lounge displays an impressive 19th-century bar and there's a good restaurant nearby, Max and Thelma's.

🛈 198 🅿 🖀 🕄 🎐 📺 🕃 AE, MC, V

### 🏨 SHERIDAN HOUSE INN
**$$–$$$$$**
460 E. SHERIDAN AVE.
TEL 928/635-9441 or
888/635-9345
www.grandcanyonbbinn.com
This large house on a pine-forested hillside offers visitors a home-style atmosphere. Guests enjoy a gourmet breakfast, a casual dinner, hiking, and many extras.

🛈 10 🅿 🕃 Closed mid-Jan.–mid-Feb. 📺 🕃 AE, MC, V

### 🏨 THE RED GARTER BED & BAKERY
**$$–$$$**
137 W. RAILROAD AVE.
TEL 928/635-1484 or
800/328-1484
www.redgarter.com
The saloon in this 1897 Victorian Romanesque-style building downtown now serves tasty pastries. A madam and her ladies once entertained guests in the bordello rooms upstairs, now converted to a bed-and-breakfast with 1890s decor.

🛈 4 🅿 🕃 Closed Dec.–Jan. 🕄 🕃 All major cards

### 🍴 CRUISER'S CAFÉ 66
**$–$$**
233 W. ROUTE 66
TEL 928/635-2445
At this 1930s former gas station, you can fill up on family fun and thick juicy burgers, barbecued ribs, and sizzling fajitas. The imaginative Route 66 decor includes

antique gas pumps and automobile paraphernalia.
🛏 100 🕐 Closed L 📶
🅰 AE, MC, V

🍴 **ROD'S STEAK HOUSE**
$–$$
301 E. ROUTE 66
TEL 928/635-2671 or
800/562-5545
Traditional western food like fine mesquite-broiled steaks, barbecued ribs, broiled trout, and seafood is served here, along with homemade soups, yeast rolls, and pies.
🛏 150 🕐 Closed Sun. Oct.–Feb.; closed first 3 weeks of Jan.
📶 🅰 MC, V

🍴 **PANCHO MCGILLICUDDY'S**
$
141 W. RAILROAD AVE.
TEL 928/635-4150
The Mexican menu includes some American favorites. Musicians entertain on summer evenings, and some weekends the rest of the year.
🛏 125 🕐 Closed L Mon.–Fri. in winter 🅰 AE, MC, V

## WESTERN ARIZONA

### KINGMAN

🏨 **HOTEL BRUNSWICK**
$–$$$
315 E. ANDY DEVINE AVE.
TEL 928/718-1800
FAX 928/718-1801
www.hotel-brunswick.com
Beautifully restored, this 1909 hotel offers rooms decorated with quilts and antiques. Of the 24 rooms, 15 have private baths. Hubb's Café offers fine dining and Mulligan's Bar is a quiet place to relax.
🛏 24 🚻 📶 🅰 All major cards

🏨 **BEST WESTERN KINGS INN & SUITES**
$$
2930 E. ANDY DEVINE AVE.
TEL 928/753-6101 or

800/750-6101
FAX 928/753-6192
The modern motel offers spacious regular rooms, as well as mini-suites, and suites. Many amenities, including an indoor spa and a sauna.
🛏 102 🅿 📶 🏊 🏋
🅰 All major cards

🏨 **HUALAPAI MOUNTAIN PARK**
$–$$
HUALAPAI MOUNTAIN RD.
TEL 877/757-0915
www.hualapaimountainpark.com
Cabins are tucked away in the mountains of this country park 14 miles southeast of Kingman. All have kitchenettes and most have either a fireplace or woodstove, but you need to bring your own bedding and kitchenware. Make reservations for summer weekends. The office is closed on weekends, but you can call the park ranger then at 928/757-3859.
🛏 14 🅿 🅰 MC, V

🍴 **HUBB'S CAFÉ**
$–$$
315 E. ANDY DEVINE AVE.
TEL 928/718-1800
The attractive restaurant in the 1909 Hotel Brunswick specializes in French cuisine.
🛏 70 🕐 Closed Sun. & L 📶 🅰 All major cards

🍴 **PORTOFINO RISTORANTE ITALIANO**
$
2215 HUALAPAI MOUNTAIN RD. (ON THE LEFT 0.4 MILE S. OF ANDY DEVINE)
TEL 928/753-0542
Chef Antonio Pagano prepares unusual pasta dishes such as *fettucini tutto mare*, which includes fettucini shrimp, scallops, and baby clams in a white wine sauce, or meat dishes like ribeye steak served with sun-dried tomatoes and mushrooms in red wine sauce.
🛏 50 🅿 🕐 Closed L Sat. & Sun. 📶 🅰 AE, MC, V

### PRICES

**HOTELS**
An indication of the cost of a double room without breakfast is given by $ signs.
$$$$$   Over $280
$$$$   $200–$280
$$$   $120–$200
$$   $80–$120
$   Under $80

**RESTAURANTS**
An indication of the cost of a three-course dinner without drinks is given by $ signs.
$$$$$   Over $80
$$$$   $50–$80
$$$   $35–$50
$$   $20–$35
$   Under $20

### LAKE HAVASU CITY

🏨 **LONDON BRIDGE RESORT**
$$–$$$$
1477 QUEENS BAY
TEL 928/855-0888 or
800/624-7939
FAX 928/855-9209
www.londonbridgeresort.com
The size and English-style architecture of this resort near London Bridge set it apart. All units are time-share, but the studios and one- and two-bedroom units are often available for rent. Guests congregate around the three pools and spa or at the Bridgewater Café. It's worth stepping inside the elegant lobby to see a replica of the ornate Gold State Coach. The 1762 original has conveyed all of the British monarchs since George III to their coronations in Westminster Abbey.
🛏 120 🅿 🚻 📶 🏊 🏋 🅰 All major cards

🏨 **NAUTICAL INN**
$$–$$$$
1000 MCCULLOCH BLVD.
TEL 928/855-2141 or
800/892-2141
FAX 928/453-5808
www.nauticalinn.com

All of the rooms have lake views and a private patio or balcony. Two-bedroom townhouses include kitchens and patios. Captain's Table serves all meals and brunch on Sundays. Tiki Terrace Sports Bar and Grill offers casual dining. Both restaurants have an outdoor terrace. The inn lies beside an 18-hole golf course on the island, reached via London Bridge.
🛏 120 🅿 🅰 ☲ ☷ 🛎 All major cards

### 🏨 HOLIDAY INN
$$–$$$
245 LONDON BRIDGE RD.
TEL 928/855-4071 or
888/428-2465
FAX 928/855-2379
Rooms have lake or mountain views. Suites are available too.
🛏 162 🅿 🔄 🅰 ☲ 🛎 All major cards

### 🍴 SHUGRUE'S
$–$$$
ISLAND MALL
TEL 928/453-1400
You cross London Bridge to reach Shugrue's and diners enjoy views of the grand structure while feasting on steaks, seafood, or pasta. Specialties include pepper steak topped with Jack Daniels, and broiled swordfish almondine. Shugrue's also runs the nearby Barley Brothers Brewery and Grill.
🍽 130 🅿 🅰 🛎 All major cards

### 🍴 CITY OF LONDON ARMS RESTAURANT
$–$$
422 ENGLISH VILLAGE
TEL 928/855-8782
The English setting is perfect for ordering fish and chips. Other options include pizza and sandwiches for lunch, and beef, chicken, and seafood dishes for dinner. The pub has a microbrewery and a patio. Sunday buffet.
🍽 350 🕐 No Sun. buffet July 4–Labor Day 🅰 🛎 All major cards

## PARKER

### 🏨 BLUEWATER RESORT & CASINO
$$–$$$$
11300 RESORT DR.
TEL 928/669-7000 or
888/243-3360
FAX 928/669-7075
www.bluewaterfun.com
The rooms and suites here all have balconies or patios and overlook the blue Colorado River north of Parker. A huge atrium shelters four pools, a spa, and waterfalls. The Feast offers a choice of buffet or menu offerings. The River Willow Restaurant features fine dining in the evening (closed Mon. & Tues.).
🛏 200 🅿 🔄 🅰 ☲ 🛎 AE, MC, V

### 🏨 HAVASU SPRINGS RESORT
$$–$$$$
2581 HWY. 95
TEL 928/667-3361
FAX 928/667-1098
www.havasusprings.com
On Lake Havasu, 16 miles north of Parker and 20 miles south of Lake Havasu City, this resort offers three motels, apartments, RV park, restaurant, nine-hole golf course, swimming beaches, and boat rentals, including houseboats.
🛏 44 🅿 🅰 ☲ 🛎 AE, MC, V

## YUMA

### 🏨 BEST WESTERN INNSUITES
$$–$$$$
1450 S. CASTLE DOME AVE.
TEL 928/783-8341 or 888/986-2784
FAX 928/783-1349
Guests enjoy large studios and suites, a breakfast buffet, and many amenities.
🛏 166 🅿 🅰 ☲ 🛎 All major cards

### 🏨 LA FUENTE INN & SUITES
$$
1513 E. 16TH ST.

TEL 928/329-1814 or 800/841-1814
FAX 928/343-2671
www.lafuenteinn.com
Rooms and suites at this attractive Spanish-colonial inn face a courtyard.
🛏 96 🅿 🅰 ☲ 🛎 All major cards

### 🍴 CALIFORNIA BAKERY COMPANY
$–$$
284 S. MAIN ST.
TEL 928/782-7335
In the high-ceilinged dining room, you can enjoy meat, seafood, and pasta dishes.
🍽 200 🕐 Closed Sun.–Mon. & summer 🅰 🛎 AE, MC, V

### 🍴 GARDEN CAFÉ
$
250 MADISON AVE.
TEL 928/783-1491
This charming café beside the Century House Museum downtown offers a pleasant spot for breakfast or lunch, surrounded by gardens and serenaded by birds from nearby aviaries.
🍽 20 inside, 120 outside 🕐 Closed Mon. & summer 🅰 🛎 AE, MC, V

### SOUTH-CENTRAL ARIZONA

## MESA

### 🏨 SHERATON MESA
$$$$
200 N. CENTENNIAL WAY
TEL 480/898-8300 or 800/456-6372
FAX 480/964-9279
www.sheratonmesa.com
The 12-story hotel offers comfortable rooms with good amenities, including two restaurants.
🛏 273 🅿 🔄 🅰 ☲ 🛎 All major cards

### 🏨 SHERATON SAN MARCOS RESORT
$$$$
1 SAN MARCOS PLACE,
CHANDLER

---

🔄 Elevator  🅰 Air-conditioning  ☲ Indoor/☲ Outdoor swimming pool  🛎 Health club  🛎 Credit cards  **KEY**

TEL 480/812-0900
FAX 480/899-5441
www.sanmarcosresort.com
In 1913, this was your only choice for an Arizona resort with a full complement of amenities! Today's guests enjoy the old Arizona charm, along with fine dining, an 18-hole golf course, swimming pools, and tennis.

ⓘ 295 P ⬌ ⑤ ⊠
🍷 🍽 All major cards

### 🏨 SAGUARO LAKE RANCH RESORT
$$$
13020 BUSH HWY.
TEL 480/984-2194
FAX 480/380-1489
Overlooking the Salt River northeast of Mesa, this rustic resort makes a great base for horseback riding, hiking, mountain biking, and jeep tours. Nearby Saguaro Lake has boating and fishing. Summer rates include breakfast; the American plan available in the cooler months includes three meals.

ⓘ 25 P ⏱ Closed late May–late Sept. ⑤ ⊠
🍽 All major cards

### 🍴 ROCKIN' R RANCH
$$
6136 E. BASELINE RD.
TEL 480/832-1539
After a good feed of cowboy food, the wranglers entertain you with songs and stories. You have a choice of barbecued beef or chicken as the main entrée. Open Saturdays and some weekdays, depending on the season.

🪑 769 P ⏱ Closed Sun.–Wed. in winter, Sun.–Fri. in summer ⑤ 🍽 AE, MC, V

## PHOENIX

### SOMETHING SPECIAL

### 🏨 ARIZONA BILTMORE
Frank Lloyd Wright inspired many of the architectural details of this lavish resort, opened in 1929. You have a choice of standard rooms, resort rooms, and villa suites. Guests enjoy the landscaping, restaurants, five pools (one with a 90-foot waterslide), two 18-hole golf courses, tennis courts, children's activities, and a health spa/athletic club. The central location is handy for shopping and sightseeing. the elegant Wright's Restaurant specializes in contemporary American cuisine, while the Biltmore Grill offers a variety of cuisines.
$$$$$
24TH ST. & MISSOURI AVE.
TEL 602/955-6600 or
800/950-0086
FAX 602/381-7646
www.arizonabiltmore.com

ⓘ 728 P ⬌ ⑤ ⊠
🍷 🍽 All major cards

### 🏨 HYATT REGENCY PHOENIX
$$$$$
122 N. 2ND ST.
TEL 602/252-1234 or
800/ 233-1234
FAX 602/254-9472
www.hyatt.com
Rooms and suites here in the heart of downtown have a Southwest decor.

ⓘ 712 ⬌ ⑤ ⊠ 🍷
🍽 All major cards

### 🍴 ROYAL PALMS HOTEL
$$$$$
5200 E. CAMELBACK RD.
TEL 602/840-3610 or
800/672-6011
FAX 602/840-6927
www.royalpalmshotel.com
Spanish-mission architecture, courtyards, and enclosed gardens create a restful atmosphere. Antiques and tasteful design grace the luxurious rooms, casitas, and

suites. T. Cook's prepares exceptional cuisine (see below).

ⓘ 116 P ⬌ ⑤ ⊠
🍷 🍽 All major cards

### 🏨 HOLIDAY INN EXPRESS HOTEL & SUITES
$$$
620 N. 6TH ST.
TEL 602/452-2020 or
800/465-4329
FAX 602/252-2909
The inn has a convenient location on the northeast side of downtown.

ⓘ 90 P ⬌ ⑤ ⊠ 🍷
🍽 All major cards

### 🏨 LOS OLIVOS HOTEL & SUITES
$$–$$$
202 E. MCDOWELL RD.
TEL 602/258-6911 or
800/776-5560
FAX 602/258-7259
The hotel offers a choice of standard rooms or suites in a handy location near museums and other downtown attractions.

ⓘ 48 P ⬌ ⑤ ⊠
🍽 All major cards

### 🍴 LON'S
$$$
5532 N. PALO CRISTI
TEL 602/955-7878
A Mexican hacienda provides an attractive setting for American and Continental cuisine at the Hermosa Inn, northeast of Phoenix in Paradise Valley. Views of Camelback Mountain from the patio. Sunday brunch.

🪑 190 P ⏱ Closed L Sat.–Sun. ⑤ 🍽 All major cards

### 🍴 T. COOK'S
$$$
ROYAL PALMS HOTEL
5200 E. CAMELBACK RD.
TEL 602/808-0766
Superb Mediterranean-inspired food in a romantic atmosphere makes this a special place. Breakfast and Sunday brunch too.

🛏 235 🅿 🅢 🅢 All major cards

### VINCENT GUERITHAULT ON CAMELBACK
$$–$$$
3930 E. CAMELBACK RD.
TEL 602/224-0225
Exceptionally fine Southwestern cuisine comes in a French country atmosphere.
🍴 200 🅿 🕐 Closed Sat.–Sun. L also Sun.–Mon. June–Sept. 🅢 🅢 All major cards

### GREEKFEST
$–$$
1940 E. CAMELBACK RD.
TEL 602/265-2990
Greek and Byzantine flavors entice diners at this popular restaurant.
🍴 120 🅿 🕐 Closed Sun. 🅢 🅢 All major cards

### COMPASS
$
HYATT REGENCY PHOENIX
122 N. 2ND ST.
TEL 602/440-3166
Dine on American and Continental cuisine and enjoy views of the mountain-ringed Valley of the Sun by day and the twinkling lights at night from Arizona's only revolving restaurant. It's on the 24th floor of the Hyatt Regency Phoenix. Brunch on Sunday.
🍴 130 🕐 Closed L Sat. & Sun. 🅢 🅢 All major cards

### ELIANA'S
$
1627 N. 24TH ST.
TEL 602/225-2925
Delicious El Salvadoran food features plantains and stuffed tortillas. The chile rellenos are pan-fried green bell peppers stuffed with meat, potatoes, and cheese.
🍴 65 🅿 🕐 Closed Mon. 🅢 🅢 All major cards

### SCOTTSDALE

### THE BOULDERS
$$$$$
34505 N. SCOTTSDALE RD.

TEL 480/488-9009 OR
800/553-1717
FAX 480/488-4118
www.wyndham.com/boulders
Casitas and villas in elegant southwestern decor that features natural woods and Mexican tile floors are nestled among the picturesque granite boulders. The resort has two 18-hole golf courses, a driving range, as well as three pools, tennis courts, trails, and the Golden Door Spa. Dining options include the refined, yet rustic, Latilla Room serving classic American food with contemporary regional flavors.
ℹ 208 🅿 🅢 🅢 🅥 🅢 All major cards

### SOMETHING SPECIAL

### THE PHOENICIAN
The 250 landscaped acres here at the foot of Camelback Mountain showcase one of the world's most luxurious resorts. The spacious rooms, casitas, and suites have a host of amenities. Guests can fill their days with the 27-hole golf course, tennis garden, nine pools, waterfalls, fitness center, and health spa. Children will enjoy the 165-foot waterslide and Funicians Club activities. Savor French cooking at the elegant Mary Elaine's, Continental cuisine in The Terrace Dining Room, or eat Southwestern style at Windows on the Green.
$$$$$
6000 E. CAMELBACK RD.
TEL 480/941-8200 or
800/888-8234
FAX 480/947-4311
www.thephoenician.com
ℹ 654 🅿 🅢 🅢 🅢 🅥 🅢 All major cards

### ECONOLODGE SCOTTSDALE
$$–$$$
6935 E. 5TH AVE.
TEL 480/994-9461 or
800/553-2666
FAX 480/947-1695
www.econolodge.com
This motel has spacious

rooms and a central location in the Fifth Avenue shopping district.
ℹ 92 🅿 🅢 🅢 🅢 🅥 🅢 All major cards

### MARY ELAINE'S
$$$$–$$$$$
THE PHOENICIAN
6000 E. CAMELBACK RD.
TEL 480/423-2444
Dinner at this sophisticated French restaurant on the top floor of the main building at the Phoenician features appetizers like Caspian beluga caviar and Caesar scallop salad, as well as entrées like garlic-and-herb-crusted rack of lamb niçoise.
🍴 180 🅿 🕐 Closed Sun. (also Mon. in summer) 🅢 🅢 All major cards

### RESTAURANT OCEANA
$$$$
8936 E. PINNACLE PEAK RD.
TEL 480/515-2277
You may feel that you're dining wharfside while enjoying a menu of "definitive seafood" that changes daily. Extensive wine list.
🍴 60 🅿 🕐 Closed L & Sun.–Mon. D in summer 🅢 🅢 All major cards

### LA HACIENDA
$$$
7575 E. PRINCESS DR.
TEL 480/585-4848
Gourmet Mexican cuisine comes to you in a ranch-house setting at the Scottsdale Princess Resort, 12 miles north of Scottsdale.
🍴 180 🅿 🕐 Closed L & May 🅢 🅢 All major cards

### MARQUESA
$$$
7575 E. PRINCESS DR.
TEL 480/585-4848
The romantic Spanish atmosphere provides a perfect setting for the fine Catalonian and Mediterranean flavors. Located in the Scottsdale Princess Resort, 12 miles north of Scottsdale, the

HOTELS & RESTAURANTS

Marquesa is open Sundays for a magnificent brunch. 🛏70 🅿 ⊘Closed L & Sun.–Mon. D, may also close in summer 🅲 🔘All major cards

## 🍴 RAWHIDE STEAKHOUSE
$–$$
23023 N. SCOTTSDALE RD.
TEL 480/502-5600 or 800/527-1880
www.rawhide.com
Set in a lively re-creation of an 1880s Old West town, the steakhouse offers many meat dishes plus trout, shrimp, and a veggie plate. On some evenings, you can join an outdoor Sundown Cookout. 🛏300 🅿 ⊘Closed L 🅲 🔘AE, MC, V

## 🍴 SUSHI ON SHEA
$–$$
7000 E. SHEA BLVD.
TEL 480/483-7799
Sushi, teriyaki, sukiyaki, and noodle dishes are served in a contemporary setting. 🛏89 🅿 ⊘Closed L 🅲 🔘All major cards

## 🍴 SUGAR BOWL
$
4005 N. SCOTTSDALE RD.
TEL 480/946-0051
Sweet tooths will feel like they're in heaven at this old-fashioned ice-cream parlor. You can also order home-style American food. 🛏100 🅲 🔘MC, V

## TEMPE

## 🏨 TEMPE MISSION PALMS HOTEL
$$$$$
60 E. 5TH ST.
TEL 480/894-1400 or 800/547-8705
FAX 480/968-7677
www.missionpalms.com
The large guest rooms have windows or French doors to enjoy Arizona's fresh air and are decorated in rich hues of the desert Southwest. Some Jacuzzi suites are available.

🛏303 🅿 🔲 🅲 🚲 🍽 🔘All major cards

## 🏨 TWIN PALMS HOTEL
$$$$
225 E. APACHE BLVD.
TEL 480/967-9431 or 800/367-0835
FAX 480/968-1877
www.twinpalmshotel.com
This seven-story hotel has a great location adjacent to Arizona State University and Mill Avenue. Guests can keep fit with privileges at the A.S.U. recreation facilities nearby. ⓘ140 🅿 🔲 🅲 🚲 🍽 🔘All major cards

## 🏨 PHOENIX/TEMPE UNIVERSITY TRAVELODGE
$$
1005 E. APACHE BLVD.
TEL 480/968-7871 or 800/578-7878
FAX 480/968-3991
www.travelodge.com
This motel is located just east of Arizona State University. ⓘ90 🅿 🔲 🅲 🚲 🍽 🔘AE, MC, V

## 🍴 HOUSE OF TRICKS
$$–$$$
114 E. 7TH ST.
TEL 480/968-1114
Bob and Robin Trick offer creative American food in a restaurant converted from a pair of Craftsman bungalows. Most customers head for the shaded patio. 🛏112 🅿 ⊘Closed Sun. & first 2 weeks of Aug. 🅲 🔘All major cards

## 🍴 PITA JUNGLE
$
1250 E. APACHE BLVD.
TEL 480/804-0234
Tasty Mediterranean and American dishes including falafel, and spicy mango shrimp are served at this healthful restaurant. Vegetarians will find plenty of choice. 🛏84 🅿 🅲 🔘All major cards

## WICKENBURG

## 🏨 FLYING E RANCH
$$$$$
2801 W. WICKENBURG WAY
TEL 928/684-2690 or 888/684-2650
FAX 928/684-5304
www.flyingeranch.com
Cowboys still work cattle across a nearby spread. Guests enjoy the informal Western atmosphere where they ride horses, relax around the pool, work out in the exercise room, or socialize in the lodge. Rooms, which come in different sizes, have Western furnishings. Rates include family-style meals. ⓘ17 🅿 ⊘Closed May–Oct. 🅲 🚲 🍽 🔘None

## 🏨 KAY EL BAR GUEST RANCH
$$$$$
RINCON RD. (BOX 2480, WICKENBURG, AZ 85358)
TEL 928/684-7593 or 800/684-7583
FAX 928/684-4497
www.kayelbar.com
The adobe buildings of this early 1900s ranch give it an Old West feel. Guests can ride, hike, and enjoy the pool

and hot tub. There's a choice of historic lodge rooms, a cottage, and the larger Casa Grande room. Everyone dines family-style.
☐ 12 ☐ ☐ Closed May–Oct. ☒ ☒ MC, V

### ☐ RANCHO DE LOS ☐ CABALLEROS
**$$$$$**
1551 S. VULTURE MINE RD.
TEL 928/684-5484 or
800/684-5030
FAX 928/684-2267
www.sunc.com
The most elegant of the guest ranches round Wickenburg, it offers an 18-hole golf course as well as horseback riding, tennis, swimming, children's programs, and fine dining. Rooms and suites have a Southwest decor. The restaurant prepares American and Continental cuisine; it's open to the public (reserve) and you'll need to dress up for dinner (jacket for men).
☐ 79 ☐ ☐ Closed mid May–mid-Oct. ☒ ☒ ☒ ☒ None

### ☐ BEST WESTERN RANCHO GRANDE
**$$–$$$**
293 E. WICKENBURG WAY
TEL 928/684-5445 or
800/854-7235
FAX 928/684-7380
www.bwranchogrande.com
This centrally located motel has Spanish colonial-style architecture and a choice of room sizes.
☐ 80 ☐ ☒ ☒ ☒ All major cards

### EASTERN ARIZONA

## ALPINE

### ☐ TAL-WI-WI LODGE
**$$**
110 COUNTY RD.
TEL 928/339-4319
FAX 928/339-1962
www.talwiwilodge.com
This rustic lodge, 3 miles north of Alpine, is a good

base for exploring the surrounding mountain and forest country. Some of the rooms have a hot tub or woodstove.
☐ 20 ☐ ☐ Closed L, also breakfast & D Mon.–Thurs. Dec.–April ☒ MC, V

## HOLBROOK

### ☐ RAMADA LIMITED
**$$**
2608 E. NAVAJO BLVD.
TEL 928/524-2566 or
800/272-6232
FAX 928/524-6427
www.ramada.com
In addition to the modern rooms, guests can enjoy the indoor pool and spa.
☐ 41 ☐ ☒ ☒ ☒ All major cards

### ☐ WIGWAM MOTEL
**$**
811 W. HOPI DR.
TEL 928/524-3048 or
800/414-3021
Have you slept in a wigwam lately? This modest motel from the late 1940s has become a Route 66 icon, thanks to its unusual architecture. Inside the cozy interiors, you'll find one or two double beds and original hickory furniture. A small museum displays Indian artifacts and petrified wood. Vintage cars on the grounds add to the nostalgic feeling.
☐ 15 ☐ ☒ ☒ MC, V

### ☐ BUTTERFIELD STAGE CO.
**$–$$**
609 W. HOPI DR.
TEL 928/524-3447
Specialties at this family-oriented restaurant include chicken and dumplings, beef stroganoff, grilled steaks, lamb chops, and baked or deep-fried seafood.
☐ 155 ☐ ☐ Closed L ☒ ☒ AE, MC, V

## HON-DAH

### ☐ HON-DAH RESORT
**$$–$$$$**
777 HWY. 260 (AT HWY. 73)
TEL 928/369-0299 or
800/929-8744
FAX 928/369-0382
www.hon-dah.com
The immense lobby and spacious rooms and suites are sure to impress. The smoky casino may not. Restaurants offer fine dining and some buffets, including a big Sunday brunch.
☐ 128 ☐ ☒ ☒ ☒ All major cards

## PINETOP-LAKESIDE

### ☐ LAKE OF THE WOODS
**$$–$$$$$**
2244 W. WHITE MTN. BLVD.
TEL 928/368-5353
www.privatelake.com
Cabins of many sizes and styles nestle under the pines near the resort's private lake; all have fireplaces and cooking facilities. Take a canoe or rowboat out on the lake. The resort also has a sauna, spa, games, and a playground.
☐ 30 ☐ ☒ ☒ MC, V

### ☐ CHARLIE CLARK'S STEAKHOUSE
**$$**
1701 E. WHITE MTN. BLVD.
TEL 928/367-4900
In business since 1938, this popular restaurant specializes in steak, prime ribs, and seafood.
☐ 300 ☐ ☒ ☒ All major cards

### ☐ CHRISTMAS TREE
**$–$$**
455 N. WOODLAND RD.
TEL 928/367-3107
You can expect good home-style dinners—chicken and dumplings is a specialty—amid Christmas decor.
☐ 95 ☐ ☐ Closed Mon.–Tues. & Halloween to Thanksgiving ☒ DC, MC, V

## SAFFORD

### 🏨 RAMADA INN
**$$–$$$**
420 E. HWY. 70
TEL 928/428-3200 or
800/272-6232
FAX 928/428-3288
Some of the rooms have spa
tubs or you can go for a suite.
🛏 102 🅿 ❄ ⛱
🏊 All major cards

## WINSLOW

### SOMETHING SPECIAL

### 🏨 LA POSADA
Architect Mary Colter not only designed this great railroad hotel, she created a story behind it, suggesting that it was a grand 18th-century Spanish hacienda. Arched halls, antiques, a ballroom, rustic furniture, and exotic gardens helped create the effect. Staying here, you felt as though you were the personal guest of a Spanish don. When the hotel opened in 1930, Winslow was a crossroads of the West—a major stop on transcontinental railroad, airline, and highway routes. The hotel closed in 1959, a victim of the decline in railroad passenger traffic, and lay forgotten for four decades. Now it's open again and welcoming guests. The Turquoise Room (see below) serves fine meals. Even if you're not staying at the hotel, it's worth taking the self-guided tour of the public areas.
**$$–$$$**
303 E. 2ND ST.
TEL 928/289-4366
FAX 928/289-3873
www.laposada.org
🛏 20 🅿 ❄ 🏊 All major cards

### 🍴 TURQUOISE ROOM
**$**
LA POSADA
303 E. 2ND ST.
TEL 928/289-2888
Menus change frequently to keep tastes fresh, but

chef/owner John Sharpe serves southwestern fare and Fred Harvey-inspired dinners such as filet mignon wrapped in applewood-smoked bacon on a bed of red caboose-mashed potatoes with wild mushroom sauce.
🍽 100 🅿 🕐 Closed Mon.
❄ 🏊 MC, V

## SOUTHERN ARIZONA

## AMADO

### 🍴 REX RANCH
**$$$**
131 AMADO-MORTOSA RD.
TEL 520/398-2914 or
800/547-2696
FAX 520/398-8229
www.rexranch.com
The peaceful setting is great for bird-watching, or as a base for Tubac, Tumacacori, and the Santa Rita Mountains. The ranch offers a full-service spa and arranges horseback riding and mountain biking. The restaurant serves European and Southwestern cuisine.
🛏 27 🅿 ❄ ⛱ 🏊 All major cards

## BENSON

### 🍴 SKYWATCHER'S INN
**$$–$$$$**
TEL 520/586-7906 or
520/615-3886 (TUCSON)
www.communiverse.com/skywatcher
Stargazers will love staying at this bed-and-breakfast inn at the Vega-Bray Observatory. The observatory has a planetarium, exhibits, and instruments that guests can use during stargazing sessions. Each room is individually decorated with Egyptian, garden, or galaxy themes.
🛏 4 🅿 ❄ 🏊 MC, V

## BISBEE

### 🏨 BISBEE GRAND HOTEL
**$$–$$$**
61 MAIN ST.
TEL 520/432-5900 or

800/421-1909
Richly decorated Victorian rooms carry you back to the romance of the 1890s. A saloon downstairs adds to the atmosphere with its high pressed-tin ceiling and an 1880s bar from Tombstone. All rooms have private baths, though some are located across the hall.
🛏 15 🏊 All major cards

### 🏨 COPPER QUEEN
**$$–$$$**
11 HOWELL AVE.
TEL 520/432-2216 or
800/247-5829
FAX 520/432-4298
www.copperqueen.com
The Copper Queen Mining Company built this hotel in 1902 and it's still impressive today. The four-story building contains different styles and sizes of rooms; most have been attractively restored. The restaurant serves American and Continental food. Murder-mystery weekends and a very colorful saloon provide other diversions.
🛏 47 ❄ 🏊 ⛱ 🏊 All major cards

### 🏨 HIGH DESERT INN
**$$**
8 NACO RD.
TEL 520/432-1442 or
800/281-0510
FAX 520/432-1410
www.highdesertinn.com
Rooms have contemporary styling, and the restaurant prepares international dishes.
🛏 5 🕐 Closed L & Mon.–Wed. D ❄ 🏊 All major cards

### 🏨 LE CHÊNE HOTEL & BISTRO
**$$**
1 HOWELL AVE.
TEL 520/432-1832
FAX 520/432-1833
www.lechenebistro.com
This hotel—the name is French for "the oak"—features spacious rooms, most with views. Downstairs is a traditional French bistro.

**HOTELS & RESTAURANTS**

⓵ 6 ⓢ Bistro closed L & Sun.–Mon. D 🅢 🅢MC, V

## DOUGLAS

### 🏨 GADSDEN HOTEL
**$–$$**
1046 G AVE.
TEL 520/364-4481
FAX 520/364-4005
The amazing lobby of this grand hotel, built in 1907, has marble columns decorated with gold leaf supporting a vaulted ceiling that has stained glass skylights. A white marble staircase sweeps up past a Tiffany stained-glass mural. More than 200 cattle brands cover the walls of the Saddle and Spur Tavern. The restaurant serves American and Mexican food.
⓵ 144 🅟 🖃 🅢 🅢All major cards

## PEARCE

### 🏨 SUNGLOW GUEST RANCH
**$$–$$$$**
14066 S. SUNGLOW RD. (OFF TURKEY RD.)
TEL 520/824-3334
FAX 520/824-3176
www.sunglowranch.com
In the western foothills of the Chiricahua Mountains, the ranch offers birding, hiking, astronomy, and trail rides. Rooms, all with patios, are decorated in Southwestern style; larger units have a fireplace and living room. The dining room is open to the public by reservation.
⓵ 9 🅟 🅢All major cards

## SANTA RITA MOUNTAINS

### 🏨 SANTA RITA LODGE
**$$**
TEL 520/625-8746
FAX 520/648-1186
www.santaritalodge.com
Nestled in the woods of Madera Canyon at an elevation of 5,000 feet, the lodge is a great base for bird-watchers and lovers of the

outdoors. Both rooms and cabins are cozy with wood-paneled walls and kitchenettes. You can join bird walks from March to August.
⓵ 12 🅟 🅢 🅢AE, MC, V

## SASABE

### 🏨 RANCHO DE LA OSA
**$$$$$**
TEL 520/823-4257 or 800/872-6240
FAX 520/823-4238
www.ranchodelaosa.com
Near the border village of Sasabe, 66 miles from Tucson, this historic ranch offers horseback riding, a pool, a whirlpool, birding, hiking, mountain biking, and miles to roam. Rugged adobe buildings contrast nicely with the glamorous interiors decorated with nineteenth-century antiques to re-create the feel of the working cattle ranch it once was.
⓵ 18 🅟 ⓢ Closed Aug.–mid-Sept. 🅢 🅢MC, V

## TOMBSTONE

### 🏨 BEST WESTERN LOOKOUT LODGE
**$$**
W. US 80
TEL 520/457-2223 or 877/652-6772
FAX 520/457-3870
Views from the large rooms take in the surrounding desert and the Dragoon Mountains.
⓵ 40 🅟 🅢 🅢 🅢All major cards

### 🏨 TOMBSTONE BOARDING HOUSE
**$$**
108 N. 4TH ST.
TEL 520/457-3716 or 877/225-1319
tombstonebandb@theriver.com
Two 1880s adobe houses offer comfortable rooms with private bath while keeping their historic atmosphere. It's in a quiet neighborhood, yet the Wild West action on Allen St. lies just two blocks

south. Rates include full breakfast The dining room makes a romantic spot for a Sunday champagne brunch or dinners when you have a choice of meats, fish, or vegetarian dishes.
⓵ 7 🅟 ⓢ Restaurant closed Mon 🅢MC, V

## TUCSON

### 🏨 🍴 ARIZONA INN
First opened in 1930, the inn offers a wonderful combination of old Arizona charm and modern amenities. Gardens create a peaceful refuge amid the pink stucco buildings. Spacious rooms contain period furniture, some made by disabled World War I veterans. The lounge has piano music nightly. In the restaurant you can savor continental cuisine like oven-roasted pork chops with herbed mozzarella and soft polenta, or roasted corn and butternut squash cannelloni.
**$$$$$**
2200 E. ELM ST.
TEL 520/325-1541 or 800/933-1093
FAX 520/320-2182
www.arizonainn.com
⓵ 86 🅟 🅢 🅢 🅥 🅢All major cards

### 🏨 CANYON RANCH HEALTH RESORT
**$$$$$**
8600 E. ROCKCLIFF RD.
TEL 520/749-9000 or 800/742-9000
FAX 520/749-7755
www.canyonranch.com
You can experience top-quality treatment and fitness programs at this health spa near Sabino Canyon. Packages of four nights or longer include luxurious rooms, healthy gourmet meals (no alcohol), and spa services.
⓵ 180 🅟 🅢 🅢 🅥 🅢All major cards

HOTELS & RESTAURANTS

## 🏨 🍴 LOEWS VENTANA CANYON RESORT

$$$$$

7000 N. RESORT DR.

TEL 520/299-2020 or 800/234-5117

FAX 520/299-6832

www.loewshotels.com

This luxurious oasis beneath the rugged Santa Catalina Mountains features two 18-hole golf courses, two pools, waterfall, tennis, health spa, and a kids club. Spacious rooms have balconies from which you can enjoy the mountain views or overlook the city. The Ventana Room serves some of Tucson's best food.

🛏 398 🅿 🚭 😊 🏊
🚇 🚳 All major cards

## 🏨 TANQUE VERDE GUEST RANCH

Guests here enjoy both the height of luxury and the great outdoors at the foot of the Rincon Mountains, 10 miles east of Tucson. Riders and hikers can head into the nearby Saguaro National Park or Coronado National Forest. Many of the large rooms and casitas have fireplaces and shaded patios, but don't expect a TV. The ranch offers riding stables, pools, tennis, exercise room, saunas, and children's programs, as well as a nature center, trails, and wildlife observation areas.

$$$$$

14301 E. SPEEDWAY BLVD.

TEL 520/296-6275 or 800/234-3833

FAX 520/721-9426

www.tanqueverderanch.com

🛏 74 🅿 😊 🚇 🏊 🚲
🚳 AE, MC, V

## 🏨 EL PRESIDIO BED & BREAKFAST INN

$$-$$$

297 N. MAIN AVE.

TEL 520/623-6151 or 800/349-6151

FAX 520/623-3860

Antiques and art decorate the guest rooms of an 1866 adobe house in El Presidio Historic District. The central location is just a short stroll from restaurants and the Tucson Museum of Art.

🛏 4 🅿 😊 Closed July
🚇 🚳 None

## 🍴 TACK ROOM

$$$

7300 E. VACTOR RANCH TRAIL

TEL 520/722-2800

In a hacienda, the Tack Room offers superb Southwestern and Continental dinners.

🪑 130 🅿 😊 Closed Mon. & 1st 2 wks July 🚇 🚳 All major cards

## 🍴 JANOS

$$-$$$

WESTIN LA PALOMA RESORT

3770 E. SUNRISE DR.

TEL 520/615-6100

Janos serves sophisticated French-inspired Southwestern food at the Westin La Paloma resort. J Bar, next door, offers less expensive Latin American and Caribbean food (same telephone).

🪑 160 🅿 😊 Closed Sun.
🚇 🚳 All major cards

## 🍴 KINGFISHER

$$

2564 E. GRANT RD.

TEL 520/323-7739

Fresh seafood is the star attraction, but you'll also find meat and vegetarian dishes.

🪑 180 🅿 😊 Closed L Sat.–Sun. 🚇 🚳 All major cards

## 🍴 LA FUENTE

$-$$

1749 N. ORACLE RD.

TEL 520/623-8659

A garden setting provides an enjoyable spot for Mexican dining. Mariachi or other bands serenade evening diners.

🪑 275 🅿 😊 Closed Mon. in summer 🚇 🚳 None

## 🍴 LA COCINA

$-$$

201 N. COURT

TEL 520/622-0351

Good Southwestern and Mexican food rejuvenates sightseers and shoppers downtown at the Old Town Artisans shopping plaza. Dine in the courtyard or inside.

🪑 70 😊 Closed D 🚇
🚳 All major cards

## 🍴 EL CHARRO

$

311 N. COURT AVE.

TEL 520/622-1922

Sonoran Mexican food has been satisfying diners here in this historic stone house since 1922.

🪑 190 🚇 🚳 All major cards

## 🍴 GOVINDA'S NATURAL FOOD BUFFET

$

711 E. BLACKLIDGE DR.

TEL 520/792-0630

Excellent vegetarian food is served buffet-style with a different theme each day. The dining rooms are small, but there's an attractive patio. A Hare Krishna community runs this restaurant, so no alcohol is allowed.

🪑 32 🅿 😊 Closed L Sun.–Tues. & D Sun.–Mon.
🚇 🚳 MC, V

# SHOPPING

Arizona artists translate the hues of earth and sky in countless ways, and the arts and crafts that you'll see tend to reflect the cultures and landscapes of the Southwest. Navajo and Hopi, the most prolific artisans of Arizona's many tribes, incorporate sacred symbols into their ceramics, weavings, woodcarvings, and other work. Colorful Mexican crafts entice visitors to shop in border towns.

## GRAND CANYON COUNTRY

### GENERAL SUPPLIES

**General Store** South Rim (S of visitor center), tel 928/638-2262. Huge store, good for books, camping supplies, film, groceries, clothing, and souvenirs; there's a deli too. Smaller general stores in the Grand Canyon area are in Tusayan and at Desert View.
**Marble Canyon Lodge** Marble Canyon, tel 928/355-2225. Native American crafts as well as supplies for camping, river running, and fishing.

### ARTS, CRAFTS, & SOUVENIRS

You'll find a gift shop almost everywhere you turn in Grand Canyon Village and Tusayan on the South Rim of the Grand Canyon. Most motels, hotels, and helicopter tour offices have one. Also, many Navajo families sell their work at tiny roadside stalls along Ariz. 64 between Cameron and Desert View. The largest cluster is at a viewpoint of the Little Colorado River between Mileposts 285 and 286.
**Hopi House** South Rim just E of El Tovar. An outstanding selection of Native American art on two floors of a pueblo-style building, opened in 1905.
**Verkamp's Curios** South Rim just E of Hopi House, tel 928/638-2242, www.verkamps .com. John Verkamp tried his hand at selling tourist curios out of a tent in 1898, but closed after several slow weeks. He returned in 1905, after the railroad arrived, and set up shop here. The store is still run by his family. Inside the large sales room, you'll find a selection of Native American work plus lots of souvenirs.

### REGIONAL BOOKS & MAPS

**Grand Canyon Association shops** South and North Rims, tel 928/638-2481, www.grandcanyon.org. Large selection of Canyon books, posters, videos, music, and postcards on the South Rim at Kolb Studio, Canyon View Information Plaza, Yavapai Observation Station, Tusayan Museum, and Desert View. Another shop is on North Rim near Bright Angel Point.
**Carl Hayden Visitor Center** Glen Canyon Dam, tel 928/608-6404. The shops here and at Navajo Bridge (near Lees Ferry) carry many regional and nature books as well as maps, posters, videos, music, and postcards.
**Front Page** 48 S. Lake Powell Blvd., Page, tel 928/645-5333. Good for regional books and general reading.

## NORTHEASTERN ARIZONA

### GENERAL SUPPLIES

Trading posts on the Navajo and Hopi reservations often sell groceries and other everyday items. See, for example, Cameron Trading Post and Van's Trading Company, below.

### ART, CRAFTS, & SOUVENIRS

You'll have many opportunities to purchase art and crafts directly from the Navajo and Hopi in this region. Navajo usually sell from roadside stalls. Hopi have small shops in their villages and sometimes sell out of their homes—look for signs. Both tribes also have large cooperative stores. See "Native American Arts" (pp. 40–42).
**Cameron Trading Post** US 89, Cameron, tel 928/679-2231 or 800/338-7385,

www.camerontradingpost.com. A huge sales floor in the main building has almost any kind of souvenir a tourist could wish for; groceries are sold too. Most of the museum-quality Native American art is in a two-story building in front.
**Goulding's Trading Post** Monument Valley, Utah (just N of the Arizona border on US 163, then W 1.5 miles), tel 435/727-3231 or 800/874-0902, www.gouldings.com. The sales gallery offers many fine Native American pieces.
**Hopi Arts & Crafts** Second Mesa (W of the Hopi Cultural Center), tel 928/734-2463. The Silvercrafts Cooperative Guild offers a great selection of silver inlay work and other Hopi art. You can often see silversmiths at work. Closed Sunday.
**Hubbell Trading Post National Historic Site** Ganado, tel 928/755-3475, www.nps.gov/hutr. This historic trading post hasn't changed much over the years. Navajo still drop in to trade. You can pick up canned goods, clothing, or shop for superb rugs and jewelry.
**Navajo Arts & Crafts Enterprise** Shops in Cameron (tel 928/679-2244), Chinle (tel 928/674-5338), Kayenta (tel 928/697-8611), and Window Rock (tel 928/871-4090). This business has been promoting and selling high-quality work by Navajo artisans since 1941.
**Thunderbird Lodge** Canyon de Chelly National Monument, tel 928/674-5841 or 800/679-2473, www.tbirdlodge.com. Large gift shop offering very high-quality work.
**Tsakurshovi** 1.5 mile E of Hopi Cultural Center, Second Mesa. Joseph and Janice Day run this little trading post, packed with high-quality Hopi work. There's a good selection of arts and crafts, including traditional kachina dolls, plus books, and Native American music. The owners are full of advice on Hopi art and visits to the Hopi lands.
**Tuba Trading Post** Tuba City (turn N 1 mile from US 160 to

SHOPPING

the center of town), tel 928/283-5441. Good selection of Native American artistry in an attractive building. The trading post dates from 1870 and the unusual two-story octagon was added in 1920.

**Van's Trading Company** US 160, W of Tuba City, tel 928/283-5343. This large trading post sells Native American arts and crafts, groceries, and just about everything else.

### NORTH-CENTRAL ARIZONA

#### ARTS, CRAFTS, & SOUVENIRS
**Art Barn** 2320 N. Fort Valley Rd., Flagstaff (2 miles NW of downtown Flagstaff on US 180), tel 928/774-0822. Regional artists, including several Native Americans, run this large sales gallery behind the Pioneer Museum. Artwork includes paintings, prints, sketches, photography, ceramics, jewelry, Navajo rugs, and Hopi kachina dolls. There's a bronze foundry and frame shop here, too.
**Garland's Indian Jewelry** 4 miles N of Sedona on Ariz. 89A, tel 928/282-6632. The gallery specializes in Native American jewelry, though you'll also find Hopi kachinas, Navajo sandpaintings, baskets, pottery, and other work. It's at Indian Gardens in Oak Creek Canyon.
**Garland's Navajo Rugs** 411 Ariz. 179, Sedona, tel 928/282-4070. This large gallery claims to have over 5,000 rugs, plus other Native American work.
**Hillside Sedona** 671 Ariz. 179, Sedona, tel 928/282-4500. Sculpture gardens decorate this group of galleries and restaurants.
**Museum of Northern Arizona** 3101 N. Fort Valley Rd., Flagstaff (3 miles NW of downtown Flagstaff), tel 928/774-5213, www.musnaz. org. A large gift shop sells top-quality Native American art and crafts. In summer, the sales exhibition "Enduring Creations" features the finest work by Hopi, Navajo, Zuni, Pai, Hispanic, and Western

artists. Also in summer, weekend shows highlight a style of Southwestern art with sales and demonstrations. The regular museum exhibits are a good introduction to Native American arts and history. The bookstore has an excellent selection of Native American and nature books.
**Sedona Arts Center** N. Hwy. 89A at Art Barn Rd., Sedona, tel 928/282-3865, www.sedona artscenter.com. Galleries display works by both emerging and well-known artists. Nearly all work is for sale, and there's a gift shop as well.

#### BOOKS
**Bookman's Used Books** 1520 S. Riordan Ranch St. (off S. Milton Rd.), Flagstaff, tel 928/774-0005. The giant selection also includes magazines, music, and new books. There's an Internet café, too.
**Hastings Books Music & Video** 1540 S. Riordan Ranch St., Flagstaff, tel 928/779-1880. South of Bookman's, this store offers discounted new titles.
**Northland Publishing** 2900 N. Fort Valley Rd. (US 180), Flagstaff, tel 928/774-5251, www.northlandpub.com. Many fine Native American, regional, cookery, and children's titles come from this publisher. Books at bargain prices in the sales room, open Monday to Friday.
**The Worm Books & Music** 207 N. Hwy. 89, Sedona, tel 928/282-3471. A great selection of regional and new age titles, general reading, topographic maps, and music.
**The Worm Bookstore** 128 S. Montezuma St., Prescott, tel 928/445-0361. Regional books, general reading, and maps.

#### SHOPPING CENTERS
**Flagstaff Mall** 4650 N. Hwy. 89, Flagstaff, tel 928/526-4827. This indoor mall houses Dillard's, Sears, JC Penny, and more than 60 specialty shops.
**Tlaquepaque** 336 Hwy. 179, Sedona, tel 928/282-4838, www.tlaq.com. Shady courtyards,

flowers, fountains, and Spanish-colonial architecture create a lovely setting. Tlaquepaque (T-lockey-pockey), named for a suburb of Guadalajara in Mexico, offers many shops and some good restaurants. Southwestern and Native American art predominate, but you'll find some surprises, too!

### WESTERN ARIZONA

#### ARTS, CRAFTS, & SOUVENIRS
**Algodones, Mexico** tel 928/783-0071 or 800/293-0071 (Yuma Convention & Visitors Bureau). This Mexican town offers good shopping for crafts just 8.5 miles from Yuma. Head west 6.5 miles into California on I-8, and then turn south 2 miles at the Algodones/Andrade Exit. There's parking just before the border, then it's only a short walk to the shops.

### SOUTH-CENTRAL ARIZONA

#### BOOKS
**The Book Store** 4230 N. 7th Ave., Phoenix, tel 602/279-3910. You'll find lots of used books, out-of-town newspapers, and magazines here.

#### OUTDOOR EQUIPMENT
**Recreation Equipment, Inc.** 1405 W. Southern Ave. at Priest, Tempe, tel 480/967-5494, www.rei.com. (Another branch at 12634 N. Paradise Village Pkwy. West in Paradise Valley, tel 602/996-5400.) REI has an excellent selection of outdoor recreation gear, plus free clinics.

#### SHOPPING CENTERS
**Arizona Mills** 5000 Arizona Mills Circle, Tempe, tel 480/491-7300. Mix movie theaters, restaurants, and a game arcade into a factory-outlet mega-mall and you get "Shoppertainment." Theaters include both a giant-screen Imax and a 24-screen. Arizona tourist information is here too.

**Biltmore Fashion Park**
E. Camelback Rd. at 24th St.,
Phoenix, tel 602/955-8401 or
602/955-1963, www.shopbilt
more.com. Luxury names such
as Gucci, Cartier, and Saks Fifth
Avenue in a park along with 70
other shops and restaurants.
**Borgata of Scottsdale** 6166
N. Scottsdale Rd., Scottsdale, tel
480/998-1822, www.borgata
.com. Medieval towers and arch-
ways styled after 14th-century
Italian San Gimignano grace this
elegant center.
**El Pedregal Festival
Marketplace** 34505 N.
Scottsdale Rd., Scottsdale, tel
480/488-1072, www.elpedregal
.com. A festival atmosphere adds
to the fun of visiting this center,
which offers boutique shopping,
restaurants, and a branch of the
Heard Museum.
**Metrocenter** 9617 N. Metro
Pkwy., Phoenix (just W of I-17
Dunlap and Peoria Ave. exits), tel
602/997-2641, www.shopsimon
.com. This is the big one—five
department stores, a 14-screen
movie theater, and more than
200 specialty shops and eateries.
**Old Towne Shopping
District and Historic Catlin
Court Shops** Around Glendale
Ave., E of 59th Ave., Glendale.
(Glendale Visitor Center, 5800
W. Glenn Dr., #140, tel 877/800-
2601, www.tourglendale.az.com.)
Antique shops and specialty
stores attract shoppers to this
area of downtown Glendale,
northwest of Phoenix. The
Historic Catlin Court Shops,
many in Craftsman bungalows,
offer more shops and galleries
just to the north in the four
blocks east of 59th Ave. between
Myrtle and Palmaire Aves.
Cerreta Candy Company whips
up sweet attractions and tours,
5345 W. Glendale Ave., tel 623/
930-1000, www.cerreta.com.
**Old Town Scottsdale** Main St.
& Brown Ave., Scottsdale,
www.downtownscottsdale.com
or www.scottsdalecvb.com.
(Scottsdale CVB, just E of Brown
Ave., can advise on shopping and
events, 7343 Scottsdale Mall, tel
800/805-0471.) Porch-fronted

shops sell Native American
work, cowboy and other
Western art, crafts, and Western
clothing. Many restaurants are
here too. The Main St. Arts &
Antiques District runs west of
Old Town along the two blocks
of Main St. between Scottsdale
Rd. and Goldwater Blvd. More
galleries, boutiques, and restaurants lie northwest of Old
Town on Fifth Ave. and in the
Marshall Way Arts District.

### EASTERN ARIZONA

### ARTS, CRAFTS, &
### SOUVENIRS
**Arizona Indian Arts
Cooperative** 523 W. 2nd St.,
Winslow, tel 928/289-3986.
Native American artists sell both
traditional and contemporary
work in a historic Lorenzo
Hubbell Company Trading Post.
**Jim Gray's Petrified Wood
Company** Hwy. 77 & 180,
Holbrook, tel 928/524-1842.
Logs of petrified wood surround
this huge store at the southern
edge of town. An impressive
array of petrified wood, agates,
crystals, and fossils is on display.

### SOUTHERN
### ARIZONA

### ARTS, CRAFTS, &
### SOUVENIRS
**Nogales, Mexico** (The
Nogales-Santa Cruz Chamber of
Commerce provides advice on
shopping in Mexico as well as
sights, services, and events on
the Arizona side at Kino Park,
Nogales, AZ 85621, tel 520/287-
3685, www.nogaleschamber
.com.) Mexican artists and
craftspeople turn out an aston-
ishing array of colorful work,
sold at shops a short stroll from
the U.S.–Mexico border. Park at
one of the pay lots on the Arizona side of Nogales. Mexican
salespeople speak English and
accept U.S. dollars. Be sure to
shop around and bargain, or at
least ask for a discount! Popular
items include glassware, ceramics, onyx chess sets, em-

broidered clothing, leather
goods, woodcarvings, and
Tiffany-style lampshades. There's
a Mexican tourist office just
across the border. No permit is
needed to visit the border area,
but non-U.S. and non-Canadian
citizens should check with
immigration on the U.S. side
about reentry before crossing.
**Old Town Artisans** 201 N.
Court Ave., Tucson, tel 520/623-
6024 or 800/782-8072, www
.oldtownartisans.com. Galleries
in an 1850s adobe building
contain colorful works by Native
American, Mexican, and Western
artists (see p. 202).

### BOOKS
**Bookman's Used Books**
1930 E. Grant Rd., Tucson, tel
520/325-5767; and 3733 W. Ina
Rd., Tucson, tel 520/579-0303.
You'll find masses of books, magazines, and music at these stores.
**Singing Wind Bookshop**
(near Benson from I-10
Ocotillo Exit 304 turn N 2.3
miles on Ocotillo Rd., then turn
right on Singing Wind Rd. for
half a mile; there's a gate halfway
in), tel 520/586-2425. A
bookstore at a ranch? Yes,
enthusiastic book lovers
operate a well-stocked shop
with many regional titles. It's a
good idea to call before coming,
but the Singing Wind is usually
open 9 a.m.–5 p.m.

### SHOPPING CENTERS
**El Con Mall** 3601 E. Broadway
Blvd., Tucson, tel 520/327-8767.
Tucson's first enclosed mall has a
great selection of department
and specialty stores.
**Foothills Mall—Outlets,
Entertainment & More** 7401
N. La Cholla Blvd., Tucson, tel
520/219-0650 or 742-7191. A
15-screen movie theater, a food
court, and several restaurants
complement the specialty shops
and factory-outlet stores.
**Tucson Mall** 4500 N. Oracle
Rd., Tucson, tel 520/293-7330.
Six anchor stores, more than
200 department and specialty
stores, a food court, and
restaurants fill this large mall.

# ENTERTAINMENT

Outdoor events usually follow the seasons to take advantage of the desert's winter sun and the high country's summer breezes. Indoors, you can enjoy music and theater all year, especially in the cities. Sports fans can visit exciting rodeo events, watch the Cactus League Spring Training, or see regular games by pro and college teams.

## GRAND CANYON COUNTRY

**Grand Canyon IMAX Theatre** Tusayan, tel 928/638-2468 or 928/638-2203. Frequent showings of *The Grand Canyon: The Hidden Secrets* (images of the canyon, its wildlife, and history).

**Grand Hotel Dinner Theater** Tusayan, tel 928/638-3333 or 888/634-7263. Native American groups and cowboy entertainers perform in the Canyon Star restaurant.

**Navajo Village** Page, tel 928/645-2741 or 888/261-7243, www.navajovillage.net. Navajo demonstrate crafts, explain aspects of Navajo culture, serve a traditional dinner, and tell stories.

## NORTH-CENTRAL ARIZONA

**The Museum Club** 3404 E. Route 66, Flagstaff, tel 928/526-9434, www.museumclub.com. This Route 66 roadhouse has hosted generations of country music bands and their fans. The current owners have added other styles of popular music too. The log building began as a trading post and taxidermy museum and became a nightclub in 1936. Inside you'll find Route 66 exhibits, a dance floor among five ponderosa pines, and a gleaming 19th-century bar.

**Northern Arizona University** Flagstaff, tel 928/523-5661 or 888/928-7214, www.nau.edu. N.A.U. sponsors theater, music, dance, and sporting events on campus and also hosts the Flagstaff Symphony (www.flagstaffsymphony.org).

**Prescott Fine Arts Association** 208 N. Marina St., Prescott, tel 928/445-3286, www.pfaa.net. The association sponsors plays, musicals, and concerts along with a gallery.

**Yavapai College** 1100 E. Sheldon St., Prescott tel 928/776-2033, www.yavapai .cc.az.us. A variety of concerts, plays, and events on campus.

## SOUTH-CENTRAL ARIZONA

**Arizona Opera** Phoenix, tel 602/266-7464, www.azopera .com. Productions are staged from Oct. to April at Symphony Hall in the Phoenix Civic Plaza.

**Ballet Arizona** Phoenix, tel 602/381-1096 (box office), 381-0184 (administration), or 888/322-5538, www. ballet arizona.org. Classical and modern productions from Oct. to April at the Orpheum or Phoenix Symphony Hall.

**Desert Sky Pavilion** Phoenix, tel 602-254-7200, www .azconcerts.com. This 20,000-seat outdoor amphitheater in far west Phoenix hosts many big-name music events.

**Gammage Center for the Performing Arts** Arizona State University, Tempe, tel 480/965-3434 (box office), www.asu.edu. Varied offerings of theater, dance, and concerts take place in this distinctive building designed by Frank Lloyd Wright.

**Herberger Theater Center** 222 E. Monroe St., Phoenix, tel 602/252-8497 (box office) or 602/254-7399 (administration), www.herbergertheater.org or www.aztheatreco.org. Arizona Theatre Company and other groups stage musicals and classical and modern plays.

**Phoenix Symphony** tel 602/495-1999 or 800/776-9080, www.phoenixsymphony.org. Concerts in Symphony Hall in Phoenix and Scottsdale Center for the Arts (see below) during the Sept. to May season.

**Phoenix Theatre & Cookie Company** 100 E. McDowell Rd., Phoenix, tel 602/254-2151, www.phoenixtheatre.net offers a range of plays for adults plus children's programs.

**Red River Music Hall** 730 N. Mill Ave., Tempe, tel 480/829-6779 or 800/466-6779, www.redrivermusichall.com. Jazz. In winter, there's also country music and a Christmas show.

**Scottsdale Center for the Arts** 7380 E. 2nd St., Scottsdale, tel 480/994-2787, www. scottsdalearts.org. Theater performances, films, and contemporary art shows.

## SOUTHERN ARIZONA

**Arizona Theatre Company** 330 S. Scott Ave., Tucson, tel 520/622-2823 (box office) or 884-8210 (administration), www.aztheatreco.org. The company peforms in the restored 1927 Temple of Music & Art.

**Gaslight Theatre** 7010 E. Broadway Blvd., Tucson, tel 520/886-9428. Dastardly villains fight heroes over helpless heroines in old-style melodramas.

**Tucson Convention Center (TCC)** 260 S. Church Ave., Tucson, tel 520/791-4101, www .ci.tucson.az.us/tcc. The Music Hall, Leo Rich Theatre, and Arena host many events. Performing groups include: **Arizona Friends of Chamber Music,** tel 520/577-3769; **Arizona Opera,** tel 520/293-4336, www.azopera.com; **Ballet Arizona,** tel 888/322-5538, www.balletarizona.org; **Theater League's** musicals, tel 800/776-7469, www. theaterleague.org; and **Tucson Symphony,** tel 520/882-8585, www.tucson symphony.org.

**University of Arizona** Tucson, tel 520/621-1162, www. arts.arizona.edu (Fine Arts Box Office, students), tel 520/621-3341, www.uapresents.arizona. edu (Centennial Hall). Many theater productions and concerts take place on campus.

# ACTIVITIES

Arizona's outdoors offers the grandeur of deep canyons and vast open spaces, lush alpine forests, and unusual desert life. There are ski slopes for winter and water sports for hot summer's days. Hiking and camping are a great way to get close to nature, or you can sign up for tours of the skies, the back roads, the rivers, or the lakes.

## GRAND CANYON COUNTRY

### GUIDED HIKES & TOURS
**Grand Canyon Field Institute** P.O. Box 399, Grand Canyon, AZ 86023, tel 928/638-2485, fax 928/638-2484, www .grandcanyon.org/fieldinstitute. Small groups explore the Grand Canyon region's natural world and cultural history with day hikes, van tours, and classes.

### RIVER RUNNING
**Wilderness River Adventures** 50 S. Lake Powell Blvd., Page, tel 928/645-3279 or 800/528-6154, www.visitlake powell.com. Motorized raft trips run through Glen Canyon on the Colorado River. Half-day trips during the March–Oct. season.
**Hualapai River Runners, Hualapai Lodge** Peach Springs, tel 928/769-2219 or 888/255-9550, www.river-runners.com. The Hualapai tribe offers one-day motorized raft trips through the lower Grand Canyon from Diamond Creek, followed by a helicopter ride to Grand Canyon West, then by road back to Peach Srpings. March–Oct. season.

### SCENIC FLIGHTS OVER THE GRAND CANYON
Fixed-wing and helicopter flights go year-round from the airport just south of Tusayan on the South Rim. The shortest helicopter flights just go across to the North Rim and back.

**Air Grand Canyon** tel 928/638-2686 or 800/247-4726. High-wing Cessnas.
**AirStar Airlines** tel 928/638-2139 or 800/962-3869, www.airstar.com. High-wing Cessnas.
**AirStar Helicopters** tel 928/638-2622 or 800/962-3869,

www.airstar.com.
**Grand Canyon Airlines** tel 928/638-2407 or 800/528-2413, www.grandcanyonairlines.com. High-wing Twin Otters.
**Kenai Helicopters** tel 928/638-2764 or 800/541-4537, www.flykenai.com.

### TRAIL RIDES
For more than a century, sure-footed mules have carried prospectors and visitors in and out of the Grand Canyon. Riders need to be able to control their mules, mount and dismount without assistance, and be prepared for long hours in the saddle. Check carefully the list of requirements, which include a weight of under 200 pounds (91 kg), no pregnant women, sturdy shoes (no open-toed footwear), and hat tied beneath your chin. Show up before the check-in time or you could lose your space. From the South Rim, rides go on day trips and on overnight excursions to Phantom Ranch at the bottom of the canyon. On the North Rim, there's a one-hour ride on the rim and half- or full-day trips down the North Kaibab Trail.
**Bright Angel Lodge** tel 928/638-3283 for reservations four days in advance for South Rim mule rides. Otherwise contact the desk in the lobby. If you're cannot make advance reservations, try signing up early for the wait list.
**Grand Canyon Lodge** (near Bright Angel Point), tel 928/638-9875 (mid-May to mid-Oct.) or 435/679-8665 (before June 1). Contact the desk in the lobby for mule rides on the North Rim. Reservations recommended.
**Grand Canyon National Park Lodges** 14001 E. Iliff Ave., Suite 600, Aurora, CO 80014, tel 303/297-2757, www.amfac.com. Make reservations for South

Rim mule rides well in advance (9–12 months peak times).

Just outside the park, **Allen's Outfitters** (tel 435/644-8150 or 435/689-1979) runs pack trips from mid-May to early Sept. from stables near the North Rim, and year-round in Kanab.
**Apache Stables** Reservations at the desk in Moqui Lodge (by the South Entrance), tel 928/638-2891, www.apache stables.com. Horse and mule rides from March to Dec. by the South Rim.

## NORTHEASTERN ARIZONA

### GUIDED HIKES & TOURS
**Monument Valley Navajo Tribal Park** Navajo guides operating at the visitor center will show you the backcountry. Travel on horseback, on foot, or in a vehicle for as short or as long as you'd like. Pack trips are possible too (bring your own food and camping supplies). Vehicle tours can also be arranged through Goulding's Lodge and the motels at Kayenta.
**Canyon de Chelly National Monument** tel 928/674-5500. Ask at the visitor center for a Navajo guide or information on tours that take visitors into the sheer-walled canyons on horseback, on foot, or in vehicles.
**Thunderbird Lodge** tel 928/674-5841, www.tbirdlodge .com. Popular half-day and full-day vehicle tours into Canyon de Chelly and Canyon del Muerto.

## NORTH-CENTRAL ARIZONA

### HORSEBACK RIDING
**A Day in the West** Sedona, tel 928/282-4320 or 800/973-3662, www.adayinthewest.com.
**Flying Heart Barn** on US 89, 3.5 miles north of I-40 Exit 201 near Flagstaff, tel 928/526-2788. Rides on and around the San Francisco Peaks.
**Legends of Sedona Ranch** tel

**ACTIVITIES**

928/282-6826 or 800/848-7728, www.redrockjeep.com.
**Trail Horse Adventures** Sedona, tel 928/282-7252 or 800/723-3538, www.trailhorseadventures.com.

### SCENIC FLIGHTS
**AeroVista** tel 928/282-7768 or 800/637-8749, www.aerovista.com. Flights in high-wing Cessnas over the mountains and canyons surrounding Sedona. **Northern Light Balloon Expeditions** Sedona, tel 928/282-2274 or 800/230-6222, www.sedona.net/fun/balloon. Hot-air balloons float over the early morning landscape. **Red Rock Biplane Tours** tel 928/204-5939 or 888/866-7433. Trips in an open-cockpit biplane.

### SKIING & CHAIRLIFTS
**Arizona Snowbowl** tel 928/779-1951, www.arizonasnowbowl.com. Chairlifts take skiers up the San Francisco Peaks. In summer, you can take a chairlift up for a panorama of northern Arizona.

### TOURS & EXCURSIONS
**Earth Wisdom Jeep Tours** tel 928/282-4714 or 800/482-4714, www.sacredsites.com/earthwisdom.html. Backcountry jeep trips reveal the Red Rock Country's beauty. **Nava-Hopi Tours** 114 W. Route 66, Flagstaff, tel 928/774-5003 or 800/892-8687, www.navahopitours.com. Half-and full-day tours to most major sites. **Prescott Historical Tours** tel 928/445-4567, fax 928/445-0517. Tours through historic Prescott led by a costumed guide. **Sedona Red Rock Jeep Tours** tel 928/282-6826 or 800/848-7728, www.redrockjeep .com. Excursions to scenic and archaeological sites.

WESTERN ARIZONA

### BOAT TOURS
**Black Canyon River Raft Tours** 1297 Nevada Hwy., Boulder City, Nevada, tel

702/293-3776 or 800/696-7328, www.rafts.com. Raft trips down the Colorado River from Hoover Dam (not Dec.–Jan.) **Bluewater Charters** Lake Havasu City, tel 928/855-7171 or 888/855-7171. Jetboat trips go north from Lake Havasu City. *Colorado King I* tel 928/782-2412. Cruises on the Colorado River from Fisher's Landing on Martinez Lake, near Yuma. *Desert Princess* tel 702/293-6180, www.lakemeadcruises .com. Tours through Lake Mead from Boulder Beach in Nevada.

### CANOEING & KAYAKING
**Jerkwater Canoe & Kayak Company** Topock, tel 928/768-7753 or 800/421-7803, www.jerkwater.com. Rentals along the Lower Colorado River.

SOUTH-CENTRAL ARIZONA

### BALLOONING
**Aerozona Adventure** tel 480/991-4260 or 888/991-4260, www.azballoon.com. Balloons rise over the Valley of the Sun. **Unicorn Balloon Company of Arizona** tel 480/991-3666 or 800/468-2478, www.unicornballoon.com.

### HORSEBACK RIDING
Many stables arrange lessons, cookouts, overnight trips, and boarding. **All Western Stables** tel 602/276-5862. **MacDonald's Ranch** tel 480/585-0239, www.macdonalds ranch.com. **Papago Riding Stable** tel 480/966-9793. Hop a horse and head into the desert foothills. **Trail Horse Adventures** tel 480/982-6353, www.trail horseadventures.com. Ride into the Superstition Mountains from a stable in Apache Junction.

### RIVER RUNNING
**Desert Voyagers** tel 480/998-7238 or 800/222-7238, www.desertvoyagers.com. **Salt River Recreation** tel 480/984-3305,

www.saltrivertubing.com. The **Salt River Canyon Wilderness** north of Globe contains thrilling white water when there's enough of it—spring is the best bet. Rafting companies include **Blue Sky Whitewater** tel 928/425-5252 or 800/425-5253, www.go bluesky.com; **Far Flung Adventures** tel 928/ 452-7272 or 800/231-7238, www.farflung-.com; **Sun Country Rafting** tel 928/425-842 or 800/272-3353, www.raftarizona .com; and **Mild to Wild** tel 800/ 567-6745, www.mild2wildrafting .com.

### TOURS & EXCURSIONS
**Arrowhead Desert Jeep Tours** Phoenix, tel 602/942-3361, www.go.to/aztours. Backcountry tours into the rugged desert. **Wild West Jeep Tours** Scottsdale, tel 480/922-0144, www.wildwestjeeptours.com. Backcountry tours.

EASTERN ARIZONA

### HORSEBACK RIDING
**Lee Valley Stables** Sunrise, tel 928/735-7454. A variety of rides and overnight trips.

### SKIING
**Sunrise Park Resort** tel 928/735-7669 or 800/772-7669, www.sunriseskipark.com. From Nov. to April Sunrise Ski Area has more than 65 ski runs.

SOUTHERN ARIZONA

### TOURS & EXCURSIONS
**Gray Line Tours** 181 W Broadway, Tucson, tel 520/622-8811 or 800/276-1528, www.graylinearizona.com. Day trips around Tucson. Also two- and three-day excursions. **High Desert Adventures** tel 520/586-9309, www.highdesert adventures.com. Explore prehistoric and ghost towns on a guided back-road trip. **Trail Dust Jeep Tours** tel 520/747-0323, www. traildustadventures.com.

# ILLUSTRATIONS CREDITS

Abbreviations for terms appearing below: (t) top: (b) bottom: (l) left; ( r) right; (c) center

Cover, all pictures, including spine, Gettyone/Stone

1, Richard Hamilton Smith. 2/3, Larry Ulrich/Gettyone/Stone. 4, Sally Black Ruscitti/Blacklight Photo. 9, Lee Foster. 10, Elk Photo. 11, Brian McGilloway/Robert Holmes. 12, Images International Stock Photography. 13, Buddy Mays. 14/15, David Hiser/Gettyone/Stone. 16/17, Stephen Trimble. 18/19, Dewitt Jones/ Gettyone/Stone. 21, Kerrick James/ PhotoFile. 22t, Powerstock Zefa Ltd. 22bl, Tom Bean/Gettyone/Stone. 22br, Tom Bean/Gettyone/Stone. 24/25, Larry Ulrich/National Geographic Society. 26/27, Markham Johnson/ Robert Holmes. 29, David Muench/ Gettyone/Stone. 30/31, Private Collection/Bridgeman Art Library. 32, Richard Cummins. 33l, Hulton Archive. 33r, Maxine Cass. 34, Corbis UK Ltd. 35, Arizona State Archives. 36/37, Paul Chesley/National Geographic Society. 38/39, Private Collection/Christie's Images/ Bridgeman Art Library. 40, Edward S. Curtis/Niedersächsische Staats-und Universitätsbibliothek, Göttingen. 41, Sun Valley Photography. 42, Gerald L. French/PhotoFile. 43, James Lemass. 44, Courtesy The Frank Lloyd Wright Archives, Scottsdale, AZ. 45l, Hulton Archive. 45r, Buddy Mays. 46, Hulton Archive. 47, Nik Wheeler. 49, Elk Photo. 50, Tom Bean/Gettyone/Stone. 52, Richard Cummins. 52/53, James Lemass. 54, Elk Photo. 55t, Elk Photo. 55b, L. Fordyce/Eye Ubiquitous. 56/57, Images International Stock Photography. 58, Stephen Trimble. 58/59, Tom Bean Photography. 60/61, Chad Ehlers/Gettyone/Stone. 61, Hugh Rodney/Eye Ubiquitous. 62, David Muench/Gettyone/Stone. 63, Images International Stock Photography. 64, David Brown/Images Colour Library. 65, Dewitt Jones/Robert Holmes. 66, Bruce Dale/National Geographic Society. 67t, Simon Harris/Robert Harding Picture Library. 67b, Bruce Dale/National Geographic Society. 68/69, George H. H. Huey. 69, Bill Weir. 70, Tom Bean Photography. 71, David Hiser/Gettyone/Stone. 72/73, Gerald L. French/PhotoFile. 74, Bill Weir. 75, Ric Ergenbright/National Geographic Society. 76, Coco McCoy/Rainbow. 78/79, Chris Simpson/Gettyone/Stone. 79, Mark Wagner/Gettyone/Stone. 80/81,

Catherine Karnow. 81, George H. H. Huey/National Geographic Society. 82, Elk Photo. 83, Stephen Trimble. 84, Suzanne Anderson/National Geographic Society. 85, Dewitt Jones/Robert Holmes. 86/87, Mecky Fögeling. 87, Stephen Trimble. 88, Edward S. Curtis/Niedersächsische Staats-und Universitätsbibliothek, Göttingen. 89t, Suzanne Anderson/ National Geographic Society. 89bl, Dewitt Jones/Robert Holmes. 89br, Dewitt Jones/Robert Holmes. 90, Place Stock Photo. 91, Richard Cummins. 92, Renee Lynn/Gettyone/Stone. 93, Marc Muench/Gettyone/Stone. 94, Kerrick James/PhotoFile. 96, Elk Photo. 97, Wolfgang Kaehler Photography. 98, Dan McCoy/Rainbow. 99, Willard Clay Photography, Inc. 100/101, Bill Weir. 101, Larry Ulrich Stock Photography, Inc. 102, David Hiser/Network Aspen. 103, Gerald L. French/PhotoFile. 104, Wolfgang Kaehler Photography. 105, Richard Cummins. 106, Kerrick James/ PhotoFile. 107, Images International Stock Photography. 108, Tom Mackie. 109t, David Muench/Gettyone/Stone. 109b, Kerrick James/PhotoFile. 110, Images International Stock Photography. 111, Richard Cummins. 113, Images International Stock Photography. 114, L. Fordyce/Eye Ubiquitous. 115, George H. H. Huey. 116, Images International Stock Photography. 117, Bill Weir. 118, Images International Stock Photography. 119, Richard Cummins. 120, ImageArtist Stock Photography. 121, Bill Weir. 122, Kiana Dicker. 123, Kerrick James/PhotoFile. 124/125, Gerald L. French/PhotoFile. 126, Judith Jango-Cohen/Janelco Photographers. 126/127, Dick Dietrich/ Dietrich Stock Photo Inc. 128, Kerrick James/PhotoFile. 129, Rob Boudreau/Gettyone/Stone. 130, Bill Weir. 130/131, Bill Weir. 132, Kerrick James/PhotoFile. 133, Kerrick James/ PhotoFile. 135t, Nik Wheeler. 136/137, Kerrick James/PhotoFile. 137, Kerrick James/PhotoFile. 138, Nik Wheeler. 139, ImageArtist Stock Photography. 140, ImageArtist Stock Photography. 141, Nik Wheeler. 142, Nik Wheeler. 143, Dave Bartruff/PhotoFile. 145, Richard Cummins. 147, Tom Mackie. 148, Tom Bean Photography. 149t, Richard Cummins. 149b, Images International Stock Photography. 150, Chris Coe/Axiom. 151, Richard Cummins. 152, J. Greenberg/Trip & Art Directors Photo Library. 152/153, Kiana Dicker. 154, Fred Young. 155, Richard Cummins. 156, Richard Cummins. 157, T. Bognar/Trip & Art Directors Photo Library. 158, Buddy Mays. 159, Susan Davison. 160, James

Lemass. 161, Richard Cummins. 162, Richard Cummins. 163, Kerrick James/ PhotoFile. 164, Kerrick James/ PhotoFile. 165t, Buddy Mays. 165b, Bill Weir. 166, Images International Stock Photography. 167, Images International Stock Photography. 168, Richard Cummins. 169, Richard Cummins. 170t, Elk Photo. 170b, Sally Black Ruscitti/Blacklight Photo. 171, L. Fordyce/Eye Ubiquitous. 172, Images International Stock Photography. 173, Gerald L. French/PhotoFile. 174t, Marjory J. Siewert/Wild Nature Photos. 174b, Bill Weir. 175, Owens Advertising and Publications. 176t, Bill Weir. 176b, Frank Balthis. 178, James Lemass. 178/179, Bill Weir. 180, Mecky Fögeling. 181, Jack Dykinga/ Gettyone/Stone. 182, Kerrick James/ PhotoFile. 183b, J. Dennis/Trip & Art Directors Photo Library. 184, David Hiser/Network Aspen. 185, David Hiser/Network Aspen. 186, Sun Valley Photography. 187, Sun Valley Photography. 188, F. A. Rinehart/Hulton Archive. 188/189, Hulton Archive. 189, Bill Hess/ National Geographic Society. 190/191, Laurence Parent Photography. 191, Bill Weir. 193t, Stewart Aitchison. 193b, Stewart Aitchison. 194, Bill Weir. 195, Philip Condit II/Gettyone/Stone. 196, Anne Laird/Powerstock Zefa Ltd. 197, Tom Bean Photography. 198/199, James Lemass. 199, Images International Stock Photography. 200, Images International Stock Photography. 202, Elk Photo. 204t, Catherine Karnow. 204b, Bill Weir. 205, Images International Stock Photography. 206/207, Catherine Karnow. 208, Richard Wagner/Wild Nature Photos. 209, Catherine Karnow. 210, James Lemass. 211, Images International Stock Photography. 212, Chris Coe/Axiom. 213, Bill Weir. 214, Images International Stock Photography. 215, Bill Weir. 218, Elk Photo. 219, Bob Hobby/Impact Photos. 220, George H. H. Huey/National Geographic Society. 220/221, George H. H. Huey/National Geographic Society. 222, Kerrick James/PhotoFile. 223, Richard Wagner/Wild Nature Photos. 224, Images International Stock Photography. 225, Elk Photo. 226, Fort Huachuca Museum. 227, Laurence Parent Photography. 228, Kiana Dicker. 229t, Kerrick James/PhotoFile. 229b, M. Barlow/Trip & Art Directors Photo Library. 230/231, Kerrick James/PhotoFile. 231, Elk Photo. 232, George H. H. Huey. 233, AZ State Parks/Bill Weir. 234, ImageArtist Stock Photography. 235, Dewitt Jones/ Robert Holmes.

The world's largest nonprofit scientific and educational organization, the National Geographic Society was founded in 1888 "for the increase and diffusion of geographic knowledge." Since then it has supported scientific exploration and spread information to its more than nine million members worldwide.

The National Geographic Society educates and inspires millions every day through magazines, books, television programs, videos, maps and atlases, research grants, the National Geography Bee, teacher workshops, and innovative classroom materials.

The Society is supported through membership dues, charitable gifts, and income from the sale of its educational products. Members receive NATIONAL GEOGRAPHIC magazine—the Society's official journal—discounts on Society products, and other benefits.

For more information about the National Geographic Society, its educational programs, publications, or how to support its work, call 1-800-NGS-LINE (647-5463), or write to: National Geographic Society, 1145 17th Street, N.W., Washington, D.C. 20036 U.S.A.

Printed in the U.S.A.

**Published by the National Geographic Society**
John M. Fahey, Jr., *President and Chief Executive Officer*
Gilbert M. Grosvenor, *Chairman of the Board*
Nina D. Hoffman, *Executive Vice President,*
*President, Books and School Publishing*
Elizabeth L. Newhouse, *Director of Travel Publishing*
Barbara A. Noe, *Senior Editor and Project Manager*
Allan Fallow, *Senior Editor*
Cinda Rose, *Art Director*
Carl Mehler, *Director of Maps*
Joseph F. Ochlak, *Map Coordinator*
Gary Colbert, *Production Director*
Richard S. Wain, *Production Project Manager*
Carol Lutyk, *Editorial Consultant*
Lawrence Porges, *Editorial Coordinator*
Verena Phipps, Jane Sunderland, *Contributors*

Edited and designed by AA Publishing (a trading name of Automobile Association Developments Limited, whose registered office is Millstream, Maidenhead Road, Windsor, Berkshire SL4 5GD Registered number: 1878835).
Virginia Langer, *Project Manager*
David Austin, *Senior Art Editor*
Betty Sheldrick, *Senior Editor*
Keith Russell, Mike Preedy, *Designers*
Inna Nogeste, *Senior Cartographic Editor*
Richard Firth, *Production Director*
Steve Gilchrist, *Prepress Production Controller*
Cartography by AA Cartographic Production
Picture Research by Zooid Pictures Ltd. and Carol Walker, AA Photo Library
Drive maps drawn by Chris Orr Associates, Southampton, England
Illustrations drawn by Maltings Partnership, Derby, England
Sonoran desert illustration by Ann Winterbotham

ISSN 1536-8629

Printed and bound by R.R. Donnelley & Sons, Willard, Ohio.
Color separations by Leo Reprographic Ltd., Hong Kong
Cover separations by L.C. Repro, Aldermaston, U.K.
Cover printed by Miken Inc., Cheektowaga, New York.

Visit the society's Web site at http:/www.nationalgeographic.com

The information in this book has been carefully checked and to the best of our knowledge is accurate. However, details are subject to change, and the National Geographic Society cannot be responsible for such changes, or for errors or omissions. Assessments of sites, hotels, and restaurants are based on the author's subjective opinions, which do not necessarily reflect the publisher's opinion. The publisher cannot be responsible for any consequences arising from the use of this book.

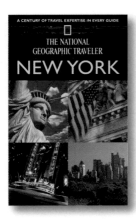
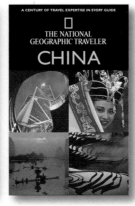
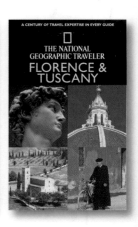